Essays on Bertrand Russell

Essays on
Bertrand Russell

EDITED BY
E. D. KLEMKE

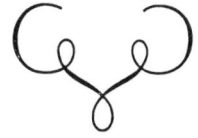

University of Illinois Press
URBANA, CHICAGO, AND LONDON

To Bob Leali, Jr.

PREFACE

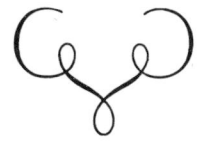

HARDLY anyone who has taken the trouble to wrestle with his major philosophical works can have doubts as to the status and rank of Bertrand Russell in contemporary philosophy. He has been referred to as "the dominant figure of the century" by Gustav Bergmann—one who has read Russell with care and constantly acknowledged his stature and importance.

Bertrand Arthur William Russell was born in 1872. He entered Cambridge University at the age of eighteen and there met Alfred North Whitehead, J. E. McTaggart, and G. E. Moore, among others. For three years he was mainly occupied with the study of mathematics, but in his fourth year, he emphasized work in philosophy and studied under Henry Sidgwick, James Word, and G. F. Stout. He left Cambridge in 1894 and spent some time in foreign countries. He returned and held a position as lecturer in philosophy at the University of Cambridge from 1910 to 1916. The bulk of his philosophical works —including a large number of books and countless papers—cover a span of almost seven decades. He died on February 2, 1970, at the age of 97.

In 1944, a volume was devoted to Russell's philosophy in the Library of Living Philosophers Series.[1] Since that time, a number of essays have appeared which deal with various aspects of Russell's thought. As I have already edited a collection of *Essays on Frege*,[2] it

[1] Paul A. Schilpp, ed., *The Philosophy of Bertrand Russell* (Evanston: Northwestern University Press, 1944).

[2] E. D. Klemke, ed., *Essays on Frege* (Urbana: University of Illinois Press, 1968).

was suggested that I bring together a similar collection of essays on Russell. Even more so than in the case of the earlier volume, I thought it desirable to include a number of new papers, which were written expressly for this volume. These are essays 5, 6, 7, 16, 17, 18, 19, 24, 25, and 26.

I have arranged the essays under three main headings: (1) Russell's ontology, (2) his theories of reference and of descriptions, and (3) his philosophy of logic and of mathematics. To some extent, the categorization is not quite adequate. Thus, a paper in the section on the theory of descriptions, for example, may in certain aspects deal with issues in ontology as well. Since some of the essays deal not with Russell's thought but with various criticisms of Russell, perhaps a more accurate title would have been *Essays on Bertrand Russell and His Critics*. However, for convenience, I have chosen the shorter title.

I am grateful to all the writers, editors, and publishers who so kindly granted permission to allow essays and selections to be reprinted in this volume. I would also like to express my appreciation to those who wrote and contributed new essays expressly for this book and to all those who gave advice or helped with the many tasks of getting the manuscript prepared for publication. I am particularly indebted to Professors Gustav Bergmann, Moltke S. Gram, Herbert Hochberg, Arthur Jacobson, Leonard Linsky, and Henry Veatch; Messrs. Truman Metzel, G. Moor, Richard Reed and Robert Bimbaum; Mrs. Mary Facko for typing the manuscript; Miss Jane Phillips of the University of Illinois Press; and President Rolf Weil, Dean Otto Wirth, and Dean George Watson of Roosevelt University.

Finally, I would like to express my appreciation to Bob Leali, Jr., who has helped in so many ways that I cannot adequately express my gratitude.

E. D. Klemke
Roosevelt University
Chicago, Illinois
March, 1970

CONTENTS

ix

PART ONE

Russell's Ontology

I

Russell's Ontological Development

W. V. Quine

THE twentieth century began, as many of you know, in 1901. Russell was 28 and had published three books: one on politics, one on mathematics, and one on philosophy. Late next summer the century will be two-thirds over. Russell's books have run to forty, and his philosophical influence, direct and indirect, over this long period has been unequaled.

Russell's name is inseparable from mathematical logic, which owes him much, and it was above all Russell who made that subject an inspiration to philosophers. The new logic played a part in the philosophical doctrines that Russell propounded during the second decade of this century—doctrines of unsensed sensa and perspectives, logical constructions and atomic facts. These doctrines affect our thinking today both directly and through supervening schools of thought. The impact of logical empiricism upon present-day philosophy is to an important degree Russell's impact at one remove, as the references in Carnap and elsewhere generously attest. Moreover Wittgenstein's philosophy was an evolution from views that Russell and the young Wittgenstein had shared. The Oxford philosophy of ordinary language must admit, however, bleakly, to a strong strain of Russell in its origins.

I think many of us were drawn to our profession by Russell's books. He wrote a spectrum of books for a graduated public, layman to specialist. We were beguiled by the wit and a sense of new-found clarity

Reprinted with the kind permission of the author and the editor from *Journal of Philosophy*, 63 (1966): 657–667.

with respect to central traits of reality. We got memorable first lessons in relativity, elementary particles, infinite numbers, and the foundations of arithmetic. At the same time we were inducted into traditional philosophical problems, such as that of the reality of matter and that of the reality of minds other than our own. For all this emergence of problems the overriding sense of new-found clarity was more than a match. In sophisticated retrospect we have had at points to reassess that clarity, but this was a sophistication that we acquired only after we were hooked.

Russell spoke not only to a broad public, but to a broad subject matter. The scatter of his first three books set a precedent to which his books of the next six decades conformed. Some treat of education, marriage, morals, and, as in the beginning, politics. I shall not venture to guess whether the world is better for having heeded Russell in these farther matters to the degree that it has, or whether it is better for not having heeded him more. Or both.

Instead I shall talk of Russell's ontological development. For I must narrow my scope somehow, and ontology has the virtue of being central and not unduly narrow. Moreover, Russell's ontology was conditioned conspicuously by both his theory of knowledge and his logic.

In *Principles of Mathematics*, 1903, Russell's ontology was unrestrained. Every word referred to something. If the word was a proper name, in Russell's somewhat deviant sense of that phrase, its object was a *thing*; otherwise a *concept*. He limited the term 'existence' to things, but reckoned things liberally, even including instants and points of empty space. And then, beyond existence, there were the rest of the entities: "numbers, the Homeric gods, relations, chimeras, and four-dimensional spaces."[1] The word 'concept', which Russell applied to these nonexistents, connotes mereness; but let us not be put off. The point to notice, epithets aside, is that gods and chimeras are as real for Russell as numbers. Now this is an intolerably indiscriminate ontology. For, take impossible numbers: prime numbers divisible by 6. It must in some sense be false that there are such; and this must be false in some sense in which it is true that there are prime numbers. In this sense are there chimeras? Are chimeras then as firm as the good prime numbers and firmer than the primes divisible by 6?

Russell may have meant to admit certain chimeras (the possible

---

1 (London: Allen & Unwin, 1956), pp. 44, 449.

ones) to the realm of being, and still exclude the primes divisible by 6 as impossibles. Or he may, like Meinong, have intended a place even for impossible objects. I do not see that in *Principles of Mathematics* Russell faced that question.

Russell's long article on Meinong came out in *Mind* in installments the following year.[2] In it he criticized details of Meinong's system, but still protested none against the exuberance of Meinong's realm of being. In the same quarterly three issues later, however, a reformed Russell emerges: the Russell of "On Denoting" (1905), fed up with Meinong's impossible objects. The reform was no simple change of heart; it hinged on his discovery of a means of dispensing with the unwelcome objects. The device was Russell's theory of singular descriptions, that paradigm, as Ayer has said, of philosophical analysis. It involved defining a term not by presenting a direct equivalent of it, but by what Bentham called *paraphrasis:* by providing equivalents of all desired sentences containing the term. In this way, reference to fictitious objects can be simulated in meaningful sentences without our being committed to the objects.

The new freedom that paraphrasis confers is our reward for recognizing that the unit of communication is the sentence and not the word. This point of semantical theory was long obscured by the undeniable primacy, in one respect, of words. Sentences being limitless in number and words limited, we necessarily understand most sentences by construction from antecedently familiar words. Actually there is no conflict here. We can allow the sentences a monopoly of full "meaning," in some sense, without denying that the meaning must be worked out. Then we can say that knowing words is knowing how to work out the meanings of sentences containing them. Dictionary definitions of words are mere clauses in a recursive definition of the meanings of sentences.

Bentham was perhaps the first to see the sentence thus as the primary vehicle of meaning. Frege took up the tale.[3] But Russell, in his theory of singular description, was the first to put this insight to precise and effective use. Frege and Peano had allowed singular description the status of a primitive notation; only with Russell did it become an "incomplete symbol defined in use." What suggested the expedient to

---

[2] "Meinong's Theory of Complexes and Assumptions," *Mind*, 13 (1904): 204–219, 336–354, 509–524.

[3] *Grundlagen der Arithmetik* (Breslau, 1884; New York: Oxford, 1950), §60.

Russell was not in fact Bentham's work, it seems, but a use of operators in the differential calculus.[4]

Russell's preoccupation with incomplete symbols began with his theory of singular descriptions in 1905. But it continued and spread, notably to classes. For background on classes we must slip back a few years. Classes were an evident source of discomfort to Russell when he was writing *Principles of Mathematics*. There was, for one thing, his epoch-making paradox. Burali-Forti had found a paradox of classes as early as 1897, but it concerned infinite ordinal numbers, and could be accommodated, one hoped, by some local adjustment of theory. On the other hand. Russell's simple paradox of the class of all classes not belonging to themselves struck at the roots. It dates from 1901, when, as Frege expressed it to Russell, arithmetic tottered.

Russell's accommodation of the paradoxes, his theory of types, came only in 1908. In *Principles*, 1903, we find no more than tentative gropings in that direction. But *Principles* evinces much discomfort over classes also apart from the paradoxes. The further source of discomfort is the ancient problem of the one and the many. It seems strange now that Russell saw a problem in the fact that a single class might have many members, since he evidently saw no problem in the corresponding fact that a single attribute, or what he then called a class-concept, might apply to many things. What made the difference was that, in the bipartite ontology of *Principles of Mathematics*, classes counted as things rather than as concepts; classes existed. Russell observed against Peano that "we must not identify the class with the class-concept," because of extensionality: classes with the same members are the same (68). Since the class was not the class-concept, Russell took it not to be a concept at all; hence it had to be a thing. But then, he felt, it ought to be no more than the sum of the things in it; and here was his problem of the one and the many.

We saw that in 1905 Russell freed himself of Meinong's impossibles and the like by a doctrine of incomplete symbols. Classes were next. In his 1908 paper "Mathematical Logic as Based on the Theory of Types" there emerges not only the theory of types but also a doctrine of incomplete symbols for explaining classes away. This latter doctrine is designed precisely to take care of the point Russell had made against Peano in connection with extensionality. Russell's contextual defini-

---

[4] Cf. *Principia Mathematica*, I (2nd. ed., 1925): 24.

tion of class notation gave the benefit of classes, namely extensionality, without assuming more than class-concepts after all.

Seeing Russell's perplexities over classes, we can understand his gratification at accommodating classes under a theory of incomplete symbols. But the paradoxes, which were the most significant of these perplexities, were not solved by his theory of incomplete symbols; they were solved, or parried, by his theory of types. One is therefore startled when Russell declares in "My Mental Development" that his expedient of incomplete symbols "made it possible to see, in a general way, how a solution of the contradictions might be possible."[5] If the paradoxes had invested only classes and not class-concepts, then Russell's elimination of classes would indeed have eliminated the paradoxes and there would have been no call for the theory of types. But the paradoxes apply likewise, as Russell knew, to class-concepts, or propositional functions. And thus it was that the theory of types, in this its first full version of 1908, was developed expressly and primarily for propositional functions and then transmitted to classes only through the contextual definitions.

The startling statement that I quoted can be accounted for. It is linked to the preference that Russell was evincing, by 1908, for the phrase 'propositional function' over 'class-concept'. Both phrases were current in *Principles of Mathematics;* mostly the phrase 'propositional function' was visibly meant to refer to notational forms, namely open sentences, while concepts were emphatically not notational. But after laying waste Meinong's realm of being in 1905, Russell trusted concepts less and favored the more nominalistic tone of the phrase 'propositional function', which bore the double burden. If we try to be as casual about the difference between use and mention as Russell was fifty and sixty years ago, we can see how he might feel that, whereas a theory of types of real classes would be ontological, his theory of types of propositional functions had a notational cast. Insofar, his withdrawal of classes would be felt as part of his solution of the paradoxes. This feeling could linger to 1943, when he wrote "My Mental Development," even if its basis had lapsed.

We, careful about use and mention, can tell when Russell's so-called "propositional functions" must be taken as concepts, more specifically as attributes and relations, and when they may be taken as mere open

[5] P. A. Schilpp, ed., *The Philosophy of Bertrand Russell* (1944; New York: Harper & Row, 1963), p. 14.

sentences or predicates. It is when he quantifies over them that he re-ifies them, however unwittingly, as concepts. This is why no more can be claimed for his elimination of classes than I claimed for it above: a derivation of classes from attributes, or concepts, by a contextual defi-nition framed to supply the missing extensionality. On later occasions Russell writes as if he thought that his 1908 theory, which reappeared in *Principia Mathematica*, disposed of classes in some more sweep-ing sense that reduction to attributes.

Just how much more sweeping a reduction he was prepared to claim may have varied over the years. Readers have credited him with ex-plaining classes away in favor of nothing more than a nominalistic world of particulars and notations.[6] But Russell early and late has ex-pressly doubted the dispensability of universals. Even if we were in-geniously to paraphrase all talk of qualities, for instance, into an idiom in which we talk rather of similarity to chosen particulars instancing those qualities, still, Russell more than once remarked, we should be left with one universal, the relation of similarity. Now here, in con-trast to the class matter, I think Russell even concedes the Platonists too much; retention of the two-place predicate 'is similar to' is no evi-dence of assuming a corresponding abstract entity, the similarity rela-tion, as long as that relation is not invoked as a value of a bound vari-able. A moral of all this is that inattention to referential semantics works two ways, obscuring some ontological assumptions and creating an illusion of others.

What I have ascribed to confusion can be ascribed to indifference; for we are apt to take pains over a distinction only to the degree that we think it matters. Questions as to what there is were for Russell of two sorts: questions of existence in his restricted sense of the term, and residual questions of being—questions of what he came to call "subsis-tence." The questions as to what subsists evidently struck him as less substantial, more idly verbal perhaps, than questions as to what exists. This bias toward the existential would explain his indiscriminate be-stowal of subsistence in *Principles of Mathematics*. True, he called a halt in 1905 with his theory of descriptions; but on that occasion he was provoked by the impossibility of Meinong's impossibles. And he had even put up with those for a time. Moreover, Russell continued to be very prodigal with subsistence even after propounding his the-ory of descriptions. We find him saying still in 1912 that "nearly all

6 Hans Hahn, "Ueberflüssige Wesenheiten" (Vienna, 1928).

the words to be found in the dictionary stand for universals."[7]

I am suggesting that through his fourth decade Russell took a critical interest in existential questions but was relatively offhand about subsistential ones. This bias explains his glee over eliminating classes and his indifference over the status of the surviving propositional functions; for we noted that in *Principles* the classes occupied, however uneasily, the existential zone of being. To hold that classes, if there be any, must exist, while attributes at best subsist, does strike me as arbitrary; but such was Russell's attitude.

Russell's relative indifference to subsistence shows again in his treatment of meaning. Frege's three-way distinction between the expression, what it means, and what if anything it refers to, did not come naturally to Russell. In "On Denoting," 1905, he even argued against it. His argument is hard to follow; at points it seems to turn on a confusion of expressions with their meanings, and at points it seems to turn on a confusion of the expression with the mention of it, while elsewhere in the same pages Russell seems clear on both distinctions. The upshot is that "the relation of 'C' to C remains wholly mysterious; and where are we to find the denoting complex 'C' which is supposed to denote C? . . . This is an inextricable tangle, and seems to prove that the whole distinction between meaning and denotation has been wrongly conceived" (50).[8]

In other writings Russell commonly uses the word 'meaning' in the sense of 'reference'; thus " 'Napoleon' means a certain individual" and " 'Man' means a whole class of such particulars as have proper names."[9] What matters more than terminology is that Russell seldom seems heedful, under any head, of a subsistent entity such as *we* might call the meaning, over and above the existent object of reference. He tends, as in the 1905 paper "On Denoting," to blur that entity with the expression itself. Such was his general tendency with subsistents.

For my own part, I am chary of the idea of meaning and, furthermore, I think Russell too prodigal with subsistent entities. So it would be odd of me to criticize Russell for not recognizing meanings as subsistent entities. However, the outcome that wants criticizing is just that, for want of distinctions, Russell tended to blur meaninglessness with failure of reference. This was why he could not banish the king of France without first inventing the theory of descriptions. To make

---

[7] *The Problems of Philosophy* (New York: Holt, 1912), p. 146.
[8] Pagination of *Logic and Knowledge* (New York: Macmillan, 1956).
[9] *Analysis of Mind* (London: Allen, 1921), pp. 191, 194.

sense is to have a meaning, and the meaning is the reference; so 'the king of France' is meaningless, and 'The king of France is bald' is meaningful only by being short for a sentence not containing 'the king of France'. Well, even if the theory of descriptions was not needed in quite this way, it brought major clarifications and we are thankful for it.

Russell's tendency to blur subsistent entities with expressions was noticed in his talk of propositional functions. It is equally noticeable in what he says of propositions. In *Principles of Mathematics* he describes propositions as expressions, but then he speaks also of the unity of propositions (50), and of the possibility of infinite propositions (145), in ways ill suited to such a version. In "Meinong's Theory," 1904, he speaks of propositions as judgments (523). There is similar oscillation in *Principia Mathematica*.

But by the time of "The Philosophy of Logical Atomism," 1918, the oscillation has changed direction. At one point in this essay we read, "a proposition is just a symbol" (185);[10] at a later point we read rather, "Obviously propositions are nothing. . . . To suppose that in the actual world of nature there is a whole set of false propositions going about is to my mind monstrous" (223). This repudiation is startling. We had come to expect a blur between expressions and subsistent entities, concepts; what we get instead of subsistence is nothingness. The fact is that Russell has stopped talking of subsistence. He stopped by 1914. What would once have counted as subsisting has been disposed of in any of three ways: identified with its expression, or repudiated utterly, or elevated to the estate of out-and-out existence. Qualities and relations come to enjoy this elevation; Russell speaks in "The Philosophy of Logical Atomism" of "those ultimate simples, out of which the world is built, . . . that . . . have a kind of reality not belonging to anything else. Simples . . . are of an infinite number of sorts. There are particulars and qualities and relations of various orders, a whole hierarchy" (270).

Russell's abandonment of the term 'subsistence' was an improvement. It is a quibbling term; its function is to limit existence verbally to space-time and so divert attention from ontological commitments of other than spatiotemporal kind. Better to acknowledge all posits under an inclusive and familiar heading. Posits too dubious for such recognition will then be dropped, as were propositions in some sense.

10 Pagination of *Logic and Knowledge*.

As for propositions, in particular, we saw Russell in this essay taking them as expressions part of the time and part of the time simply repudiating them. Dropping then the ambiguous epithet, we might take this to be Russell's net thought: there are no nonlinguistic things that are somehow akin to sentences and asserted by them.

But this is not Russell's thought. In the same essay he insists that the world does contain nonlinguistic things that are akin to sentences and asserted by them; he merely does not call them propositions. He calls them facts. It turns out that the existence of nonlinguistic analogues of sentences offends Russell only where the sentences are false. His facts are what many of us would have been content to call true propositions. Russell himself called them that in 1904,[11] propositions then being judgments; and in the 1918 essay now under discussion he allows them full-fledged existence. "Facts belong to the objective world" (183). True, he says a page earlier that "when I speak of a fact I do not mean a particular existing thing"; but he is here distinguishing between fact and thing only as between sorts of existents, paralleling the distinction between sentences and names. Facts you can assert and deny; things you can name (270). Both exist; 'thing' has ceased to be coextensive with 'existent'.

Russell in this 1918 essay acknowledges Wittgenstein's influence. Russell's ontology of facts here is a reminder of Wittgenstein, but a regrettable one. Wittgenstein thought in his *Tractatus* days that true sentences mirrored nature, and this notion led him to posit things in nature for true sentences to mirror; namely, facts.

Not that Wittgenstein started Russell on facts. Russell was urging a correspondence between facts and propositions in 1912,[12] when he first knew Wittgenstein; and he equates facts with true judgments as early, we saw, as 1904. Russell had his own reason for wanting facts as entities, and Wittgenstein abetted him.

Russell was receptive to facts as entities because of his tendency to conflate meaning with reference. Sentences, being meaningful, had to stand to some sort of appropriate entities in something fairly like the relation of naming. Propositions in a nonsentential sense were unavailable, having been repudiated; so facts seemed all the more needed. They do not exactly serve as references of false sentences, but they help. For each true or false sentence there *is* a fact, which the sentence asserts or denies according as the sentence is true or false. This two-

---

[11] "Meinong's Theory," *Mind*, p. 523.
[12] *The Problems of Philosophy*, pp. 198 ff.

to-one variety of reference became for Russell even a central trait distinguishing sentences from names, and so facts from things.[13]

Russell continued to champion facts, right through his *Inquiry into Meaning and Truth* and into *Human Knowledge*, 1948. In *Human Knowledge* the term applies not only to what true statements assert, but to more: "Everything that there is in the world I call a 'fact' " (143).

Russell's predilection for a fact ontology depended, I suggested, on confusion of meaning with reference. Otherwise I think Russell would have made short shrift of facts. He would have been put off by what strikes a reader of "The Philosophy of Logical Atomism": how the analysis of facts rests on analysis of language. Anyway Russell does not admit facts as fundamental; atomic facts are atomic as facts go, but they are compound objects.[14] The atoms of Russell's logical atomism are not atomic facts but sense data.

In *Problems of Philosophy*, 1912, Russell had viewed both sense data and external objects as irreducible existents. We are acquainted with sense data beyond peradventure, he held, whereas our belief in external objects is fallible; still, speaking fallibly, both are real. Our belief in external objects is rooted in instinct, but it is rational of us, he held, to accept such dictates of instinct in the absence of counterevidence (39). This cheerful resignation echoes Hume and harmonizes also with the current Oxford way of justifying scientific method: scientific method is part of what 'rational' means.

Two years later, in *Our Knowledge of the External World*, Russell was more sanguine. Here it was that sense data became logical atoms for the construction of the rest of the world. Already in *Problems* he had talked of private worlds of sense data and the public space of physics, and of their correlations. Now we find him using these correlations as a means of identifying external objects with classes of sense data. He identifies the external object with the class of all the views of it in private worlds, actual and ideal. In so doing he also pin-points each of the private worlds as a point in public space.

It was a great idea. If executed with all conceivable success, it would afford translation of all discourse about the external world into terms of sense data, set theory, and logic. It would not settle induction, for

---

[13] "The Philosophy of Logical Atomism," in *Logic and Knowledge*, pp. 187, 270; pagination of *Logic and Knowledge*.

[14] *Ibid.*, pp. 198 f., 270; *Our Knowledge of the External World* (London: Allen & Unwin, 1914), p. 54.

we should still be in the position of predicating sense data from sense data. But it would settle the existence of external things. It would show that assumption superfluous, or prove it true; we could read the result either way.

It would neatly settle the ontology of the external world, by reducing it to that of the set theory of sense data. In *Our Knowledge of the External World*, moreover, Russell wrote as though he had eliminated classes, and not just reduced them to attributes (cf. 224 f.); so he would have looked upon the project, if successful, as resting on an ontology of sense data alone (cf. 153). But by 1918 he thought better of this point, as witness the recognition of "qualities and relations . . . a whole hierarchy" lately quoted.

In *Our Knowledge of the External World* Russell expressed no confidence that the plan he sketched could be fully realized. In his sketch, as he remarked, he took other minds for granted; moreover he broached none of the vast detail that would be needed for the further constructions, except for a few illustrative steps. But the illustrations gave a vivid sense that the concepts of *Principia Mathematica* could be helpful here and the many ingenious turns and strategies of construction that went into *Principia* could be imitated to advantage. A strategy much in evidence is definition by abstraction—what Whitehead came to call *extensive abstraction*, and Carnap *quasianalysis*.

It was left to Carnap, in 1928, to be inspired to press the plan. Russell's intervening works, "The Philosophy of Logical Atomism," *The Analysis of Matter*, and *The Analysis of Mind* might in view of their titles have been expected to further it, but they did not. The dazzling sequel to *Our Knowledge of the External World* was rather Carnap's *Der logische Aufbau der Welt*. Carnap achieved remarkable feats of construction, starting with sense data and building explicitly, with full *Principia* techniques and *Principia* ingenuity, toward the external world. One must in the end despair of the full definitional reduction dreamed of in recent paragraphs, and it is one of the merits of the *Aufbau* that we can see from it where the obstacles lie. The worst obstacle seems to be that the assigning of sense qualities to public placetimes has to be kept open to revision in the light of later experience, and so cannot be reduced to definition. The empiricist's regard for experience thus impedes the very program of reducing the world to experience.[15]

---

[15] This ironic way of putting the matter is due to Burton Dreben.

Russell meanwhile was warping his logical atomism over from its frankly phenomenalistic form to what, influenced by Perry and Holt, he called "neutral monism."[16] Neutrality here has a bias, as it often has in politics; Russell's neutral particulars are on the side of sense data. Still, a drift has begun, and it continues. It does not reach the physicalistic pole, even in *Human Knowledge;* but there is an increasing naturalism, an increasing readiness to see philosophy as natural science trained upon itself and permitted free use of scientific findings. Russell had stated the basis for such an attitude already in 1914: "There is not any superfine brand of knowledge, obtainable by the philosopher, which can give us a standpoint from which to criticize the whole of the knowledge of daily life. The most that can be done is to examine and purify our common knowledge by an internal scrutiny, assuming the canons by which it has been obtained."[17]

16 Cf. *Analysis of Mind*, p. 25; *Analysis of Matter* (1927; New York: Dover, 1954), Chapter 37.
17 *Our Knowledge of the External World*, p. 71.

2

Russell on Particulars

Gustav Bergmann

THE following remarks have been stimulated by an argument Russell develops through three chapters (VI–VIII) of his recently published *Inquiry into Meaning and Truth*. In this part of the book he examines the possibility of an analysis of the kind commonly known as a sense data analysis, without, however, referring to particulars, that is, in terms of universals only. Indicating the lines that he thinks such an analysis would have to follow, he arrives, tentatively, at the conclusion that it could be carried out successfully. Presently I shall criticize Russell's proposals, and I shall also be critical of the reasons he gives for the importance of this kind of analysis. To restate the last point, I believe, contrary to Russell's opinion, that a "particular-free" analysis would not tend to throw any light on those philosophical puzzles—if puzzles they are—which he thinks it would solve. I shall also contend that such an analysis is, in fact, impossible, though I agree with Russell that, for reasons different from his, its possibility would be philosophically rather significant. In the first section I shall, in my own manner, formulate the problem and what I take to be its significance. In the second section I shall present what I believe is a proof of the impossibility of a particular-free analysis. In the third section I shall briefly state my criticism of what Russell does and of his reasons for doing it.

Reprinted with the kind permission of the author and the editor from *The Philosophical Review*, 56 (1947): 59–72.

I

By a sense data analysis I mean an attempt to describe all percepts, though not necessarily all contents of consciousness, by means of a language whose simplest or basic sentences are of the kind exemplified by "this is green" or "this is later than that," where the descriptive universals "green" and "later" have their ordinary (phenomenal) meanings, and where the referents of "this" and "that" are objects of the sort many philosophers call simple momentary givennesses or sense data. The referents of "this" and "that," thus used, are often called *Particulars*. Since "particular" has also a purely linguistic meaning I shall, in the present note, capitalize the term whenever it occurs in its nonlinguistic sense. As far as the notion of a sense data analysis is concerned, there is the further proviso that the descriptive universals that can be properly predicated about particulars are the only undefined universals needed. In other words, a sense data analysis always undertakes to define such descriptive predicates as "stone" and "tree," that is, the universals predicated of (the percepts of) physical objects. For the most part, though not always, there is also the explicit claim that predicates such as "color," occurring in "green is a color," that is, quite literally, all predicates of higher type, can be thus eliminated. Important and controversial as all this is, for the purpose at hand we can let it go. For, if the referents of the basic sentences of an ordinary sense data language can be described in a particular-free manner, then it follows that whatever can be said or, if you please, reconstructed in an ordinary sense data language can also be said or reconstructed in a language of that special kind. And whether or not this is so is, following Russell, the one question I have undertaken to examine. But in order to state precisely what is meant by "particular-free," one must first consider the linguistic meaning of "particular" and distinguish it carefully from that of "Particular."

As far as I know no philosopher has ever proposed the use of a language that is not of the subject-predicate form in the ordinary linguistic sense[1] of "subject" and "predicate," a sense common to Indo-Germanic grammar and the formal languages of the kind developed in *Principia Mathematica*. In these languages expressions that can occur both as subjects and as predicates are, in a purely linguistic sense

---

[1] It should be noticed, though, that "predicate," as here used, includes relations.

of the term, called universals. The universal "green," for instance, occurs as subject in "green is a color," as predicate in "this is green." Expressions that occur as subjects, but not as predicates (and which are not, in Russell's sense, descriptions) are called *particulars*. Whenever I write "particular" with a lower-case initial, it ought to be understood in this grammatical sense. Now I am ready to state Russell's problem. He does not suggest that we abandon the subject-predicate schema. Thus the analysis he proposes is not particular-free; nor is it, if I understand him correctly, Particular-free. The point is this. In an ordinary sense data analysis the referents of the particulars are the Particulars. What Russell suggests is an analysis in which the referents of the particulars are Universals, or, more precisely, the referents of those universals that occur in the basic sentences of an ordinary sense data language. It will be noticed that I have now extended the device of upper- and lower-case initials to "universal." Also, it will be seen that "particular-free" is really not a good name for the kind of analysis Russell proposes; yet I shall, for want of a better term, continue to use it occasionally. If, then, in such an analysis the referents of the particulars are to be Universals, one might ask whether, conversely, the Particulars are to be designated by universals. This would indeed be so. But I feel that before attending to these matters I should state the advantage which, in the opinion of some philosophers, might be gained from a particular-free analysis.

The awkwardnesses in which particularity involves us are many. There is, first, a difficulty concerning the psychological or, as I would rather say, the *phenomenological* status of Particulars. As it is usually put, the point is that the content of even the simplest awareness is never one or, in the relational case, several *quid*, but always, whether property or relation, a *quale*, that is, a Universal. Against such views one could defend the unqualitied Particular by pointing out its indispensability in fixing the location of the qualities. But those who are skeptical of Particulars might insist that such location is itself a matter of relational structure and that the pertinent spatial and temporal relations, themselves Universals, are, upon correct analysis, found to obtain among qualities. At this point some would, perhaps, speak more cautiously of exemplified qualities; as far as I can see, this caution neither adds to nor detracts from the argument.[2] If, then, one is on

[2] The reason for my belief that such caution or qualification is irrelevant can be stated in a very ancient terminology: exemplification (predication) is a relation *secundae intentionis*.

such groups skeptical of Particulars, one may incline toward the opinion that the particulars of an ordinary sense data analysis are, in a manner of speaking, artifacts of language. And there is, of course, no better way of proving this contention than to construct a usable and adequate language whose ground layer of particulars refers not to Particulars but to Universals. The case of these skeptics would be further strengthened if what comes, within the new language, closest to being the proper name of a Particular should turn out to be a construction, in the sense in which whatever can be obtained by the method of extensive abstraction is sometimes called a construction. However, I do not mean to recommend such vague and, to my mind, dangerous usage of "construction." Outside of mathematics, extensive abstraction consists simply in the definition of descriptive universals from undefined ones; the referents that exemplify such terms are, of course, not in any reasonable sense constructed. To say the same thing differently, the distinction between defined and undefined descriptive predicates, fundamental as I believe it to be, does not imply the kind of discrimination, either phenomenological or ontological, that is connoted by a certain usage of "construction."[3] Yet an analysis in which the names of the Particulars, or what comes closest to them, turn out to be defined predicates would, I believe, realize and, at the same time, clarify a further tenet of those who do, on the grounds now considered, object to Particulars.

There is, second, another cluster of awkwardnesses tied up, not with the phenomenological status of the Particulars but, rather, with the *linguistic* or, if one wishes to speak loosely, with the logical status of the particulars. So it is natural enough that these difficulties have lately come in for a good deal of attention on the part of logical positivists. It seems, though, that a good case can be made by historians who trace the issue back to Hegel, to the idealistic tradition in general and, perhaps, even to the Eleatics. I have reference to the argument about proper names; and "proper name" is, within an ordinary sense data analysis, a synonym for "particular." Readers of Russell's *Inquiry* will remember that he uses at one place the expository device of calling Particulars by such names as "John" and "Henry," thus replacing the idiomatic "this is green" by "Henry is green." More formally one writes, instead of "John" and "Henry," letters such as '*a*' and '*b*'. This brings us face to face with the difficulty

[3] For a fuller discussion of these issues see my essay on "Undefined Descriptive Predicates," *Journal of Philosophy and Phenomenological Research*, 7 (1947).

that '*a*' and "Henry" do not connote anything in the sense in which "green" and all other descriptive universals do connote an identifiable character "This" and "here," as Hegel already knew, designate everything and, therefore, nothing. To put it the way Pierce did, proper names are indexical, and not presentative signs. So far the argument has run parallel, though in a different vein, to the one I have called phenomenological. Pierce's formulation leads on to a further difficulty, the one that makes us prefer '*a*' or "Henry" to "this" and similar spoken gestures. Uneasiness about these gestures as such is one of the philosophical motives behind the recent insistence on the so-called metalinguistic approach and its impressive technical development. Quite untechnically speaking, the idea is that spoken gestures represent, informally or idiomatically, the semantical tie and transcend, by the same token, the language which they thus relate to its referents. So they cannot, according to this view, occur in formal or philosophically correct language. The '*a*' and '*b*' we are forced to use for proper names in formal languages have indeed the virtue of making it clear that an index taken out of its context does not indicate anything. Nor are these signs either presentative, like all names of Universals, or structural in the sense in which the connectives and the copula are structural, nonreferential, or logical. They constitute, besides the structural and the presentative signs, a third class by itself, representing, properly according to one view, the category of particularity or, improperly according to another, what does not really belong in the language itself. If one is of the latter opinion, what is more natural than to ask whether one could not build on adequate language in which all nonstructural signs are fully and unambiguously presentative, that is, a language whose particulars are on a par with its universals in that they all refer to identifiable characters or Universals? Thus one is again led to the particular-free language Russell wishes to design.

These, I feel, are two groups of *good* reasons for being interested in the problem of a particular-free analysis. Its possibility would, as it were, definitely settle the points I have mentioned; or, perhaps, I had better say it would settle them as definitely as one could ever hope to settle any philosophical issue. This, however, does not mean that the actual impossibility of a particular-free analysis indicates the unsoundness of the views which such analysis, if possible, would conclusively establish. Its impossibility merely shows that particularity is indeed a fundamental or categorial feature of our world. The mistaken belief that this state of affairs is irreconcilable with a positivistic metaphysics has something to do with the *bad* reasons that led Russell to investigate the problem. But of these matters I propose to speak later.

II

A particular-free language cannot even adequately describe perceptual fields so simple that they can be described by basic sentences of an ordinary sense data language. In order to prove this, I shall show that the usual statements which are needed to describe such a field, that is, statements whose particulars refer to Particulars, cannot be adequately reconstructed within a language whose particulars refer to the Universals that present themselves in these fields. If one shows this, one has, I take it, also shown that our world as it is, or, for that matter, any world in this one categorial aspect like ours, cannot be so described. Specifically, I shall consider, within the specious present, a series of qualitied points. A linear arrangement of patches of different shapes, colors (hues), and brilliancies exemplifies a perceptual field of the kind I have in mind. It will be noticed that, like Hume's atoms, my points are really extended. This is merely a simplifying assumption and must not be taken to indicate agreement with Hume's views on continuity, divisibility, and infinity. Agreement or disagreement with Hume on these matters is equally irrelevant. For, if one could in a particular-free manner describe a world, spatially and temporally discontinuous but otherwise like ours, then one should also be able so to describe our own continuous universe. The same holds true for the number of undefined descriptive characters, that is, in the illustration I have chosen, the number of, by assumption, unanalyzable shapes, hues, and brilliancies. For again, particularity is not in any manner connected with the number of undefined descriptive characters, whether this number be finite, denumerable, or that of the continuum. But before making any assumption concerning this number I had better explain more carefully the formal aspect of what one would have to do if one were to carry out Russell's program.

The particulars of the language from which one starts form a class, a. Its members—let us call them a_1, a_2, a_3, and so on—refer by assumption to such Universals as green, blue, round, square, bright. The undefined descriptive universals of the language are of three kinds. Either they are (1) spatial or (2) of the kind exemplified by "this green is brighter than that red," where "this" and "that" do, of course, not refer to particular instances of these colors, which are Particulars, but to particular shades of them, which are Universals. Or they are (3) nonrelational predicates such as "color," "shape," and "brilliancy." As far as I can see, the predicates of the second kind are not at all relevant for the problem at hand, and I shall not, therefore, mention them further. The predicates of the third kind I shall neglect for the moment but shall return to them presently. So there are only the spatial relations left. Of these there are, under our simplifying assumptions, but two; one of coincidence, call it "S," and one of order, call it "P." "a_1Sa_2" reads "a_1 coincides with a_2"; "a_1Pa_2" reads "a_1 precedes a_2." The statement "a_1Sa_2" will be true if the field of which it is predicated contains at least one point that exemplifies both Universals mentioned. S is, accordingly, symmetrical and reflexive, but not transitive. To fix the ideas, let us further assume "a_1Pa_2" to mean that a_1 is to the left of a_2. This statement will thus be true whenever it is made about a field that contains at least two points so that the left one has the character a_1 while the right one has the character a_2. Though the points themselves are serially ordered, it is easily understood that P does not have the properties of asymmetry, irreflexivity, and transitivity which are characteristic of serial order. For in a field in which at least two points have the same character a_1, one has "a_1Pa_1"; in a three-point field of the type $a_1a_2a_1$ (say, green-blue-green) one has "a_2Pa_1" and "a_1Pa_2," but not, as one would if P were transitive, "a_2Pa_2."

To describe in our peculiar language a field of the kind considered is to state or know all the instances of the relations S and P that obtain in it. For this, as far as spatial arrangement is concerned, is all there is to be known, or, if you please, all that can be said in such a language. To ask whether our ordinary language and everything we can actually say or know in it about these fields can be reconstructed in a particular-free manner amounts, therefore, to proposing the following *bundling problem.* Assume that a given class a is the field of two given relations, the first of which, S, is symmetrical and reflexive, while no condition restricts the generality of the second, P. Do such a, S, and P, if known or given, uniquely determine a *series* $a_1, a_2, a_3, \ldots$ of subclasses of a, which may have members in common and which satisfy the following three conditions? (1) There is a subclass to which both a_1 and a_2 belong, if and only if a_1Sa_2. (2) There are at least two subclasses, a_1 and a_2, so that a_1 is a member of a_1 and a_2 a member of a_2, and so that a_1 precedes a_2 in the serial order of the subclasses, if and only if a_1Pa_2. (3) If the relation P holds between one element of a subclass a_1, and one element of a subclass a_2, then it holds also, in the same order, between any two elements of these two classes. Intuitively speaking, the "bundles" or subclasses are of course our points; they are classes or predicates of our peculiar particulars; and the question is whether these predicates can be defined—by extensive abstraction, as one says—in terms of the two known relations. For these to be known or given means, as far as the formal aspect of the matter is concerned, that, in the case of S, a set of pairs of elements of a, and, in the case of P, a set of such ordered pairs are known or given in exactly the same sense in which the data of a mathematical problem are said to be known or given.[4] What it means for S and P to be given phenomenologically is a different matter, and one that does not concern us here. Also, it is virtually obvious that the bundling problem has, in the general case, either no solution or more than one; only under special conditions will the solution be unique. Yet an explicit argument is a little long-winded; so I shall present it in three steps.

1. In agreement with what has been said before, I shall assume that the class a of identifiable characters is finite. The class of all bundles or points that are different from each other in the sense that they do not exemplify the same characters is, therefore, also finite. So are, in this case, the sets of pairs and ordered pairs that determine S and P respectively. There is, however, no limit to the number of points in fields completely characterized by a finite a, S, and P. This can be used to demonstrate the inadequacy of our language. Assume that, for a finite a, S, and P, the series $a_1, a_2, \ldots, a_k$ constitutes one solution of the bundling problem, and assume, furthermore, that P consists of all the ordered pairs that one can form from the elements of a. It is easy to see that for such a P the series $a_1, a_2, \ldots, a_k, a_1, a_2, \ldots, a_k$ and, generally, those obtained by repeating the original series of k points any number of times are also solutions. I shall, as a next step, show that there are solutions of bundling problems with this particular P.

2. Consider the case of five characters, a, b, c, d, e; and make both S and P consist of all possible pairs. Form the ten possible triples of characters; write them in lexicographical order, abc, abd, $\ldots$, cde and call them, in this order, $a_1, a_2, \ldots, a_{10}$. Everybody can, with a little patience, see for himself that the series a_1, a_3, a_4, a_5, a_9 is a solution of this particular bundling problem. But so is the series $a_1, a_3, a_4, a_5, a_7, a_9$, the series $a_1, a_3, a_4, a_5, a_9, a_7$, and others. Though it is not difficult to formu-

---

[4] It is not required that the two members of a pair are different.

late a general rule, it is hardly worth while to do so. At any rate, one sees that the ambiguity is even more radical than we have already been led to expect by the possibility of iteration. All this means, of course, that *there are fields which differ in number, order, and kind of points, and among which we could not discriminate by means of our peculiar language.* So this language is, in an obvious and obviously pertinent sense of the term, inadequate. Yet there is one objection to this conclusion which is, I believe, worth considering.

3. Some might agree with me that such relatively contingent features as continuity and the number of characteristics have nothing to do with the much deeper-lying categorial feature of particularity, but might, at the same time, feel that there are other features, of comparable depth, which I have neglected and which, if included in its assumptions, would so modify the bundling problem as to make it yield, at least within reasonable range, unique solutions. It so happens that there is, indeed, one feature that one could not unnaturally connect with particularity and which also lies—in the opinion of many, though not in my own—sufficiently deep to justify the expectation that its introduction might make a difference. I am thinking of the fact that the same monochromatic patch or point cannot exemplify two different colors; that it cannot, generally speaking, bear two undefined characters of the same "dimension." Recognizing these dimensions means, within our particular-free language, to introduce the third kind of universals, such as "color" and "shape," which I have mentioned at the beginning of the section. To introduce them formally and so to introduce the critical feature amounts to (1) dividing the class a into mutually exclusive subclasses β_i, and (2) postulating that the relation S does not obtain between any two different members of a β-class. But even under this additional assumption very simple bundling problems have no adequate solution. Consider the case of two β-classes, each of which has two members. One may think of two shapes (a_1, a_2) and two colors (b_1, b_2). Choose now S and P so that they consist of all the pairs that are possible under the additional assumption and you will find that a_1b_2, a_2b_1, a_2b_2, a_1b_1 and a_1b_2, a_2b_1, a_1b_1, a_2b_2 are two series of points (not to be confused with pairs, though each of them happens to bundle two characters!) which satisfy the conditions of this particular bundling problem. That means, of course, that we could not, in our peculiar language, discriminate between two fields that contain the same four points, all different from each other, in different orders. Again, the result could be generalized; but again, it is hardly

worth the trouble to do so. For we have already, and as far as I can see conclusively, proved the inadequacy of a particular-free language.

III

It will, perhaps, be best to begin the discussion of Russell's argument with a broad and interpretative outline that reveals what I have permitted myself to call the bad reasons for his interest in a particular-free analysis. So I shall do this first; afterwards and in conclusion, I shall gather some detailed comments and criticisms.

1. Everybody who is but superficially acquainted with Russell's philosophical career knows that the problem of ontological realism has never ceased to occupy and, I dare say, to vex him. It is almost as if he were torn between what he would probably call phenomenological subjectivism or empirical idealism on the one hand and the charms of a realistic sanction for what we all accept, in a commonsense manner, as the teachings of physics and physiology on the other. According to these teachings one might say, in a slight paraphrase of certain passages in the *Inquiry*, that whenever I have a cat-percept, then there also *is* a cat—at least as a rule, and we are not concerned here with the exceptions. For Russell the realist, such being there of a cat is a piece of empirical *impersonal* knowledge; Russell the phenomenalist insists that "what we directly know when we say [in a perceptual judgment] 'this is a cat' is a state of ourselves."[5] There is nothing new in all this, neither within Russell's work nor otherwise. New and, in a certain sense, interesting is the way by which the Russell of the *Inquiry* proposes to escape the classical dilemma. His point of attack is the "this" in the perceptual judgment "this is a cat" or, for that matter, in the basic sentence "this is green." He first spends some time in pointing out the mutual substitutability of "this" and such expressions as "I-now." The oversimplified and, in my opinion, outright mistaken conception of the Self and the perceptual act which probably underlies this part of the argument is not now my concern. The point is that for Russell the indexical signs, or *egocentric particulars* as he calls them, are the carriers of the subjectivity, in the full classical sense of "subjectivity." Also, Russell thinks—and this has something to do with what I have called linguistic reasons for the interest in our problem—

---

[5] *An Inquiry into Meaning and Truth* (London: Allen & Unwin, 1940), p. 142.

that all particulars are in a sense like "this" and thus infected by the same subjectivity. If, therefore, indexical particulars could be eliminated from our perceptual judgments, then, he feels, "there can be empirical impersonal knowledge, and two men who believe (say) that hydrogen is the lightest element *may* be both believing the same proposition."[6] In case there should be any doubt left that the realism issue is behind all this, let me add that we read, in the same paragraph, "that it is the ideal of science to dispense with egocentric particulars." Here, then, is the main motive and key to the understanding of Russell's proposal to do away with indexical particulars.

There is also, as a subsidiary motive, the antisubstantialist argument. If one regards "this is red" as a subject-predicate proposition, then one finds, according to Russell, "that 'this' becomes a substance, an unknowable something in which properties inhere, but which, nevertheless, is not identical with the sum of its properties."[7] Historically, that is, in view of the role particularity has played in the Aristotelian tradition, the connection is quite understandable and *prima facie* plausible. Also, it is understandable that an "empirical" realist wants to dissociate himself from substantialist views. Structurally, however, Russell's antisubstantialist argument against the Particulars is merely the ontological version, as it were, of what I have called, in an earlier section, the phenomenological reasons for uneasiness about Particulars. This has something to do with my considering Russell's two motives, both the antisubjectivist and the antisubstantialist, bad reasons. And the time has indeed come where I must state my grounds for this rejection. I must say, then, with due respect to Russell, that these grounds are, at the present stage of the analytical enterprise, obvious. Another way of saying the same thing is that they are implicit in the *purely phenomenological way in which the whole issue of particularity and particular-free analysis can be treated* and in which I have actually treated it in this note. The possibility of a particular free analysis is, indeed, an issue within phenomenology and, as positivists would expect, amenable to linguistic elucidation. But if the issue is one *within* the given, then the result of such elucidation, whatever it may be, cannot possibly bear on questions which concern the status of the given and are thus, in a sense, *about* it. Russell's solution of the classical dilemma, startling at first, is, therefore, purely verbal; and *verbal*, I am afraid, is not what modern analysts mean by *linguistic*.

[6] *Ibid.*, p. 157.
[7] *Ibid.*, p. 120.

2. The outstanding characteristic of Russell's specific proposal for the construction of a particular-free language is the introduction of spatial coordinates as nonrelational Universals. His exposition of the idea suffers from an abrupt and unnecessary substitution of "physical" for phenomenological material. But if allowance is made for this complication, the thing amounts to this. To lie on a certain distinguished curve in the visual field is, according to Russell, a nonrelational Universal (quality) exemplified by all the points or patches on such a curve. If this were so, then one could indeed, instead of speaking of a certain point being red, refer to the bundle consisting of redness and the (spatial) qualities characteristic of the co-ordinate-curves at whose intersection the point mentioned lies. Here several comments come to mind.

To begin with a purely historical observation, one wonders whether Russell realizes that his proposal revives the doctrine of *local signs*, which has played such an important part in the nineteenth-century discussion of space perception. The term is Lotze's, but the one who most articulately insisted that there are qualities of the kind Russell introduces and, also, that they are intrinsically and irreducibly spatial was Helmholtz's vigorous opponent, Emil Hering. Second, as far as the actual phenomenological givenness of such characters is concerned, there is no other argument than that to which the great British tradition eventually resorts in such cases: go and see whether you find it in yourself! I don't; but perhaps that is merely because I am, and not just on phenomenological grounds, convinced of the essentially relational nature of space. There is, third, another point that disturbs Russell and which, if I understand him at all, comes down to this. Either one assumes that no two different points exemplify the same co-ordinate-qualities or the device does not do what it is supposed to do, namely, to use Russell's language, guarantee the nonidentity of discernibles. But if one does make this assumption then one faces what is, for Russell, a further difficulty. That no two points have the same co-ordinate-qualities is a piece of generalized knowledge, that is, according to a line of thought that goes through the whole of the *Inquiry*, knowledge that is not certain and, perhaps, not even empirical. Yet this particular piece of knowledge is of the kind Russell would prefer to consider as certain; just as he prefers an analysis in which what he conceives to be the identity of indiscernibles becomes analytic. To clear up these difficulties, which are, I believe, more apparent than real, one would have to analyze our ideas of certainty and identity;

I do not propose to take up either in this note. It should be noticed, though, that I was, in the second section, able to discuss the impossibility of discriminating, within our peculiar language, among fields that contain the same bundle once, twice, or any number of times *without* ever bringing up the philosophical issues connected with the notion of identity.[8] And I have, in doing this, also taken account of spatial relations and not, like Russell, arbitrarily restricted myself to the intrinsic properties of the points, that is, to the qualities in the bundles. The last remark leads to my fourth and last point. I wish to call attention to the extraordinary manner in which Russell neglects the relational aspects of space and proposes to construct it, in a fashion that reminds one of Hume, Hartley, and James Mill, out of qualities conceived in the analogy of sensations. Certainly this does not go well with the incipient holism that is so noticeable at many places throughout the *Inquiry*. But then, such reluctance to do justice to the fundamental importance of relational Universals is, I am afraid, not peculiar to Russell; rather, it is characteristic of both the materialistic and empiricist traditions. This, however, is a large subject, one that I have taken up elsewhere.[9]

[8] The injection of the identity issue is thus but another unnecessary complication of the argument. Also, Russell's conception of identity is inadequate, really a fusion between three different notions. Concerning these matters, see my "Notes on Identity," *Philosophy of Science*, 10 (1943): 163–166; 11 (1944): 123–124.

[9] See note 3.

3

The Revolt Against Logical Atomism

Gustav Bergmann

Explaining metaphysics to the nation—
I wish he would explain his explanation.

Byron, *Don Juan.*

PHILOSOPHICAL movements rise
and fall, not excluding those that set out to end all movements or even
philosophy itself. Having run its course, a movement is either found
wanting or judged to have made a contribution. In either case, it is
vigorous while the clever young men gather around its banner. And,
of course, there are always many clever young men eager to enlist.
Oxford is now the centre of a vigorous movement. Surely it is not the
whole of contemporary British philosophy. Yet hardly anyone now
philosophizing in Britain or, for that matter, in this country, is un-
aware of it.

Urmson's[1] recent book hails from Oxford. For at least two reasons
it makes an excellent text for a critical study. One reason is that it is
very good of its kind. The other is its major theme. Urmson tries to
show, successfully I think, that the two main slogans of Oxford are

Reprinted with the kind permission of the author and the editor from
The Philosophical Quarterly, 7 (1957): 323–339, and 8 (1958): 1–13.

[1] *Philosophical Analysis: Its Development between the Two World Wars* (Oxford: Clarendon Press, 1956).

reactions against certain ideas of the classical analysts. The word 'slogan' is his. The phrase 'the classical analysts' is mine. I shall use it to refer to the members of the movement or movements over which Russell and Wittgenstein[2] presided, with G. E. Moore as the most important figure in the near background.

Urmson presents the case for Oxford. I shall take the other side. When I call his book good I therefore do not mean that I agree with everything he says. Far from so. But with a good deal of it every analytical philosopher can agree. This is to his credit. Also, he attends to what is important and does not niggle about what is not. He gives the other fellow a fair run for his money and doesn't wear him out by elaborating the obvious. These are rare virtues.

Logical Atomism is the metaphysical system at one time propounded by Russell and Wittgenstein. Among its numerous propositions, its several parts (theories), and the method by which it is established there are many structural connections. Its two major parts are the *picture theory of language* and the *verification theory of meaning*. Its method is reductive analysis by means of an *ideal language*. The structural connections between the whole, its two major parts, and the method are such that if one of the latter three is overthrown, all four collapse. Thus, even the method does not make sense unless one accepts some of the propositions it is designed to establish. The two major theories have in fact been overthrown. *Reductive analysis* has been shown to be unfeasible even if disengaged from the ideal language method. Logical Atomism thus collapsed. The two new slogans point in the direction of the right theory of meaning and the right method. In broad strokes, this is Urmson's argument. I shall now block out my own.

As it stands, the doctrine in question is indeed untenable, if only because it is an *unreconstructed* metaphysics. Properly reconstructed, its propositions fall into three classes. Some would seem to be true. I say 'seem' because one should never be too certain about propositions as sweeping as these. Some are almost certainly false. Some others become mere explications of philosophical uses. As such they are neither true nor false but, rather, adequate or inadequate. The ideal

---

[2] I.e., throughout this essay, the author of the *Tractatus*, not of the *Investigations*. In another long essay, I traced the tragedy of the second book to a fundamental shortcoming of the first. See "Intentionality," in *Semantica* (Archivo di Filosofia, 1955), pp. 176–206; hereafter cited as "Int."; reprinted in *Meaning and Existence* (Madison: University of Wisconsin Press, 1959), pp. 3–38.

language method is philosophically neutral. The programme of reductive analysis has not been shown to be unrealizable. I have argued all this before.[3] In this paper I propose to supplement the argument by defending those parts of the doctrine which I believe to be sound against the criticisms Urmson marshals against them. It will be best if I first get two general matters out of the way.

The ideal language is not really a language but merely the skeleton of one. Some dismiss the method on this ground alone. Urmson has not joined their tedious company. One good turn deserves another. I shall keep out of this study a point which goes rather deep, namely, that the ideal language must not even be thought of as the skeleton of what is called the inner monologue.[4] Perhaps it is worth noticing that a last-ditch defender of the notion goes (in the right direction) much further than its most scornful critics.

Urmson not only examines structural connections, he also suggests historical ones. With many of these no one need quarrel. Every now and then I disagree with his emphasis. Some historical connections I think he overlooks. In either case I shall say my piece without, however, offering much, if anything, in the way of evidence. So, perhaps, a historical connection I believe he missed is merely a structural one I see. Little harm will be done. Happily, neither Urmson nor I are primarily interested in philology, not even in Wittgenstein philology.

I

All physical objects consist of atoms. An atom, being a simple, does not itself consist of anything. This shows how 'atom' is used in (classical) physics. All other uses are controlled by the ideas of simplicity and consisting. In the proposition 'The world consists of simples' the words 'simple' and 'consist' are used philosophically. That makes it a philosophical proposition. It may be taken to state somehow, at its barest, the thesis of Logical Atomism. As it stands, it makes no sense. No unreconstructed philosophical proposition does. But this is not to say that one cannot recover the sense it is intended to make. The result is an explicated or *reconstructed* philosophical proposition. Explication and result must both be free from philosophical uses; otherwise we

---

[3] See "Int." and *The Metaphysics of Logical Positivism* (London: Longmans, Green and Co., 1954); hereafter cited as *MLP*, with Arabic numerals referring to the numbers of the essays in this volume.

[4] See "Int.," especially pp. 187–190, 193–194.

would be weaving a Penelopean pall. Philosophical (metaphysical) propositions are reconstructed by the ideal language method (hereafter, briefly: the method). I shall begin by describing it, most concisely to be sure and only selectively for my purpose, yet in sufficient detail to show that even in the most detailed description no word would be used philosophically. If I can show this, then I shall also have shown that the method does not commit its practitioners to any philosophical proposition, either reconstructed or unreconstructed. First, though, four comments on what has been said already.

A reconstructed philosophical proposition says something about the world and is, therefore, literally either true or false. In spite of all the other huge differences, in this one respect there is no difference between a philosophical proposition and, say, 'Peter is tall'. This I believe. According to Oxford, a philosophical proposition, neither true nor false, is at best a confused way of calling attention to the "logic" of non-philosophical uses occurring in propositions that are not, in my sense, the reconstructions of philosophical ones. This is the first comment. 'Confused' is the cue for the second.

All philosophical problems, or, as they say, puzzles are the result of linguistic confusion. The formula, very fashionable at Oxford, is but another way of saying that there are no philosophical propositions. I find this use of 'confusion' very confusing. To use ordinary language, to speak commonsensically, not to use any word philosophically, are one and the same thing. To confuse two or several things is either not to distinguish among them or to mistake one for another. Depending on occasion of utterance and grammatical context, some words and phrases of ordinary language have different "ordinary" meanings. The play of words that that permits has, I believe, often called attention to philosophical problems. But this is not to say that the classical philosophers confused the "ordinary" meanings. Attempting to say what is very difficult to say, they rather groped for new meanings. Whatever linguistic confusion there was, and there was plenty, is the effect rather than the cause of such gropings.

When is a word used philosophically? Some philosophers maintained that bodies do not exist. Either they were raving mad or they used 'exist' in the peculiar way I call philosophical. This is a clear case. We all know many clear cases, through experience and from the tradition. If in doubt, explore. The question must be faced each time it arises. But there is no need to answer it once and for all, by a definition. This should be obvious to the men of Oxford, committed as they are to the two propositions (these are not the two new slogans) that we can only start from common sense and that some things cannot and need not be argued directly. This is the third comment. It leads to the last.

Ordinary language is not just small talk. Scientific and moral (not, ethical!) discourse are part of it. In such areas the establishment of and the distinctions among several non-philosophical uses are often crucial. Call this the task of non-philosophical linguistic analysis. It can be performed without the sharp tool of an ideal language. One does not cut butter with a razor. Nor need one be concerned with drawing a razor-sharp line between non-philosophical linguistic analysis and philosophy. It suffices again that there are clear cases of either. Also, the former is often of propaedeutic value for the latter (and therefore quite properly done by philosophers). At Oxford they think that there is no such thing as the latter. So they overdo the former, a good thing in itself, until it becomes trivial and boring.

Language has many uses. We ask questions and issue commands. There is poetry. Some sentences are descriptive or, as one says, statements of fact. ('Fact' is also used philosophically. I speak, as always, commonsensically.) There is no doubt that philosophical propositions are meant to be descriptive. Lest this sound high-handed, consider ethics, where there is a good deal of talk about imperatives. Whatever the philosopher's position,[5] the sole purpose of such talk is to describe the facts involved in imperatives. Thus we are led to restrict our attention to descriptive statements. This the method does. *If* it should fail of its purpose, we can always return to inquire whether the restriction was the cause of the failure.

In unimproved languages unreconstructed philosophical statements are grammatically correct. This suggests the idea of an improved language. Notice the distinction between *improved* and *ideal*. An improved language is called ideal if and only if it is thought to fulfill *three conditions*: (1) Every non-philosophical descriptive proposition can in principle[6] be transcribed into it; (2) No unreconstructed philosophical one can; (3) All philosophical propositions can be reconstructed as statements about its syntax (see below) and interpretation (see below). (3) is the heart of the matter. (1) and (2) are auxiliary;

---

[5] One who asserts that 'This is good' is not a statement of fact uses 'fact' philosophically. For the explication of this use see Section Two.

[6] The phrase *in principle* refers as usual to the "skeleton" feature of ideal languages.

if they were not fulfilled, one could not possibly know that (3) was. Any attempt to "prove," directly and separately, as it were, that an improved language is the ideal one is patently absurd. This one "proves," indirectly, as well as one may by using it as a tool in philosophizing. All one can and need show is that the *four improvements* on which the method insists are not on commonsensical grounds impossible of achievement and that their being achieved does not depend on any philosophical proposition being true. This I shall now do.

First. Whether the *sentence* 'It's raining' is true or false depends on when and where it is *asserted.* The sentence 'It rained in Iowa City on October 12, 1956' is (as it happens) true whenever or wherever it is uttered or asserted or what have you.[7] Call it for the moment complete. Every scientific report is complete. The method requires that every sentence of an improved language be in this sense complete. *Second.* Consider the ellipsis 'We are far'. Sometimes, when I utter it, it is understood that I mean 'We are far from Iowa City'. (Had I driven instead of walked, I might on the same occasion have asserted its negation.) The convenience is achieved by using 'far' once as a one-term, once as a two-term predicate. This makes for "loose" grammar. Part of the price paid for the looseness is that not only unreconstructed philosophical propositions but also some unquestioned nonsense is in natural language grammatically correct. Remember Russell's 'Quadruplicity drinks procrastination'. Thus we are led to the idea of a (written) language in which grammatical correctness depends only on the shapes and the arrangement of the words. An improved language must fulfil this requirement. It is, as one says, syntactically constructed. *Third.* Consider two men speaking the same natural language. The first utters a sentence containing a word or phrase not familiar to the second. The second asks to be enlightened. The first, without pointing or resorting to any other non-verbal means, produces another sentence, with the same meaning,[8] in which the critical word or phrase no longer occurs. This can be done in many cases. Without either circularity or an infinite regress it obviously cannot be done in all cases. This leads to the following requirement. Each word of an improved language is of one and only one of two kinds,

---

[7] "Vagueness" so-called is a different issue.

[8] I know as well as the next man that in *one* of the *several* meanings of 'meaning' no substitution leaves meaning unchanged. See "Int." and, for an elaboration, G. Bergmann and H. Hochberg, "Concepts," *Philosophical Studies*, 8 (1957): 19–27.

called *primitive* and *non-primitive* respectively; for each sentence containing words of both kinds there is one and only one, with the same meaning, containing only primitive ones. *Fourth.* The second and the third requirements bring us up against the fact that a system of marks, to be a language, must be "tied" to what it is about. Call this "tying" interpretation. An improved language must be interpreted by interpreting either (1) all of its primitives, or (2) all of the sentences that contain only primitive words, or (3) by a procedure combining (1) and (2). This is the fourth requirement. It is a consequence of the third. Also, it is the only limitation which the method as such imposes on interpretation. In particular, it is not required that an improved language be interpreted by interpreting separately all, or even any, of its primitives.

No practitioner of the method ever interpreted his improved language by assigning *all* its primitives to things according to the rule *unum nomen—unum nominatum.* On the other hand, *all* interpretations ever proposed consist in part in assigning *some* primitives (they are called *non-logical*) to things. That could not be done unless the following were true.

P. *There are* several *things with which we become acquainted if they are* once *presented to us.* If *one such thing is presented to us again, we recognise it.* Construe 'thing' and 'being presented to us' as 'physical object' and 'being perceived by us' and P becomes a truism. Notice, though, that P contains no such specification. Provided only that he stays within the limits of common sense (uses no word philosophically), the kind of presentation on which a philosopher insists for the things to which he assigns his nonlogical primitives as labels is still his choice. The choice is of course determined by what he thinks is required by his purpose of reconstructing all philosophical propositions, or, what amounts to the same, solving all philosophical problems by means of his improved language. Of this later.

According to one very influential philosophy, namely, Hegel's, P is "really" false; commonsensical belief in its truth, an illusion. Since Dewey's instrumentalism is merely a scientistic version of Hegelianism, it is not surprising that he, too, rejects P. But P is also the "metaphysical presupposition" Oxford implicitly attacks whenever it attacks either the method, which as we just saw does not imply it, or the classical analysts, who indeed "presupposed" it. This, at the deepest level, is the "atomism" against which the movement rebels. *Pluralism,*

I think, would be more accurate. In Urmson all this is relatively explicit. That is one of his merits. To another structural connection between Oxford and Hegel I shall attend later. For a historical connection, it comes to mind that not so long ago Oxford was a centre of Hegelianism.[9] As far as P itself is concerned, I find myself at the limits of "direct" argument. A world in which P is false is beyond my imagination.

All practitioners of the method insist that *some* primitives, they call them *logical*, are *not* the names of anything and must, therefore, be interpreted differently. The connectives, for instance, they interpret by truth conditions (the so-called truth tables). This was in fact of tremendous importance to them. So I am not a little surprised by Urmson writing at least once (p. 95) as if he didn't know that. Perhaps it is merely a slip of the pen. Even so, it is significant. What it signifies is that Oxford has either repressed or forgotten a philosophical problem that was to all classical analysts of burning interest, namely, the explication of the nature of deductive logic (analyticity), i.e., of logic in the traditional sense, not in the all-comprehensive sense in which 'logic' is now used at Oxford. The matter will come up again. For the rest, since I must limit myself and since Urmson ignores the problem, I too shall ignore it in this study.[10]

The primitives of an improved language are in an obvious sense its simples. There is in each language still another kind of simplicity. Some sentences remain sentences if one omits from them one or several strings, each consisting of one or several consecutive words, without changing the order of the remaining ones. Sentences not remaining sentences if a word is omitted are called *atomic*. If, as in all known

[9] Confirmation of this diagnosis comes from Italy, where a keen and intelligent interest in recent and contemporary British and American philosophy is part of a remarkable cultural recovery. As far as I know, the bulk of this literature appears in three journals, *Rassegna di filosofia, Rivista di filosofia, Rivista critica di storia della filosofia*. With the historical astuteness that is part of their heritage, these newcomers discover similarity upon similarity between instrumentalism and Oxford. Some also stress the continuity with Hegel, perhaps in hope of making the importations more palatable. Most recently still another twist, depressingly foreseeable, has been added. Oxford's casuistic approach and its emphasis on "ordinary language" are said to secure *l'istoricità e l'umanità* that are so dear to Italian philosophers.

[10] As I introduced them here, the appellations 'logical' and 'nonlogical' are mere names. Their justification lies in the role they play in the classical analysts' admirable but not quite adequate attempts to explicate analyticity, which I decided to ignore in this study. For the inadequacy of Wittgenstein's attempt, see *MLP*3; for the role it plays in his ontology, Section IV below.

cases, an improved language contains both logical and non-logical words, two kinds of atomic sentences can be distinguished. Call an atomic sentence that contains only non-logical words *atomic in the narrower sense*; one that contains at least one logical word, *atomic in the broader sense*. Consider as illustration an improved language of the *Principia Mathematica* (*PM*) kind. Let 'a', 'b'; 'f_1', 'r_1'; 'F_1' stand for non-logical primitives of type zero, one, two, respectively. '$f_1(a)$', '$r_1(a, b)$', '$F_1(f_1)$' are all atomic in the narrower sense. '$(x)f_1(x)$' is atomic in the broader sense. To understand the last example, one must understand that '$f_1(x)$' is not a sentence. In the formalisms mathematicians study such expressions are often called sentences. This is technical jargon by which one must not be misled. In a language only closed expressions are sentences. It will be expedient and save words if in the sequel I replace 'atomic in the narrower sense' and 'atomic in either the narrower or the broader sense' by 'atomic' and 'atomic$_1$', respectively.

II

Urmson knows of course that, as he uses the phrase, Logical Atomism is not one proposition but many. Yet he misses some distinctions which he might have noticed had he used the phrase less freely. I shall now without either asserting or denying any of them state several propositions, investigate their connections or lack of such, then base a string of explications (reconstructions) on them. Since they are all involved in "Logical-Atomism," I shall guard against the dangers of the phrase by avoiding it, except occasionally for demonstration purposes. Instead, I shall associate each of these propositions with a letter symbol. It will save bulk if I write 'L' for 'ideal language'.

A$_1$. *L contains no primitive pseudopredicates.*
A$_2$. *L contains no non-logical primitive pseudopredicates.*

Let 'p_1' and 'p_2' be any two sentences of L, 'α' and 'β' two primitives such that 'αp_1' and '$p_1\beta p_2$' are both sentences. 'α' is called a modifier; 'β', a connector of sentences. A pseudopredicate is, by definition, a modifier or connector of sentences that is not a connective. A$_1$ is obviously stronger than A$_2$.

A$_3$. *Every sentence of L is a truth-function of atomic sentences.*

A_4. *Every sentence of L is a truth-function of atomic$_1$ sentences.*

A_5. *Every sentence of L is a truth-function of every sentence occurring in it.*

A_3 is stronger than A_4 which is in turn stronger than A_5 which is equivalent to A_1. '$(x)f_1(x)$' and '$(\exists x)f_1(x)$' are not truth functions of atomic sentences. A_3 is therefore false for all L that contain the lower functional calculus. More interestingly, perhaps, A_4, too, is false in this case. To see that, consider (1) '$(\exists x)[f_1(x).f_2(x)]$', (2) '$(\exists x)f_1(x)$', (3) '$(\exists x)f_2(x)$'.[11] Since (1) *contains* both (2) and (3), it is not atomic$_1$. Yet it is not a truth-function of atomic$_1$ sentences. On the other hand, neither (2) nor (3) *occur* in (1). Because of this difference between occurring and being contained, A_5 holds not only in the lower functional calculus but in any language, call it PM', obtained from *Principia Mathematica* (PM) by adding non-logical primitives.

The next three propositions assume that every atomic sentence of L is of the subject-predicate form. (As I use the term, predicates may be relational.) It would be easy to weaken this condition, but the game is not worth the candle. In case A_1 holds for L the parenthetical clauses in A_7 and A_8 can be suppressed.

A_6. *L contains particulars.*

Unless it is a pseudopredicate, a non-logical primitive of L occurs either in subject or in predicate places. If nothing else has been said, it may therefore, either in different sentences or even in the same, appear in either place. Or, L may be so constructed that it contains non-logical primitives which occur only in subject places. A particular is, by definition, a non-logical primitive of this kind. Notice, first, that I use 'particular' syntactically, not philosophically. Notice, second, that the definition does not presuppose a Russellian theory of types in L. Notice, third, that one could be an "atomist" in the sense of using the method, "accepting" P, and asserting A_1 and yet consistently deny A_6. An example of such an L is easily constructed. The type hierarchy of PM' is of the order type 0, 1, 2, ... Supplement PM' with variables and non-logical primitives so that the hierarchy is of the order type . . . $-2, -1, 0, 1, 2$ . . . . Since what matters logically in PM is not the absolute order numbers but merely the "width" of a sentence, i.e., the difference between the highest and the lowest type occurring in it, this addition requires no change in logic (in the narrower, not Ox-

---

[11] Assume the operator to be primitive.

ford's sense of logic). It is worth realizing how different from ours a world could be in which both P and our logic hold. One who does realise that will not easily use 'atomic' as broadly as Urmson.

A$_7$. *(Unless they are pseudopredicates) the non-logical primitives of L are all particulars.*

A$_8$. *(Unless they are pseudopredicates) the non-logical primitives of L are all either particulars or occur only in predicate places taking particulars as subjects.*

A$_7$ and A$_8$ require no explanation. The first is of course stronger than the second. There are no deductive connections, either jointly or singly, between the two classes A$_1$, A$_2$, A$_3$, A$_4$, A$_5$, and A$_6$, A$_7$, A$_8$. I turn to the promised string of explications, associating each with a letter symbol and marking each philosophical use to be explicated by italicizing the word or phrase on its first occurrence.

E$_1$. A *fact (state of affairs)* is what is referred to by a sentence of *L*. An *atomic fact* (state of affairs) is what is referred to by an atomic sentence of *L*. 'State of affairs' has the virtue, if it be a virtue to make philosophical uses sound less strained, that in the case of a false sentence it grates less to speak of states of affairs not being the case or not prevailing. E$_2$. An *existent* is what *exists*. The proposed explication: An existent is what is or could be named by a non-logical primitive of *L*. To explain first the 'could', what could be so named depends of course on how the philosopher construes, with an eye on his purpose, the 'presented' in P. This I deliberately left open, stipulating only that he remain within the limits of common sense. His purpose, to repeat, is to show that his improved language is ideal. As to the adequacy of the explication,[12] the philosophical uses of 'exist' are ontological. Ontology is above all the search for "simples," simples that are "things," neither too broadly facts nor too narrowly individuals (see below). The non-logical primitives of an improved language are those of its primitives that name things. To say about a thing that it is or could be named by a linguistic simple of the ideal language is to explicate the ontological use of 'simple' and, at the same time, say something about

---

12 As Russell knew, who invented this reconstruction but did not hold fast to it, it illuminates most strikingly the realism-phenomenalism controversy. For the mind-body tangle, see *MLP*6. One may wonder whether it works equally well for ontologies containing subsistents (eternal things, nonexistents). It works in the case of Leibniz. See "Russell's Examination of Leibniz Examined," *Philosophy of Science*, 23 (1956): 175–203.

this thing.[13] E_3. There are no *internal relations*. Reconstructed, this thesis asserts A_2. E_4. An *individual* is what is or could be named by a particular. The explication adds weight to what has been said about A_6. The method, P, and A_5 jointly do not imply that there are individuals, or, as is often said with a philosophical use of 'particular', that there are "particulars." E_5. Only individuals exist. This is the thesis of "nominalism." I reconstruct it as asserting A_7. "Elementarism" reconstructed asserts A_8.

III

So far I have not asserted a single philosophical proposition. Now I shall state what I believe to be true. This gives me two opportunities; the opportunity, first, of saying what I shall presently need in the way I shall need it; the opportunity, second, of demonstrating in a case I know rather intimately the several senses in which one can consistently be a "logical atomist" without being one in others. According to the method, this statement, like any such statement, must answer two questions. Which things are named or could be named by the non-logical primitives of my *L*? What is the syntax of this *L*? The first question naturally divides into two. How do I construe the 'presented' in P? Which things do I find thus presented to me?

'Presented' I construe as 'wholly presented in an act of direct acquaintance'. In this sense of the phrase, we are directly acquainted only with mental or, as one says, phenomenal things, such as percepts, but not with physical objects. Oxford demurs. Who mentions mental things speaks philosophically and not, as I insisted one must when specifying P, commonsensically. I disagree. Does one who mentions a memory image speak philosophically? Of course not. Oxford retorts that one can in the language of seeming and appearing speak about mental things without ever mentioning a single one. Of course one can.[14] This is wholly beside the point. He who eliminates by non-

[13] Concerning the objection from a plurality of ideal languages, see below, Section IV.

[14] This is the sort of thing which it is now fashionable at Oxford to prove with the utmost of care and circumstantiality. That is part of what makes for the tedium. Besides, philosophical analysis of the "logic" of seeming and appearing leads very quickly to the common sense root of the realism-phenomenalism issue. Moore, Broad, and Price knew and explained that very well. (It will have been noticed that when I use 'logic' as it is used at Oxford I quarantine the word by double quotes.)

philosophical linguistic analysis the non-philosophical uses of words that have also been used philosophically merely prevents himself from discovering the philosophical problems. Nothing illustrates more strikingly the nihilism of Oxford.

I am directly acquainted with such things as, e.g., sensa and some of the characters they exemplify; roughly and briefly, with all those things the *left* wing of the empiricist tradition claimed to be directly acquainted with. But I also find among the things wholly presented to me individual awarenesses and, among the characters these individuals exemplify, knowings, doubtings, rememberings, meanings and so on. Only the *right* wing of the empiricist tradition claimed to be directly acquainted with this sort of thing. Urmson, very deplorably, uses 'empiricist' so that only the left wing would be empiricist, thus excluding, on this ground alone, Locke, the Scotch school, Brentano, and G. E. Moore. In this he follows uncritically the persuasive use of the classical analysts.[15]

Among the things wholly presented to me are characters. For instance, when I have a green sensum, two things are wholly presented to me, namely, first, an individual, the sensum, which I name by a particular, and, second, a character exemplified by this individual which, since I recognize it from a previous presentation, I call by the name I gave it before. Notice, though, that in any improved language (one could say, in any language) the non-logical primitives are all "mere labels." In this respect it makes no difference whatsoever that the things named by the particulars of my ideal language do not happen to recur.

I turn to the syntax of my L. From what has just been said it is clear that I accept A_6, reject A_7 (nominalism). I also believe that A_8 (elementarism) is true. This, however, is not important. More precisely, if I found that I had to abandon A_8, I would not on this ground alone have to change any other of my views. That is perhaps of some importance, since it reveals a structural connection, quite independently of who believes what. I reject A_1, assert A_2. Specifically, my L contains one and only one logical pseudopredicate. It transcribes the meaning 'means' has in such sentences as 'the *proposition* . . . means

---

[15] There is rhyme to this unreason. To run with the left wing, we shall presently see, prevents one from having an adequate philosophy of mind. Thus one is pushed toward philosophical behaviourism. Oxford, too, is implicitly behaviourist. The false radicalism of the left wing springs, in an intriguingly complex yet lucid pattern, from the Epicurean root of the empiricist tradition. See *MLP* 17.

. . .', uttered on occasions when we do not wish to mention either psychological matters or what the *sentences* of a natural language refer to. Sentences of L containing this logical pseudopredicate are not truth functions of all the sentences that occur in them. This is why I must reject A_5. These sentences, however, are the only ones which violate A_5. On the other hand, the pseudopredicate occurs only in the transcriptions of what one says when speaking *non*-behaviouristically about minds. It follows that A_5 holds for "almost all" of my L. In a formal sense, the difference is thus small. Philosophically, I submit, it is the difference between an adequate and an inadequate philosophy of mind.[16]

Now for the promised demonstration of the dangers of the phrase "Logical Atomism." As Urmson uses it, I am a "logical atomist" because (1) I practise the method; (2) I accept P, whatever it may mean to accept the obvious; and assert (3) A_2, (4) A_6, and (5) A_8. I am not a "logical atomist" because I reject (a) A_5 (A_1), (b) A_3, (c) A_4, and (d) A_7. With one exception, Urmson ignores all these distinctions. He recognizes the difference between A_3 and A_4, though none too clearly, since he misses that between A_4 and A_5.

The classical analysts all suffered from four grave weaknesses. They invented the method and on occasion practised it superbly. But they did not see it either steadily or whole. The fully articulated idea of reconstruction escaped them. This made them all unreconstructed metaphysicians; either overtly, as in Russell's case; or paradoxically, as in Wittgenstein's before he threw away the ladder. This is their first weakness. Urmson agrees that they were metaphysicians. As metaphysicians, virtually all of them were or tended to be phenomenalists. In other words, they chose for what I believe were on the whole the right reasons, the construction I put on P. Urmson thinks that a weakness. I don't. But, since they could not hold on to the glimpse they had of the method, they were at times tempted to say such things as that physical objects did not exist or were logical constructions without remembering that in such statements 'exist' and 'logical construction' are used philosophically. This both Urmson and I consider a weakness. It is of course but an example of the first weakness.

In the style of the left wing the classical analysts all arbitrarily ignored some of the things that are wholly presented to us. This is their

[16] For details see *MLP, passim* and, at considerable length, "Int."

second weakness. I rather doubt whether (given their frame of reference) Urmson agrees. Very probably not; for this weakness is structurally related to and, I suggest, a partial cause of a third, to which
Oxford fell heir. The classical analysts all either were or tended to be
metaphysical behaviourists.[17] This is their third weakness. They were
pushed into it by, among other things, excluding from what is
wholly presented to us everything that pertains specifically to mind.
Urmson agrees that their metaphysical behaviourism is a weakness. But
since Oxford itself, as I shall presently show, is implicitly behaviouristic, he naturally misses the structural and historical connection I
suggest. So he must cast about for another. He finds it in the classical
analysts' commitment to an L not richer than PM' and, therefore, to
A_5, which prevents one from transcribing, except behaviouristically,
such non-truthfunctional statements as 'Peter knows that it rains'.
Urmson has a point. There is undoubtedly a structural connection as
well as a partial cause. But I think he overestimates it, partly because
he misses the one I suggest, partly because of the Oxford distaste for
symbolic logic, which tempts him into making PM the scapegoat for
all the analysts' sins. One need not share this distaste to insist, as I do,
that some of the classical analysts eventually became the servants of
the symbolisms they mastered.

The classical analysts all suffered from implicit nominalism. This is
their fourth major weakness. They inherited it from both the left and
the right wing of the empiricist tradition. Presently we shall see that
Urmson points at two sore spots which, as I shall then show, are
symptoms of this secret malady. But I shall also argue, from what he
says on these two occasions, that he himself is affected by the ailment.

Price[18] in a charming essay once proposed a witty formula. Logical
Positivism is Hume plus mathematical logic. Let me say it differently.
Classical analysis is Hume's data, an incomplete "ideal" language and,
perhaps most important, the vision of the method. As I see it, the
formula for the next step in the empircist tradition is: all the data, a

---

17 A metaphysical behaviourist asserts that there are no minds without realizing that he is using 'there are', as 'exists', philosophically. The almost pathetic
clash between the philosophical behaviourism (materialism) and the phenomenalism of the classical analysts should by now be obvious to everybody. Carnap
escaped from it into an implicit realism (physicalism). Russell's waverings are
notorious. For some distinctions between the eminent scientific sense and the
egregious philosophical nonsense in "behaviourism," see "The Contribution of
John B. Watson," *Psychological Review*, 63 (1956): 265–276.

18 *Horizon*, 109 (1939): 69.

complete ideal language, and a firm grasp of the method. The men of Oxford did not see this step. That is why they rebelled against the tradition.

IV

Urmson comments specifically and in detail on Wittgenstein's ontology, on his picture theory of language, and on his views about the nature of universals. Following suit, I shall examine Wittgenstein's views on these matters as well as what Urmson says about them. To do that effectively, I must first briefly attend to Wittgenstein's logic or, what amounts virtually to the same thing, the syntax of his *L*.

What was the *L* Wittgenstein proposed? A precise answer is not easy. Everyone agrees, though, that his *L* contained the lower functional calculus. He therefore ought to have rejected A_3. Again, everyone agrees that he nevertheless embraced A_3 and tried to gloss over the difficulty by "construing" *all*- and *some*-sentences as infinite conjunctions and disjunctions, respectively. Urmson rehearses the obvious objection to this dodge. Every sentence of *L* is of finite length; yet there might be an infinite number of individuals. Two other objections, which Urmson does not mention, go deeper. Granting, for the sake of the argument, that a complete enumeration, finite or infinite, has been achieved, how could we ever know that it was complete? Even granting that we know it to be complete, mere conjunction or disjunction does not, as 'all' and 'some' do, either state or imply this completeness. In the circumstances, one must search for the structural reasons and intellectual motives behind Wittgenstein's strange insistence on A_3. Urmson finds them in Wittgenstein's ontology. Presently I shall examine the merit of his diagnosis. First, though, I want to suggest another reason (and probable motive) which he misses.

As I mentioned before, the classical analysts were all greatly preoccupied with finding a satisfactory interpretation for the logical primitives of their *L*; a satisfactory interpretation being one that permits an adequate explication of the nature of analyticity or logical truth (in the narrower sense). All details of execution apart, in the case of the connectives Wittgenstein had hit upon the heart of the matter, namely, the truth tables. In the case of the quantifiers, the key is what is now known as validity theory. When the *Tractatus* was written, validity theory was as yet unborn. This alone suffices to account for

Wittgenstein's reluctance to admit quantifiers as logical primitives. As I also mentioned before, Oxford has lost sight of the classical analysts' preoccupation with logic. Small wonder, then, that Urmson misses this reason and, very probably, motive. So he must cast about for others. He finds them in an interpretation of Wittgenstein's ontology which, as I shall now try to show, is in itself questionable, to say the least. I say questionable rather than wrong, because this is not the place for detailed textual criticism and exegesis. I grant that Urmson could quote some passages in support of his view. A massive preponderance of evidence, I believe, favours mine.[19] This, I said, I shall not show. But I also believe that my view, unlike Urmson's, agrees with the spirit of the *Tractatus* as well as with that of the ontological enterprise. About this, naturally, I shall have something to say.

Ontology, we remember, is the search for simples, in some philosophical sense of 'simple', of which "everything else" consists, in some philosophical sense of 'consist'. Urmson's explication of Wittgenstein's ontology has two parts. (*a*) A "simple" is an atomic state of affairs which is the case, or, what amounts to the same thing, what a *true* atomic sentence (of *L*) refers to. (*b*) "Everything consists of simples" means that every statement of fact, either true or false, is a truth function of atomic statements, either true or false. Upon this explication A_3 is indeed crucial. The explication I propose, in agreement with E_2, has no parts. A "simple" is what is named or could be named by a non-logical primitive (of *L*). Upon this explication A_3 becomes ontologically irrelevant. (Wittgenstein, we remember, had another plausible reason for clinging to A_3.) Also, I can do without a separate explication of 'consist'. "Everything consists of simples" will naturally be taken to mean that no logical word (of the proposed *L*) names anything.

Now for three non-textual reasons why I consider Urmson's explication inadequate. *One*. According to Wittgenstein, Urmson agrees, even atomic states of affairs have "constituents." The referent of 'ar_1b,' for instance, has three, two individuals and one (relational) character. Whatever has constituents patently is not simple! *Two*. Notice the jarring necessity of introducing the qualifying 'true' into (*a*), though not into (*b*). Urmson agrees that it jars; so I shall not explain why it does. But, alas, he also blames Wittgenstein for a shortcoming that is merely one of his own inadequate explication. *Three*. The "simples"

19 E.g., 2.01, 2.02, 2.027.

ontologists look for always were and still are "things" and not "facts."
I conclude that in explicating Wittgenstein as he does, Urmson im-
putes to him three grave and implausible lapses of style. My admira-
tion for the author of the *Tractatus* leads me to plead that even if the
evidence Urmson could adduce were much stronger than I believe
it to be, he should be given the benefit of the doubt. Generally, I find
no satisfaction whatsoever in putting the most unfavourable of all
possible constructions upon any classical text. But then, I do not have
to prove, as they do at Oxford, that all metaphysics is nonsense.

A sentence (of *L*) shows, by sharing it, the *logical structure of the
state of affairs* to which it refers. This is the gist of Wittgenstein's *picture theory*. Urmson's statement of it is admirably to the point. So is
his diagnosis of the intellectual motive behind it. "What metaphysicians try to say is ineffable; it merely shows itself. In particular, they
try in vain to describe the world's structure. This structure shows itself in *L*; but, since one cannot properly speak about *L*, it remains
ineffable."[20] Urmson rejects the theory as metaphysical. Again, I
agree that as it stands it needs reconstruction. Against this helpful
background of triple agreement I shall now show four things. First.
Properly explicated, the theory becomes in one respect tautological
and, therefore, ontologically trivial. Second. It has a core which is true
and neither tautological nor trivial. Third. Urmson partly misses,
partly misunderstands this non-trivial core. Fourth. Accurate understanding of the theory leads to the refutation of a criticism of both it
and the method in general. Urmson, who rehearses the criticism,
thinks it unanswerable.

First. The phrase italicized in the first sentence of the last paragraph
is used philosophically. Thus it must be explicated. I explicate it to
mean the syntactical structure of the sentence referring to the state of
affairs in question. To understand the notion of syntactical structure,
consider once more 'ar_1b'. It is a sequence of three marks, from left to
right; a mark whose shape makes it, by definition, a particular; followed by a mark whose shape makes it, by definition, a two-term
predicate of the first type; followed by a different particular. This and
nothing else is the syntactical structure of 'ar_1b'. The notion is thus
commonsensical, not philosophical. It refers to a (kind of) physical
pattern; in the case of a written language, to a geometrical design.
Thus explicated, the "theory" becomes tautological.

[20] These are, in spite of the quotation marks, my words, not Urmson's. But I
have no doubt that he would concur.

Second. Take any sentence (of L) containing non-logical primitives, say, Hume's paradigm of a law, '$(x)[f_1(x) \supset f_2(x)]$'; replace all its non-logical primitives ('f_1', 'f_2') by variables of the proper types ('f', 'g'); define '$R_1(f, g)$' as '$(x)[f(x) \supset g(x)]$'. 'R_1' refers to a logical relation[21] of the second type. What has been done in this case can be done in all cases. It follows that the *constituents of two states of affairs exemplify the same logical relation if and only if the sentences referring to them exemplify the same syntactical structure.* This is the non-trivial core of the theory. I don't think that Wittgenstein himself saw it clearly.

Third. Urmson characteristically bases his comments on a sentence (3.1432) which, as I read the *Tractatus*, is merely an isolated and accidental blunder.[22] Assume the particulars to be blocks; the two-term relational predicates, flat discs; make the linear order vertical downwards; replace consecutiveness by contiguity. In this peculiar language we have, instead of 'ar_1b', the sentence: block resting on disc resting on block. Urmson claims, first, that the "sentence" does not exemplify the logical structure of the fact, and second, that this structure would be exemplified by one block resting on (or being in a certain direction at a certain distance from) another. In this he makes two related mistakes. He confuses the character ordinarily named by 'r_1' and, in our peculiar language, by the disc, with a syntactical (geometrical) character exemplified by our peculiar names. And he confuses a character of this latter kind, namely, a syntactical (geometrical) relation exemplified by the names, with the logical relation exemplified by the things named. His mistakes are interesting for two reasons. For one, if I may for once speak allusively, they show that the ghost of Bradley's famous conundrum still walks in Oxford. For another, the reluctance to have characters named by non-logical primitives ('r_1', or the disc), thus putting them in this respect on a par with individuals, betrays symptomatically an implicit nominalism.

Fourth. If there are several ideal languages, the "structure" of which among them is that of the "world"? This is the root of the criticism Urmson thinks fatal. *Mutatis mutandis* it can be directed at the method

21 A logical relation is a defined relation in the definiens of which no nonlogical primitive occurs. For simplicity's sake I limit myself here to sentences that contain only primitives. The limitation is easily done away with. Nor is there in all this any limitation to atomic sentences.

22 [The sentence reads: "Instead of, 'The complex sign "aRb" says that a stands to b in the relation R', we ought to put, 'That "a" stands to "b" in a certain relation says *that aRb*.'"]

as such. Assume for the sake of the argument that there are several L.[23] Since they can all serve as ideal languages, they all have the same expressive possibilities. Hence certain isomorphisms must obtain among their syntactical (geometrical) structures. This use of 'isomorphism' is commonsensical (geometrical) and not philosophical. The detailed exploration of the isomorphism involved can therefore safely be left to the mathematical logicians. Philosophically relevant are of course only those syntactical features of *an* L which, as one says, are invariants of this isomorphism. The objection thus suggests a certain mathematical sophistication in the formulation of the method. After the sophistication has been introduced,[24] the objection collapses.

Wittgenstein's individuals are rudimentary Aristotelian substances. This is Urmson's third major comment on Wittgenstein. He has a point. His argument is based on Wittgenstein's claim that some such sentences as 'Nothing is (at the same time all over) red and blue' are analytic or, as one so misleadingly says, linguistic truths. Again, Wittgenstein does make this claim. It is, as I believe I can show, inconsistent with the bulk of what he says and therefore one of the major blemishes of the *Tractatus*, but it is certainly not merely an accidental blunder.[25] The issue is subtle; so I shall separate its strands. 1. A substance is or has a nature.[26] Its nature determines the characters it exemplifies and therefore, in particular, which characters are "incompatible" (e.g., green and red), which "necessarily" connected (e.g., being coloured and being extended). 2. To insist on the analyticity, of the statements in question may be taken for a round-about way of asserting that individuals are or have natures. If so, then the particulars naming them are indeed not "bare particulars" or "mere labels." 3. Most classical analysts—though not, I think, Wittgenstein, except in those isolated but not accidental passages—fail to recognize a truth on which I insisted before, namely, that all non-logical primitives, whether they name individuals or characters, are "mere labels." This failure puts

[23] There obviously are, at least in the sense that the sentences of two symbolisms which look at first quite different, such as *PM* and Quine's version of it in *Mathematical Logic*, can be put into one-one correspondence with all deductive connections preserved.

[24] *MLP* p. 43; also "Two Criteria for an Ideal Language," *Philosophy of Science*, 16 (1949): 71–74.

[25] This is confirmed by the *Aristotelian Society* paper of 1929. For an analysis of four inconsistencies in the *Tractatus*, see *MLP*3.

[26] By the difference between *is* and *has* there hangs a tale. For an analysis of the substance notion, see "Russell's Examination of Leibniz Examined."

them in double jeopardy. On the one hand, they are tempted either to ignore individuals completely[27] or to make them into rudimentary substances. On the other hand, they are prevented from realizing that some characters are sometimes wholly presented to us. This drives them to nominalism. That much for the issue. Urmson, though he senses its structure, does not make it explicit. One reason why he doesn't is that (given the frame of reference) he approves of Wittgenstein's lapse into substantialism. From where I stand the reasons for his approval are not hard to find. Urmson shares Oxford's implicit nominalism and its Hegelian commitment to the logical nature of such truths as that nothing is both red and blue. Of this later.

V

The silence that now virtually blankets Russell's name at Oxford, the failure or unwillingness to do justice to his epochal work shocks me profoundly. One wonder whether the somewhat frenzied revival of Frege is not merely the other side of the same coin.[28] Urmson's account is an honourable exception. Some of the criticisms he directs explicitly against Russell I met implicitly in what went before. Presently I shall attend to what he says and doesn't say about the very peculiar use Russell makes of definite descriptions. First, though, I shall examine two broader issues; the nature of *basic propositions* and the problems of *reconstruction*. Russell thought and wrote about them as much as anyone; yet they are not specifically Russellian. On both of these issues the classical analysts ran into difficulties they could not conquer. On this I agree with Urmson. He also argues that the difficulties are unconquerable. I disagree. To show cause I shall therefore in each case first state the problem and indicate its solution and only then turn to what the classical analysts and Urmson say about it.

'Basic proposition' was used philosophically. Thus it must be explicated. I explicate it to mean *atomic sentence of L*. The phrase, we see, is expendable. If I use it at all, it is only for the sake of continuity. 'Basic' provides the cue for what is involved. The classical analysts set

---

[27] See the discussion of basic propositions in Section V.

[28] This is not to deny Frege's historical significance, his ingenuity, and his occasional profundity. To do that would be foolish indeed. Incidentally, Frege was studied closely in Vienna a generation ago; quite properly so, since there was then much more to be learned from him than now.

themselves the task of "proving" that veridical basic propositions possess a peculiar and peculiarly excellent kind of "certainty." This was their mistake. The task is not to prove anything, but rather to explicate *one* of the *several*[29] philosophical uses of 'certain'. This can indeed be done by means of the atomic sentences of *L*. The explication has two parts. (*a*) No atomic sentence follows deductively from any other. (*b*) The constituents of an atomic state of affairs, if they are presented to us at all, are wholly presented in an act of direct acquaintance. The strictness of the construction put on P secures the adequacy of the explication. This is *one* of the *several* reasons why P must be so strictly construed. It is also one of the motives for the classical analysts' (unreconstructed) phenomenalism.[30] Urmson diagnoses this motive correctly. I would add that even though explication of the philosophical uses of 'certain' is part of the task, the quest for some superior sort of certainty, which is so prominent in our tradition, did and still does more harm than good. But this is not to say that one cannot avoid the errors caused by the preoccupation with "certainty" without going to the extreme of rejecting P.

The troubles the classical analysts ran into with basic propositions have a common root in their implicit nominalism. More specifically, their troubles can all be traced to *three themes*. 1. They worried about the "communicability" of basic propositions. 2. One attempt to secure "certainty" succeeded only too well by seeming to make these propositions into "tautologies." 3. Another attempt led to "doubt" about their certainty.

Ad 1. The language in which we communicate with each other consists (in the spoken case) of physical noises emitted by physical objects, i.e. our bodies, in the direction of other such objects, i.e. the bodies of those whom we address. Thus, even if *L* were what it is not,[31] namely (the skeleton of) the inner monologue, it could not conceiv-

---

[29] In another philosophical use, certain is what is analytic. There are still others. Notice also that if certainty were a character of states of affairs rather than of acts, 'certain' would be a (nonlogical) pseudopredicate. This, however, is a finer point which I can safely neglect for my present purpose.

[30] This, as so much else, comes to a head in Russell's *Inquiry into Meaning and Truth*, which appeared shortly after the close of the period Urmson covers in detail. Such generalities as 'nothing is both blue and red' are neither atomic sentences nor deducible from such. In the *Inquiry* Russell wonders whether one who claims to know that this sentence is true is still an "empiricist." Thus he identifies empiricism with some sort of scepticism, which is one of the two silliest of all philosophies. (The other is materialism.)

[31] See fn. 4.

ably be the language in which we communicate with each other. *About* this latter language we can "speak" in *L*, but only after reconstructing in *L* (see below) the world of physical objects and events, including behaviouristic psychology. Once this is understood, the worry about the "communicability" of *any* sentence of *L* vanishes. The classical analysts did not understand this. Had they been consistent phenomenalists, they would therefore have worried about the communicability of *all* sentences of *L*. What then, one must ask, is the special feature of atomic sentences that caused them to worry just about these sentences? The answer is not difficult. Every atomic sentence contains at least one particular. The classical analysts thought that particulars were the only "mere labels." The idea of a label leads to that of pointing. Naturally one cannot point at phenomenal things for the benefit of others. So one cannot "communicate" about "particulars." I explained before the connections between nominalism on the one hand and, on the other, the error that only particulars are mere labels combined with an unresolved distrust of all mere labels. *Ad* 2. Assume that one who shares the illusion that '*a*' is and 'f_1' is not a mere label starts from '$f_1(a)$'. Since he distrusts mere labels, he somehow suppresses the particular. The remaining predicate is of course no longer a sentence referring to a state of affairs but a mere label naming a character. Our friend, however, not too alert to any of these distinctions, thinks that he is still dealing with the sentence from which he started. The error leads to another. He now thinks of that sentence itself as merely a label attached to a state of affairs. This is absurd; states of affairs have no names. Again, our friend is not aware of the absurdity. Nor does he grasp firmly that whether or not a sentence is a tautology depends on its syntactical structure and on nothing else. But he remembers that in attaching a label one cannot possibly go wrong. So he "concludes" that what he still mistakes for the sentence from which he started cannot possibly be false and is therefore a "tautology." *Ad* 3. This theme is the converse of the second. Those who followed it accepted particulars as mere labels but felt that predicates were more than just that. Thus they were led to believe that an atomic sentence refers to something more than could ever be wholly presented in an act of direct acquaintance. This belief caused them, quite understandably, to question the "certainty" of basic propositions. Failure to recognize that some characters are wholly presented to us is of course a major source of nominalism.

These are the three themes. The classical analysts all made either one or several of the mistakes connected with them. Urmson very astutely senses the importance of the themes. He does not see how one can decline these gambits and thereby avoid the mistakes. So he argues that the difficulties the classical analysts could not conquer are unconquerable.

Reconstruction is what Carnap called *Aufbau*.[32] Consider physical objects, say, chairs. No physical object is ever wholly presented to us in an act of direct acquaintance. It follows that in an L such as the classical analysts' (or mine) non-logical primitives cannot serve as the names of physical objects. The task of reconstruction is to design in L the definitions of terms that can so serve. Since Urmson falters on this occasion, let me recall that all reconstruction is schematic or, as one says, in principle only. Anything else exceeds our strength. For all philosophical purposes, though, i.e., for the explication and solution of all philosophical problems, the schema suffices. A reconstructionist might even turn the tables on certain of his critics by adducing, correctly I think, the very impossibility of reconstruction in detail as a partial explication of what they mean when, speaking philosophically, they insist that "a real chair is more than a collection of sensa." Be that as it may, even schematic reconstruction has more philosophically relevant features than I could possibly touch on in this study. Some of these features the classical analysts did not understand. Or they did not understand them very well. Thus they ran into problems they could not solve. Urmson thinks these problems are insoluble. My best plan, therefore, is to select the features connected with these problems. It will save bulk if I stick to chairs and write '*ch*' for the definiendum whose definiens the reconstruction must provide.

First I shall introduce a few symbols (A); then attend to their interpretation (B); then propose a schematic definition of '*ch*' (C); then explore what can be learned from it (D). The schema (C) does not make explicit all the features that can, and for certain purposes must, be made explicit. Thus it is most schematic indeed. Yet, what can be learned from it will suffice to conquer the difficulties Urmson thinks are unconquerable. This must of course be shown. If I can show it, then I shall also have shown, in an instance, why reconstruction in principle suffices. And this is the sort of thing that can only be shown by exhibiting instances.

(A) Write '*a*' and '$(\exists x)$' as abbreviations for '$a_1, a_2, \ldots a_n$,' and

[32] This use of 'reconstruct' and its derivations is of course different from that in a 'reconstructed philosophical proposition'.

'$(\exists x_1, x_2, \ldots x_n)$' respectively. Similarly, let 'y' and '$\{y\}$' stand for a series of m variables all different from $x_1, x_2, \ldots x_n$ though not necessarily all of type zero and for a prefix binding all these variables but consisting of both kinds of operators, respectively. Let 'chp' and 'chl' be molecular predicate expressions such that '$chp(a)$' and '$\{y\}chl(a, y)$' are (closed) sentences. It follows that '$(\exists x)[chp(x).\{y\}chl(x, y)]$' is also a (closed) sentence. (B) Let '$chp(a)$' be the sentence referring to what is called the sensory core of a (schematic) chair percept. Let '$\{y\}chl(a, y)$' be a generality stating (schematically) what other individuals there are and the relations in which they must stand to each other and to $a_1, a_2 \ldots a_n$ if what '$chp(a)$' refers to is (the sensory core of) a veridical chair percept.[33] (C) Define

$$\text{'}ch(x)\text{' as '}chp(x).\{y\}chl(x,y)\text{'}.$$

(D) 1. If 'ch' transcribes in principle the English word "chair," then the transcriptions of "There are chairs" and "This is a chair" are '$(\exists x)ch(x)$' and '$ch(a)$', respectively. Notice, first, that 'ch' *is a predicate*, and, second, that *L contains no terms, either primitive or defined, that refer to individual chairs*. 2. '$ch(x)$' is essentially the conjunction of a molecular and a law statement. The latter manages to state what it does only because it contains predicates referring to spatial and temporal relations.[34] 3. The second conjunction term of '$ch(a)$' thus states, as it must, that there are individuals it does not mention which stand in certain relations among themselves and to certain others which it mentions. But there is no reason whatsoever why it should also contain (the schematic reconstruction of) the statement that there are individuals with which I or Jones or anybody else will be acquainted or would be acquainted if certain conditions, in turn to be schematically reconstructed, were fulfilled.

Urmson rehearses quite a few of the usual objections. Two of them he thinks are unanswerable. He reminds us, first, that whether or not a physical object is ever perceived, or under certain conditions would be perceived, either by myself or by anybody else is wholly extraneous to its being what it is, namely a physical object, and that, therefore, a reconstruction is not even in principle adequate unless it does

---

[33] '$\{y\}$' may contain predicate variables. If it does, it may not be possible to gather the operators into a prefix. This, however, is merely a technicality. For some details, see *MLP7*.

[34] Rather detailed analyses, about as detailed as one can reasonably expect, have been given by Price and Ayer.

justice to this feature. Quite so. He adds that every "phenomenalistic" reconstruction must in this respect be inadequate. Let us see. Berkeley's first crude sketch of the idea certainly was. Nor did the classical analysts know how to rid their reconstructions of the Berkeleyan flavour. As far as they are concerned Urmson therefore has a point. The reason why they did not know how to solve this problem is, once more, that, not having learned the lesson Moore tried to teach them, they did not know how to distinguish between there being something and this something being sensed or perceived by somebody. Thus they couldn't get rid of Jones. That the problem is in fact soluble I have shown in D_2 and D_3 above.[35]

Urmson's second major objection is more interesting. A chair, to put the matter with Berkeleyan crudeness, is a pattern exemplified by an infinity of individuals. Urmson believes that even if this kind of infinity could in principle be controlled by the quantifiers in the second conjunction term, there is still another kind to which no reconstruction, either "phenomenalistic" or otherwise, could possibly do justice. For this argument the differences between English and L make no difference; so I shall write 'chair' instead of 'ch'. There is an infinite (more precisely, indefinite) number of true generalities in which 'chair' occurs. Chairs do not talk. Chairs do not leave their places by themselves. And so on.[36] Now, so the argument begins, all these truths are part of the "meaning" of 'chair'. A reconstruction, it continues, is successful if and only if the term proposed has by virtue of its definition the same "meaning" as the one it is to replace. Hence, so the argument concludes, what I call the second conjunction term would have to state all these truths; thus it would have to be of infinite length, which is impossible. The way to meet this argument is to challenge the philosophical relevance of this meaning of 'meaning' and to claim, as I do, that its study may safely be left to psychological and historical linguists. Obviously, it is forever open and growing, and therefore by its very nature not reconstructible. Historically, we recognize in

[35] Urmson expressed the opinion that even if 'ch' could be adequately defined, it would be impossible to transcribe the sentence "There is a chair in this room." Let '$rm(b)$' be the transcription of "This is a room." Since it is analogous to that of "This is a chair," we may by hypothesis assume that it is adequate. Let 'sp' be a predicate of the first type stating certain spatial relations among its arguments. '$rm(b).(\exists x)\ [ch(x).sp(x,b)]$' reconstructs in principle the sentence which Urmson claims it is in principle impossible to reconstruct.

[36] Sentences stating that chairs are available for perception, either by myself or by Jones or by anybody else, are of course among these truths.

it the "meaning" of the flower in the crannied wall. More soberly, what Urmson wants us to reconstruct is the holistic meaning of the idealists. We have come upon Oxford's second major structural similarity with Hegelianism. The other, we saw, is the rejection of P. More of all this presently.

That much for the two major issues, basic propositions and reconstruction, which, though Russell thought and wrote so much about them, are not specifically Russellian. I turn briefly to the third issue I mentioned at the beginning of this Section, Russell's peculiar use of definite descriptions.

Definite descriptions, Urmson points out, are among Russell's favourite illustrations for what can be achieved by reconstruction. This is correct. Urmson believes that to be misleading. For two reasons this is also correct. *First*, definite descriptions are often employed in cases where what they refer to either could be labelled or is of a kind that could be labelled. Thus they are not good examples of what can be achieved by reconstruction. This reason Urmson sees. *Second*. Defined terms can without further ado be used like undefined ones. Without a familiar existential premiss one cannot so use definite descriptions. If one does, he gets into familiar troubles.[37] In this major respect definite descriptions are thus not on a par with definitions; yet reconstruction proceeds by definition. This reason Urmson does not see. Since logic isn't much studied at Oxford, that is perhaps not surprising. It is surprising, though, that while he spends a good deal of time pointing at the mote, he does not see the beam in Russell's eye. So I shall, *third*, point at the beam. As every one knows and as I had occasion to mention, Russell throughout his career chafed against the (unreconstructed) phenomenalism he did not know how to escape. One of the false leads he followed again and again he found in definite descriptions. The physical object, though it cannot be named, can be referred to by a definite description. Now there is indeed no reason why, say, '*ch*' could not be replaced by a definite description.[38] This, however, is not what Russell meant. What he expected definite description to yield were substitutes for particulars naming individual

---

[37] Technically, the identity '$(\imath x)f_1(x) = (\imath x)f_1(x)$' is not analytic as, of course, it is for all genuine terms. Notice also that, even in a nonextensional calculus, '$\hat{x}f_1(x) = \hat{x}f_1(x)$' is analytic. By lumping both these cases under the common heading of incomplete symbols Russell fathered a confusion of which we still have to see the last.

[38] Of a higher type, as in 'the colour of my daughter's eyes'.

physical objects. This makes no sense for two reasons. For one, physical objects are not the sort of things that could, in his L and upon his construction of P, be named by particulars. For another, we saw (D₁ above) that L does not and need not contain any terms or expressions referring to individual physical objects.

VI

The classical analysts and their Oxford critics, including Urmson, all fail to distinguish among several uses, philosophical and otherwise, of 'meaning'. In the case of the critics this is profoundly ironical. For, do they not propound that meaning is use and therefore, varying with the latter, could not possibly be univocal? As to meaning itself, there is, first, the idea of a meaning *criterion*, i.e., of a criterion by which to decide which utterances *have* meaning. There are, second, the several *theories*[39] as to what meaning *is*, or, as I would rather say, the explications of the several uses of 'meaning'. There is, third, the claim made for one of these explications, the so-called reference theory, which, with a different emphasis, goes by the name of *verification theory*. This theory explicates quite adequately *one* of the several uses of 'meaning'. It does not explicate *the* meaning of 'meaning', for the very good reason that there is no such thing. Some classical analysts who thought that there was, also thought that the reference theory was its explication. For this they should be criticized. Oxford, however, whose theory of meaning is just as monolithic,[40] does not criticize them on this ground. Rather, it criticizes the reference theory as such. Its real target, though, is once more the "presupposition" I called P. This is the outline of my argument. Now for some details.

One who states a meaning criterion specifies, whether he knows it or not, the syntax and the non-logical primitive vocabulary of an improved language which he claims to be ideal. Since the classical analysts knew this after a fashion, they did not really use 'meaning criterion' philosophically but, rather, commonsensically about philosophy. The confusion they nevertheless produced, in their own minds and others', by their use of the phrase stems for the most part from

---

[39] The use of 'theory' for both philosophical doctrines and scientific theories invites confusion and should therefore be avoided. But it will do no harm and simplify the exposition if I for once follow the practice.

[40] See Section Seven.

their failure to distinguish between a criterion and a theory. This is one thing. The inadequacy of the criterion, or, less confusingly, of the ideal language which the classical analysts proposed is another thing. This inadequacy, we saw, stems from their left-wing radicalism, which caused them to exclude everything specifically mental from the things named by the non-logical primitives of their L. There is a hackneyed argument that refutes the "positivistic" criterion by showing that it is meaningless by its own standard. Of course it is. But why bother? Is it not much more telling that by this standard all statements about minds, our own and others', are also meaningless? Few victories are more demoralizing for the victor than those won with big guns over little sparrows. Urmson expounds with considerable zest and relish the hackneyed refutation.

There are many meanings of 'meaning'. Four of them are of special importance in first philosophy. Each of them occurs in ordinary as well as in (unreconstructed) philosophical discourse.[41] No classical analyst clearly grasped all four; all classical analysts failed at times to distinguish clearly even among those they knew. This was another source of their errors. Two of these four meanings I cannot and need not discuss in this study. One of them I call *logical*. In this use, two sentences (of L) have the same meaning if and only if they are analytically equivalent. The other is the *intensional* meaning I have mentioned before[42] and transcribe by the one logical pseudopredicate of my L. At the two remaining uses we must look more closely.

Meaning is *context*. This is the gist of the context theory. Upon this explication the meaning of a mental content, say, the percept of a word, phrase, or sentence, is the response it elicits in the perceiver. Among these responses there are or may be bodily states, overt bodily actions, and other mental contents, be they auditory images of other words or, perhaps, visual images of things and actions. This is the prebehaviouristic variant of the theory. Berkeley, we are told, anticipated it. More recently its most distinguished expositor was Titchener. If you limit the responses which constitute the "context" to overt ones and behaviouristically defined bodily states, then you have the behaviouristic variant. The latter dominates, quite properly, contemporary psychology. There is no doubt that the theory describes cor-

---

[41] This is therefore an instance of nonphilosophical blending into philosophical analysis. See Section One.

[42] See fn. 8. Notice also that, technically, the logical meaning of a sentence *is* a class of such.

rectly *one* use of 'meaning'. Psychologists, when they speak as psychologists, always use it this way. Notice, for later reference, that this kind of meaning varies with the context. Thus it makes no sense to speak of *the* (contextual) meaning of a word, phrase, or sentence.

Meaning is *reference*. This is the gist of the reference theory. Upon this explication the meaning of the English word "horse" is a certain character exemplified by all horses. The meaning of a sentence is the state of affairs to which it refers. Again, there is no doubt that we all sometimes use 'meaning' this way.[43] To see that the so-called verification theory amounts to the same thing, consider the familiar formula: The meaning of a sentence is the method of its verification. Or, less misleadingly, if we want to find out whether a sentence is true we must somehow make contact with the state of affairs to which it (or its negation) refers. The phrase "somehow make contact" is vague. Yet it will do. For my purpose the many niceties, some of which are very nice indeed, don't matter. It will even do if we limit ourselves to an atomic sentence of *L*, where there is surely no "method," since the verification is, as one says, immediate and direct. What matters is one thing and one thing only. The theory makes no sense unless one "presupposes" that every sentence of *L* has one and only one referent.[44] This "presupposition," though it is as we saw not equivalent to P, is yet, as we also saw, very closely related to it. *Oxford rejects the verification, or, rather, the reference theory of meaning because it rejects P.* Urmson makes this rather clear even though, from where I stand, his exposition suffers from two serious defects. He is not aware of any of the distinctions I made; and he feels bound to reject the obvious.

VII

Don't ask for the meaning, ask for the use. Every statement has its own logic. These are, in Urmson's words, the two new slogans. He

[43] So certainly does a teacher of German who tells us in English that he taught his pupils what "Pferd" means by pointing to a horse while pronouncing the word. *As far as communication is concerned*, his method has of course its limits. Thus its results must be checked by making sure that the pupils acquired the right "referential" contexts. Oxford, under the spell of the second Wittgenstein, makes a mountain out of this molehill.

[44] Remember what was said in Section One about 'It rained in Iowa City on October 12, 1956'.

thinks that they state, however concisely, two major ideas or guiding principles of the movement. I agree. Structurally as well as historically, he further tells us, they are both reactions against the ideas of the classical analysts. I again agree. I even believe that they epitomize very aptly all the guiding principles of the movement. There, however, agreement ends. I shall use the first slogan to show that what is being done at Oxford is not philosophy but a curiously twisted kind of psychology of language, even though a gifted follower may occasionally and accidentally, as it were, lapse into philosophy. A person's implicit metaphysics is one he holds and propounds without knowing that he is doing just that. For a philosopher it is, in an obvious sense, the worst of all. I shall use the second slogan to show that implicitly the movement embraces Hegelian idealism, which, even if explicitly held, is very bad metaphysics.

Meaning is use. This is but another current version of the first slogan. More explicitly, if you want to know what a word, phrase, or sentence means, don't look for an entity called its meaning, be it a referent or anything else, but inquire instead how it is used. Oxford thus propounds what I called a monolithic theory of meaning. Nor is there any doubt, from what Urmson says and from what is being said at Oxford, that this "new" theory is one we encountered before, namely, the old context theory. With some honourable exceptions, Oxford embraces the behaviouristic variant. This explains why most of what it has to say about language is as tedious and trivial as most of what the behaviourists have as yet been able to say. The cause of this more or less explicit behaviourism is the dislike and distrust, so unhappily prevalent at Oxford,[45] of anything mental.

One who expounds the context theory expounds matters psychological and sociological and nothing else. That is obvious. At least it is obvious to the many philosophers who consider the movement a dead end. Urmson, who is well aware of their opinion, speaks of a breakdown in communication. To say the same thing more gently, we have once more arrived at the limit of "direct" argument. So I shall attempt only two things. First I shall show how my diagnosis fits with what was said before. Then I shall try to explain why the men of the movement do not recognize what they are doing for what it is. The explanation I shall propose will fasten on differences in environment and

---

45 This trait Oxford shares with some of the classical analysts. I cannot here trace it in detail. But there are some hints scattered through this study. See also *MLP* p. 74.

tradition. Anything else would be invidious. For there are usually brilliant men on both sides of such fences.

The thesis that there are no philosophical propositions is not easily expanded. What passes for its expansion is therefore not likely to be philosophy. Some nihilists among the classical analysts soon became nonphilosophical students of artificial languages with materialism (physicalism) as their implicit metaphysics. At Oxford one cultivates the psychological study of language. The only nihilist whose practice was better than his teaching was the author of the *Tractatus*; and even he succumbed. The contextual meaning of an English word, phrase, or sentence depends on the circumstances in which it is used. So may therefore, if it has one, its referent. This shows how Oxford's espousal of the context theory fits with its rejection of improved languages in which, as we saw, reference does not depend on context. It also fits with the rejection of the reference theory. Uncritically argued, this rejection leads in turn to the Hegelian rejection of P. These are some respects in which my diagnosis that Oxford propounds the psychologists' context theory as still another monolithic theory of meaning fits with what was said before. There are still others. But we need not tarry.

Those who complain that our age is hostile to philosophy merely whistle in the dark. First philosophy has not been the major intellectual concern of any age; it has always been hard pressed by the dominant nonphilosophical concern of the day; this concern has usually been mistaken for philosophy; the latter has usually been blamed for not being what it is not. For quite some time now psychology and, more generally, behaviour science has been the dominant intellectual concern. A generation ago, under the influence of Dewey, they were in the U.S.A. mistaken for philosophy. Instrumentalism is on the wane. Behaviour science still dominates the American intellectual scene. Until most recently British academic culture strenuously ignored it.[46] Oxford was and still is the centre of this resistance. An analogy comes to mind. Those who repress too long a natural appetite tend to debauch themselves when they finally succumb. Oxford, as I see it, now enjoys its debauch.[47] The style of the revelry is coloured

[46] The only two theoretical psychologists of note Britain has produced since Alexander Bain, E. B. Titchener and William McDougall, both made their careers in the U.S.A.

[47] The direction of the export trade in old fallacies on which Broad so caustically commented is thus reversed for once.

by the spirit of the place. This spirit is philosophical rather than scientific and the overt hostility toward behaviour science still persists. That is why what is being done is not really science but a kind of armchair psychology which is mistaken for philosophy. The philosophical climate in Britain when the movement first found itself was not speculative but, rather, analytic with the accent on language. That is why what is done is nonphilosophical linguistic analysis. On the continent, where both spirit and climate are different, the dominant interest takes the even more curious form of the "philosophical anthropology" of the existentialists.[48]

I made it plausible, I think, why Oxford does what it does. I still have to explain what Urmson calls the breakdown in communication by explaining why it cannot see that what it does is psychology. The explanation has two sides, one negative, one positive, as it were. Since *modern* psychology is still a humble newcomer on the British academic scene, the men of Oxford do not really know what it is and does. So they are incredulous when they are told that what they do is logically (I use the word as they do) the same sort of thing. The positive side is of some historical interest. The central problem of *classical* psychology is the so-called decomposition by analytical introspection of all mental contents into introspectively irreducible constituents. This is of course not what they do at Oxford. Yet classical psychology is the only psychology they really know. So they are once more incredulous if they are told that what they do is psychology. Thereby hangs a nice point in historical semantics. The introspectively irreducible constituents of classical introspection are, in an obvious sense, psychological atoms (simples). Some classical psychologists put some quite arbitrary and unrealistic restrictions on the kinds of atoms of which they claimed all mental contents consist.[49] Thus their psychological "atomism" fell into well-deserved disrepute. Probably this is one of the reasons why at Oxford 'atomism' is still a bad word. So it may well be that a lingering distaste for psychological atomism was one of the sources of strength for the revolt against "Logical Atomism."

48 This fits very well with the common Hegelian root of instrumentalism, existentialism, and Oxford. Hegel's greatness, such as it was, lay after all in his intuitive grasp of the socio-psychological (historical) process.

49 For this they had (mostly implicit) philosophical reasons. See *MLP* 17. The connection with left-wing empiricism (Hume, James Mill) is obvious. For the continuity between Würzburg, the last school of classical psychology (except Gestalt) and the Wittgenstein of the *Investigations*, see "Int."

Every statement has its own logic. This is the second slogan. Negatively, it rejects classical logic as too narrow and vitiatingly abstract. Positively, it claims that there is such a thing as logic, sometimes also called logical grammar. Its task is the clarification of "meaning." Oxford thus maintains the distinction between matters of fact and of logic. This is all to the good. The trouble is that, as Oxford wants to make it, the distinction cannot consistently be made. I shall show in two ways, first how the difficulty arises, then why it is unconquerable.

Sometimes, when asserting what is false, we still make sense; we know how to use the language[50] and are merely in factual error. On this we can all agree. But consider now the sentence 'There is something which is (at the same time all over) both red and blue'. Oxford observes that no one who knows (English grammar and) the meanings of (how to use) 'red' and 'blue' is likely to assert this sentence though he may, of course, mention it as a paradigm of nonsense, in some vague and unanalysed sense of 'nonsense'. As long as not too much is made of the observation, we can again agree. Oxford, however, makes this improbability or "impossibility" (of assertion) its criterion of logical error. There the trouble starts. It becomes apparent as soon as one raises an obvious question. Where is the line that divides logical from factual error? Oxford does not face this question. So they do not notice that it has no answer. Or, rather (if one accepts the criterion) the only consistent answer is that every error, or at least, every error concerning a generality either is or with increasing knowledge (growing meanings) eventually becomes a logical error. Theoretically, therefore, *cadit distinctio*. Practically, Oxford engages in a kind of armchair observation of linguistic behaviour. The psychologism of the practice is patent. Three comments will reinforce the point.

First. According to the view predominant among the classical analysts the sentence I chose as an illustration, even though patently false or, if you please, absurd, is not "contralogical."[51] This is so because upon that view, which despite all defects in execution I believe to be correct, whether or not a sentence (of L) is analytic depends on its syntactical structure and nothing else. The sentence I chose as an

---

[50] This is short for: know how to use the words occurring in the sentence or sentences under consideration. Whenever there is no danger of confusion I shall use the shorter version.

[51] I use this barbarous word because I do not want to explain in detail what becomes apparent at this point, namely, that Oxford ignores the distinction between falsehood, contradiction, and syntactical nonsense.

illustration is synthetic and therefore, in the relevant sense of 'factual', a factual falsehood. Also, the line between the analytic and the synthetic is sharp (in *L*). So the unanswerable question never arises. Second. From Oxford we hear on this point nothing but a good deal of hermetic talk about the essential openness and stratification of language. This talk is merely another string of psychological and historical comments. Its profundity is mostly specious and hardly justifies the aplomb. Historically, all this stratified hemming and hawing about "analytic-synthetic" reminds one of the relative *a priori* of the Neokantians. Third. We have come upon further evidence that the "meaning" Oxford proposes to clarify is the holistic meaning of the idealists. Remember what was said about Urmson's major criticism of reconstruction.

The second way of exposing the unconquerable difficulty starts from a scrutiny of the alleged criterion for the contralogical and, therefore, also the logical. I shall first restate the criterion, underlining the three expressions, two words and a phrase, that stand for the three crucial ideas. "A sentence is *contralogical* if and only if one who *knows how to use the language* would not *assert* it." This proposition, I submit, is so "fundamental," particularly if one construes 'knowing' and 'asserting' behaviouristically, that upon the Oxford view it may reasonably be taken to encode (part of) the meanings of the three expressions. Still upon this view, it is therefore a "logical" truth of the kind some others, in a different version of the same confusion, call a (partial) implicit definition. Assume now, in order to simplify the exposition, what upon this view one really must not assume, namely, that we have an independent criterion by which to decide whether or not an utterance is an assertion. Assume next that someone asserts a sentence which strikes you as "absurd." There are two possibilities. Either the sentence is contralogical and he does not know how to use the language. Or the sentence is logical and he knows how to use the language. The "criterion" does not permit you to decide which of these alternatives is the case. So it is not really a criterion. The unconquerable difficulty is that a "tautology" cannot do the job of a "statement of fact." It is essentially the same difficulty which the proponents of the (idealistic) coherence theory of truth encounter.

Every factual error is or eventually becomes one of logic. An analytic sentence must do the job only a synthetic one can do. These, we just saw, are two conclusions Oxford cannot escape. Structurally, they are the very heart of Hegelianism. The purpose of this philosophy, if I may so put it, is to enhance the role of the logical (rational) at the expense of the factual (empirical). Let me recall in three easy steps how the purpose is achieved. First. Every factual sentence is merely a most imperfect predication; apparently about an "empirical" referent; really about the one true subject, the Absolute. (Hence the rejection of P.) Second. Knowledge grows through the discovery of more and more adequate meanings. (Or, as I would rather put it, we gain knowledge by designing successively more and more adequate definitions.) Three. In the ideal limit knowledge consists of a system of "axioms" that are both synthetic and analytic. They are analytic because they are true merely by virtue of the ideally adequate definitions of the terms they contain. They are synthetic because somehow they comprehend all of factual truth. Nor need one worry about the apparent contradiction. In the Absolute, as in the God of negative theology, all contradictories coincide. This, such as it is, is Hegel's (and Dewey's[52]) way out. Made explicit, I don't think it is to Oxford's taste. Yet they have no other.

VIII

Some members of the movement are very clever. Of course. Mistakes made by clever people are often interesting, particularly in philosophy, partly because of the ingenuity of their authors, partly because they force us to grasp the truth more firmly and state it more neatly. Also, alas, they are at times rather influential. There is thus much, much more to be said about the mistakes of Oxford. But enough has been said to arrive at a judgment.

The movement's metaphilosophy is nihilistic. There are no philosophical propositions. In this respect they are no less radical than Wittgenstein and Carnap. Only, the author of the *Tractatus* fortunately did propound philosophical propositions. In its practice, tediously overdoing nonphilosophical linguistic analysis, the movement is futilitarian. Its implicit metaphysics is materialistic (behaviouristic) in content and idealistic (Hegelian) in structure. The first to achieve this

---

[52] See also M. Brodbeck, "The New Rationalism: Dewey's Theory of Induction," *Journal of Philosophy*, 46 (1949): 781–791.

strange combination was Marx. From what I can tell, Sartre achieves it too. This profound similarity between Oxford and existentialism has struck me for quite some time. The two surfaces, of course, conditioned by vast differences of temper and tradition, are vastly different. At the two centres is the same failure of nerve, the same paralysis of that rarest of all gifts, the metaphysical genius.

4

Things and Descriptions

Herbert Hochberg

IN *An Inquiry into Meaning and Truth*, Russell proposed to consider a phenomenal thing like a square white patch as a collection of qualities. He did so to avoid an alternative view which would hold that the patch consisted of a bare particular (substratum) related to qualities (universals) by the special relation (ontological tie) of exemplification. To Russell his alternative eliminated an "unknowable" that had bothered philosophers since, if not before, Aristotle's introduction of prime matter.[1] Russell recognized that a problem arises in trying to distinguish adequately one collection of qualities from another—two white squares, for example. In short, he faces the problem of individuation. This we shall take up later, for I hope to show that certain arguments purporting to establish that substrata must be recognized in order to deal adequately with the problem of individuation are unsound.[2] Before doing so we shall

Reprinted with the kind permission of the author and the editor from *American Philosophical Quarterly*, 3 (1966): 1–9.

[1] Bertrand Russell, *An Inquiry into Meaning and Truth* (London: Allen & Unwin, 1956), pp. 97–99.

[2] Arguments for particulars occur in G. E. Moore, "Identity," *Proceedings of the Aristotelian Society*, 1 (1901) and Bertrand Russell, "On the Relations of Universals and Particulars," reprinted in *Logic and Knowledge*, ed. R. C. Marsh (London: Allen & Unwin, 1956). Moore's particulars are quality instances and Russell's may also be, but the arguments are essentially the same as those for bare particulars that later are suggested throughout G. Bergmann, *Logic and Reality* (Madison: University of Wisconsin Press, 1964), and in essays by E. Allaire and R. Grossmann in *Essays in Ontology* (The Hague: M. Nijhoff, 1963).

discuss some related questions that arise in the analysis of the idea of *one thing*.

Consider a white square that has only the additional property designated by "P^1," with "W^1" and "S^1" standing for "white" and "square." If "Socrates" were the name of the white square, then, on Russell's view, that term may be considered as an abbreviation for *either* a definite description of a second order class or property specifying that only P^1, W^1, and S^1 are members of it *or* for the set sign "$\{W^1,S^1,P^1\}$." [Let (a) stand for the description and (β) for the set sign.] Thus Socrates, like all individuals, becomes a class or property of properties.[3] Such a proposal involves several difficulties. To say that Socrates is white would be to assert either "$W^1\epsilon(a)$" or "$W^1\epsilon(\beta)$."[4] But both statements are analytic truths. To put it loosely, classes being what they are, the assertion that there is one and only one class having as its only members W^1, S^1, and P^1 and that W^1 is a member of that class is analytic, as is the assertion that white is a member of a class defined by enumeration to include white. The same would hold for assertions ascribing S^1 and P^1 to Socrates. Since the sentences asserting the existence of such a class, using either (a) or (β), are also analytic truths, that there is such a thing as Socrates also becomes an analytic truth. There are even stranger consequences. Assume that there were no white circles and no black squares, but that there was a black circle indicated either by a description analogous to (a) or by the set sign "$\{B^1, C^1, P^1\}$" where "B^1" and "C^1" stand for "black" and "circle." Having such terms and properties one could then construct (descriptions or) class signs like "$\{B^1,S^1,P^1\}$" and "$\{W^1,C^1,R^1\}$." Again, classes being what they are, statements ascribing existence to such classes would also be analytically true. To put it paradoxically, on the view that reduces things to classes of qualities, nonexistent things become necessary existents. The problem lies in the incompatibility of the logical properties of classes with the analyzing of things into classes of qualities. To avoid all this one would have to have some way of distinguishing between classes that *were* things and classes that simply were classes. A special property, say *existence*, at the level of prop-

---

[3] The description is $(\imath F^2)\{[W^1\epsilon F^2 \ \& \ S^1\epsilon F^2 \ \& \ P^1\epsilon F^2] \ \& \ (f^1)[(f^1\epsilon F^2) \equiv ((f^1= W^1)\text{v}(f^1=S^1)\text{v}(f^1=P^1))]\}$. For purposes of this paper 'F^2' can be read as either a second level class or property and 'ϵ' as either the class membership sign or the predicative "is."

[4] Sometimes '(a)' and '(β)' will be used to refer to and sometimes to abbreviate the description and set sign.

erties like W^1 would not do. Instead one might suggest the introduction of a higher level property that *existent* classes would exemplify. That some such thing must be done points up the peculiarities of the position. This point also serves to contrast sharply Russell's view, which turns the sentence "Socrates is white" into a statement of class membership, with the view that predication in language reflects an ontological tie between elements of a fact or of a complex thing. Class membership as a linguistic device reflects no such tie, nor is there any on Russell's view.[5] This is precisely what leads to the problems we just considered. To avoid such problems some device must be introduced which connects the members of *some* classes of qualities into individual entities. But then this connection will furnish the ontological tie, not class membership.[6]

One who holds that exemplification is a relation between a bare particular and a universal property might also claim that so viewed exemplification is something he comprehends in that he is acquainted with such an ontological connection. Class membership, however, is a logical relation he understands only in terms of predication and not in terms of direct acquaintance. Such a claim introduces a principle of acquaintance as a crucial theme in one's metaphysics. The issues surrounding such a principle will not concern us here.[7] A proponent of exemplification and bare substrata might also contend that the ontological tie must connect or relate entities that are *independent* of the

[5] Class membership is not significant for ontological questions. Part of what is involved we have just seen. That Russell's view can be stated in terms of properties rather than classes does not affect this. With "Socrates" as a second order property defined as in n. 3, predication would not reflect any ontological tie, since all ascriptions of properties to Socrates would become disjunctive identity statements that are either analytic truths or falsehoods. Where a predication is so transformed one may say no ontological connection is involved as no connection among entities is required for the statement to be true.

[6] A referee has suggested the use of a second order property of "co-exemplification" that the first order properties exemplify when there is an individual thing. This, however, would mean that Socrates was no longer a class of qualities, but qualities *in a certain relation*. Such a relation would then furnish the ontological tie and hence turn the view into one we consider later. This is disguised since such a view would also require an exemplification tie so that the qualities could *exemplify* the *relation* of *co-exemplification*. Moreover, predication would no longer be trivial as in n. 5, unless, of course, one defined "co-exemplification" by extension. Russell problematically spoke of "compresence" in this connection. See note 11.

[7] For a claim of acquaintance with substrata and the ontological tie see G. Bergmann, *Logic and Reality*, pp. 47–48.

relation. This is not so for class membership, where a class is specified in terms of its members. In part this reflects the concern over the analyticity of sentences like "Socrates is white" on Russell's view; but it also reflects other concerns that we shall take up later. A consequence of statements like "Socrates is white" and "Socrates is square" being analytic is that all statements truly ascribing properties to Socrates are logically equivalent and, in that sense, say the same thing. Furthermore, if, contrary to the simplified case we are considering, Socrates was discovered to have additional properties, then we could not, on Russell's view, truly predicate them of him unless we altered our analysis of Socrates. One can only truly ascribe properties to Socrates that are included in the specification of the class which Socrates is. One might then conclude that to say anything about Socrates is not only redundant, but involves knowing everything about the patch. If one adds relational properties to the class then one is on the road to internal relations and Bradley's Absolute. This holistic theme will also occupy us later in another context.

Quine has proposed the replacement of proper names by definite descriptions. He has some explicit motives for doing this. One that is not so explicit may be the same as Russell's. If we use a "regular" description instead of (a) to define "Socrates" we would have (γ), "$(\imath x)[W^1x \ \& \ S^1x \ \& \ P^1x]$." If one uses (γ) instead of the proper name "Socrates" one might feel that he is not required to recognize an entity that the proper name designates which is distinct from, independent of, and in addition to the properties specified in the description. For, following Russell, the meaning of a description is specified by the predicates in the description; a description is not a "denoting" sign. The description can refer to something indirectly without, like a name, being connected to that thing.[8] A name to be used independently of any description of what it names must be connected to something directly and not by means of other terms. The thing named and the connection of the name to it provide the ground for a sentence in which the name occurs, being about the thing named or referring to some fact. A description may be said to be about something in a different way. It is connected indirectly through the specified properties. This may lead one to hold that the use of a description, when there is a thing fulfilling it, reflects a consideration or analysis of that thing in terms of its properties. A name, not making

[8] Russell, in keeping with his formula that a description is an incomplete symbol, would probably not accept this formulation.

use of any properties of a thing, lends itself to the idea that it refers to something about the thing other than the properties of it—the substratum or bare particular. The use of descriptions, as opposed to names, would go along with a view that considered an individual to be composed solely of universals or properties in combination. The description (γ) does not reflect the turning of Socrates into a class of properties, but it may be thought to reflect his analysis into a *composite* of qualities. On the bare particular analysis, Socrates would be a bare particular tied by exemplification to universals white, square, and P^1. On the class analysis the white patch is simply a class of qualities. A third analysis is to consider the white patch as a composite of qualities in a special structural connection or tie that would correspond to exemplification on the bare particular analysis. On this alternative the ontological tie would hold only between universals and not between universals and a further kind of thing, a substratum. The analysis of the term "Socrates" by (γ) may be taken to reflect this view. Such a view recognizes particulars, but not as either simples or substrata. Since this alternative recognizes an ontological tie that connects qualities into things, one may hold that it does not get rid of particulars in the way that Russell did. On Russell's view the lack of an ontological tie may be considered to reduce individuals to their constituent universals in a way that the present alternative does not do. [It is perhaps relevant to recall that Russell considered classes to be "logical fictions."] However, the present alternative does get rid of *bare* individuals or substrata. If defensible, it thus reaches Russell's goal.

Before pursuing the above point let us compare the use of (γ) with the use of a proper name like "Socrates." Consider three sentences, using (γ), to assert "Socrates is white," "Socrates is square," and "Socrates is P^1." None are analytic truths. Nor would a sentence asserting that the description (γ) is fulfilled be an analytic truth. This points to a radical difference between (γ) and (a). Furthermore, the problem about the nonexistent black square does not arise in the case of (γ). Yet the three statements asserting that Socrates is white, square and P^1 are logically equivalent to each other and to the assertion that the description (γ) is fulfilled. In this sense all these statements, using (γ), say the same thing.[9] But this is neither surprising nor detrimental.

[9] The sense in which these formulations say the same thing is like the sense in which "$2 + 2 = 4$" and "$7 + 3 = 10$" say the same thing. Also with respect to intentional contexts none of these statements say the same thing as any other one.

To name Socrates is only to indicate him. Where the term "Socrates" is a name, the sentences "Socrates is white" and "Socrates is square" each state that what is indicated by that name has a certain, and different, property. A description does not *merely* indicate. It indicates by means of properties purporting uniquely to determine an object. Hence, to ascribe such properties to the object, indicated by means of them, is to do something different from indicating by means of a name. Moreover, there is an analogous, though not explicit, feature in the use of names. When seeing a white square and naming it or referring to it by a purely indicating sign like "this" or a proper name, we do so in virtue of something we notice about it. That is, one does not come across a substratum or particular apart from properties. One confronts it, if at all, exemplifying properties. In applying a name to a bare particular or substratum proponents of such things think of distinguishing them from the properties they exemplify. This may be looked upon as just another way of saying that the sign used as a proper name has only an indicating function. Hence, a bare particular becomes a hypostatization of this function of a sign. The use of descriptions makes explicit the fact that where something is indicated properties of that thing play a role. Proposing the use of definite descriptions in place of proper names may thus reflect the rejection of bare particulars as elements of one's ontology. This may be gotten at, alternatively, by holding that proper names name complexes of qualities, yet are simple, primitive signs. One who argues in this way rejects the notion that language must picture objects and hence that simple signs cannot designate complex objects. The proponent of descriptions, as opposed to names, as indicators of complexes of qualities might then be thought to accept, *to a degree*, such a "picture principle" of language while rejecting bare particulars as entities. Since his individual objects are composites of universals, the signs corresponding to such individuals must be composites of signs which refer to the universals involved. The composite sign is linked to the complex object it corresponds to since the signs it is composed of refer to the entities the object is composed of. Furthermore, while descriptions, as complex signs, would correspond to complexes of qualities as complex entities, they would do so only to a certain degree. That is, a description need not contain predicates indicating all the qualities of the indicated object. An object described by (γ) on the present alternative could have further properties. Thus another problem that arose on Russell's view does not arise. Suppose, a bit more realistically than our simplifying assumption that Socrates has properties in addition to W^1, S^1, and P^1, but that predicates referring to these additional properties do not enter into his description in (γ). To ascribe any such additional properties to him will not in the least be to say "the same thing" as ascribing properties included in the description. Nor will any two such ascriptions say the same thing as each other. Thus a further difference to Russell's view is involved. Moreover, one must not be misled by the following argument. Suppose W^1, S^1, and P^1 suffice to individuate Socrates, then if in addition he has R^1 and Q^1, the set of properties W^1, S^1, P^1, R^1, and Q^1 will also individuate him. Let (γ^1) stand for a description constructed from this latter set of predicates. Then the identity "$(\gamma) = (\gamma^1)$" will hold. We could then replace the definition of the term "Socrates" by the more extensive descriptive phrase. One could do this for all the descriptive properties of Socrates and hence turn any statement ascribing one of these to him into a statement logically equivalent to any other statement ascribing a different property to him. The point to be made in reply is that the above identity statement is synthetic.

Those who advocate a bare particular analysis and the naming of such things still, generally, hold that one indicates past objects or things one is not now acquainted with, and hence not capable of being simply and directly indicated, by definite descriptions. Hence, to say about such things that they have or had certain qualities involves the same seeming redundancies. On a bare particular analysis one avoids these seeming redundancies at the price of introducing two kinds of entities. First, there is the mysterious bare particular which is named. Second, this entity combines, by predication, with a universal to form a fact which determines the truth of a sentence asserting that the thing has the quality. Such a true sentence may even be thought to refer to this further thing, the fact. On the alternative analysis, since the white patch is considered a combination of qualities no further entity is involved. A true sentence ascribing a quality specifies a constituent of the complex indicated by the descriptive phrase. It does not assert that something is related to what is indicated and hence refer to a third, complex, entity comprising the two relata in a relation of predication. Holding that Socrates is a composite of qualities one might say that it is the complex thing that makes the sentence true.

All this brings us to the question of individuation, for it is on this issue that the bare particular analyst bases his case. Supposedly, alternative views cannot account for individuation and difference.

Quine sought to solve the problem of individuation by introducing peculiar individuating properties and basing descriptions on predicates referring to such properties—"Pegasizing." He made one mistake in holding that such primitive properties could be introduced for unfulfilled descriptions. Thus he had signs whose only function was an indicating one with nothing being indicated. But we are not here concerned with questions about references to non-existent "things." Talking about existent things having a unique property, which serves solely to individuate them, simply puts proper names (and bare particulars) at the predicate level. Such properties of individuation are certainly as puzzling and mysterious as bare substrata, and, like these latter, are hypostatizations, in a more devious way, of the simple indicating function that some terms may have.

Russell tried another approach. Consider two white patches, Socrates and Plato. Assume that they are alike in all non-relational descriptive properties and that Socrates is to the left of Plato. To distinguish them qualitatively Russell assigned to each the property of being at a place in the visual field. Some would object to this on the grounds (*a*) that they are not acquainted with such properties of things, and (*b*) that space is relational, while on Russell's proposal it is not.[10] But is Russell's suggestion so outlandish? Given a succession of phenomena cannot one recognize that a patch is in the same part of the visual field as a previous one, just as he recognizes that it is the same color as the previous one? However, given a succession of exactly similar visual fields one might also have to have recourse to similar properties of a temporal kind. Perhaps such properties cannot stand up to philosophical probing. But this question can be waived here, for one has had recourse to such properties due to the acceptance of certain arguments that forbid the use of relational properties for purposes of individuation. These arguments, I wish to show, are not cogent and, consequently, one may employ relational predicates in descriptive phrases to indicate Socrates and Plato.

Suppose that in order to distinguish the descriptions of Socrates and Plato, where Socrates and Plato are two exactly similar patches with Socrates being to the left of Plato, one proposes to include in the description of Socrates the predicate "being to the left of Plato." This would immediately be seen to be inadequate since the definition of such a predicate would have to include the descriptive phrase indicating

[10] G. Bergmann, "Russell on Particulars," reprinted in *The Metaphysics of Logical Positivism* (London: Longmans, Green & Co., 1954), and in this volume.

Plato. This in turn would have to include the predicate "being to the right of Socrates" or it would not have been uniquely specified as distinct from Socrates, for, recall, all its non-relational properties are shared with Socrates. But this problematic situation is easily changed. Suppose one introduces the property L, with "R" standing for "right of," by

$$Lx = df(\exists y)(Ryx \,\&\, Wy \,\&\, Sy)$$

and suppose further that no white patch is to the right of Plato. For a thing to have L is to have a white square to its right. To the use of such a property the proponent of bare particulars retorts that to use a relation we must already have terms standing in that relation, and hence to use a relational property as a constituent property in forming a definite description is illegitimate. This argument is confused on two counts.

First, it confuses "being about" a white patch in the sense of saying that something is white with formulating a descriptive phrase to indicate or be about the thing. Thus in formulating the descriptive phrase to indicate Socrates one refers to Plato only in that one talks about something being to the right of Socrates. It is not a question of using the descriptive phrase for Plato in the construction of a relational property to individuate Socrates and of using the descriptive phrase for Socrates in the construction of such a property for Plato. Consequently no circularity is involved.

Second, one might, to use a cryptic and loose phrase, say that *logical* and *temporal* priority are confused. Perhaps the point can be clarified in the following way. One must indeed notice Socrates as distinguished from Plato. One can also refer to these different things by different names. This does not mean, having done this, that one cannot consider an analysis of the things in terms of properties and of the names in terms of descriptions composed of predicates referring to those properties. Two patches are noticed to be different and in a spatial relation. To notice them in a spatial relation does involve that instance of the relation depending on there being things related. But this does not mean that the things related do not also depend on that instance of the relation. Without there being some spatial relation between them "they" would be one and not two. Nor does it mean that such mutual dependence prohibits the use of the relation in an analysis of the things. One might think otherwise if he confuses a relation with an instance of it and thinks that "L" must be defined in terms of "being to the right of Plato" instead of in terms of "*R*." Also, if one holds that exemplification is the ontological tie or relation and that such a tie must hold between independent relata, he might hold that all relations require ontologically independent relata. It is understandable why one would hold that exemplification requires independent and simple relata. Recall the sentence "Socrates is white." If the subject term is held to refer to a composite entity that contains whiteness, and thus *depends* on the universal, one might feel that predicating "white" of Socrates is redundant, or empty or analytic. This we discussed earlier. Furthermore, one who adheres to a picture principle of language would naturally believe that predication in language ought to reflect the ontological tie between the simple elements of an ontology. On the view adhering to substrata, universals, and exemplification it seems to. On the alternative view it apparently does not since the description (γ) refers to a complex in which both the tie and the universal are constituents. The ontological tie on this view combines simple universals into things; it does not combine a substratum and a universal into a fact. This difference is behind the fear that predication without substrata is empty. Be that as it may, that relations are not presented without relata does not mean that one cannot analyze particulars in terms of qualities and relations. Ontology is not phenomenology. Thus even if one may notice something without being aware of what relations it stands in or properties it has, that fact has no bearing on the issue. To the bare particular analyst it might. Thus he may argue for numerical difference as distinct from conceptual difference by holding that he can apprehend our two patches as different without noticing how they differ. One might then think that if he notices *simply* that two things differ, they must differ in *simples*. Since they do not differ, in our example, in simple nonrelational properties, and, since relational properties "involve" terms (and hence are thought incapable of grounding simple difference), they must differ in simple bare particulars. From what one simply notices, one is thus led to a kind of ontological simple. Since, via a principle of acquaintance, one convinces oneself that a bare particular is an object of acquaintance, the circle is closed and the knot is tied. The bare particular is the ontological representative of apprehended difference and the ground of numerical difference. We may protest that all this is far too simple. For some might feel that they just don't know what it is to apprehend two particular things as different without apprehending them to be different in some way. But that aside, the above argument confuses what I apprehend with the analysis of what is apprehended. To put the matter slightly differently we may say that without there being a difference in property (including relations) between Socrates and Plato there would be no apprehension of simple difference. That this is so points up that what "makes" them different is one question. Whether they may be apprehended as simply different is another. It is relevant to notice that for the bare particular analyst there is the possibility of having Socrates and Plato be different while not differing in any properties or relations, for bare particulars may be simply different, and, I take it, could be apprehended as such. That this does not happen is, from the perspective of the bare particular analyst, a fact about our world. Looked at from another perspective it reveals an inherent absurdity in the bare particular analysis. In any case, as I am said to notice something being simply different from something else, it is then thought that this difference must not, ultimately, be grounded or analyzed in terms of properties or relations. In addition to the problematic nature of this assumption, there is the sheer question-begging element involved in the notion of "something." If "something" is taken as a bare particular then, of course, from the very role such a thing plays it is simply different from another such thing. But if the something is taken as the patch from which we start our ontological analysis, then the matter is not closed. We may still consider it to be a composite of qualities. If at this point one argues that it cannot be analyzed as a composite of qualities, because it is just seen as a distinct thing, not as a composite, I hardly know what to say, except to repeat that ontology is not phenomenology. Of course Plato and Socrates are apprehended as distinct things. This is where analysis begins. But this does not mean that the bare particular analysis is the correct one. Some may think that it does—that to say that bare particulars account for the difference of Plato and Socrates is simply to say that the latter are different. This explains why one may also convince himself that he is acquainted with bare particulars. It also points up that in attempting to defend bare particulars as entities and as objects of acquaintance ontology may be reduced to triviality.

We may then reject the arguments we have considered in favor of bare particulars and allow a description which employs a property like *L* to indicate Socrates. For objects, one need not recognize numerical difference as distinct from conceptual difference. For what *makes* Socrates differ from Plato may be held to be a quality occurring in his description. In this context, we might note something about numerical difference. Suppose in order to reflect that relation we introduced into a language schema a predicate "D," as a primitive predicate distinct from "$\neq$," the latter being defined in the Russell-Leibniz fashion as "$\sim (F)$ $(Fx \equiv Fy)$." Whatever else the property D would involve it would be such that (δ) "$(x)(y)[x \neq y \supset Dxy]$" would be true. Otherwise one *would* have conceptually different things being numerically the same. But it is difficult to consider what that would mean. I cannot. This is part of the peculiarity about "D." It is, supposedly, a primitive predicate, yet (δ) is hardly an empirical generalization. Hence (δ) becomes either a synthetic *a priori* truth, a partial or implicit definition, an addition to the analytic statements of the language, or what have you. In short it becomes some form of necessary truth. Consider two things that are numerically different, a_1 and a_2. a_1 will not be numerically different from itself, hence there will be a context involving the property D that distinguishes a_1 from a_2. That something does not differ numerically from itself will, I take it, be a "necessary" truth like (δ). Hence, it will "follow" from two things being numerically different that they are conceptually different. For, to put it paradoxically, D is a concept among concepts. Therefore, (ϵ) "$(x)(y)[Dxy \supset x \neq y]$" will also be a kind of necessary truth. [Just as "follow," above, reflects a kind of "inference."] Thus "D" and "$\neq$" are, in some sense, "logically" equivalent notions. All this points up both the redundancy and peculiarity of "D," as a primitive predicate, and why numerical difference is represented in the language schema, not by "D," but by the occurrence of different signs for different things. Numerical difference, like conceptual difference, is said to be "logical," but in a different sense. The relation expressed by "$\neq$" is logical in that it is defined in terms of logical signs—connectives, variables, and quantifiers. Numerical difference is logical by analogy to predication. The latter is reflected in a language schema by a syntactical device, say juxtaposition and the type distinction, to show that what is reflected is a structural or ontological tie rather than an ordinary relation and to acknowledge and avoid the puzzles associated with Bradley. But the problems about "D" are not on a par with Bradley's puzzles about predication. Any ontology must acknowledge some *connection* or *tie*, corresponding to predication, and distinguish it *in kind*, to avoid Bradley's problems, from what it connects or ties. Numerical difference is another matter. To put it cryptically one doesn't need either it or bare particulars in the way in which one needs a tie like predication. Hence the peculiarities about "D" reflect, not a general or logical feature of ontology, but puzzles arising from a particular solution to the problems of ontology. This may be ignored by assimilating numerical difference to predication as a basic logical or structural or categorial feature of reality.

To the view that Socrates and Plato are composites of qualities, including relations, it may be objected that this forces one to acknowledge that a thing changes when what it is related to changes. In short one is involved with *internal relations*. Thus if L is included in the set of properties that constitute Socrates, the replacement of Plato by a red square would mean that Socrates was no longer what he was. Yet, if one is talking about phenomenal things he may well, for a variety of reasons, hold that such things neither change nor persist through change. That Socrates does not persist through a change—the disappearance of Plato—would be perfectly in keeping with this contention. Even if one does not restrict himself to phenomenal entities, but rejects continuants, the point would be the same. Actually, the bare particular analyst faces the same problem in his own way. Given that Socrates and Plato are bare particulars and that the latter disappears then to hold that Socrates persists through time forces him (1) to acknowledge that qualities, relational or otherwise, are attributed *at a time* rather than simply predicated, (2) to hold that the persistence of Socrates is not to be taken literally since another particular exactly like Socrates is what is to the left of the red square after the change, or (3) to divide, but not reduce, Socrates into parts coincident with the period before and after the change; this would involve there being three bare particulars—Socrates and his temporal parts—related in certain ways. (1) and (3) introduce continuants. (2), in rejecting continuants through relational change, reflects the point about internal relations. Here we are not concerned to explore the issues surrounding (1), (2), and (3) on a bare particular analysis. The point simply is that the same sorts of problems face such an analyst. Further, certainly a variant of (1) is possible on the analysis of Socrates into a composite of qualities if one makes use of predication *at a time*. Unlike (3), however, a composite, as opposed to a bare particular, is not literally the same composite through a change of a constituent. But the peculiarity of (3) reveals the problem of acknowledging continuants on a bare particular analysis. The issue is then whether there are continuants through relational change. If one is convinced that there are no continuants at all, then the analysis of Socrates into a composite of qualities including relations would cause no anxiety. If one is convinced that there are continuants, then perhaps he will argue for bare particulars on such a ground. But this is to base his contention on arguments differing from those we are rejecting in this paper.

A proponent of bare particulars may raise two further objections to the view we are considering. First, he might hold that the use of descriptions begs the question since (1) zero level variables are employed, and (2) the connection of predication is used. But, while zero level variables are used, composites of qualities not bare particulars are, as some say, the "values of the variables." And, the linguistic relation of predication need not reflect the ontological connection between a bare particular and a quality. What it *reflects* is the ontological connection between qualities in a composite. Further, it is used to specify a member of that composite in a true sentence about it. Second, he might point out that to hold that things are composites of qualities is to turn predication between zero and first level signs into something different from predication between first and second level predicates. To say that green is a color is not to say that green, a simple, is a composite containing color as a constituent. Yet one might wonder if exemplification between a bare particular and a universal is the same thing as exemplification between two universals. It is the same in the sense that it holds between simples in both cases and that in both cases the simples are thought to combine into facts. It is different in that the simples are of logically different types. Moreover, only the substrata and first level universals are held to be constituents of the things we started out to analyze. This crucial difference indicates that exemplification, on the substrata analysis, does not function uniformly. The question invites detailed analysis. The point here is that it is not obvious that the bare particular analysis requires fewer ontological ties. If that analysis does require fewer such ties then this would be a point in favor of it. But this is a different argument for bare particulars than those we are rejecting.

A definite description need not specify all the properties of what is described, only those sufficing to individuate. One might feel that it should mention all, eventually, since then the descriptive term will reflect, in language, what sort of entity is being described—its structure so to speak. For, it will show that it is a composite and what it is composed of, just as, on a bare particular analysis, a proper name referring to a bare particular reflects, in language, that it is and what it is—a simple particular. Thinking of the predicates in a description as furnishing a meaning for the descriptive phrase, one then thinks the addition of predicates to a description reflects the growth of meaning. Including relations of all kinds can lead one to hold that to know what a thing is, i.e., to know what the term indicating it means, is to know everything. Hence including relational properties in the descriptions of things leads one to Bradley's holistic Absolute. Also, one is led to the complete redundancy of all statements about something when using such a comprehensive description. Alternatively taking a bare particular as the meaning-referent of a proper name avoids such redundancy. But one must not be misled by the way this matter is put. A fulfilled description indicates or is connected with a thing by means of the predicates in the description. We can then distinguish two aspects of a description: first, its indicating role and, second, its meaning in the sense in which the latter is specified by the predicates it contains. In view of the second, one may be led to hold that of two descriptions of the same thing the one that specifies more properties provides more meaning. But all this could mean is that since one answers the question "What is this?" by listing properties a more complete description provides a fuller answer to that question. If we keep separate the questions (*a*) "What is it?" in the sense of what are its non-relational properties; (*b*) "What is it?" in the sense of all the things one can say about it; (*c*) "What is it?" in the sense of what properties need be specified in order to individuate it; (*d*) "What is it?" in the sense in which the answer is simply "a composite of qualities"; (*e*) "What is it?" in the sense in which one asks "What is being indicated?" and in which the answer might be simply "this"; then no harm is done. Mixing different senses of this "question" can lead one, on the one hand, to invent bare particulars, and, on the other, to Bradley's Absolute. That one could indicate a complex of qualities by the term "this" or a proper name does not mean that there need be an additional simple entity which is what is really named. To think so is to accept uncritically the principle that a simple term must indicate a simple thing. One who feels forced to indicate a composite of qualities by a complex sign such as a definite description also, in a way, accepts this principle. But such a principle is not bound to the view that things are complexes of qualities. One may on rejecting this principle indicate such complexes of qualities by proper names—signs with a purely indicating function. This is another matter, though we may note here that it is an alternative that could avoid the consideration of relational properties in the complex that constitutes the thing.[11] (Two complexes of non-relational qualities would just be different as bare particulars are just different.) One might suggest that both the bare particular analyst and the holist accept the principle that language must picture reality in an extreme form. Just as one invents a simple thing to correspond to a simple term, the other holds that the corresponding term must reflect all the complexity of the complex thing. Hence, in order for a description to indicate a composite of qualities it must indicate all of them, including relations. As our knowledge of a thing grows *what the thing is* is revealed by the term that indicates it—by its *meaning* or *definition*, which is specified in terms of its constituent predicates. We then arrive at absolute idealism and the notion that all statements about a thing are redundant or analytic. All that is then left to be said about "what it is" is that it is what it is—"Reality is reality." This illusion and that of bare particulars are opposite extremes of the same kind of mistake.

11 What I have called "Russell's view" is not, literally, what he proposed, since he treats the sign "Socrates" as an undefined sign (a proper name) to avoid turning sentences like "Socrates is white" into analytic truths. But as he analyzed objects into classes of coexistent qualities and did not recognize the need for (or role of) an ontological tie, his use of names for classes is specious. To argue this point is beyond the scope of this paper, though part of what is involved is touched on in notes 5 and 6. The use of proper names for objects considered as complexes, but not classes, of qualities is discussed in "Things and Qualities" in the proceedings of the Oberlin philosophical meetings for 1964.

5

Russell's Theory of Relations

William J. Winslade

METAPHYSICIANS have usually treated relations in one of two ways: as real features of the world or as mental entities. Among those who classify relations as real are Aristotle, Aquinas, McTaggart, and Wittgenstein; among those who classify relations as mental are Ockham, Locke, Leibniz, and Bradley. Russell clearly should be listed with those who think that at least some relations are real features of the world, not merely products of the mind. Russell went further than most philosophers in emphasizing that "the question of relations is one of the most important questions that arise in philosophy, as most other issues turn on it: monism and pluralism . . . idealism and realism, in some of their forms; perhaps the very existence of philosophy as a subject distinct from science."[1] Although Russell may have exaggerated the importance of relations, the adequacy of his ontology depends to a great extent upon the soundness of his theory of relations.

In this paper I will examine six of Russell's ontological commit-

I am indebted to Ann Winslade for her many helpful comments and suggestions and to Henry B. Veatch who aroused my interest in this problem.

[1] Bertrand Russell, "Logical Atomism," reprinted in *Logic and Knowledge*, ed. Robert C. Marsh (New York, 1956), p. 333. Subsequent references will be to works by Russell unless otherwise indicated.

ments concerning the nature of relations. They can be summarized as follows:

(1) Relations are real features of the world.
(2) Relations cannot be reduced to properties.
(3) Relations have a sense.
(4) Relations and pluralism are interdependent.
(5) Relations are constituents of relational facts.
(6) Relations are unparticularized universals.

My procedure will be to discuss each thesis separately as well as to bring out the ways in which the theses are related to each other. In reconstructing Russell's theory of relations, I will call attention to his insights, but I am primarily interested in assessing the consistency of the theory. I will argue that the thesis that relations are unparticularized universals is inconsistent with the thesis that relations are constituents of relational facts. If relations and relata form facts, relations cannot be unparticularized universals. There is some evidence, however, that Russell finally came very close to resolving the inconsistency.

Some preliminary comments about the nature of Russell's metaphysics and my attempt to deal with it are called for. Russell developed his theory of relations in attempting to describe the structure of the world (not just of the concepts) of ordinary experience. The ontology of relations was discussed for the most part in the object language of particulars, properties (qualities), and relations. With some hesitation I have adopted Russell's terminology in order to represent accurately his metaphysical views. Certain logical, linguistic, and epistemological assumptions and theories that Russell held have been introduced in order to explain his ontology of relations. Although Russell used the word 'relation' broadly because he apparently thought that all transitive verbs express relations,[2] I use 'relation' in a restricted way to include only relational expressions of comparison ('larger than', 'similar to'), of space and time ('to the right of', 'earlier than'), or of production ('author of', 'father of'). For if any linguistic forms denote real relations, some of these do.

(1) Russell advanced the thesis that relations are real features of the world in opposition to idealists and other philosophers who either

---

[2] "On the Relations of Universals and Particulars," reprinted in *Logic and Knowledge*, p. 108. See also *The Problems of Philosophy* (New York, 1959), p. 92. For a criticism of Russell on this point see Anthony Kenny, *Action, Emotion and Will* (London, 1963), pp. 151–170.

neglected relations altogether or thought that relations were mental entities. The denial of the nonmental reality of relations was based on the belief that our minds "produce" relations when we make judgments that objects are related. Both Leibniz and Bradley, for example, maintained that relations are at best mental entities. While Leibniz distrusted relations because they are neither substances nor accidents, Bradley expressed contempt for relations because he was convinced that relations are ultimately self-contradictory. Many philosophers who were less skeptical were nevertheless unwilling to treat relations as real features of the nonmental world.

The prejudice against relations was a consequence of the linguistic and logical presuppositions of many traditional philosophers who used subject-predicate logic. According to the traditional doctrine, every true descriptive statement could be expressed by copulating a predicate adjective with a single subject. This doctrine, Russell contended, had two serious limitations. First, it led to a neglect of verbs and prepositions which express relations.[3] Second, it led to a failure to realize or at least to allow for the difference of logical form between relational statements such as 'this is smaller than that' and nonrelational statements such as 'this is round'.[4]

As a result of the bias against relations in subject-predicate logic, relations were usually ignored in substance-accident ontologies. Russell argued that a metaphysics of things and qualities, modeled on subject-predicate logic, provided an incomplete "account of the world of science and daily life."[5] He went on to say that "a complete description of the existing world would require not only a catalogue of the things, but also a mention of their qualities and relations."[6] Russell insisted that the "independent reality"[7] and the "absolute and metaphysical validity"[8] of relations must not be overlooked.

Certain aspects of Russell's theories of denotation, meaning, and truth reinforced his belief that relations are real features of the world. With considerable oversimplification, I will summarize those doctrines which bear on the present issue. Russell thought that descriptive ex-

[3] *The Problems of Philosophy*, pp. 92–93.
[4] *Our Knowledge of the External World* (New York, 1956), p. 42.
[5] *Ibid.*
[6] *Ibid.*, p. 47.
[7] *A Critical Exposition of the Philosophy of Leibniz*, 2nd ed., with appendix (London, 1937), pp. 14–15.
[8] *The Principles of Mathematics*, 2nd ed., with introduction (London, 1937), p. xviii.

pressions—expressions for properties and relations—in true descriptive statements denote entities. The fact that descriptive expressions denote entities accounts for their meaning as well as their contribution to the truth of the statement. Russell could not understand how descriptive statements could be meaningful or true unless expressions for properties and relations sometimes denote real things. Consider Russell's example: "Suppose, for instance, that I am in my room . . . the word 'in' has a meaning; it denotes a relation which holds between me and my room. This relation is something, although we cannot say that it exists *in the same sense* in which I and my room exist."[9]

In the preceding passage, Russell said that relations do not exist in the same sense that persons or physical objects exist; he also claimed that relations "have a being which is in some way different from that of . . . minds and from that of sense-data."[10] Russell held that relations are found in the world of universals, among those entities which are neither material nor mental and which subsist rather than exist. The distinction between existence and subsistence, which Russell inherited from Meinong, is extremely difficult to interpret. For the moment I will put this problem aside, but I will return to it in the subsequent discussion of the thesis that relations are unparticularized universals.

Up to this point I have merely been trying to show why Russell thought that relations are real features of the world. I have mentioned his reactions to philosophers who denied the reality of relations, his assumption that no adequate theory about science or ordinary experience can be constructed unless relations are real, and his belief that relational expressions must denote to be meaningful or to be used as descriptive elements in true sentences. Perhaps Russell's reactions were too extreme, his assumption unwarranted, or his belief mistaken. Russell's claim that relations are real does have an appeal, however; for it is difficult to imagine a world—such as a Leibnizian or Bradleyan world—in which there are no real relations. But even if we suppose that relations are real features of the world, it remains to be seen whether Russell's further claims about the nature of relations are acceptable.

(2) The thesis that relations cannot be reduced to properties is one of Russell's most famous insights. Yet sometimes instead of arguing for this claim, Russell merely characterized relations with the following words: 'independent', 'absolute', 'ultimate', and 'irreducible'.

9 *The Problems of Philosophy*, p. 90.
10 *Ibid.*, p. 91.

At other times he said that relations are indefinable and implied that their irreducibility was self-evident.[11] Contrary to Leibniz, Russell asserted that relations are "distinct from and independent of subject and accident."[12] Considerations such as these suggest that Russell thought not only that relations cannot be reduced to properties, but also that relations cannot be reduced to any other entity or set of entities. Although Russell might have taken the general thesis that relations are irreducible for granted, he argued only for the specific thesis that relations cannot be reduced to properties.

In *The Principles of Mathematics*[13] Russell gave serious consideration to the Leibniz's "monadistic" and Bradley's "monistic" theories of relation. According to both theories, which were based on subject-predicate logic and substance-accident metaphysics, relations could be reduced to properties. The monadistic theory reduced relations to properties of related terms; the monistic theory reduced relations to properties of larger wholes. Accordingly, the nonmental reality of relations was denied by Russell's opponents on the grounds that relations could be reduced to properties. Russell maintained, however, that relations are "ultimate and not reducible to adjectives of their terms or of the whole which they compose."[14]

Although Russell's classic argument for this claim was fully worked out in *The Principles of Mathematics*, for our purposes it can be summarized as follows. Relational propositions, especially those expressing asymmetrical relations, cannot be analyzed without a loss of meaning into subject-predicate propositions. Consider, for example, '*A* is greater than *B*'; the meaning of 'greater than' cannot be captured by two subject-predicate propositions, one attributing a magnitude to *A* and the other attributing a different magnitude to *B*. According to Russell, "mere difference of magnitude is not *all* that is involved. . . . We shall have to say that one magnitude is *greater* than the other, and thus we shall have failed to get rid of the relation [denoted by] 'greater'."[15] Since Russell believed that in this respect the structure of logic mirrors the structure of the world, he concluded that relations cannot be reduced to properties.

---

[11] "Meinong's Theory of Complexes and Assumptions," *Mind*, New Series, 13 (1904): 204, 209.
[12] *A Critical Exposition of the Philosophy of Leibniz*, p. 13.
[13] *Ibid.*, pp. 221 ff.
[14] *Ibid.*, p. xviii.
[15] *Our Knowledge of the External World*, p. 45.

What, then, is the connection between (1) the thesis that relations are real features of the world, and (2) the thesis that relations cannot be reduced to properties? Russell could not argue that (1) entails (2) without begging the question against his opponents. Russell apparently thought that (2) entails (1), for he sought to support (1) by arguing for (2). But there are two reasons why this is not the case. First, Russell produced no argument for the general thesis that relations are irreducible entities; relations might be reducible to some entity or set of entities other than properties. Second, even if relations cannot be reduced to properties, it is still possible that relations are mental entities. The connection between (1) and (2) is weaker than entailment. The argument for (2) partially supports (1), however, for it explains why traditional efforts to reduce relations to properties in order to deny that relations are real features of the world have failed. Furthermore, (2) clarifies Russell's views on the nature of relations by further specifying what Russell meant by saying that relations are real features of the world.

The thesis that relations cannot be reduced to properties needs to be analyzed further. For it implies that relations and properties are essentially different, but it does not tell us how they are different. The thesis that relations have a sense provides a partial explanation, but the thesis that relations and pluralism are interdependent more fully explains why relations cannot be reduced to properties.

(3) Russell's thesis that relations have a sense is found in the chapter on "Relations" in *The Principles of Mathematics*: "A relational proposition may be symbolized by aRb, where R is the relation and a and b are the terms; and aRb will then always, provided a and b are not identical, denote a different proposition from bRa. That is to say, it is characteristic of a relation of two terms that it proceeds, so to speak, *from* one *to* the other. This is what may be called the *sense* of the relation, and is, as we shall find, the source of order and series." Russell went on to say that "we may distinguish the term *from* which the relation proceeds as *referent*, and the term *to* which it proceeds as the *relatum*. The sense of a relation is a fundamental notion, which is not capable of definition."[16]

The fact that relations have a sense is best illustrated by asymmetrical relations. Consider the relational fact expressed by 'a is larger than b'. The sense of the relation denoted by 'is larger than' goes from a to

---

[16] *Ibid.*, pp. 95–96.

b. That is, *a* is the referent and *b* is the relatum of the relation. Although it is a fact that *aRb*, it is not a fact that *bRa*. The sense of the relation goes from *a* to *b* because the proposition expressed by '*aRb*' is contingently true. The converse proposition expressed by '*bRa*', though intelligible, is false. This example illustrates Russell's claim that '*aRb*' and '*bRa*' express different propositions, for if one is true and the other is false, the propositions cannot be the same.

One might think that Russell should say that the sense of asymmetrical relations differs from the sense of symmetrical relations, if the latter have a sense at all. The sense of an asymmetrical relation goes "one way" in contrast to the sense of a symmetrical relation which seems to go "two ways." But if Russell's claim that '*aRb*' and '*bRa*' express different propositions (except when *a*=*b*) is correct, then the sense of the symmetrical relation *R* would be different in *aRb* and *bRa*. The difference might be analogous to the difference between going from Edinburgh to London and from London to Edinburgh on the same road. The road, like a symmetrical relation, goes both ways, but a traveler goes in a different direction depending upon his starting point. It can be argued, however, that at least some symmetrical relations do not have a sense; I will come back to this issue in a moment.

If all relations have a sense, it would be easy to distinguish relations from properties. I have illustrated what Russell meant by saying that relations have a sense. But what could be meant by asking, for example, 'What is the sense of the property of being round?' The question does not make sense. It is simply inappropriate to ask whether a given property has a sense, just as it is inappropriate to ask whether the square root of two is red, white, or blue. But it is appropriate to ask whether a given relation has a sense. We have seen that at least some relations do have a sense. Therefore, at least some relations are different from properties. But it could be objected that the sense of a relation is not sufficient to explain the essential difference between relations and properties unless all relations have a sense. One might reply to this objection that the fact that it is appropriate to ask whether a relation has a sense is sufficient to distinguish in principle between the relations and properties. As far as I can tell this criterion is adequate, but it is still not entirely clear why relations differ from properties. The subsequent discussion of the thesis that relations and pluralism are interdependent will bring out why it is appropriate to ask whether a given relation has a sense. The existence conditions of relations are such that it is always appropriate to ask whether a given relation has a sense. Relations cannot exist, it will be argued, in the absence of a plurality of relata; relations cannot have a sense without a referent and a relatum. Properties cannot have a sense because the existence conditions of relations are such that the question 'Do properties have a sense?' does not arise and cannot be intelligibly raised.

Although Russell could have taken the position that I have just sketched, he probably would have attempted to respond in a different way to the objection that the fact that some relations have a sense is not sufficient to distinguish relations from properties. Russell probably would have replied that all relations have a sense, for he made such a claim (without argument) in *The Problems of Philosophy*.[17] It is far from clear, however, that the claim is true.

Russell held that all relations order their relata. For example, the relation of being larger than by one orders the numbers in the natural number series. According to Russell, the sense of a relation is "the source of order and series." Many relations, especially many dyadic relations, clearly do have a sense, for example, those denoted by 'father of', 'taller than', 'before', 'above'. But it is not at all clear that the relations denoted by 'between' or 'sibling of', for example, have a sense. If y is between x and z, what is the sense of the relation denoted by 'between'? One could argue that 'y is between x and z' does not express a proposition different from 'y is between z and x'. Of course the order of sign arrangement is different, but it does not follow that in this example that the difference of sign expresses a difference of sense. Different propositions have not been expressed unless every formal difference entails a difference of meaning. Similarly, the relation denoted by 'sibling of' does not have a sense. If a and b bear the sibling relation to each other, then 'aSb' and 'bSa' do not express different propositions. Both 'between' and 'sibling of' denote relations which order their relata, but neither relation has a sense. Russell was correct in thinking that all relations order their relata, but not because the sense of a relation is "the source of order" (even if it is the source of series). All relations necessarily order their relata. What it means to say that a relation holds is simply that a certain order has been established among certain relata. But not all relations have a sense; hence the sense of a relation could not in general be "the source of order."

17 *Ibid.,* p. 127.

Even if a given relation has a sense, that fact is independent of the fact that it orders its relata.

Russell was correct to emphasize that relations are the kind of thing that can have a sense, but wrong to suppose that all relations do in fact have a sense. Russell failed to distinguish a characteristic of the concept of a relation from a characteristic of entities falling under the concept. The important question is not whether all or only some relations have a sense, but what the existence conditions of relations are which make it intelligible to ask whether a given relation has a sense. The thesis that relations and pluralism are interdependent, as I have already suggested, can provide the explanation we are looking for.

(4) The thesis that relations and pluralism are interdependent grew out of a reaction to the ontologies of Leibniz and Bradley. Russell claimed that Leibniz's denial of the nonmental reality of relations made his assumption of a plurality of substances "peculiarly difficult, and involved him in all the paradoxes of the pre-established harmony."[18] Contrary to Bradley, Russell argued that the reality of relations established that pluralism rather than monism is a correct theory about the structure of the world. In view of Russell's opposition to Leibniz and Bradley, it is reasonable to suppose that Russell assumed that relations and pluralism are interdependent in the sense that each entails the other. Whether or not this is true, it should now be clear why Russell thought that the question of relations is important to the monism-pluralism controversy.

It is worth noting, however, that the thesis that relations and pluralism entail each other would satisfy neither Leibniz nor Bradley. It may be true that Leibniz's commitment to pluralism and to the denial of the nonmental reality of relations led to paradoxes in his system, but pluralism without relations may be conceivable, and perhaps even a Leibnizian world is conceivable. Although Leibniz's theory is paradoxical if it is taken to be a description of the existing world, it was designed to convince us that we should change our view of the world. Leibniz sought to explain, not to describe, the structure of the world. Similarly, Bradley held that the belief in pluralism and relations seems plausible only because we have not properly distinguished between appearance and reality. Bradley's position is that we must banish com-

[18] *A Critical Exposition of the Philosophy of Leibniz*, p. 15.

mon sense notions like thing, quality, and relation in attempting to account for the structure of the world. Russell's objections to Leibniz and Bradley presuppose that there are relational facts, and that, therefore, relations and pluralism are interdependent. But this presupposition is precisely what Leibniz and Bradley thought was false.

However the dispute between Russell and his opponents should be decided, I am concerned primarily with the implications of the thesis that relations and pluralism are interdependent. Let us assume that there are relational facts and that relations and pluralism are interdependent. In the discussion of the thesis that relations are constituents of relational facts, I will try to explain more precisely the way in which relations are dependent upon a plurality of relata. The point that I wish to make here is that the thesis that relations and pluralism are interdependent explains the essential difference between relations and properties.

Although Russell held both that pluralism entails the reality of relations and that the reality of relations entails pluralism, only the latter need be considered in connection with the difference between relations and properties. 'The reality of relations entails pluralism' can be interpreted to mean that the existence of relational facts requires a plurality of relata. For example, if A is taller than B, then there must exist (or have existed at some time) at least two entities. A cannot, at the same time, be taller than itself (although A at time t_2 might be taller than A at t_1). A cannot, for instance, be above, below, or in anything unless there is at least one relatum to which A can be related. Although this point is obvious, it is important because it provides a criterion for distinguishing relations from properties.

The basis of the distinction between properties and relations is that as constituents of facts each has different existence conditions. Russell made this point in passing when he distinguished between propositions "attributing a property to a single thing" and propositions "expressing a relation between two or more things."[19] Contrast, for example, the different existence conditions of the facts expressed by 'this is green' and 'this precedes that'. Properties, but not relations, can exist if only one particular exists. Relations can exist only if two or more relata exist. In this respect all relations differ from all properties. It follows that the thesis that relations and pluralism are interdependent both provides the ontological grounds for the thesis that relations cannot

19 *The Problems of Philosophy*, p. 94.

be reduced to properties and accounts for the difference in logical form between relational and nonrelational propositions. Finally, it should now be clear why relations, but not properties, can in principle have a sense.

Although I have tried to show why relations cannot be reduced to properties, it might be objected that properties can be reduced to relations. That is, one might argue that properties are merely monadic relations. Russell himself saw no objection to a formal reduction of lower order relations to higher order relations, that is, monadic to dyadic, dyadic to triadic, etc.[20] Regardless of what is technically possible, the notion that properties can be reduced to relations rests on a confusion between exemplification and real relations. Exemplification, if it is anything at all, is a nonrelational tie between a particular and a property; it is not a relational constituent of a nonrelational fact. Even if exemplification were a real relation, it would not follow that properties can be reduced to relations. Instead, properties would become relata. If a nonrelational fact such as that expressed by 'this is green' consists of a particular, a property, and a relation of exemplification, the particular and the property are the relata; exemplification is the only relation. I will say more about exemplification in the discussion of the thesis that relations are unparticularized universals. What I have said here is sufficient to show that properties cannot be reduced to relations.

Another objection that has more force is that my claim that a plurality of relata is a necessary condition of the existence of relations ignores the relation of identity. The relation of a thing to itself, the objection might proceed, does not require a plurality of relata. Although I think that a case can be made to show that identity is not an ordinary relation, if a relation at all, I will not attempt to deal with this difficult issue here. Instead I will simply exclude the relation of identity from the scope of my analysis. I do wish, however, to call attention to McTaggart's suggestion that if identity is a relation, it requires some form of plurality. "For a relation *always connects something with something*. Even when it only connects something with itself, the term so connected with itself is—to use a metaphor which is not, I think, misleading—at both ends of the relation, and this does involve a certain aspect of plurality, though not, of course, a plurality of sub-

[20] "The Philosophy of Logical Atomism," reprinted in *Logic and Knowledge*, pp. 183–184.

stances. This may be more obvious if we notice that it is impossible to express any relation without either having two terms, or using one term twice."[21]

(5) I have said that the thesis that relations are constituents of relational facts is presupposed by the thesis that relations and pluralism are interdependent. I will first try to explain why Russell thought there are relational facts. Then I will try to describe the structure of relational facts, that is, how relations and relata can be said to constitute facts.

According to Russell, a metaphysical theory purports to tell us "what sort of structure we may reasonably suppose the world to have."[22] Russell's use of the word 'structure' is tied to his view that the world is composed of facts as well as things.[23] "It is important to observe that facts belong to the objective world . . . [which] is not completely described by a lot of 'particulars', but . . . also . . . [by] things that I call facts, which are the sort of things you express by a sentence, and that these, just as much as particular chairs and tables, are part of the real world."[24] Among the facts in the world are "ultimate relational facts";[25] Russell said that "it is quite clear that there are relational facts. The sentences, 'Philip was the father of Alexander' and 'Alexander preceded Caesar', clearly assert facts about the world. . . . I think it is as certain as anything can be that there are relational facts such as [is expressed by] '*A* is earlier than *B*'."[26]

Although Russell said that sentences can "express" or "assert" facts, he did not think that sentences are names of facts. Nor did Russell say that the existence of relational facts rests on logical grounds. Instead, he claimed that his "decision in favour of pluralism and relations [ultimate relational facts] is taken on empirical grounds."[27] One does not know precisely what Russell meant by 'empirical grounds' because he did not elaborate on this claim.

One possible line of interpretation is suggested by Russell's theory of perception. "Let us consider a complex object composed of two parts *a* and *b* standing to each other in the relation *R*. The complex object '*a*-in-the-relation-*R*-to *b*' may be capable of being perceived;

---

21 J. M. E. McTaggart, *The Nature of Existence* (Cambridge, 1921), I:80.
22 "Logical Atomism," p. 338.
23 "The Philosophy of Logical Atomism," pp. 183–184.
24 *Ibid.*, p. 184.
25 "Logical Atomism," p. 338.
26 *My Philosophical Development* (New York, 1959), p. 172.
27 "Logical Atomism," p. 339.

when perceived it is perceived as one object."[28] What does it mean to say that facts are perceived as one object? Apart from the judgments that are made about perception, what exactly is perceived? Since for Russell facts are just as much part of the "objective" or "real" world as chairs and tables, it would be reasonable for him to say that we can, for example, see (some) facts. But can we see the constituents, and in particular the relational constituents of facts?

Suppose we see that this dot is to the right of that dot. We see the two dots standing in a certain relation. Do we see the relation? If relations are perceived at all, they are not perceived *simpliciter*, that is, in isolation from their relata. I may see this dot to the right of that dot, but I do not see a nonlinguistic entity denoted by 'to the right of' apart from seeing the two dots.[29] Perhaps the relation is seen *in* seeing the two dots. In that case the relation is seen, but not as an isolated entity. On the other hand, perhaps the relation is seen *as* an aspect of a fact. Seeing relations may involve, as G. J. Warnock has suggested,[30] noticing, attending, realizing, and getting to know relations as features of facts.

Although it would be too much of a digression to discuss fully Russell's views on the perception of facts,[31] it should be noted that his position is especially puzzling with regard to relations. Russell thought that we could be "acquainted" with relations, but he held that relations as such are apprehended only by thought, not perceived by the senses. One reason why Russell denied that relations are objects of perception is that he claimed that relations, as universals, are nonempirical entities. How one becomes "acquainted" with relations, however, was never made clear. In trying to make this clear Russell appealed to but did not spell out a doctrine of abstraction. In any case, I will argue later that if relations are universals, a question arises that is more basic than whether relations can be perceived: How can relations be constituents of relational facts?

If there are grounds for claiming that there are relational facts, how do relations and relata constitute facts? Russell's analysis of the structure of relational facts has two aspects. The first concerns the ontolog-

[28] *Principia Mathematica*, 2nd ed. (Cambridge, 1935), p. 43.

[29] See J. L. Austin, "Are There A Priori Concepts?" *Philosophical Papers*, ed. J. O. Urmson and G. J. Warnock (Oxford, 1961), p. 18.

[30] "Seeing," reprinted in *Perceiving, Sensing, and Knowing*, ed. R. J. Swartz (New York, 1965), pp. 59–60.

[31] See D. F. Pears, *Bertrand Russell and the British Tradition in Philosophy* (London, 1968), esp. Chapters 11, 12, and 13.

ical priority of relata to relations (or the ontological dependence of relations on relata). The second concerns the instantiation of relations by relata, which Russell expressed metaphorically by saying that "all that is truly relational is the hooking of the relation to the terms."[32] In the discussion of the thesis that relations are unparticularized universals, the hooking metaphor will be interpreted; I will here consider only the question of ontological priority (dependence).

In the analysis of the thesis that relations and pluralism are interdependent it was argued that the existence of relations requires a plurality of relata. To say that relata are ontologically prior to relations is to emphasize not that there must be more than one relatum but that the existence of relations depends upon the existence of relata. What is most important in connection with ontological priority is not which specific existence conditions hold, but the conditional existence of relations. The specific existence conditions vary. For example, if *A* is taller than *B*, the simultaneous existence of the relata is not necessary; suppose *A* is presently taller than *B*, his great-great-great-grandfather who is now deceased. But the simultaneous existence of both *A* and *B* is necessary if *A* is to the right of *B*. But although the specific existence conditions for different kinds of relational facts may vary in some respects, the fact that relations are dependent upon relata does not vary. In every case, the relata are ontologically prior to the relations. Russell recognized this, as the following passage illustrates: "If we say 'Alexander preceded Caesar', we feel (perhaps mistakenly) that Alexander and Caesar are solid. But what about the word 'preceded'? We could, at a pinch, imagine a universe consisting only of Alexander or only of Caesar or only of the pair of them. But we cannot imagine a universe consisting only of [the denotation of] 'preceded'."[33]

Russell used another linguistic clue to make the point about the dependence of relations on relata: "A relation-word is only used correctly when relata are supplied."[34] By this Russell meant that relation words do not "point to something extra-linguistic" unless they are elements in a sentence which makes a true descriptive statement about the world. Just as relation words can denote only in the context of sentences, relations can enter into relational facts only if their relata exist. Relations, to use Frege's terminology, are incomplete or unsaturated entities; as constitutents of facts relations are dependent upon

---

[32] "Logical Atomism," p. 335.
[33] *My Philosophical Development*, p. 236.
[34] *Ibid.*, p. 237. See also "Logical Atomism," p. 337.

relata. Although properties are also unsaturated, they, unlike relations, presuppose the existence of only a single object. Relations presuppose at least two relata—they are *doubly* unsaturated.

A natural objection to Russell's analysis of the structure of relational facts is to say that Russell was misled by the structure of language. Even if it were granted that relational expressions do denote real features of the world, it might be argued that there is no good reason to suppose that relations have characteristics (for example, unsaturatedness) analogous to those of relational expressions. Russell would reply not only that he was not misled by the structure of language but also that the structure of sentences "must have some relation to the structure of facts, at any rate in those aspects of syntax which are unavoidable and not peculiar to this or that language."[35] And he would surely insist that expressions for relations—or technical equivalents—cannot be eliminated from any language adequate for describing the world of ordinary experience. Although Russell admitted that he did not know how to demonstrate this conviction, it is difficult to prove that it is false.

(6) The thesis that relations are unparticularized universals follows from Russell's separate claims that relations are unparticularized and that relations are universals. Because Russell did not himself conjoin these two claims, they will be discussed separately, even though there may be reason to believe that Russell might have confused, or at least not clearly distinguished, the two issues. It will be argued that each claim leads to difficulties which undermine Russell's analysis of the structure of relational facts. If relations are unparticularized universals, no satisfactory account can be given of the thesis that relations and relata constitute facts. However, there are a few of Russell's remarks which point to a possible way out of the difficulties.

Russell explicitly claimed that "there are no such entities as particularized relations."[36] He used different language to make the same point

---

[35] *My Philosophical Development*, p. 157.

[36] "Meinong's Theory of Complexes and Assumptions," p. 345. Russell here made the claim that there are no particularized relations to avoid admitting negative facts into his ontology. Although he later changed his mind about negative facts, I do not discuss the problem of negative facts for three reasons. First, at no time did Russell officially renounce the doctrine that relations are unparticularized. Second, the problem about negative facts was not the only factor that led to the unparticularity doctrine (see fn. 41 and the accompanying text). Third, the problem of negative facts would introduce unnecessary complications into my argument.

when he said that "relations have no instances" for "verbs do not, like adjectives, have instances."[37] It is important to recall that for Russell "adjectives . . . express qualities or properties of single things, whereas . . . verbs tend to express relations between two or more things."[38] One might be tempted to interpret Russell's remarks in a way that would provide support for the thesis that relations cannot be reduced to properties; that is, one might be tempted to infer that the fact that relations are unparticularized and properties are particularized provides a criterion for distinguishing in principle between relations and properties. Such an interpretation of the claim that relations are unparticularized might be thought to tie it closely to the doctrine of external relations. For the doctrine of external relations amounts to a formulation of the thesis that relations cannot be reduced to properties.[39] This interpretation might be plausible if Russell had retained the belief that relations are unparticularized and properties are particularized. But although he later reiterated his belief that relations are unparticularized, he went on to deny that "there is any difference in this respect between relations and qualities."[40] Hence the doctrine that relations are unparticularized is not a basis for the doctrine of external relations, that is, the thesis that relations cannot be reduced to properties. Why, then, did Russell claim that relations are unparticularized?

Russell thought that unless relations were unparticularized, the same relation could not hold between different relata.[41] For example, Russell would say that in 'five is larger than four' and in 'three is larger than two' the same relation is denoted by 'is larger than'. He thought that if relations had instances, then only similar relations, not the same relation, could hold among different sets of relata. To avoid the nominalism he thought was entailed by denying that the *same* relation can occur in different relational facts, Russell invoked the doctrine that relations are unparticularized. He thought that only if relations are not particularized by their relata, can the same relation occur in different relational facts. His radical realism, whether or not it is warranted, helps to explain why he accepted the unparticularity doctrine.

37 *The Principles of Mathematics*, p. 52.

38 *The Problems of Philosophy*, pp. 94–95.

39 "Logical Atomism," p. 335.

40 "Replies to Criticisms," *The Philosophy of Bertrand Russell*, ed. P. A. Schilpp (Evanston and Chicago, 1944), p. 684.

41 *The Principles of Mathematics*, p. 52. Russell was still bothered by the same issue in *An Inquiry into Meaning and Truth* (Baltimore, 1962), p. 325.

Another aspect of Russell's radical realism helps to explain what he meant by saying that relations are unparticularized. One could argue that the claim that relations are unparticularized means that there are no facts in which relations are constituents. But this would flatly contradict Russell's claim that there are relational facts. What Russell apparently meant is that relations are entities of a radically different sort from relata. Following Meinong, Russell at one time thought that entities that do not exist must subsist. Although Russell later limited access to the world of subsistent beings as a result of his theory of descriptions, his theory of universals incorporated the distinction between existence and subsistence. According to Russell, relations are universals which subsist rather than exist. Consider the fact that Edinburgh is north of London. Russell thought that 'north of' denotes a relation which "is neither in space nor time, neither material nor mental; yet it is something."[42]

Russell's belief that relations subsist rather than exist might help to explain what Russell had in mind when he claimed that relations are unparticularized. If relations are subsistent entities, then it is not surprising that they are not particularized by existing relata, for subsistents and existents are worlds apart. But it immediately becomes clear that difficulties arise. If relations are unparticularized universals, how can they be constituents of facts at all? I will first criticize the claim that relations are unparticularized, whether or not they are universals, and then criticize the claim that relations are universals.

The claim that relations are unparticularized implies that relations are not ontologically dependent upon their relata. That is, relata are not ontologically prior to relations because relations are found in a realm of being which is wholly separated from and independent of existing relata. But this clearly conflicts with Russell's analysis of the structure of relational facts. As constituents of relational facts, relations are dependent upon their relata. One might be tempted to suppose, however, that Russell later rejected the doctrine that relations are unparticularized. He denounced as absurd the idea that relata are independent of their relations, and presumably would deny that relations are independent of their relata. If relations are unparticularized, it would seem to follow that a "relation is a third term which comes between the other two terms and is somehow hooked onto them, [and] that is obviously absurd, for in that case the relation has ceased

[42] *The Problems of Philosophy*, p. 98.

to be a relation, and all that is truly relational is the hooking of the relation to the terms. The conception of the relation as a third term between the other two sins against the doctrine of types, and must be avoided with the utmost care."[43]

If relations are unparticularized, no reasonable interpretation of the hooking metaphor can be given. The force of the hooking metaphor is that relations are not only dependent on their relata, but also are particularized by them. Otherwise, there would be no grounds for saying that a statement of the form 'aRb' is true or false. That is, unless relations are particularized, Russell's theory can account for neither the structure nor the existence of relational facts. It is not surprising, therefore, that Morris Weitz[44] thought that Russell gave up the "very curious doctrine" of unparticularized relations. Oddly enough, Russell denied that he had given up his belief that relations are unparticularized. Furthermore, he claimed that he had held the view that relations have no instances continuously since 1902.[45] Hence Russell did not get off the hook by officially renouncing his position.

The unparticularity doctrine made it impossible for Russell to explain how relations and relata form facts. D. F. Pears has suggested that Russell "cannot explain the general phenomenon of attachment" of relations and relata. According to Pears, Russell "treats this as something ultimate which the philosopher has to accept without being able to explain it."[46] But the difficulty is more serious than that. For if, as Russell said, what is "truly relational is the hooking of the relation to the terms," does it make any sense at all to say that relations are not particularized or have no instances? Alternatively, it could be argued that the hooking metaphor itself violates the theory of types. For if it is absurd to say that relations are independent of their relata, then it must also be absurd to say that what is truly relational is the "hooking." Unless my earlier argument that relata are ontologically prior to relations is unsound, Russell's doctrine that relations are unparticularized is either inconsistent with the thesis that relations are constituents of relational facts or else it is simply unintelligible in virtue of Russell's own theory of types.

A similar inconsistency concerning the structure of relational facts

---

[43] "Logical Atomism," p. 335.
[44] "Analysis and the Unity of Russell's Philosophy," *The Philosophy of Bertrand Russell*, pp. 68–69.
[45] "Replies to Criticism," p. 684.
[46] *Bertrand Russell and the British Tradition in Philosophy*, pp. 170–171.

arose as a result of Russell's early theory of universals. Just as Russell did not explain how relations could be unparticularized and yet attached to relata, he did not explain how relations could be universals and yet "shared" by particulars. Again, when he was confronted with an inconsistency in his theory, Russell failed to resolve it. He tried to avoid the problem of explaining how particulars can share (exemplify) universals by eliminating particulars from his ontology rather than by attempting to interpret exemplification. There is no need to discuss this problem in detail since Alan Donagan has already done so in his excellent article "Universals and Metaphysical Realism."[47] I will, however, briefly summarize Russell's early theory of universals in order to show that it is inconsistent with his account of the structure of relational facts.

144732

According to Russell, universals—relations and properties—are entities which are shared by particulars. A relation is shared by, say, two particulars if it is tied to the particulars by "an ultimate simple relation"[48] which Russell called predication. (Like Donagan, I think it is preferable to call this alleged relation between particulars and universals exemplification and to reserve the word 'predication' for a grammatical relation between a predicate and that of which it is predicated.) Donagan has shown that if exemplification is treated as a relation which holds between relations and particulars, Russell cannot avoid the charge that a vicious infinite regress ensues. Donagan's suggestion that exemplification might be nonrelational, however plausible or implausible it may be, is not Russell's position. Russell simply turned away from the problem of exemplification. He claimed that exemplification was a problem only if there are particulars. He then proceeded to attempt to eliminate particulars from his ontology.

Russell said that "there is no need for particulars as subjects in which qualities inhere. Bundles of qualities . . . can take the place of particulars."[49] As a result of the elimination of particulars, Russell discarded the notion that "proper names denote some unique object"[50] and that we are acquainted with the alleged denotations of proper names. For example, Russell once held that words such as 'this' were used to denote particulars. Now, however, "instead of saying, 'This is red', we shall have to say, 'Redness is compresent with centrality'; if the

[47] *The Monist*, 47 (1963): 211–246.
[48] "On the Relations of Universals and Particulars," p. 123.
[49] *My Philosophical Development*, p. 161.
[50] *Ibid.*, p. 167.

red thing concerned is in the center of our field of vision."[51] Russell
went on to say that "much more important than such subject-
predicate propositions are propositions asserting relations. A language
cannot express all that we know about the world unless it has means
of saying such things as, 'A is before B', 'A is to the right of B', 'A is
more like B than C'."[52] Even if bundles of qualities take the place of
particulars, the problem of exemplification has not been eliminated.
For it must now be asked how the relation from A to B in 'A is before
B' holds between A and B if 'is before' denotes a relation and 'A' and
'B' denote qualities. Exemplification remains a problem whether A and
B are particulars or bundles of qualities. Even if the problem of exemplification could be solved, Russell would have to deal with the attachment problem. If relational facts consist of "bundles" of qualities
(quasi-particulars) and relations, how are the qualities attached to
the relations to form facts? Thus even if Russell eliminated particulars,
he did not thereby eliminate the inconsistencies in his theory of
relations.

Although the structure of relational facts cannot be explained if
relations are unparticularized or if relations are other-worldly universals, Russell sometimes characterized his theory of universals in a way
that seems to avoid the inconsistencies. Russell's remarks about the
proper use of relation-words in *My Philosophical Development* suggested such a radical departure from his previous position that it is
very doubtful that he was still expressing a theory of universals. What
he said entails that relations are real features of the world, that relations
and relata are entities of different kinds, that relata are ontologically
prior to relations, and that relations are particularized by their relata,
but not that relations are universals which are neither material nor
mental that subsist rather than exist. Consider the following passages:

> There certainly are complex wholes which have a structure, and we
> cannot describe the structure without relation-words. But if we try
> to descry some entity denoted by these relation-words and capable of
> some shadowy kind of subsistence outside the complex in which it is
> embodied, it is not at all clear that we can succeed.[53] . . . just as the
> names in such sentences [those expressing relations] point to objects,
> so the relation-words must point to something extra-linguistic. It is a

51 *Ibid.*, p. 170.
52 *Ibid.*, p. 171–172.
53 *Ibid.*, p. 173.

fact that Alexander preceded Caesar, and this fact does not consist merely of Alexander and Caesar. Relation-words, it is clear, serve a purpose in enabling us to assert facts which would otherwise be unstatable. So far, I think, we are on firm ground. But I do not think it follows that there is, in any sense whatever, a 'thing' called 'preceding'. A relation-word is only used correctly when relata are supplied.[54]

Furthermore, whether or not technical devices can be used to eliminate relation-words from a language adequate for describing the world of ordinary empirical things, qualities, and relations, Russell was convinced that "a technical device should be possible which would preserve the differences of ontological status between what is meant by names on the one hand, and predicates and relation-words on the other."[55]

Russell did not officially renounce the doctrine that relations are unparticularized universals. If only the foregoing passages are taken to be Russell's current views, however, such a renunciation is called for. Otherwise, his theory is still inconsistent. If my arguments are correct, I have shown that Russell's theory of relations is consistent only if the thesis that relations are unparticularized universals is eliminated. I have not shown that the other parts of Russell's theory are true, but I have tried to make them intelligible.

[54] *Ibid.*, p. 237. Russell's use of 'in any sense whatever' could be taken to suggest that Russell has given up the thesis that relations are real features of the world. But I think it is more properly interpreted to mean that he has given up the idea that relations are unparticularized universals.

[55] *Ibid.*

6

The Philosophy
of Logical Atomism:
A Realism *Manqué*

Henry Veatch

FAR be it from me in this essay to assume the role of one who comes to bury Russell, not to praise him. But this, of course, is not to deny that "the evil that men do lives after them; the good is oft interred with their bones." Shall we not add, then, "So let it be with Russell?"

In any case, it would surely not appear to be an entirely implausible thesis with respect to the history of recent philosophy that while Russell in the period of his logical atomism was indeed a realist and even a metaphysical realist, his descendants, or at least those who have come after him in recent English philosophy, have been anything but realists or metaphysicians either one. Accordingly, in this paper I should like to argue that while it might be going too far to claim that the realism of Russell's logical atomism contains the seeds of its own destruction, still there is something about Russell's brand of realism and his manner of understanding it that makes him powerless to defend himself against the now fashionable repudiation of realism, particularly on the part of the latter-day linguistic analysts. And so it is in this wise that one might feel tempted to say that evil that Russell did, or at least did not prevent, lives after him.

First, though, let me say just a word in explanation of the rather bold assertion that in the period of his logical atomism Russell was a metaphysical realist. In saying that he was a realist, I mean no more than that, as he himself puts it, "the world contains facts, which are what they are whatever we may choose to think about them,"[1] and that "facts belong to the objective world: they are not created by our thoughts or beliefs except in special cases."[2] And in saying that Russell was a metaphysician, I mean no more than that in putting forth particulars on the one hand and universals and relations on the other as making up the ultimate furniture of the world, Russell was engaging in just that sort of ontological investigation or enquiry that is typical of a certain kind of metaphysical enterprise. If you will, it might be called an enterprise in categorial analysis, "categories" being here understood in an Aristotelian rather than in a Kantian sense. Thus Aristotle's classification of the things or entities of the real world as being either substances or various accidents of substance might be meaningfully compared with Russell's classification of things as either particulars or universals.[3] Or again, Aristotle's principle to the effect that while accidents are present in substances and, with certain restrictions, are predicable of them, primary substances are neither present in nor predicable of anything else—this principle would indeed seem to be somewhat analogous to Russell's insistence that whereas "a relation can never occur except as a relation, never as a subject,"[4] "particulars have this peculiarity . . . that each of them stands entirely alone and is completely self-subsistent."[5] In other words, in such contexts Russell, no less than Aristotle, might be said to be concerned with the ultimate categories of things and with the respective characters and interrelationships of such categories; and in this sense Russell's concern, quite as much as Aristotle's might be said to be a concern with metaphysics, or perhaps, since the term is rather more fashionable now-a-days and a little less highly charged, with ontology.[6]

To begin with, then, let us consider but very briefly the salient re-

---

[1] Bertrand Russell, "The Philosophy of Logical Atomism," reprinted in *Logic and Knowledge*, ed. Robert C. Marsh (New York: Macmillan Co., 1956), p. 182. Subsequent references will be to works by Russell unless otherwise indicated.

[2] *Ibid.*, p. 183.

[3] Cf. Russell's explicit comparison of particulars, in his sense, with Aristotle's substances, *ibid.*, pp. 201–202.

[4] *Ibid.*, p. 206.

[5] *Ibid.*, p. 201.

[6] Russell's own use and yet suspicions of the term *metaphysics* scarcely need documenting. Cf. *ibid.*, Section 8.

spects in which Russell's successors, particularly among the linguistic analysts, might be said to have forsaken the somewhat straight and narrow path of metaphysical realism. To cite a comparatively insignificant, but still rather illuminating example, consider the somewhat rambling essay by Professor Cavell, entitled "Must We Mean What We Say?" That essay, it will be recalled, was provoked by an earlier paper of Professor Mates that had been quite severely critical of the position of the ordinary language philosophers. But what is interesting and significant for our purposes in Cavell's essay is a comparatively short passage where the author finally brings himself to face up squarely to the issue of what might be called the normative or binding character of ordinary language uses. Thus why is it—to use a couple of Cavell's own examples—that "we do not say 'I know . . .' unless we mean that we have great confidence . . .", or that "when we ask whether an action is voluntary we imply that the action is fishy"?[7] Mates had implied that what might be called "the necessity" of such uses must be due either to mere stipulations to the effect that words like "know" and "voluntary" were to be used in this way, or, if the use could not trace its origin to any such stipulation, then it must be simply an empirical matter (to be confirmed by a properly scientific study of language), that in a language such as English words like "know" and "voluntary" are in fact always used in the ways indicated.

But Cavell will have none of this. As he sees it, a statement such as "when we ask whether an action is voluntary we imply that the action is fishy" (call it S), once it is seen to be true is seen to be "necessarily true," to be "a priori."[8] Yet the truth of S is surely not an analytic truth. Moreover, being a necessary truth, it could not be synthetic a posteriori either. Accordingly, the only alternative left, apparently, is to recognize that it is a truth that is synthetic a priori. "When I am impressed," Cavell says, "with the necessity of statements like S, I am tempted to say that they are categorial—about the concept of action *überhaupt*. . . . This would account for our feeling of their necessity: they are instances (not of Formal, but) of Transcendental Logic."[9]

And with this the cat is out of the bag! For by such an admission Cavell has exposed for all to see—albeit somewhat unwittingly per-

---

[7] Stanley Cavell, "Must We Mean What We Say?" reprinted in *Ordinary Language*, ed. Vere C. Chappell (Englewood Cliffs, N.J.: Prentice-Hall, 1964), p. 85.

[8] *Ibid.*

[9] *Ibid.*, p. 86.

haps—the true character of that philosophical progress or regress from the now unfashionable metaphysical realism of Russell's logical atomism to the recently fashionable ordinary language philosophy of the sort that took its rise from the later Wittgenstein. For it isn't so much a case of any mere "linguistic turn," as a result of which philosophical attention might be said to have been shifted from such things and facts in the real world as language might be said to be about or to refer to, to the very language or logic or logico-linguistic uses that might be presumed to have such an intentional or referring character. No, the turn is no mere linguistic turn, so much as it is an actual transcendental turn. And just as Kant in the first *Critique* sought to shift philosophic attention from a metaphysical or ontological concern with the nature and character of things in the real world to a transcendental concern with what he claimed were the transcendental conditions of there being a world in the first place, or of there being things and objects of experience at all, so likewise, *mutatis mutandis*, the latter-day linguistic analysts have succeeded in pretty well displacing anything like a metaphysical realism of the type of logical atomism in favor of a new-born transcendental philosophy which, if it be not of direct Kantian inspiration, is at least in a very general way on the Kantian model.

Yes, to point up the implications of this brief excursus of ours into what Professor Bergmann would call "structural history," we might even hazard the following somewhat speculative *Gedankenexperiment*. Suppose that a neo-Wittgensteinian of roughly the persuasion of the so-called ordinary language philosophers were to undergo a conversion from being an ordinary-language partisan to being an ideal-language partisan, this would still not preclude him from plying his trade as a transcendental philosopher who had duly made the transcendental turn and was duly concerned that he thus continue to keep right in step. No, for even supposing that his newly accomplished conversion had now made him newly, or perhaps again, tolerant of the categorial scheme of Russell's logical atomism—after all, this scheme does derive quite directly and by Russell's own admission from the propositional structures contained in the lower functional calculus of the ideal language of *PM*—still all that one now needs to do is simply to transpose Russell's categorial scheme from its original setting of a metaphysical realism to a new and transcendental setting of a more or less Kantian type, and one will have it made, so to speak, so far as one's remaining faithful to a philosophy of the type of the transcendental turn is concerned. Indeed, that very same type of synthetic a priori necessity which we found Cavell wishing to attach to so-called ordinary uses of words like "know" and "voluntary" may now be simply transferred to the regular Russellian requirements regarding the uses of function-terms (universals and relations) and argument terms (particulars) in the familiar *PM* logical scheme.

Nevertheless, it is high time that we gave over these somewhat fanciful projections by the way of structural history, and got back to the principal thesis of the present paper. For that thesis might be simply put as a question: Granting that the subsequent course of English philosophy after the period of logical atomism has followed the transcendental turn and has departed ever farther and farther from the metaphysical realism of the early Russell, is there not something about the way Russell conceived the categorial structure of his metaphysics that would render his categorial scheme peculiarly susceptible to just this sort of transcendental displacement and distortion?

To keep our exposition as simple as possible, let us recur to but a single illustration, and to one already alluded to above. For as we noted, it was somewhat in the manner of Aristotle with his account of the dependence of accidents upon substances and of the independence of substances with respect to accidents that Russell insists that particulars are such as to require that each of them should stand entirely alone and be completely self-subsistent, whereas relations on the other hand are entirely incapable of occurring as subjects. Now without pausing to pursue further just what more specifically Russell may have meant by such a pronouncement, or without developing the further features of his categorial scheme as a whole, let us simply ask by what warrant Russell is able to make these categorial assertions about particulars and about relations. Indeed, if we exfoliate our question more or less in the manner of Cavell, we must begin by recognizing that unquestionably for Russell assertions of this kind, having to do with particulars and relations, are no less than necessary truths; they are a priori. And yet are they a priori in the manner of analytic truths? But they could hardly be this, because analytic truths are not truths about the world; whereas these truths that Russell propounds concerning particulars and relations are no less than categorial assertions about the ultimate furniture of the world. Nor, of course, could they be mere synthetic a posteriori statements, for then they would not be a priori. Are they, then, a priori in the sense of being synthetic a priori truths?

But if we interpret Russell in accordance with this option, there would then seem to be no way in which Russell could be spared the necessity of having to make the transcendental turn. For was it not the main burden of the first *Critique* to show that the only way to account for the possibility of synthetic judgments a priori is through the apparatus of a transcendental philosophy? And did not Cavell find himself forced, somewhat naively to be sure and apparently almost in spite of himself, to acknowledge that the only way to account for that feeling of necessity that attaches to our categorial assertions is to regard them as being "instances (not of a Formal, but) of Transcendental Logic"? Clearly, therefore, if one were to interpret Russell as regarding his categorial assertions about particulars and relations as being synthetic a priori truths, then not only would Russell have no way of defending his would-be metaphysical realism against those who would make the transcendental turn in philosophy; in addition, he would have already actually committed himself and his own logical atomism to just such a turn away from a realistic metaphysics and into the way of transcendentalism.

Such a criticism of Russell, however, does seem patently over-hasty and unfair. For presumably at no time during his logical atomism period did he commit himself unequivocally to a view of categorial truths as being synthetic a priori—at least not in Kant's sense of that notion.[10] For that matter, he would seem to have been somewhat uneasy and reluctant about even approaching the question as to the peculiar character and warrant of categorial truths in terms of the traditional analytic-synthetic dichotomy. May one say, then, that Russell was clearly aware of the fact that if categorial statements about the ultimate furniture of the world are to sustain anything like a genuine metaphysical realism, they must needs be of a kind that are neither analytic nor synthetic a priori—that is to say, they must be on the order of necessary truths of fact or necessary truths about the world, and necessary truths that pertain not to any mere "empirical reality" in Kant's sense, but to things-in-themselves?

Unfortunately, a reading of Russell's actual texts would hardly confirm the judgment that Russell was very clear as to just how the necessary and a priori character of categorial statements in his philosophy was to be explained and justified. For instance, there is the well-known passage in "The Philosophy of Logical Atomism" where, with characteristic aplomb, Russell simply lays it down that:

[10] At least, I find the statements made in Chapter 8 of *The Problems of Philosophy* (New York: Oxford, 1959) rather indecisive on this score.

Particulars = terms of relations in atomic facts. Df.

That is the definition of particulars and I want to emphasize it because the definition of a particular is something purely logical. The question whether this or that is a particular, is a question to be decided in terms of that logical definition. In order to understand the definition it is not necessary to know beforehand 'This is a particular' or 'That is a particular'. It remains to be investigated what particulars you can find in the world, if any. The whole question of what particulars you actually find in the real world is a purely empirical one which does not interest the logician as such. The logician as such never gives instances, because it is one of the tests of a logical proposition that you need not know anything whatsoever about the real world in order to understand it.[11]

Now this is a curious passage, indeed. For one thing, why the insistence that the definition of a particular is something purely logical? After all, it is not the word "particular" or even Russell's own notion or concept of particular that is being defined; rather, what is to be understood by "particular" here is no less than a certain kind of ultimate category; it represents one of the basic types or kinds of things that there are in the world. But how can pure logic inform us of things in the world, or even of types of such things?

Not only that, but the concluding sentence seems downright paradoxical. For suppose that one converts Russell's definition of particulars into a straightforward proposition. "Particulars are terms of relations in atomic facts." Now presumably this would be an instance of what Russell would call a purely logical proposition. And yet a logical proposition, he says, is of a sort that "you need not know anything whatsoever about the real world in order to understand it." However, the particular proposition that is here under consideration, viz. that particulars are terms of relations in atomic facts, is most certainly a proposition about the real world. What, then, could Russell possibly mean when he seems to suggest that such a proposition being a logical proposition, it can be known to be true a priori[12] and without one's needing to know anything what-

---

11 "The Philosophy of Logical Atomism," p. 199.

12 At this point we must admit to forcing Russell's text somewhat. In the passage quoted above, he does not claim that as regards "logical propositions" one need know nothing whatsoever about the real world in order to know them to be true, but merely in order to understand them. However, although Russell does not explicitly say that it is the truth of such propositions that is in ques-

soever about the real world? Apparently, the only interpretation that readily presents itself at this point is that Russell is simply lapsing into a bit of pre-Kantian dogmatic rationalism: Various truths about the world are able to be known simply by pure reason and without one's having to have any prior experience of the world at all.

Surely, though, all of these objections and difficulties to Russell's implied proposal that such a priori knowledge as we have, so far from being either analytic or synthetic a priori, is really vouchsafed to us through logic and logic alone—surely such objections are all of them captious. For the defender of Russell will point out that in his logical atomism period Russell did have a view of logic according to which logic is capable of yielding an a priori knowledge, not about the facts of the world, to be sure, but about "the logical forms of facts."[13] Or to paraphrase this somewhat in the manner of Bergmann, one might say that logic in one sense teaches us nothing about the world, but only about "the world's form." And it is this "formal" knowledge, and presumably only such formal knowledge that Russell holds to be a priori.

Perhaps so; and yet even granting the legitimacy of such an interpretation, it scarcely helps to resolve the continuing problem that has been plaguing us. For just what is the nature and source of this supposedly a priori knowledge, which is a knowledge not of facts, but of the form of facts, and not of the world but of the world's form, and which Russell insists is a purely logical knowledge, or a knowledge based on logic alone? Yet how can this be? After all, a knowledge that is held to be a knowledge of the form of facts or of the world's form must surely be a knowledge, if not of facts, then indeed of what is im-

---

tion, it is just that that is the relevant issue, so far as his own example is concerned, of a categorial proposition about particulars being the terms of the relations in atomic facts. For Russell clearly intends to assert such a proposition as a categorial truth about the world.

Nor will it do for Russell to try to evade the issue of the synthetic a priori by claiming (as in *The Problems of Philosophy*, Chapter 10) that for him a priori propositions give no information about the actual facts of the world; that to know about these requires experience. This is simply irrelevant, for in the context of his logical atomism, he claims (1) that the actual world is populated by things that are either particulars or universals and (2) that various categorial propositions about such particulars and universals can be known to be true a priori.

[13] Cf. *Our Knowledge of the External World* (London: Allen & Unwin, 1922), p. 60.

plicit or implicated in the facts, and if not of the world, then indeed of the world's very form or structure. Such, indeed, just is the nature of such categorial knowledge as must underlie any realistic metaphysics.

How, though, can such a knowledge be said to be no more than a logical knowledge and a knowledge derived from logic alone? For the current view of formal logic is that logic involves nothing more than mere tautologies and analytic truths; and that logically true propositions, or propositions whose truth is certifiable by logic alone, are propositions which, being true simply in virtue of their logical or linguistic form, yield no information of any kind about the world or even about anything other than their own forms or structures. Hence to suppose that the purely formal knowledge that is derived from logic is at the same time a knowledge of the forms of facts or of the world's form—this latter consideration is one that, even if true, could never be vouchsafed by logic alone.

And so looking back on Russell's program for a realistic metaphysics as this was set forth in the philosophy of logical atomism, it becomes only too clear in retrospect, although it may never have occurred to Russell himself at the time, that the program was faced with a serious dilemma. For if the proposed metaphysics were to involve a genuine realism, then the categorial truths of such a metaphysics would have to have the character of being necessary truths about the world. Yet how could they be of this nature? For if they were truths vouchsafed by logic alone, then it would seem that they could not possibly be truths about the world in any sense. On the other hand, if, in order to make sure that such categorial truths were truths having some bearing on the real world, one proceeded to treat them as being synthetic a priori, then there would seem to be no escaping the transcendental turn; and with that, one's realistic metaphysics would be disastrously and irrevocably undercut. And so it is that although Russell himself may never have followed the primrose path of the transcendental turn, not a few of the neo-Wittgensteinians who have come after him have been only too ready and happy to consign themselves to such an everlasting Kantian bonfire. Nor would it appear that Russell on his own principles could really do anything to save them, or even to save himself from a like fate.

But let us turn now to a rather different set of considerations, which in their own way no less than the foregoing ones in theirs, would seem to confirm the fact that, for all of his commendable professions of realism in connection with his logical atomism, Russell was really without philosophical resource when it came to stemming the apparently all-encompassing tide, or better drift, toward a new transcendental turn in philosophy. This time the weakness in Russell's realism, I would suggest, is traceable not so much to his having been unable or unwilling to devise a proper logical status and an adequate epistemological justification for categorial truths, such as would insure their legitimacy as necessary truths about the world, and yet without collapsing them into either analytic truths on the one hand or synthetic a priori truths on the other. No, this time the comparative defenselessness of Russell's realism is traceable to certain structural flaws in the particular logico-ontological forms and structures that underlie Russell's specific program of logical atomism.

Nevertheless, if we are to demonstrate such weaknesses in Russell's position, we must first be clear as to certain of the moves which many of those who have followed the transcendental turn in philosophy have tended to make, and with respect to which Russell's logical atomism would seem to be particularly vulnerable. These moves might be loosely and variously described as involving either a kind of divorce of meaning from reference, or perhaps as a loosening or a distorting of the bearing of predicates upon subjects; or, speaking more ontologically, one might say that these moves tend to effect a kind of dissociation of both essences and accidents from the things whose essence and accidents they are supposed to be, and indeed more generally, of any and all characteristics from the entities they are presumed to characterize.

To illustrate what I mean let me first go outside of analytic philosophy altogether and call attention in a very general way to certain commonplaces that have come to be associated with developments in recent existential phenomenology. For not infrequently it has been remarked that in existential phenomenology, while there would be but little disposition to deny that there is something—call it Being, or Reality, or the In-itself—that certainly is not "created by our thoughts or beliefs," and that in this sense enjoys a certain ontological independence of our reactions to it and of what we may choose to think about it; yet at the same time this Being, or In-itself, or *Ding an Sich*, or what you will, is entirely dependent upon us for such meaning and sense and significance as it may come to have for us. Accordingly, it is we ourselves who as Kierkegaardian subjects, or as Heideggerian *Dasein*'s, or as Sartrian *pour soi*'s invest the In-itself or Being with all such determinate features, attributes, characteristics, values, dis-values, etc. as it comes to take on and to have for us.

And oddly enough, it would seem that somewhat analogous devel-opments have manifested themselves right within contemporary ana-lytic philosophy. To cite but one example, there has been an increasing tendency to repudiate anything like sense data or other supposedly indubitable experiential givens, upon which our knowledge of nature and the world might be presumed to be erected and in which it might be ultimately grounded. Instead, the fashion now is to regard all so-called data as being already "theory-laden"; and the "theories" with which the given in experience seems to be thus inescapably laden are theories which we contribute and bring to our experience ourselves. They do not represent features which we simply find in things or discover there, so much as they are reflections of our own conceptual schemes and ordering principles which we have ourselves constructed and in virtue of which our experience has been made to be an ordered experience and the world in which we find ourselves to be an actually constituted world. In short, all of this is but a mani-festation of still another variant of the transcendental turn: this time, instead of hide-bound Kantian categories, it is simply our own the-ories, conceptual schemes, language games, etc., which are regarded as functioning in the manner of transcendental conditions of our experience.

And now to return to Russell. Once again, we would say that while it might be forcing the evidence somewhat to contend that it is no less than certain features of Russell's very own account of the rela-tions of subjects to predicates or of particulars to universals that have given rise to the currently fashionable transcendental mode of con-struing the bearing of theories upon data, or of meanings with respect to referents, or of conceptual schemes with respect to their verifying evidence, still there is something about the way in which the relation of subjects (particulars) to predicates (universals and relations) is un-derstood in logical atomism that makes Russell's position peculiarly obnoxious to exploitation along transcendental lines.

Thus consider first of all how, in virtue of Russell's logical theory of the relation of subjects to predicates, his resulting ontology of so-called "logical atoms," the latter consisting of particulars on the one hand and universals or relations on the other, turns out to be an ontol-ogy in which the one class or kind of atoms, viz. the particulars, comes

to be bereft of all properties, qualities, or determinations of any kind
—"bare particulars" no less. Superficially, such a stripping bare of
particulars is accomplished through the process of logical analysis as
Russell means to practice it. Thus we are all familiar with how, in the
treatment of definite descriptions—e.g. "the present king of France"—
the description is treated as an incomplete symbol. Moreover, to bring
the symbol to completeness, one needs to expound it as being no less
than a proposition, whose subject would be a mere x or a mere something, and whose predicate would then be the recipient of all of
those determinate features that were originally packed into the incomplete symbol of the description itself: "There exists one and only one
x, such that it is King of France," etc. Or again, consider the way in
which the traditional categorical propositions (A, E, I, and O) of the
older logic are subjected to a Russellian analysis which turns them into
hypotheticals or conjunctions—e.g. "All men are mortal" becomes
"For all x's, if x is a man, x is mortal." Once again, the effect of such
logical analysis is to remove all determinate content from the original
subject, "men," and to relegate it to the predicate place. The resulting subject then turns out to be no more than so many bare x's or
something.

Notice, though, that since the subjects in such propositions are the
objective referents in the world to which the propositions may be
presumed to refer, the result is that, considered ontologically and as
they are in themselves, these real entities in the world that are thus
referred to in propositions turn out to be utterly neutral entities, and
as such neither fish nor fowl nor good red herring. Thus as Quine has
remarked,

> But in Russell's translation, 'Something wrote *Waverley* and was a
> poet and nothing else wrote *Waverley*', the burden of objective refer-
> ence which had been put upon the descriptive phrase is now taken
> over by words of the kind that logicians call bound variables, variables
> of quantification, namely, words like 'something', 'nothing', 'every-
> thing'. These words, far from purporting to be names specifically of
> the author of *Waverley*, do not purport to be names at all;[14] they refer

---

[14] It scarcely needs remarking that Russell would not accept this judgment of
Quine's, since he (Russell) does recognize so-called "logically proper names."
However, this difference between Russell and Quine does not affect the force of
the present argument.

to entities generally, with a kind of studied ambiguity peculiar to themselves.[15]

Very well, then, given this utter neutrality and characterlessness in themselves of the real entities of the world—one is almost tempted to call them "nonentities"—might it not seem plausible to suppose that such features and characters as these entities come to have for us in our everyday experience of them could only be determinations that we must have invested them with and bestowed upon them, and as a result of which they have taken on the apparent sense and meaning that they obviously and superficially do have for us? Needless to say, such a supposition is not one that Russell in his logical atomism period would have tolerated for a moment; nor does he even so much as hint at such a thing. And yet would it not seem that by his very admission of the sheer neutrality and bareness of the particulars in his ontology, he has thereby laid himself open to a possible exploitation of his ontology along just such transcendental lines?

Clearly, though, this will not do: as an explanation of Russell's susceptibility to something like the transcendental turn, it has moved much too far too fast. And particularly, what might be said to have been overlooked in our foregoing critique of Russell is that in his logic it is not only the subject terms in propositions that refer to objective entities in the world, but predicate terms do so as well. Accordingly, while bare particulars do indeed for Russell make up a part of the ultimate furniture of the world, it is only a part; and the other part consists of just those universals and relations, which, as we saw in our earlier account of Russellian logical analysis, got analyzed out of the subject place in propositions and were all of them without exception relegated to the role of predicates. Accordingly, given the objective reference of predicates as well as of subjects in Russell's logic, one cannot properly argue that for Russell, particulars being quite bare, their characteristics and determinations have to be supplied by us, after the manner of some type or other of transcendental philosophy. No, characteristics and determinations, qualities and relations, are all there in the world for Russell; they are no less real things and entities than are particulars.

Still, such considerations, sound as they are, would hardly seem to

15 W. V. Quine, *From a Logical Point of View* (Cambridge: Harvard University Press, 1953), p. 6.

suffice to save Russell's metaphysical realism from possible transcendental invasion. For qualities and relations, however much they may be a part of the ultimate furniture of the world for Russell, they are still not in the world in such manner as to be qualities and relations of particulars, in the only manner in which such an "of" might be currently relevant. For what is indispensable to the maintenance of a realism as over against a transcendentalism is that the things of the world actually be what they are in fact and in themselves, with the result that their being what they are cannot be held to be the result of our transcendentally investing them with the nature and essences and determinations that they come to have for us.

However, as I understand it, in Russell's ontology it is simply impossible that anything should be what it is, simply because in Russell's logic there is no way for one to say or think what anything is. That is to say, such a mode of understanding things in terms of what they are is, I believe, quite excluded by the very formation rules of the ideal language of *PM* logic. Put rather more technically, what this amounts to is that in the function-argument schemas of the lower functional calculus (e.g. schemas such as $f(a)$, $f(a,b)$, $f(a,b,c)$), there is no way in which a function term can be interpreted as signifying what its argument is; or, conversely, in such a logic no argument can ever be said to be its function.

Here are a few illustrations. Take the $f(a)$ schema: on the interpretation which Russell would give of this, the function term in this instance must needs stand for a quality, the argument term for a particular. For instance, let the quality in this case be wisdom, and let the particular be Russell himself. Now surely, one cannot say that Russell *is* wisdom. (Even in a volume devoted to celebrating the man's unquestioned philosophic achievements, this would be going a bit far, it would seem.) Or to take another example, let the argument term stand, say, for a particular individual leaf, and let the function term stand for one of its qualities, say, its color, and more specifically its particular shade of green. Now clearly, no "is"-relationship can ever hold between a leaf and its color: the leaf is not a color, nor can it be said to be greenness itself or even a particular shade of green. And the reason is not far to seek. The subject term in each of these examples, being a particular, it cannot properly be said to be its predicate, simply because the latter is a quality or a universal, and no particular can *be* a universal: if it were it would not be a particular at all, but rather an entirely different kind of ontological thing or entity, viz. a universal; in short, universals, on Russell's ontology, are not and cannot possibly be what particulars are.

Moreover, the same point is borne out if we take a relation as our function term, instead of a quality. For example, "Russell was the pedagogue of Wittgenstein"—$f(a,b)$. Now granted that on Russell's ontology "pedagogue of" is a real relation in the world, it is certainly not the sort of thing which the subjects in the above proposition could be said to be—i.e., it in no wise represents what they are. Thus "Russell and Wittgenstein are pedagogue of," or "What Russell and Wittgenstein are are pedagogue of"—these are both nonsense.[16]

Very well, then, what is the consequence of this exclusion from the logic of logical atomism of the "is"-relationship or of that distinctive kind of subject-predicate relationship in virtue of which we seek to understand things in terms of what they are? The consequence would seem to be that when we move from Russell's logic to his ontology, it is indeed true that universals and relations are in the world, no less than particulars. And yet the universals and relations do not stand to the particulars in the manner of determinations of what such particulars are. As a result, particulars are literally and irretrievably bare; and if one asks what they are or what determinations they have, the answer must be, "Nothing at all," or at least "Nothing of any specificity or intelligibility." Indeed, the very question as to what they are must be ruled out as a logically improper question.

And so it is that Russell's ontology raises many of the ghosts that plagued Plato's ontology. For in Plato's case—at least as Aristotle represents him—the Forms are indeed real, and yet what possible bearing can they have on the many changing particulars? And the issue is serious because the sole source of intelligibility is in the Forms; and yet as Aristotle insisted, the Forms being separately existent for Plato, the nature or essence of any particular—what it is—will not be identifiable with that of which it is the essence, so that a particular individual thing cannot properly be said even to be what it is.[17] Surely, though, if such were the difficulties which Plato experienced in his attempt to understand particulars as somehow participating in the Forms without actually being the Forms, imagine how much more

[16] This whole line of argument I have tried to work more carefully and in detail in my book *Two Logics* (Evanston: Northwestern University Press, 1969), especially Chapter I.

[17] Cf. Aristotle, the *Metaphysics*, Book Zeta, especially Chapter 6.

serious must be the difficulties of Russell's ontology in which the very "is"-relationship itself or the relation of a thing to what it is has been ruled out altogether—and that simply on the grounds of Russell's logic, as distinct from his ontology.

From all of this, now, our conclusions must needs be but tentative and even speculative. For so far as we know, none of those philosophers who have come after Russell and who have made the transcendental turn have ever proclaimed that they were trying to cover the bareness and unintelligibility of the things (in this case, particulars) of Russell's world with any new-fashioned cloak of transcendental conditions of intelligibility. Nor has Russell either, so far as we know, tried to defend himself specifically against such attempts to emend and even to supplant his realism with a new-found transcendentalism. And yet the factors would all seem to be there for just such an unfolding of structural history as we have been describing. Moreover, given that there are these structural tensions and stresses in the recent history of philosophy, then it is indeed sad to have to relate that anyone wishing to shore up a metaphysical realism, as over against a revived transcendentalism, would appeal in vain to the realism of Russell's logical atomism. For that realism, at least in the light of the current challenges, has simply to be written off as a realism *manqué*.

7

Ontology and the Theory of Descriptions

M. S. Gram

THE philosophical technique of the theory of descriptions can be stated in one sentence: Definite descriptions can in all cases be replaced by predicate expressions; hence, we can avoid commitment to the existence of any object referred to by a definite description by merely replacing the expression in question by a predicate expression. This technique can, however, be interpreted in at least two different ways. On one interpretation, the theory enables us to show that an expression purporting to name something can be replaced by an expression which does not name anything. And it is easy to see what consequence this has for ontology. If any class of expressions which purport to name something can be converted into expressions which do not have this function, it is possible to show that any entity whose existence is thought to be vouchsafed by a definite description is an ontological chimera. For merely rewriting the definite description is enough to show that the object to which it purports to refer does not exist.

But this is, as I remarked above, only one way of looking at the theory of descriptions. The other interpretation of which the theory admits begins, like the first one, by attaching ontological importance to the replacement of definite descriptions by predicate expressions. But it parts company with the first interpretation when the ontological consequences of such a move are assessed. What is being shown, according to the second interpretation, is that entities thought incorrectly to be particulars really are properties. And so what the theory of descriptions accomplishes is not the demonstration that entities thought to exist really have no ontological status at all but rather that entities thought to have one ontological status really have a quite different status. If you accept the first interpretation of the theory of descriptions, you will be in possession of a means of altogether eliminating certain entities from an ontological inventory of the world. But if you accept the second interpretation of that theory, all that you will have is a way of showing that certain entities are not particulars but properties. The difference between the two interpretations can, accordingly, be stated as follows: The theory shows either that some things thought to have extralinguistic status really have the status of predicates or that some things thought to have the extralinguistic status of particulars really have the status of properties.

Which of these two interpretations is right? I shall argue that, within the context of its employment of Russell, the theory is neutral with respect to these interpretations but that, once we take it out of that context and try to make it into a tool of general ontology, only the second interpretation is viable. And from this, I want to argue, it follows that the theory of descriptions cannot be made into a tool of general ontology. I shall argue for these claims as follows. First, I shall consider the polemical context out of which the theory of descriptions arose. What I have in mind here is Meinong's argument that there are nonexistent particulars. My purpose in doing this is to show that, although Meinong's theory can accommodate the objections that Russell wrongly thought to be fatal to it, the alternative theory that Russell advances does succeed in showing that there are no such things as nonexistent particulars. Secondly, I shall argue that what Russell's theory shows is that what Meinong wrongly believed to be nonexistent particulars are really properties and not, as proponents of the first interpretation believe, predicates. And, finally, I shall argue that the first interpretation of the theory of descriptions is philosophically objectionable. To say that expressions for particulars can be reduced to predicate expressions does not render the translation ontologically aseptic: The notion of a predicate raises all of the ontological difficulties that are associated with the notion of a property.

I. Meinong's Arguments for Nonexistent Particulars

Some philosophers have claimed that there are entities called nonexistent particulars. Meinong's version of that claim is that "there are objects of which it is true that there are no such objects."[1] I distinguish two arguments which Meinong gives for this claim and propose to call them the Argument from Reference and the Argument from Introspection. The Argument from Reference runs like this:

1. To say truly that *A* does not exist is to assert an affirmative objective. Or, equivalently, there are true objectives of nonexistence: "[T]hat a certain thing, *A*, is not—more briefly, the *Nichtsein* of *A*— is just as much an objective as the *Sein* of *A*."[2]

2. The relation of an objective to the object of which it is true is comparable to that between a whole and its parts: "[A]n objective, whether it is a *Seinsobjektiv* or *Nichtseinsobjektiv*, stands in relation to its object (*Objekt*), albeit *cum grano salis*, as the whole to its parts...."[3]

3. To say truly that *A* does not exist assumes that *A* has some ontological status; but this status cannot be that of an existent, since *A* does not, *ex hypothesi*, exist.

4. But the *A* in the factual Objective of nonbeing, the nonexistence of *A*, cannot subsist. We can say of any subsistent entity that it lacks this mode of being. But we cannot say of the *A* in the factual objective of nonbeing that it lacks the mode of being it has: To attempt to deny that *A* has the ontological status it has merely assumes that it has that mode of being as a condition of the denial; hence, the *A* in the factual Objective of nonbeing mentioned above cannot subsist.

5. Thus the entities which figure in factual Objectives of nonexistence are homeless objects (*heimatlose Gegenstände*): They neither subsist nor exist. And yet, they must have some ontological status (Meinong calls it *Aussersein*) or sentences referring to factual objectives of nonexistence would be meaningless.

6. Hence, there are nonexistent particulars which figure in factual objectives of nonbeing.

[1] Alexius Meinong, "The Theory of Objects," in *Realism and the Background of Phenomenology*, ed. Roderick Chisholm (Glencoe, Illinois, 1960), p. 83.

[2] *Ibid.*, p. 84.

[3] *Ibid.*; cf. p. 85: "[T]he Objective, which has being, always seems to require in turn an Object which has being."

The argument requires explication at two points. Meinong holds both that possible particulars relate to Objectives of nonbeing in a way that is analogous to the part-whole relation. And he also holds that possible particulars neither subsist nor exist but have *Aussersein.* Consider the latter claim first, which figures in step (4) of the Argument from Reference. Why must nonexistent particulars have *Aussersein?* Meinong argues for this by saying that entities having such a status lack any significant opposite.[4] I take Meinong to mean the following by this. To say that a particular does not exist is to assert an Objective. And an Objective has subsistence; hence, we can deny that an Objective is factual. But suppose that the particular which is a part of such an Objective does not subsist. To deny the subsistence of the particular in this Objective is to assert another Objective which would correctly assert the nonexistence of *A.* Thus every sentence formulating the correct denial of the existence of *A* must assume that *A* has some ontological status. In this sense, then, to deny that a particular has any ontological status at all is futile: The truth of the claim formulating the denial assumes that the particular in question has some ontological status as a necessary condition of the truth of such a denial. And this is what sets *Aussersein* off from subsistence and existence: To deny that an entity subsists or exists can be done without assuming that the entity in question has that status. This is not true of *Aussersein.*

Meinong says in step (2) of the Argument from Reference that the relation between a factual Objective and the entities on which it bears is analogous to that between a whole and its parts. What can Meinong be taken to mean by this? Suppose I said that the golden mountain does not exist. The golden mountain cannot be a literal part of the Objective, the nonexistence of the golden mountain. If it were, then part of the Objective would have the properties of being golden and mountainous. But the Objective can be neither of these: That the golden mountain is nonexistent is neither golden nor mountainous any more than a fact about something has any of the properties as that about which it is fact. But then in what sense does the object in question have a kind of part-whole relationship to the Objective? To speak of a kind of part-whole relation here is to say no more than that a proposition implies all of its necessary conditions. If an Objective is factual, the object on which it bears must have ontological

---

[4] *Ibid.,* p. 84: "A *Nichtsein* of the same type cannot be set in opposition to it, for a *Nichtsein* even in this new sense would have to immediately produce difficulties analogous to those which arise from *Nichtsein* in the ordinary sense."

status. Thus the use of the part-whole relation in Meinong's argument must be understood as a metaphorical statement of the implication relation. It is metaphorical because a particular or an object is not literally part of the Objective which concerns it any more than an object is part of the proposition which truly says something about that object. But the relation between an object and a factual Objective about it *is*, after all, a kind of part-whole relation just in the sense that the existence of a whole implies the existence of its parts; thus a factual Objective could not be what it is unless the object which it concerned had some ontological status.

I turn now to what I have called the Argument from Introspection. It runs like this:

(1) *A* (where "*A*" deputizes for any expression referring to a particular) must be given to me if I am to grasp (*erfassen*) the fact that it does not exist. In saying that *A* does not exist, I can describe *A*, form a conception of *A*, and distinguish it from other objects I contemplate.[5]

(2) If "*A*" refers to a nonexistent object, then that object could not be physical or mental: In both cases, the object of my contemplation would exist. What is assumed, however, is that the referent of "*A*" does not exist.

(3) Not all nonexistent objects about which I can think subsist. I can think of objects that have contradictory descriptions. Thus I can think of the round square. To say that an object subsists, however, is to imply that it obeys the Law of Contradiction. Some nonexistent objects do not obey that law.

(4) Hence there are nonexistent particulars which have the ontological status of *Aussersein*.

The crucial step in the Argument from Introspection is premise (2): Meinong is saying that nonexistent particulars cannot be reduced to physical or mental entities. The reason that such particulars cannot be physical entities is obvious. To reduce a nonexistent particular to a physical particular is to rob it of its nonexistence. The reason for rejecting mental entities as reconstructions of nonexistent particulars is less obvious. He says that a mental item lacks two characteristics that nonexistent particulars can have. For one thing, a mental item exists while a nonexistent particular by definition does not. For an-

5 *Ibid.*, p. 86.

other, the *thought* of a nonexistent particular does not have the same qualities as the particular which is the object of that thought. Thus my thought of the round square is neither round nor square. My thought of the round square does not have a self-contradictory description, for my thought of the round square exists while the round square does not. Thus Meinong concludes that there are nonexistent particulars which cannot be assimilated to mental or physical items in the world.

These, then, are the two arguments by which Meinong concludes that nonexistent particulars have a unique status in the world.[6] Are they independent of each other? They are partially dependent upon each other in that the Argument from Reference is required to assure that the entities which, according to the Argument from Introspection, are given to us in fact have *Aussersein*. The Argument from Introspection establishes only that the entities which we sometimes contemplate when we think of nonexistent particulars are not subject to the Law of Contradiction and are neither mental nor physical. It takes another premise—in this case the premise supplied by step (4) of the Argument from Reference—to establish that entities of this sort have the properties Meinong attributes to *Aussersein*. Thus the Argument from Introspection tacitly relies on a step provided by the Argument from Reference.

But there is still a sense in which both arguments are independent, for both draw the same conclusion from two different bodies of facts. The Argument from Reference turns on the fact that Objectives of nonbeing assume that objects to which they refer have ontological status. The Argument from Introspection draws the same conclusion, not from the truth conditions of certain kinds of sentences, but rather

---

[6] J. N. Findlay (*Meinong's Theory of Objects and Values*, 2nd ed. [London, 1963], p. 48) dismisses both of the arguments I have just reconstructed. Of the claim that an object must have some ontological status if we are to contemplate it, Findlay says that "Meinong does not explain why, if a chimera or a golden mountain are genuine but non-existent objects, we have to assume that they exist in order to have them before our thought." This misses the point of the Argument from Introspection: We have to assume, not that they exist, but that they have ontological status. Of the claim that non-existent objects are parts of objectives, Findlay astonishingly says that Meinong rejected this view—from which it would follow that Meinong rejected the Argument from Reference—saying that "this [the part-whole relation] is an unjustifiable application to entities called facts a principle which is only evident in the case of objects." This, too, is false: It breaks down on the fact that Meinong talks about an analogous, not a literal, application of the principle to Objectives.

from our ability to be acquainted with objects that do not exist. It would be possible to draw the conclusion that there are objects which do not exist from one body of facts and to refuse to draw that conclusion from the other phenomena; hence, in this sense the two arguments are independent of each other.

Despite the straightforward character of Meinong's arguments, philosophers have disputed exactly what Meinong was trying establish when he argued for the ontological status of nonexistent objects. Meinong was, on the face of it, arguing for a realm of objects which have ontological status although they lack being. But some philosophers have argued for a very different interpretation of Meinong's position. Linsky puts it this way: "Meinong's doctrine of *Aussersein* seems to be best interpreted as a recognition of such facts as these: That Santa Claus is denoted by the subject term of the above proposition ["Santa Claus lives at the South Pole"], that Santa Claus is not Paul Bunyan though neither Santa Claus nor Paul Bunyan exists."[7] Meinong's point, on this interpretation, is that we can refer to objects that do not exist. But what becomes of the doctrine of *Aussersein?* Linsky says that "[t]his third order of being would belong to every object 'as such'."[8] And so, to recognize this fact is merely to recognize that "one can refer to anything, whether it exists (or has being in any sense) or not."[9]

But is this a correct interpretation of Meinong's position? I think not. Linsky goes wrong when he interprets Meinong as saying that *Aussersein* belongs to every object as such and not merely to some objects as distinct from others. To interpret Meinong as saying this is to impute a contradiction to him. If *Aussersein* is something that no object can fail to have, then it follows that an object can either exist or subsist and still have *Aussersein*—which would only imply that the object in question would both exist and fail to exist. For an object which, as Meinong says, is indifferent to being or beyond being cannot, in the very nature of the case, exist. But this is not all. Meinong

[7] Leonard Linsky, *Referring* (London, 1968), p. 15. This view is also found in Rudolf Freundlich, "Die beiden Aspekte der Meinongschen Gegenstandstheorie," in *Meinong-Gedenkschrift*, vol. I (Graz, 1952), p. 25: "Dieses [das Aussersein] stellt den reinen Types des Seins dar. Es ist nämlich jenes Sein, über dessen Seins-Art noch nicht entschieden ist, gleichzeitig aber auch jenes, das jedes bestimmte Seiende begleitet und ihm zugrunde liegt." Cf. also Franz Kröner, "Zu Meinongs 'unmöglichen Gegenständen'" in the same volume, pp. 67–79.

[8] Linsky, *Referring*, p. 16.

[9] *Ibid.*, p. 18.

holds that *Aussersein* is not governed by the Law of Contradiction, while existent and subsistent objects all obey that law.[10] And this is incompatible with construing *Aussersein* as a status that all objects have. For if every object must have *Aussersein*, it would be the case that one and the same object would both be governed and not governed by the Law of Contradiction; hence, it would be possible for an object to exist and yet have a contradictory description.

The reason why some philosophers have been tempted to accept this parsimonious interpretation of Meinong is, I believe, that they have misinterpreted the argument by which Meinong tries to show that entities having *Aussersein* have no significant opposite. That argument purports to show that *Aussersein* lacks a significant opposite because the assertion that an object lacks it merely assumes that the object has it: One cannot, in other words, deny that an object has that status without tacitly attributing that status to the object in question. But this does not prove that every object must have *Aussersein*. All it proves—and all that Meinong takes it to prove—is that an object which neither exists nor subsists must have some kind of ontological status. The point which Linsky's interpretation misses but which is the only point that Meinong needs to make is, accordingly, this: To say that there is an ontological status which nothing can fail to have is not the same as to say that everything has that status. For the claim that nothing can fail to have such a status may mean that the thing in question must have it if it lacks any other status. This is the sense of Meinong's argument that *Aussersein* has no significant opposite. That argument claims only that, with regard to those objects that have *Aussersein*, one cannot deny them this status without assuming that they have it. But the argument does not claim that, with regard to any object whatsoever, one cannot deny it the status of *Aussersein* without assuming that the object in question has it. And this is what vitiates the Linsky interpretation.[11]

[10] Cf. Meinong, *Über die Stellung der Wissenschaftstheorie im System der Wissenschaften* (Leipzig, 1907), p. 16, where he says that the Law of Contradiction applies only to the real and the possible but not to entities that are neither real nor possible.

[11] There are, it must be admitted, misleading descriptions of *Aussersein* to be found in Meinong. Thus he says in Chisholm (*Realism and the Background of Phenomenology*, p. 84) that *Aussersein* belongs "to every object as such." This claim does not, however, mean that existent objects have such a status. For the notion of an object as such is ambiguous: What I have tried to do is to show that reading the phrase as a reference to every object that can be mentioned is patently incompatible with other things Meinong says.

And yet there is something in Meinong's position that lends support to Linsky's interpretation. Consider again Premise (4) of the Argument from Reference. Here Meinong claims that *Aussersein* has no significant opposite: To say that *A* lacks it is to imply that *A* has it. But if we take *Aussersein* to be a realm of extraordinary entities rather than a property that all entities have in common, then Premise (4) collapses. For if an entity having *Aussersein* is a special kind of particular, then it does have a significant opposite. To say of an entity *A* that it lacks *Aussersein* would be significant just because *A* could either exist or subsist. If we accept Linsky's interpretation, however, and say that *Aussersein* is the status an object has just in virtue of our ability to discourse about it, then Premise (4) does not collapse: To deny of *A* that it has such a property is to assume that it has that property because the denial in question is just a piece of discourse about *A*. It would seem, accordingly, that the common-property theory of *Aussersein* has not been vitiated but is rather implied by a crucial step in Meinong's argument.

As it stands, then, we have an unacceptable choice between two alternatives. If we take the realm theory of *Aussersein*, we are faced with the consequence that a crucial premise in Meinong's argument must be abandoned. But if we try to save that premise by adopting the common-property theory of *Aussersein*, we are faced by the equally unacceptable consequence that there can be objects that both exist and have self-contradictory descriptions. I believe that the realm theory is the only correct view of Meinong's position since I regard the consequence of the common-property theory as unavoidable and irreparable. The consequence of the realm theory can, however, be avoided by reformulating Premise (4) and substituting the following for it:

Premise (4'): *Aussersein* cannot be denied of an object without circularity once it has been shown that the entity in question neither subsists nor exists.

Premise (4') is weaker than Premise (4) because the latter is intended to provide a way of distinguishing between subsistence and *Aussersein*. The former assumes an independent way of doing this. But this does not constitute a sound argument against Premise (4'). Meinong does distinguish *Aussersein* from both existence and subsistence by saying that the Law of Contradiction applies to both of the latter but not to the former. But Premise (4') still gives us a property that *Aus-*

sersein has but which neither subsistence nor existence has. In order to show this, suppose that we establish that an object *A* lacks existence and *Aussersein* but has subsistence. If we then deny that *A* subsists, the claim we are making is not circular but merely false; thus we are not providing an instance of subsistence by denying of an entity that it has subsistence. The same point can be made, *mutatis mutandis*, for objects about which we know that they neither subsist nor have *Aussersein*. And if this is so, then Premise (4′) will do what Meinong expects Premise (4) to do without forcing him to embrace any of the adverse consequences of the common-property theory of *Aussersein*. It will, that is, enable him to exhibit a property that objects having *Aussersein* possess that sets them off from objects having existence or subsistence.

My conclusion, then, is that, whatever Meinong may be saying when he talks about *Aussersein*, he is definitely not saying that *Aussersein* is merely a property that attaches to things because we can discourse about them. If this were all that Meinong was saying, then what he would be offering us would not be a philosophical theory at all. It would merely be a misleading way of describing the phenomena about which philosophical theories are drafted. What Meinong is saying— whether we find it palatable or not—is that there is a realm of objects explaining the possibility of talking about things that do not exist or subsist. The philosophical problem about Meinong's position is not how we can translate his claims about *Aussersein* into ontologically aseptic language. This, if I am right, is precisely what we cannot do. The problem is, rather, whether the facts justify the conclusion that there are objects which have ontological status although they neither exist nor subsist.

II. Russell's Theory of Descriptions

I divide my discussion of Russell's theory of descriptions into a consideration of two claims. He says, wrongly, that Meinong's theory is vitiated by two objections, each of which is fatal to that theory. Russell believes, rightly, that his own theory is superior to Meinong's. Consider these claims in turn.

Russell's first objection is that Meinong's theory breaches the Law of Contradiction: "It is contended, for example, that the present King of France exists, and also does not exist; that the round square is round, and also not round, etc. But this is intolerable; and if any theory can be found to avoid this result, it is surely to be preferred."[12] Russell must have arrived at this objection by reasoning as follows: On Meinong's theory any grammatically correct denoting phrase stands for an object of some kind. Contradictory denoting phrases are grammatically well formed and therefore stand for objects; hence, such phrases as 'the round square' stand for objects having contradictory properties.

The second objection to Meinong's theory is that it requires impossible objects to have, not merely the ontological status of *Aussersein*, but also the status of existence.[13] To say, on Meinong's theory, that the existing round square exists is to say that the round square necessarily exists: The Objective of existence requires for its truth that 'the round square' refer to an object which exists. And this is merely another violation of the Law of Contradiction; it requires an entity that exists have a self-contradictory description.

Whatever the merits of Russell's theory of definite descriptions, they do not reside in these objections to Meinong's theory. For neither one of these objections is sound. Consider each of the objections once more. Is the Law of Contradiction violated by talk of self-contradictory objects? It is not. Meinong's position commits him to saying only that the Law of Contradiction applies to actual and possible objects, but not to objects having *Aussersein*.[14] What must be done to make good Russell's objection is to show that Meinong's theory requires the *existence* of impossible objects. But all that Meinong's argument commits him to is the ontological status of such objects—which is compatible with the nonexistence of objects with self-contradictory descriptions. So far, then, from constituting a refutation of Meinong's theory, Russell's objection merely states one of the facts ingredient in that theory.

What about Russell's second objection? It appears to fare better than the first: Russell supplies an example of a sentence that would apparently commit Meinong to saying that impossible objects exist. Such a sentence on Meinong's theory is true; hence, it refers to a factual Objective, the existence of the round square. The Objective

[12] Bertrand Russell, "On Denoting," reprinted in *Logic and Knowledge*, ed. Robert C. Marsh (New York, 1964), p. 45.

[13] Cf. Russell, "Review of Meinong's *Über die Stellung der Gegenstandstheorie im System der Wissenschaften*," *Mind*, New Series, 16 (1907): 439.

[14] Cf. Meinong, *Über die Stellung*, p. 17.

subsists; and the object, the round square, has *Aussersein*.[15] But this is certainly not the best answer open to Meinong. Suppose that the sentence, 'The existing round square exists', is true. The object involved in the factual Objective, the existence of the round square, would have, not existence, but rather *Aussersein*. Yet this is incompatible with the truth of the sentence. If the sentence is true, then an object having, not existence, but *Aussersein* could not enter into a factual Objective, the existence of the round square. Thus the problem is this: If the object here has *Aussersein*, it renders the sentence asserting its existence false; but if the object has existence, it violates the Law of Contradiction. This is why Meinong's reply, as it stands, is unsatisfactory.

Meinong need not, however, depend upon the view that impossible objects have *Aussersein* in order to rescue his position from Russell's objection. A conclusion favorable to Meinong's position can be made to follow if we assume, as Russell did, that the sentence, 'The existent round square exists', is false. In this case the sentence would denote a nonfactual Objective, which, on Meinong's view, would have *Aussersein*. The corresponding Objective of nonexistence would be true. But then the problem I have just raised about Meinong's answer would no longer arise. For we would no longer be attributing existence to an entity that lacks it. We would, rather, be attributing nonexistence to an entity which constitutionally does not exist. Meinong is not, accordingly, committed to recognizing the existence of a self-contradictory object merely because denoting phrases containing the word 'exists' figure analytically in the sentence. These sentences can be converted without remainder into sentences which assert the nonexistence of the entity in question. Thus the problem about the existence of an entity which cannot exist is avoided.

Russell's solution to the problem of nonexistent objects cannot, therefore, in any way depend upon the foregoing arguments against Meinong. But there is still an excellent reason to accept that solution: It can successfully account for the facts about reference to nonexistent objects without forcing us to countenance a realm of objects having *Aussersein*. The framework of the theory of descriptions is well known: The notion of a propositional function and the distinction between grammatical and logical form are its main components. Thus

[15] Cf. Meinong, *Über die Stellung*, p. 17. To this Russell said (in his review of *Die Stellung*, p. 439): "I must confess I see no difference between existing and being existent; and beyond this I have no more to say on this head."

Russell translates any sentence into a propositional function which acquires a truth value when the range of application of that function is ascertained. To say that $F(x)$ ranges over everything in the world is to say that the function $F(x)$ is always true. To say that $F(x)$ is not instantiated at all—that no substitution instance would yield a true proposition—is to say that the function is always false.

The distinction between the grammatical and logical form of sentences is the tool by which denoting expressions are reduced to propositional functions and quantifiers. The point of the distinction, quite simply, is that what appears to be the subject of some sentences (i.e., 'the round square', 'the golden mountain') is really part of the predicate. Thus in cases of definite descriptions referring to nonexistent objects, Russell's theory requires, not that we recognize an object to which those descriptions refer, but rather that we translate the expression in question into a predicate and talk about the relation of that predicate to the totality of *actual* particulars. This is how the distinction between logical and grammatical form interlocks with the notion of a propositional function: All discourse apparently demanding the recognition of nonexistent particulars can be translated without remainder into sentences in which a predicate stands in some relation to actual particulars. Russell's example of this procedure is the translation of 'the present King of France is bald'. The apparent subject expression, 'the present King of France', is translated into propositional function, 'present King of France . . .', which is related to the totality of actual particulars as follows:

For all values of x, it is the case that x is the present King of France, is bald, and, for all values of y, if they are the present King of France, they are identical with x.

If this theory is correct, Meinong's realm of *Aussersein* is not a discovery at all but rather an *ad hoc* device to support a dubious theory.

The theory I have been outlining must, however, be sharply separated from an interpretation which Russell gives to it in "On Denoting." There he holds that denoting phrases which fail to denote must be translated into predicates because such a phrase would otherwise be meaningless.

Russell puts it this way:

If we say 'the King of England is bald', that is, it would seem not a statement about the complex *meaning* 'the King of England', but about the actual man denoted by the meaning. But now consider 'the king of France is bald'. By parity of form, this also ought to be about the denotation of the phrase 'the king of France'. But this phrase, though it has a *meaning* provided 'the King of England' has a meaning, has certainly no denotation, at least in any obvious sense. Hence one would suppose that 'the King of France is bald' ought to be nonsense; but it is not nonsense, since it is plainly false.[16]

The inference in this passage is a real curiosity: Russell is saying that, if a denoting expression has a meaning but no denotation, we may infer that such an expression is nonsense. The only explanation for such a curious inference is that, in the case of denoting expressions, there is no distinction between meaning and denotation. Now on this assumption Russell sees himself forced into the following dilemma: Either he must say—what is false—that denoting expressions which lack denotation are nonsense or he must find a way of accounting for the meaningfulness of such expressions without admitting that they are irreducible to something else. What is going on here, according to Russell, is the attempt to account for the meaningfulness of definite descriptions *on the assumption that the distinction between meaning and denotation collapses when applied to definite descriptions.*[17] Thus the problem, as Russell sees it, is to account for the meaningfulness of definite descriptions in terms of their denotations. This account of the theory of descriptions is false. And the reason Russell gave such an erroneous account of what he was doing in "On Denoting" is, I hold, that he wrongly thought that there was no way of singling out the meaning as distinct from the denotation of denoting phrases. He argues for this conclusion as follows: "Thus 'C' which is what we use when we want to speak of the meaning, must be not the meaning but something which denotes the meaning. And C must not be a constituent of this complex (as it is of 'the meaning of C'): for if C occurs in the complex, it will be its denotation, not its meaning, that will occur. . . ."[18] Russell's argument here comes to this: The meaning of the expression 'C' is something we cannot talk about because we can-

[16] Russell, "On Denoting," in *Logic and Knowledge*, p. 46.

[17] Cf. *Ibid.*, p. 46, fn. 2: "In the other theory, which I advocate, there is no *meaning*, and only sometimes a *denotation*."

[18] *Ibid.*, p. 50; cf. *ibid.*, p. 50: "Thus it would seem that 'C' and C are different entities, such that 'C' denotes C; but this cannot be an explanation because the relation of 'C' to C remains wholly mysterious: and where are we to find the denoting 'C' which is to denote C?"

not isolate it and make it the subject of discourse. Let us try to say, for example, that 'C' expresses a meaning and refers to the denotation C. The only way available to us, on Russell's view, of talking about the meaning expressed by 'C' is to put 'C' in quotes, as follows: "the meaning expressed by 'C'." But the denotation of the expression enclosed in double quotes is not the meaning of 'C' but a description of the meaning of 'C'. Thus each time an attempt is made to isolate the meaning of an expression what results is a description of the meaning and not the meaning itself. This prompts Russell to conclude that we cannot isolate the meanings of expressions and, hence, that the meaning and the denotation of a denoting phrase are identical.[19]

The argument is a failure. In the first place, it does not follow that the meaning and denotation of a denoting phrase are the same merely from the premise that the meaning of such phrases cannot be isolated but only described. To show that something cannot be isolated in its pristine purity does not show that it fails to exist. This is a courtesy we pay to theoretical entities in many disciplines; and there is no reason why we should not extend it to meanings. In the second place, Russell's problem about isolating meanings and thus separating them, on the one hand, from denotations and, on the other hand, from descriptions of meanings is born of an erroneous interpretation of quotation devices. The fact is that we can never isolate meanings from expressions of them. Suppose that I want to refer to the meaning, say, of the expression 'C'. The result of my attempt to isolate the meaning from the linguistic embodiment is "C" (where the double quotes are intended to distinguish a sign design in itself from a sign design annexed to a meaning). The result is, of course, a failure if you stipulate that a meaning must be given between quotation marks without the expression with which it is associated. This is the inference that Russell draws: If a meaning or sense cannot be isolated in its pristine purity between quotation marks, then there is no distinction at all between a meaning and a denotation. This is the most conspicuous result of his problem about isolating the meaning of the expression referring to the first line of Gray's *Elegy*. He says this:

[19] Cf. *Ibid.*, p. 49. See also Ronald J. Butler, "The Scaffolding of Russell's Theory of Descriptions," *The Philosophical Review*, 63 (1954): 361 as well as A. Church, "Carnap's *Introduction to Semantics*," *The Philosophical Review*, 52 (1943): 302.

The one phrase *C* was to have both meaning and denotation. But if we speak of 'the meaning of *C*', that gives us the meaning (if any) of the denotation. 'The meaning of the first line of Gray's Elegy' is the same as 'The meaning of "The curfew tolls the knell of parting day",' and is not the same as 'The meaning of "the first line of Gray's Elegy".' Thus in order to get the meaning we want, we must speak not of 'the meaning of *C*', but of 'the meaning of "*C*",' which is the same as '*C*' by itself.[20]

Russell then concludes that "to speak of *C* itself, i.e., to make a proposition about the meaning, our subject must not be *C*, but something which denotes *C*. Thus '*C*', which is what we use when we want to speak of the meaning, must be not the meaning but something which denotes the meaning."[21] When I try to talk about the meaning of the expression "*C*", what I use is another expression in order to denote the original meaning; hence what I end up with in quotation marks is, as Russell rightly remarks, not the meaning but a phrase denoting the meaning. But what, exactly, does this establish? Russell takes it to establish that it is impossible to talk about meaning in isolation and that, accordingly, there is no distinction between meaning and denotation in the case of denoting phrases: To talk about the meaning of a denoting phrase is, for him, to talk about the denotation of a denoting phrase. But this simply does not follow. What does follow, innocuously enough, is that we can talk about the meaning of an expression only by making that meaning into a denotation. But this is not the same as to say that the meaning which can function, under certain linguistic circumstances, as a denotation is therefore identical with its denotation. All that does follow is that, in order to refer to the meaning of a given expression, we must use that expression (or its equivalent) flanked by quotation devices in order to single out the meaning as one denotation among others. But that a meaning can be a denotation does not make it any the less a meaning. Hence Russell's announced motive for translating denoting expressions into predicate expressions —that they are nonsense sequences without denotation—is simply unfounded.

This does not, however, invalidate the procedure which Russell rec-

[20] Russell, "On Denoting," in *Logic and Knowledge*, p. 49.
[21] *Ibid.*, p. 50.

ommends in the case of definite descriptions. The same problem that concerned Meinong arises all over again even if the distinction between meaning and denotation is vouchsafed for denoting expressions. We can grant, for example, that the sentence, 'The present King of France is bald', is meaningful even if there is no present King of France. But if I deny that the present King of France is bald—or, for that matter, affirm that he is bald—the question still concerns what I am denying or affirming the predicate of. To say that the denoting phrase has a meaning that is independent of its denotation does not help us here. For it is clear that I am not denying or affirming that a predicate in this case applies to the meaning of the denoting phrase. I am denying or affirming something about the *referent* of that phrase. Or again: When I contemplate the present King of France and cogitate about his being bald, I am not—in any obvious sense, at least—contemplating or cogitating about the meaning or sense of the description involved in the sentence expressing what I am thinking. Thus Meinong's problem about what we refer to or think about when we ascribe predicates to nonexistent objects arises even on the assumption that the subject expressions of sentences about nonexistent particulars are meaningful even if they lack denotation.

How, then, does the theory which Russell advances explain what it is that we attribute predicates to when we judge about nonexistent particulars or when we entertain such particulars? The theory requires us, quite bluntly, to deny that there are any such things as possible or impossible particulars. There are only actual particulars on the one hand and properties or predicates on the other. And so, when we assert that the present King of France is bald, we are asserting something about the instantiation of the predicate, '. . . present King of France', with respect to all actual particulars. We are, that is, asserting that there is an actual particular falling under the predicate in question and that, with respect to all the rest of actual particulars, any that likewise falls under the predicate here is identical with the present King of France. But since there is no actual particular which falls under the predicate here, this still does not force us to import possible particulars into the theory: What we are talking about when we talk about the subject of predication here is not a possible particular but all actual particulars. The Russellian theory accounts for accusatives of consciousness without having to fall back on possible particulars: When we think of the present King of France, the theory requires us to say that we are really thinking of a property, not a particular. Thus what Meinong calls a nonexistent particular is accounted for on Russell's theory solely by reference to existent entities.

The gains in ontological economy here are appreciable. But Russell's theory is not merely a theory equivalent to Meinong's, but one which gets along with fewer kinds of entities. For an understanding of Russell's theory of descriptions will help to expose fatal defects in Meinong's arguments. Both the Argument from Reference and the Argument from Introspection are faulty: The premises of both arguments are compatible with the denial of their conclusions. Consider how each of the arguments in question goes wrong. The mistake in the Argument from Reference occurs in step (2). Here, it will be remembered, Meinong argues that the part-whole relation applies analogously to the relation between a particular and its corresponding Objective. But this does not require that there be nonexistent particulars. All that step (2) requires in order to be true is that we admit that a true Objective of nonexistence implies the existence of whatever would make it true. This is not equivalent to saying that such an Objective implies the existence of nonexistent particulars. Thus an independent argument is required to show that the truth of step (2) in the Argument from Reference requires the recognition of nonexistent particulars. Step (2) in this argument might retain its truth value if the notion of part here were understood not as equivalent to 'nonexistent particular' but rather to 'all actual particulars'. Hence the argument is not enough to show that there are nonexistent particulars.

Consider, finally, the Argument from Introspection once again in light of the Russellian alternative. Here step (3) is crucial. The step rests on the assumption that our ability to contemplate self-contradictory descriptions of an object permits us to infer that we have a self-contradictory object before our minds. But step (3) begs the question: It assumes but does not show that self-contradictory objects are the only things that can account for our ability to contemplate things that have self-contradictory descriptions. It does not, that is, rule out the view that what we contemplate in such cases is not a particular but a complex of uninstantiable properties.

III. Objections to Russell's Theory

What I have been trying to show is that Russell's theory, once it is separated from a few unsound arguments associated with it and divorced from an interpretation Russell gives of it, is superior to the view that Meinong advances. But the Meinongian theory dies a hard death. There are three standard objections to Russell's theory of descriptions any one of which would, if sound, not only greatly weaken that theory but would present indirect evidence for the truth of Meinong's alternative.

The first objection is that Russell's theory does not succeed in translating references to impossible particulars into expressions that do not make such references.[22] Russell does, it is conceded, successfully translate references to possible particulars so that we are not committed to recognizing their existence. But he does not succeed in translating references to impossible particulars so that we need not recognize them. Consider, for example, the definite description, 'The round square'. When it is translated out of the subject place of sentences in which it figures and is replaced by corresponding predicate expressions, the contradiction contained in the definite description is not removed but only transferred to the corresponding predicate expressions.

There are two very different issues being interlarded here. There is, first, the issue of translation: Have we successfully translated a sentence containing a self-contradictory expression unless we succeed in eliminating the contradiction? But there is a second and very different question here: Can reference to an impossible particular be removed unless we remove the contradiction contained in that reference? Anyone taking the present objection seriously would have to think that the removal of the contradiction involved in referring to an impossible particular is a necessary condition of not recognizing impossible particulars. This false belief is exactly why the present objection should not be taken seriously. It is a necessary condition of giving a correct *translation* of sentences referring to impossible particulars that the contradiction in the definite description be preserved. But it is not a necessary condition of successfully eliminating reference to impossible particulars that we remove the contradiction contained in such descriptions. What must be removed is not the contradiction but the linguistic vehicle which forces recognition of impossible particulars.

The second objection questions Russell's ability to account for possible particulars. We are asked to assume that a barren woman wishes

22 Cf. Franz Kröner, "Zu Meinong's 'unmöglichen Gegenständen'," in the *Meinong-Gedenkschrift*, p. 74.

for a child.[23] What is the accusative of consciousness here? She does not want to stand in the relation of motherhood to one of the children already in the world. It would in fact be possible for the woman to be perfectly happy with all the particulars there are in the world and yet to want the inventory to be enriched by one more particular—in this case a particular that does not now exist but which might exist. What the barren woman wants, then, is not that one of the actual particulars in the world acquire the property of being her child but rather that a particular that does not now exist acquire that property. From this it allegedly follows that Russell's account of possible particulars is false. For if there are no possible particulars but only actual particulars, then the Russellian theory renders it impossible for the barren woman to wish for what she in fact wishes. She does not but, on Russell's theory, must nevertheless stand in some relation to an actual particular when she wishes of a child.

Whatever embarrassment this objection may occasion a Russellian, it gives, if anything, less aid and comfort to Meinong's theory of *Aussersein*. When the barren woman wishes for a child, it certainly cannot be a correct account of what she desires to say that she is standing in some relation to an entity which is neither spatial nor temporal, neither physical nor mental, nor even subject to the Law of Contradiction. And, what is more, if Meinong's theory were an accurate account of what the barren woman desires, what she would be desiring would be something that (logically) could not exist: To desire an entity that has the ontological status of *Aussersein* is to desire something that is not subject to the Law of Contradiction. And such an entity cannot exist just because the existence of such an entity would make it subject to the Law of Contradiction.

The point can be generalized. *Any* attempt to account for what the barren woman desires when she wishes for a child by supplying a particular other than the child itself is bound to fail. Consider what kinds of particulars are available to substitute for the child desired by the barren woman. There is, of course, a mental particular; but this can be ruled out immediately. What the woman wishes is not that a mental particular take on the property of being her child. And, for the reasons I have just given, no particular which is neither mental nor physical will serve for this purpose either. But the only particular which can

[23] Findlay, *Meinong's Theory*, p. 54.

serve is the actual child. And this is precisely the particular to which
the barren woman cannot stand in any relation. The problem must,
accordingly, be solved by supplying something other than a particular which the woman entertains. This demand can be met in either
of two ways. If you insist that she must stand in some relation to a
particular when she wishes for a child, you can say that she wishes
something about herself. What she wishes is to instantiate the property
of being a mother. But there is another way of satisfying the demand.
There is nothing wrong with saying that the woman wishes that an
actual particular instantiate the property of being her child. The objection to this is, as we know, that the woman might be satisfied with
all actual particulars and still wish for a child. But this is not clear at
all. The only thing that is clear about her dissatisfaction is that no
actual particular whatsoever might possess that property. Hence either
one of these alternatives suffices to give the barren woman a respectable accusative of consciousness. But neither one of these alternatives
makes a draft on the bankrupt account of possible particulars.

It may not be clear, as I have argued, that the woman is wishing
something about a possible rather than an actual particular. But it does
not obviously follow that her accusative of consciousness in such a
case is actual rather than possible. What she in fact wishes is that an
actual particular have a property that it does not have—from which it
would seem to follow that she is standing in relation to a possible state
of affairs as distinct from a possible particular. Thus we seem to have
rejected one possible only to have covertly introduced another.

This is true but harmless. The issue here is not whether there are any
possibles at all but rather whether there are possible particulars. Russell
does not, I concede, make this distinction in his discussion of the theory of descriptions; but it is important that it be made for him. For
there is a crucial objection that can be raised against possible particulars that cannot be raised against possible states of affairs. It is this. In
order to distinguish a particular that is actual from a particular that is
not, Meinong puts them in different realms. He puts the latter in the
realm of *Aussersein*. But from this it follows that a particular having
the property of *Aussersein* can never become an actual particular. For
what is actual can never have the properties in virtue of which Meinong calls a particular pure (i.e., *ausserseiend*). The objection, then, is
that the notion of a Meinongian nonexistent particular is not the notion of anything that can become actual without becoming a different
particular. But this is not the case with a possible state of affairs. The

particular involved in what the woman wishes is, as I have argued, actual. What is possible is the state of affairs into which the particular enters. And so, passing from possibility to actuality does not involve an exchange of one particular for another.

This does not, however, exhaust the objections to which the theory of descriptions has fallen prey. There remains what in many ways is the most formidable objection to that theory: the objection, namely, that it is circular. What the theory enables us to do is to avoid recognizing possible or impossible *particulars*. What it does not enable us to do is to avoid recognizing possible or impossible *properties*. Thus what a proponent of the theory takes away with one hand is apparently restored with the other. The theory was supposed to provide a way of showing that nonexistent particulars have no ontological status. But what happens in this putative demonstration is only that another entity —this time, a possible property—is given ontological status. Thus the ontological gain of the reduction is spurious: A nonexistent property is substituted for what was supposed to be a nonexistent particular.

The objection fails on two counts. For one thing, it is no objection to the theory to say that a particular is replaced by a property. The theory purports only to remove particulars of a certain kind. It does not purport to remove them without replacing them by any other kind of entity. For another, the entity with which a nonexistent particular is replaced is not, as the objection claims, just another nonexistent entity. The property that replaces the nonexistent particular in the reduction exists; what does not exist is an *instantiation* of that property. But this meets the requirements of the theory. What the theory requires is that we give ontological status only to what exists and, accordingly, refuse to recognize the existence of entities called possible existents. And this requirement is not violated by replacing a particular by a property. There is, of course, a host of remaining problems about the analysis of potentiality and possibility; but it is important to see that the theory of descriptions does not purport to solve all or most of them. Thus it does not offer an analysis of what it means to attribute dispositional properties to particulars. This problem lies outside the scope of the theory. For while the theory is compatible with dispositional properties, it is not compatible with possible or impossible particulars. Hence the restriction inherent in the theory is not an objection to it.

There remains one *post mortem* to the objection that the theory of descriptions duplicates the problem it was supposed to solve. I have been arguing that the reduction of nonexistent particulars to existent properties that have no instantiation implies no objection to the theory. But consider the case of a particular that does not exist because it has a self-contradictory description. The reduction would involve properties that are mutually exclusive. And if there are only existent properties, then it would appear that the theory would commit us to saying that there are existent properties that have self-contradictory descriptions. This would seem to commit us to the view that there are existent contradictions.

But there is a perfectly good sense in which contradictions do exist —only it does not follow from this commonplace that there are contradictory states of affairs. The sense in which contradictions exist, however, is completely innocuous: To assert a contradiction is to assert a combination of properties that exists. If they did not, it would be impossible for us ever to contradict ourselves. But what does not exist is the instantiation of the properties involved. The recognition that there are contradictions between properties does not, accordingly, rob the properties in question of their existence. It merely robs them of their instantiability.

IV. Implications for Ontology

The Russellian theory shows, then, that there are no nonexistent particulars. But which of the two rival interpretations outlined at the beginning of this paper underlies that theory? The answer is simple: The theory, as it stands, is compatible with either interpretation. All the theory requires is that putative nonexistent particulars be analyzed without remainder into existent entities. And this purpose can be served whether you reduce nonexistent particulars to predicates or to properties. For both of these entities are free from the ontological difficulties surrounding nonexistent particulars.

Some philosophers have, however, tried to make the theory of descriptions into a tool of general ontology.[24] When the theory is extended in this manner, what happens is this: If it is possible to translate referential expressions into predicative expressions, we are allegedly not committed to the existence of an extralinguistic entity but only to a linguistic entity called a predicate. And the reason that such a trans-

---

[24] Cf. W. V. Quine, "On What There Is," reprinted in *From a Logical Point of View* (Cambridge, Mass., 1964), pp. 1–19.

lation does not commit us to the existence of any extralinguistic entities is that predicate expressions, unlike definite descriptions, do not refer. If this is right, then any entity that is thought to exist can be shown not to exist if we can translate expressions purporting to name that entity into predicate expressions.

Will the theory of descriptions support this extension? It will not. This is not readily apparent from what I have just said. For I have argued that the theory is neutral with respect to what I have called the two rival interpretations. But there is one crucial restriction governing this neutrality: Although it makes no difference for the purposes of the theory whether we construe the entities to which we reduce nonexistent particulars as properties or predicates, we are not at liberty to claim that construing something as a predicate precludes construing it also as a property. The neutrality of the theory ends, therefore, just where the theory is supposed to become a generalized ontological technique. There is nothing in the theory demanding that a translation of a referring expression into a predicative expression commits us to saying that the predicative expression does not require the existence of a property in the world. And if this is so, then the theory has no generalized ontological application.

That the theory of descriptions provides us with a way to reduce putative extralinguistic entities to linguistic entities is not, however, a claim for which much argumentation has been presented. Philosophers believing that the theory of descriptions can be made into a method of reducing entities *non grata* into predicates have usually presented this as a program of ontological reconstruction rather than arguing for its fundamental soundness. But such a program cannot, I believe, succeed. What it aims to do is to avoid ontological commitment to entities called universals by restricting all ontological commitment to those entities that can be named. And the implication appears to be that the introduction of predicates rather than universals avoids all the difficulties attendant upon ontological controversies over universals. But the only reason that some philosophers appear to believe this is that they erroneously believe that the notion of a predicate can be explicated without raising any of the problems that common properties raise. Yet this is a myth. Whatever a predicate may be, it is always open to us to ask the same questions about it that we are inclined to ask about common properties. We can, for example, ask what there is about a predicate that makes it the same thing although it is instantiated by many different kinds of linguistic materials. And so long as we are at liberty to raise this kind of question about predicates, we have not made any ontological gains by saying that an entity is linguistic rather than extralinguistic. For both such entities admit of the same kinds of ontological questions and, therefore, provide illustrations for the ontological issue about universals.

There is, it should be noted, an occasional argument to show that the theory of descriptions must be interpreted as having the consequence against which I have been arguing.[25] A recent specimen of this kind of argument runs as follows:

(1) Paradigmatic cases of reference are uses of singular referring expressions.

(2) If two expressions refer to the same object, they are interchangeable.

(3) It is the function of predicate expressions to refer.

(4) But if (3) is true, we should be able to substitute an individual expression for the predicate expression in a proposition like '*fa*'.

(5) But if we are able to make the substitution permitted in (4), then the proposition '*fa*' can be transformed into '*ba*' (where '*b*' is substituted for '*f*')—which yields nonsense.

(6) Hence to say that a predicate expression refers to a property is false.

The strategy of this argument is to show that 'refers to a property' excludes 'ascribes a property in the use of a grammatical predicate'. If the argument is sound, then the neutrality of the theory of descriptions will have been refuted.

The argument begs the question; but it begs the question in an instructive way. What is question-begging about the argument is that it assumes but does not demonstrate that all predicative expressions must have the same grammatical features as names. This assumption comes out in steps (2) and (3) of the argument. Abstracting from the difficulties of modal contexts, step (2) is simply and straightforwardly true. But it becomes highly suspect when it is allied with step (4). Only then does it become clear what an otherwise innocuous premise would be doing in such an explosive argument. Steps (2) and (4) assume that any expression which singles out or refers to a property instead of a particular must function as a name; and a name is always an expression for a particular. But this is just where the argument goes wrong. To say that an expression standing for a property must function in all ways like an expression naming a particular is to make the assumption that renders the argument question begging. A predicate expression need not be an expression for a particular in order to single out an entity that is different from a particular. And the reason for assuming that it does is clear: Philosophers making such an assumption reason that what is thought to be an extralinguistic entity is really only a linguistic entity. What they do, then, is this: they first assume that predicative expressions do all the duties usually assigned to properties; and then they transform attempts to separate properties from predicates into an attempt to use predicates as names for particulars. Once this assumption is exposed for what it is, any interpretation of the theory of descriptions relying upon it is falsified. The present attempt to make that theory into an instrument of ontological nominalism has not succeeded.

PART TWO

Theories of Reference and Descriptions

8

On Referring

P. F. Strawson

I

We very commonly use expressions of certain kinds to mention or refer to some individual person or single object or particular event or place or process, in the course of doing what we should normally describe as making a statement about that person, object, place, event, or process. I shall call this way of using expressions the 'uniquely referring use'. The classes of expressions which are most commonly used in this way are: singular demonstrative pronouns ('this' and 'that'); proper names (*e.g.* 'Venice', 'Napoleon', 'John'); singular personal and impersonal pronouns ('he', 'she', 'I', 'you', 'it'); and phrases beginning with the definite article followed by a noun, qualified or unqualified, in the singular (*e.g.* 'the table', 'the old man', 'the king of France'). Any expression of any of these classes can occur as the subject of what would traditionally be regarded as a singular subject-predicate sentence; and would, so occurring, exemplify the use I wish to discuss.

I do not want to say that expressions belonging to these classes never have any other use than the one I want to discuss. On the contrary, it is obvious that they do. It is obvious that anyone who uttered the sentence, 'The whale is a mammal', would be using the expression 'the whale' in a way quite different from the way it would be used by any-

Reprinted with the kind permission of the author and the editor from *Mind*, 59 (1950): 320–344.

one who had occasion seriously to utter the sentence, 'The whale struck the ship'. In the first sentence one is obviously *not* mentioning, and in the second sentence one obviously *is* mentioning, a particular whale. Again if I said, 'Napoleon was the greatest French soldier', I should be using the word 'Napoleon' to mention a certain individual, but I should not be using the phrase, 'the greatest French soldier', to mention an individual, but to say something about an individual I had already mentioned. It would be natural to say that in using this sentence I was talking *about* Napoleon and that what I was *saying* about him was that he was the greatest French soldier. But of course I *could* use the expression, 'the greatest French soldier', to mention an individual; for example, by saying: 'The greatest French soldier died in exile'. So it is obvious that at least some expressions belonging to the classes I mentioned *can* have uses other than the use I am anxious to discuss. Another thing I do not want to say is that in any given sentence there is never more than one expression used in the way I propose to discuss. On the contrary, it is obvious that there may be many more than one. For example, it would be natural to say that, in seriously using the sentence, 'The whale struck the ship', I was saying something about both a certain whale and a certain ship, that I was using each of the expressions 'the whale' and 'the ship' to mention a particular object; or, in other words, that I was using each of these expressions in the uniquely referring way. In general, however, I shall confine my attention to cases where an expression used in this way occurs as the grammatical subject of a sentence.

I think it is true to say that Russell's Theory of Descriptions, which is concerned with the last of the four classes of expressions I mentioned above (*i.e.* with expressions of the form 'the so-and-so'), is still widely accepted among logicians as giving a correct account of the use of such expressions in ordinary language. I want to show in the first place, that this theory, so regarded, embodies some fundamental mistakes.

What question or questions about phrases of the form 'the so-and-so' was the Theory of Descriptions designed to answer? I think that at least one of the questions may be illustrated as follows. Suppose someone were now to utter the sentence, 'The king of France is wise'. No one would say that the sentence which had been uttered was meaningless. Everyone would agree that it was significant. But everyone knows that there is not at present a king of France. One of the questions the Theory of Descriptions was designed to answer was the question: How can such a sentence as 'The king of France is wise' be significant even when there is nothing which answers to the description it contains, *i.e.*, in this case, nothing which answers to the description 'The king of France'? And one of the reasons why Russell thought it important to give a correct answer to this question was that he thought it important to show that another answer which might be given was wrong. The answer that he thought was wrong, and to which he was anxious to supply an alternative, might be exhibited as the conclusion of either of the following two fallacious arguments. Let us call the sentence 'The king of France is wise' the sentence *S*. Then the first argument is as follows:

(1) The phrase, 'the king of France', is the subject of the sentence *S*.

Therefore (2) if *S* is a significant sentence, *S* is a sentence *about* the king of France.

But (3) if there in no sense exists a king of France, the sentence is not about anything, and hence not about the king of France.

Therefore (4) since *S* is significant, there must in some sense (in some world) exist (or subsist) the king of France.

And the second argument is as follows:

(1) If *S* is significant, it is either true or false.

(2) *S* is true if the king of France is wise and false if the king of France is not wise.

(3) But the statement that the king of France is wise and the statement that the king of France is not wise are alike true only if there is (in some sense, in some world) something which is the king of France.

Hence (4) since *S* is significant, there follows the same conclusion as before.

These are fairly obviously bad arguments, and, as we should expect, Russell rejects them. The postulation of a world of strange entities, to which the king of France belongs, offends, he says, against 'that feeling for reality which ought to be preserved even in the most abstract studies'. The fact that Russell rejects these arguments is, however, less interesting than the extent to which, in rejecting their conclusion, he concedes the more important of their principles. Let me refer to the phrase, 'the king of France', as the phrase *D*. Then I think Russell's reasons for rejecting these two arguments can be summarized as follows. The mistake arises, he says, from thinking that *D*, which is certainly the *grammatical* subject of *S*, is also the *logical* subject of *S*. But *D* is not the logical subject of *S*. In fact *S*, although grammatically it has a singular subject and a predicate, is not logically a subject-predicate sentence at all. The proposition it expresses is a complex kind of *existential* proposition, part of which might be described as a 'uniquely existential' proposition. To exhibit the logical form of the proposition, we should re-write the sentence in a logically appropriate grammatical form; in such a way that the deceptive similarity of S to a sentence expressing a subject-predicate proposition would disappear, and we should be safeguarded against arguments such as the bad ones I outlined above. Before recalling the details of Russell's analysis of S, let us notice what his answer, as I have so far given it, seems to imply. His answer seems to imply that in the case of a sentence which is similar to S in that (1) it is grammatically of the subject-predicate form and (2) its grammatical subject does not refer to anything, then the only alternative to its being meaningless is that it should not really (*i.e.* logically) be of the subject-predicate form at all, but of some quite different form. And this in its turn seems to imply that if there are any sentences which are genuinely of the subject-predicate form, then the very fact of their being significant, having a meaning, guarantees that there *is* something referred to by the logical (and grammatical) subject. Moreover, Russell's answer seems to imply that there are such sentences. For if it is true that one may be misled by the grammatical similarity of S to other sentences into thinking that it is logically of the subject-predicate form, then surely there must be other sentences grammatically similar to S, which *are* of the subject-predicate form. To show not only that Russell's answer seems to imply these conclusions, but that he accepted at least the first two of them, it is enough to consider what he says about a class of expressions which he calls 'logically proper names' and contrasts with expressions, like D, which he calls 'definite descriptions'. Of logically proper names Russell says or implies the following things:

(1) That they and they alone can occur as subjects of sentences which are genuinely of the subject-predicate form.

(2) That an expression intended to be a logically proper name is *meaningless* unless there is some single object for which it stands: for the *meaning* of such an expression just is the individual object which the expression designates. To be a name at all, therefore, it *must* designate something.

It is easy to see that if anyone believes these two propositions, then the only way for him to save the significance of the sentence S is to deny that it is a logically subject-predicate sentence. Generally, we may say that Russell recognizes only two ways in which sentences which seem, from their grammatical structure, to be about some particular person or individual object or event, can be significant:

(1) The first is that their grammatical form should be misleading as to their logical form, and that they should be analysable, like *S*, as a special kind of existential sentence.

(2) The second is that their grammatical subject should be a logically proper name, of which the meaning is the individual thing it designates.

I think that Russell is unquestionably wrong in this, and that sentences which are significant, and which begin with an expression used in the uniquely referring way, fall into neither of these two classes. Expressions used in the uniquely referring way are never either logically proper names or descriptions, if what is meant by calling them 'descriptions' is that they are to be analysed in accordance with the model provided by Russell's Theory of Descriptions.

There are no logically proper names and there are no descriptions (in this sense).

Let us now consider the details of Russell's analysis. According to Russell, anyone who asserted *S* would be asserting that:

(1) There is a king of France.
(2) There is not more than one king of France.
(3) There is nothing which is king of France and is not wise.

It is easy to see both how Russell arrived at this analysis, and how it enables him to answer the question with which we began, viz. the question: How can the sentence *S* be significant when there is no king of France? The way in which he arrived at the analysis was clearly by asking himself what would be the circumstances in which we would say that anyone who uttered the sentence *S* had made a true assertion. And it does seem pretty clear, and I have no wish to dispute, that the sentences (1)–(3) above do describe circumstances which are at least *necessary* conditions of anyone making a true assertion by uttering the sentence *S*. But, as I hope to show, to say this is not at all the same thing as to say that Russell has given a correct account of the use of the sentence *S* or even that he has given an account which, though incomplete, is correct as far as it goes; and is certainly not at all the same thing as to say that the model translation provided is a correct model for all (or for any) singular sentences beginning with a phrase of the form 'the so-and-so'.

It is also easy to see how this analysis enables Russell to answer the question of how the sentence S can be significant, even when there is no king of France. For, if this analysis is correct, anyone who utters the sentence S today would be jointly asserting three propositions, one of which (viz. that there is a king of France) would be false; and since the conjunction of three propositions, of which one is false, is itself false, the assertion as a whole would be significant, but false. So neither of the bad arguments for subsistent entities would apply to such an assertion.

II

As a step towards showing that Russell's solution of his problem is mistaken, and towards providing the correct solution, I want now to draw certain distinctions. For this purpose I shall, for the remainder of this section, refer to an expression which has a uniquely referring use as 'an expression' for short; and to a sentence beginning with such an expression as 'a sentence' for short. The distinctions I shall draw are rather rough and ready, and, no doubt, difficult cases could be produced which would call for their refinement. But I think they will serve my purpose. The distinctions are between:

(A1) a sentence,
(A2) a use of a sentence,
(A3) an utterance of a sentence,

and, correspondingly, between:

(B1) an expression,
(B2) a use of an expression,
(B3) an utterance of an expression.

Consider again the sentence, 'The king of France is wise'. It is easy to imagine that this sentence was uttered at various times from, say, the beginning of the seventeenth century onwards, during the reigns of each successive French monarch; and easy to imagine that it was also uttered during the subsequent periods in which France was not a monarchy. Notice that it was natural for me to speak of 'the sentence' or 'this sentence' being uttered at various times during this period; or, in other words, that it would be natural and correct to speak of *one and the same* sentence being uttered on all these various occasions. It is in the sense in which it would be correct to speak of one and the same sentence being uttered on all these various occasions that I want to use the expression (A1) 'a sentence'. There are, however, obvious differences between different *occasions of the use* of this sentence. For instance, if one man uttered it in the reign of Louis XIV and another man uttered it in the reign of Louis XV, it would be natural to say (to assume) that they were respectively talking about different people; and it might be held that the first man, in using the sentence, made a true assertion, while the second man, in using the same sentence, made a false assertion. If on the other hand two different men simultaneously uttered the sentence (*e.g.* if one wrote it and the other spoke it) during the reign of Louis XIV, it would be natural to say (assume) that they were both talking about the same person, and, in that case, in using the sentence, they *must* either both have made a true assertion or both have made a false assertion. And this illustrates what I mean by *a use* of a sentence. The two men who uttered the sentence, one in the reign of Louis XV and one in the reign of Louis XIV, each made a different use of the same sentence; whereas the two men who uttered the sentence simultaneously in the reign of Louis XIV, made the same use[1] of the same sentence. Obviously in the case of this sentence, and equally obviously in the case of many others, we cannot talk of *the sentence* being true or false, but only of its being used to make a true or false assertion, or (if this is preferred) to express a true or a false proposition. And equally obviously we cannot talk of *the sentence* being *about* a particular person, for the same sentence may be used at different times to talk about quite different particular persons, but only of *a use* of the sentence to talk about a particular person. Finally it will make sufficiently clear what I mean by an utterance of a sentence if I say that the two men who simultaneously uttered the sentence in the reign of Louis XIV made two different utterances of the same sentence, though they made the same *use* of the sentence.

If we now consider not the whole sentence, 'The king of France is wise', but that part of it which is the expression, 'the king of France',

---

[1] This usage of 'use' is, of course, different from (*a*) the current usage in which 'use' (of a particular word, phrase, sentence) = (roughly) 'rules for using' = (roughly) 'meaning'; and from (*b*) my own usage in the phrase 'uniquely referring use of expressions' in which 'use' = (roughly) 'way of using'.

it is obvious that we can make analogous, though not identical, distinctions between (1) the expression, (2) a use of the expression, and (3) an utterance of the expression. The distinctions will not be identical; we obviously cannot correctly talk of the expression 'the king of France' being used to express a true or false proposition, since in general only sentences can be used truly or falsely; and similarly it is only by using a sentence and not by using an expression alone that you can talk about a particular person. Instead, we shall say in this case that you *use* the expression to *mention* or *refer to* a particular person in the course of using the sentence to talk about him. But obviously in this case, and a great many others, the *expression* (B1) cannot be said to mention, or refer to, anything, any more than the *sentence* can be said to be true or false. The same expression can have different mentioning-uses, as the same sentence can be used to make statements with different truth-values. 'Mentioning', or 'referring', is not something an expression does; it is something that someone can use an expression to do. Mentioning, or referring to, something is a characteristic of *a use* of an expression, just as 'being about' something, and truth-or-falsity, are characteristics of *a use* of a sentence.

A very different example may help to make these distinctions clearer. Consider another case of an expression which has a uniquely referring use, viz. the expression 'I'; and consider the sentence, 'I am hot'. Countless people may use this same sentence; but it is logically impossible for two different people to make *the same use* of this sentence: or, if this is preferred, to use it to express the same proposition. The expression 'I' may correctly be used by (and only by) any one of innumerable people to refer to himself. To say this is to say something about the expression 'I': it is, in a sense, to give its meaning. This is the sort of thing that can be said about *expressions*. But it makes no sense to say of the *expression* 'I' that it refers to a particular person. This is the sort of thing that can be said only of a particular use of the expression.

Let me use 'type' as an abbreviation for 'sentence or expression'. Then I am not saying that there are sentences and expressions (types), *and* uses of them, *and* utterances of them, as there are ships *and* shoes *and* sealing-wax. I am saying that we cannot say *the same things* about types, uses of types, and utterances of types. And the fact is that we do talk about types; and that confusion is apt to result from the failure to notice the differences between what we can say about these and what we can say only about the *uses* of types. We are apt to fancy we are talking about sentences and expressions when we are talking about the uses of sentences and expressions.

This is what Russell does. Generally, as against Russell, I shall say this. Meaning (in at least one important sense) is a function of the sentence or expression; mentioning and referring and truth or falsity are functions of the use of the sentence or expression. To give the meaning of an expression (in the sense in which I am using the word) is to give *general directions* for its use to refer to or mention particular objects or persons; to give the meaning of a sentence is to give *general directions* for its use in making true or false assertions. It is not to talk about any particular occasion of the use of the sentence or expression. The meaning of an expression cannot be identified with the object it is used, on a particular occasion, to refer to. The meaning of a sentence cannot be identified with the assertion it is used, on a particular occasion, to make. For to talk about the meaning of an expression or sentence is not to talk about its use on a particular occasion, but about the rules, habits, conventions governing its correct use, on all occasions, to refer or to assert. So the question of whether a sentence or expression *is significant or not* has nothing whatever to do with the question of whether the sentence, *uttered on a particular occasion*, is, on that occasion, being used to make a true-or-false assertion or not, or of whether the expression is, on that occasion, being used to refer to, or mention, anything at all.

The source of Russell's mistake was that he thought that referring or mentioning, if it occurred at all, must be meaning. He did not distinguish B1 from B2; he confused expressions with their use in a particular context; and so confused meaning with mentioning, with referring. If I talk about my handkerchief, I can, perhaps, produce the object I am referring to out of my pocket. I cannot produce the meaning of the expression, 'my handkerchief', out of my pocket. Because Russell confused meaning with mentioning, he thought that if there were any expressions having a uniquely referring use, which were what they seemed (*i.e.* logical subjects) and not something else in disguise, their meaning must *be* the particular object which they were used to refer to. Hence the troublesome mythology of the logically proper name. But if someone asks me the meaning of the expression 'this'—once Russell's favourite candidate for this status—I do not hand him the object I have just used the expression to refer to, adding at the same time that the meaning of the word changes every time it is used. Nor do I hand him all the objects it ever has been, or might be, used to refer to. I explain and illustrate the conventions governing the use of the expression. This *is* giving the meaning of the expression. It is quite different from giving (in any sense of giving) the object to which it refers; for the expression itself does not refer to anything; though it can be used, on different occasion, to refer to innumerable things. Now as a matter of fact there is, in English, a sense of the word 'mean' in which this word does approximate to 'indicate, mention or refer to'; *e.g.* when somebody (unpleasantly) says, 'I mean you'; or when I point and say, 'That's the one I mean'. But *the one I meant* is quite different from *the meaning of the expression* I used to talk of it. In this special sense of 'mean', it is people who mean, not expressions. People use expressions to refer to particular things. But the meaning of an expression is not the set of things or the single thing it may correctly be used to refer to: the meaning is the set of rules, habits, conventions for its use in referring.

It is the same with sentences, even more obviously so. Everyone knows that the sentence, 'The table is covered with books', is significant, and everyone knows what it means. But if I ask, 'What object is that sentence about?' I am asking an absurd question—a question which cannot be asked about the sentence, but only about some use of the sentence: and in this case the sentence has not been used to talk about something, it has only been taken as an example. In knowing what it means, you are knowing how it could correctly be used to talk about things: so knowing the meaning has nothing to do with knowing about any particular use of the sentence to talk about anything. Similarly, if I ask: 'Is the sentence true or false?' I am asking an absurd question, which becomes no less absurd if I add, 'It must be one or the other since it is significant'. The question is absurd, because the *sentence* is neither true nor false any more than it is *about* some object. Of course the fact that it is significant is the same as the fact that it *can* correctly be used to talk about something and that, in so using it, someone will be making a true or false assertion. And I will add that it will be used to make a true or false assertion *only* if the person using it *is* talking about something. If, when he utters it, he is not talking about anything, then his use is not a genuine one, but a spurious or pseudo-use: he is not making either a true or a false assertion, though he may think he is. And this points the way to the correct answer to the puzzle to which the Theory of Descriptions gives a fatally incorrect answer. The important point is that the question of whether the sentence is significant or not is quite independent of the question that can be raised about a particular use of it, viz. the question whether it is a genuine or a spurious use, whether it is being used to talk about something, or in make-believe, or as an example in philosophy. The question whether the sentence is significant or not is the question whether there exist such language habits, conventions or rules that the sentence logically could be used to talk about something; and is hence quite independent of the question whether it is being so used on a particular occasion.

III

Consider again the sentence, 'The king of France is wise', and the true and false things Russell says about it.

There are at least two true things which Russell would say about the sentence:

(1) The first is that it is significant; that if anyone were now to utter it, he would be uttering a significant sentence.

(2) The second is that anyone now uttering the sentence would be making a true assertion only if there in fact at present existed one and only one king of France, and if he were wise.

What are the false things which Russell would say about the sentence? They are:

(1) That anyone now uttering it would be making a true assertion or a false assertion;

(2) That part of what he would be asserting would be that there at present existed one and only one king of France.

I have already given some reasons for thinking that these two statements are incorrect. Now suppose someone were in fact to say to you with a perfectly serious air: 'The king of France is wise'. Would you say, 'That's untrue'? I think it is quite certain that you would not. But suppose he went on to *ask* you whether you thought that what he had just said was true, or was false; whether you agreed or disagreed with what he had just said. I think you would be inclined, with some hesitation, to say that you did not do either; that the question of whether his statement was true or false simply *did not arise*, because there was no such person as the king of France. You might, if he were obviously serious (had a dazed astray-in-the-centuries look), say something like: 'I'm afraid you must be under a misapprehension. France is not a monarchy. There is no king of France.' And this brings out the point that if a man seriously uttered the sentence, his uttering it would in some sense be *evidence* that he *believed* that there was a king of France. It would not be evidence for his believing this simply in the way in which a man's reaching for his raincoat is evidence for his believing that it is raining. But nor would it be evidence for his believing this in the way in which a man's saying, 'It's raining', is evidence for his believing that it is raining. We might put it as follows. To say 'The king of France is wise' is, in some sense of 'imply', to *imply* that there is a king of France. But this is a very special and odd sense of 'imply'. 'Implies' in this sense is certainly not equivalent to 'entails' (or 'logically implies'). And this comes out from the fact that when, in response to his statement, we say (as we should) 'There is no king of France', we should certainly *not* say we were *contradicting* the statement that the king of France is wise. We are certainly not saying that it is false. We are, rather, giving a reason for saying that the question of whether it is true or false simply does not arise.

And this is where the distinction I drew earlier can help us. The sentence, 'The king of France is wise', is certainly significant; but this does not mean that any particular use of it is true or false. We use it truly or falsely when we use it to talk about someone; when, in using the expression, 'the king of France', we are in fact mentioning someone. The fact that the sentence and the expression, respectively, are significant just is the fact that the sentence *could* be used, in certain circumstances, to say something true or false, that the expression *could* be used, in certain circumstances, to mention a particular person; and to know their meaning is to know what sort of circumstances these are. So when we utter the sentence without in fact mentioning anybody by the use of the phrase, 'The king of France', the sentence does not cease to be significant: we simply *fail* to say anything true or false because we simply fail to mention anybody by this particular use of that perfectly significant phrase. It is, if you like, a spurious use of the sentence, and a spurious use of the expression; though we may (or may not) mistakenly think it a genuine use.

And such spurious uses[2] are very familiar. Sophisticated romancing,

---

[2] The choice of the word 'spurious' now seems to me unfortunate, at least for some non-standard uses. I should now prefer to call some of these 'secondary' uses.

sophisticated fiction,[3] depend upon them. If I began, 'The king of France is wise', and went on, 'and he lives in a golden castle and has a hundred wives', and so on, a hearer would understand me perfectly well, without supposing *either* that I was talking about a particular person, *or* that I was making a false statement to the effect that there existed such a person as my words described. (It is worth adding that where the use of sentences and expressions is overtly fictional, the sense of the word 'about' may change. As Moore said, it is perfectly natural and correct to say that some of the statements in *Pickwick Papers* are *about* Mr. Pickwick. But where the use of sentences and expressions is not overtly fictional, this use of 'about' seems less correct; *i.e.* it would not *in general* be correct to say that a statement was about Mr. X or the so-and-so, unless there were such a person or thing. So it is where the romancing is in danger of being taken seriously that we might answer the question, 'Who is he talking about?' with 'He's not talking about anybody'; but, in saying this, we are not saying that what he is saying is either false or nonsense.)

Overtly fictional uses apart, however, I said just now that to use such an expression as 'The king of France' at the beginning of a sentence was, in some sense of 'imply', to imply that there was a king of France. When a man uses such an expression, he does not *assert*, nor does what he says *entail*, a uniquely existential proposition. But one of the conventional functions of the definite article is to act as a *signal* that a unique reference is being made—a signal, not a disguised assertion. When we begin a sentence with 'the such-and-such' the use of 'the' shows, but does not state, that we are, or intend to be, referring to one particular individual of the species 'such-and-such'. *Which* particular individual is a matter to be determined from context, time, place, and any other features of the situation of utterance. Now, whenever a man uses any expression, the presumption is that he thinks he is using it correctly: so when he uses the expression, 'the such-and-such', in a uniquely referring way, the presumption is that he thinks both that there is *some* individual of that species, and that the context of use will sufficiently determine which one he has in mind. To use the word 'the' in this way is then to imply (in the relevant sense of 'imply') that the existential conditions described by Russell are fulfilled. But to use 'the' in this way is not to *state* that those conditions are fulfilled. If I begin

---

[3] The unsophisticated kind begins: 'Once upon a time there was . . .'.

a sentence with an expression of the form, 'the so-and-so', and then am prevented from saying more, I have made no statement of any kind; but I may have succeeded in mentioning someone or something.

The uniquely existential assertion supposed by Russell to be part of any assertion in which a uniquely referring use is made of an expression of the form 'the so-and-so' is, he observes, a compound of two assertions. To say that there is a ϕ is to say something compatible with there being several ϕs; to say there is not more than one ϕ is to say something compatible with there being none. To say there is one ϕ and one only is to compound these two assertions. I have so far been concerned mostly with the alleged assertion of existence and less with the alleged assertion of uniqueness. An example which throws the emphasis on to the latter will serve to bring out more clearly the sense of 'implied' in which a uniquely existential assertion is implied, but not entailed, by the use of expressions in the uniquely referring way. Consider the sentence, 'The table is covered with books'. It is quite certain that in any normal use of this sentence, the expression 'the table' would be used to make a unique reference, *i.e.* to refer to some one table. It is a quite strict use of the definite article, in the sense in which Russell talks on p. 30 of *Principia Mathematica*, of using the article '*strictly*, so as to imply uniqueness'. On the same page Russell says that a phrase of the form 'the so-and-so', used strictly, 'will only have an application in the event of there being one so-and-so and no more'. Now it is obviously quite false that the phrase 'the table' in the sentence 'the table is covered with books', used normally, will 'only have an application in the event of there being one table and no more'. It is indeed tautologically true that, in such a use, the phrase will have an application only in the event of there being one table and no more *which is being referred to*, and that it will be understood to have an application only in the event of there being one table and no more which it is understood as being used to refer to. To use the sentence is not to assert, but it is (in the special sense discussed) to imply, that there is only one thing which is *both* of the kind specified (*i.e.* a table) *and is being referred to* by the speaker. It is obviously not to assert this. To refer is not to say you are referring. To say there is *some table or other* to which you are referring is not the same as referring to a particular table. We should have no use for such phrases as 'the individual I referred to' unless there were something which counted as referring. (It would make no sense to say you had pointed if there were nothing which counted as pointing.) So once more I draw the conclusion that referring to or mentioning a particular thing cannot be dissolved into any kind of assertion. To refer is not to assert, though you refer in order to go on to assert.

Let me now take an example of the uniquely referring use of an expression not of the form, 'the so-and-so'. Suppose I advance my hands, cautiously cupped, toward someone, saying, as I do so, 'This is a fine red one'. He, looking into my hands and seeing nothing there, may say: 'What is? What are you talking about?' Or perhaps, 'But there's nothing in your hands'. Of course it would be absurd to say that, in saying 'But you've got nothing in your hands', he was *denying* or *contradicting* what I said. So 'this' is not a disguised description in Russell's sense. Nor is it a logically proper name. For one must know what the sentence means in order to react in that way to the utterance of it. It is precisely because the significance of the word 'this' is independent of any particular reference it may be used to make, though not independent of the way it may be used to refer, that I can, as in this example, use it to *pretend* to be referring to something.

The general moral of all this is that communication is much less a matter of explicit or disguised assertion than logicians used to suppose. The particular application of this general moral in which I am interested is its application to the case of making a unique reference. It is a part of the significance of expressions of the kind I am discussing that they can be used, in an immense variety of contexts, to make unique references. It is no part of their significance to assert that they are being so used or that the conditions of their being so used are fulfilled. So the wholly important distinction we are required to draw is between

(1) using an expression to make a unique reference; and

(2) asserting that there is one and only one individual which has certain characteristics (*e.g.* is of a certain kind, or stands in a certain relation to the speaker, or both).

This is, in other words, the distinction between

(1) sentences containing an expression used to indicate or mention or refer to a particular person or thing; and

(2) uniquely existential sentences.

What Russell does is progressively to assimilate more and more sentences of class (1) to sentences of class (2), and consequently to involve himself in insuperable difficulties about logical subjects, and about values for individual variables generally: difficulties which have led him finally to the logically disastrous theory of names developed in the *Enquiry into Meaning and Truth* and in *Human Knowledge*. That view of the meaning of logical-subject-expressions which provides the whole incentive to the Theory of Descriptions at the same time precludes the possibility of Russell's ever finding any satisfactory substitutes for those expressions which, beginning with substantival phrases, he progressively degrades from the status of logical subjects.[4] It is not simply, as is sometimes said, the fascination of the relation between a name and its bearer, that is the root of the trouble. Not even names come up to the impossible standard set. It is rather the combination of two more radical misconceptions: first, the failure to grasp the importance of the distinction (section II above) between what may be said of an expression and what may be said of a particular use of it; second, a failure to recognize the uniquely referring use of expressions for the harmless, necessary thing it is, distinct from, but complementary to, the predicative or ascriptive use of expressions. The expressions which can in fact occur as singular logical subjects are expressions of the class I listed at the outset (demonstratives, substantival phrases, proper names, pronouns): to say this is to say that these expressions, together with context (in the widest sense), are what one uses to make unique references. The point of the conventions governing the uses of such expressions is, along with the situation of utterance, to secure uniqueness of reference. But to do this, enough is enough. We do not, and we cannot, while referring, attain the point of complete explicitness at which the referring function is no longer performed. The actual unique reference made, if any, is a matter of the particular use in the particular context; the significance of the expression used is the set of rules or conventions which permit such references to be made. Hence we can, using significant expressions, pretend to refer, in make-believe or in fiction, or mistakenly think we are referring when we are not referring to anything.[5]

This shows the need for distinguishing two kinds (among many others) of linguistic conventions or rules: rules for referring, and

---

[4] And this in spite of the danger-signal of that phrase, *'misleading* grammatical form'.

[5] [This sentence now seems to me objectionable in a number of ways, notably because of an unexplicitly restrictive use of the word 'refer'. It could be more exactly phrased as follows: 'Hence we can, using significant expressions, refer in secondary ways, as in make-believe or in fiction, or mistakenly think we are referring to something in the primary way when we are not, in that way, referring to anything'.]

rules for attributing and ascribing; and for an investigation of the former. If we recognize this distinction of use for what it is, we are on the way to solving a number of ancient logical and metaphysical puzzles.

My last two sections are concerned, but only in the barest outline, with these questions.

IV

One of the main purposes for which we use language is the purpose of stating facts about things and persons and events. If we want to fulfill this purpose, we must have some way of forestalling the question, 'What (who, which one) are you talking about?' as well as the question, 'What are you saying about it (him, her)?' The task of forestalling the first question is the referring (or identifying) task. The task of forestalling the second is the attributive (or descriptive or classificatory or ascriptive) task. In the conventional English sentence which is used to state, or to claim to state, a fact about an individual thing or person or event, the performance of these two tasks can be roughly and approximately assigned to separable expressions.[6] And in such a sentence, this assigning of expressions to their separate rôles corresponds to the conventional grammatical classification of subject and predicate. There is nothing sacrosanct about the employment of separable expressions for these two tasks. Other methods could be, and are, employed. There is, for instance, the method of uttering a single word or attributive phrase in the conspicuous presence of the object referred to; or that analogous method exemplified by, *e.g.*, the painting of the words 'unsafe for lorries' on a bridge, or the tying of a label reading 'first prize' on a vegetable marrow. Or one can imagine an elaborate game in which one never used an expression in the uniquely referring way at all, but uttered only uniquely existential sentences, trying to enable the hearer to identify what was being talked of by means of an accumulation of relative clauses. (This description of the purposes of the game shows in what sense it would be a game: this is not the normal use we make of existential sentences.) Two points require emphasis. The first is that the necessity of performing these two tasks in order to state particular facts requires no transcendental

---

[6] I neglect relational sentences; for these require, not a modification in the principle of what I say, but a complication of the detail.

explanation: to call attention to it is partly to elucidate the meaning of the phrase, 'stating a fact'. The second is that even this elucidation is made in terms derivative from the grammar of the conventional singular sentence; that even the overtly functional, linguistic distinction between the identifying and attributive rôles that words may play in language is prompted by the fact that ordinary speech offers us separable expressions to which the different functions may be plausibly and approximately assigned. And this functional distinction has cast long philosophical shadows. The distinctions between particular and universal, between substance and quality, are such pseudo-material shadows, cast by the grammar of the conventional sentence, in which separable expressions play distinguishable rôles.[7]

To use a separate expression to perform the first of these tasks is to use an expression in the uniquely referring way. I want now to say something in general about the conventions of use for expressions used in this way, and to contrast them with conventions of ascriptive use. I then proceed to the brief illustration of these general remarks and to some further applications of them.

What in general is required for making a unique reference is, obviously, some device, or devices, for showing both *that* a unique reference is intended and *what* unique reference it is; some device requiring and enabling the hearer or reader to identify what is being talked about. In securing this result, the context of utterance is of an importance which it is almost impossible to exaggerate; and by 'context' I mean, at least, the time, the place, the situation, the identity of the speaker, the subjects which form the immediate focus of interest, and the personal histories of both the speaker and those he is addressing. Besides context, there is, of course, convention—linguistic convention. But, except in the case of genuine proper names, of which I shall have more to say later, the fulfillment of more or less precisely stateable contextual conditions is *conventionally* (or, in a wide sense of the word, *logically*) required for the correct referring use of expressions in a sense in which this is not true of correct ascriptive uses. The requirement for the correct application of an expression in its ascriptive use to a certain thing is simply that the thing should be of a certain kind, have certain characteristics. The requirement for the correct application of an expression in its referring use to a certain thing is something over and above any requirement derived from such

7 [What is said or implied in the last two sentences of this paragraph no longer seems to me true, unless considerably qualified.]

ascriptive meaning as the expression may have; it is, namely, the requirement that the thing should be in a certain relation to the speaker and to the context of utterance. Let me call this the contextual requirement. Thus, for example, in the limiting case of the word 'I' the contextual requirement is that the thing should be identical with the speaker; but in the case of most expressions which have a referring use this requirement cannot be so precisely specified. A further, and perfectly general, difference between conventions for referring and conventions for describing is one we have already encountered, viz. that the fulfillment of the conditions for a correct ascriptive use of an expression is a part of what is stated by such a use; but the fulfillment of the conditions for a correct referring use of an expression is never part of what is stated, though it is (in the relevant sense of 'implied') implied by such a use.

Conventions for referring have been neglected or misinterpreted by logicians. The reasons for this neglect are not hard to see, though they are hard to state briefly. Two of them are, roughly: (1) the preoccupation of most logicians with definitions; (2) the preoccupation of some logicians with formal systems. (1) A definition, in the most familiar sense, is a specification of the conditions of the correct ascriptive or classificatory use of an expression. Definitions take no account of contextual requirements. So that in so far as the search for the meaning or the search for the analysis of an expression is conceived as the search for a definition, the neglect or misinterpretation of conventions other than ascriptive is inevitable. Perhaps it would be better to say (for I do not wish to legislate about 'meaning' or 'analysis') that logicians have failed to notice that problems of use are wider than problems of analysis and meaning. (2) The influence of the preoccupation with mathematics and formal logic is most clearly seen (to take no more recent examples) in the cases of Leibniz and Russell. The constructor of calculuses, not concerned or required to make factual statements, approaches applied logic with a prejudice. It is natural that he should assume that the types of convention with whose adequacy in one field he is familiar should be really adequate, if only one could see how, in a quite different field—that of statements of fact. Thus we have Leibniz striving desperately to make the uniqueness of unique references a matter of logic in the narrow sense, and Russell striving desperately to do the same thing, in a different way, both for the implication of uniqueness and for that of existence.

It should be clear that the distinction I am trying to draw is primarily one between different rôles or parts that expressions may play in language, and not primarily one between different groups of expressions; for some expressions may appear in either rôle. Some of the kinds of words I shall speak of have predominantly, if not exclusively, a referring rôle. This is most obviously true of pronouns and ordinary proper names. Some can occur as wholes or parts of expressions which have a predominantly referring use, and as wholes or parts of expressions which have a predominantly ascriptive or classificatory use. The obvious cases are common nouns; or common nouns preceded by adjectives, including participial adjectives; or, less obviously, adjectives or participial adjectives alone. Expressions capable of having a referring use also differ from one another in at least the three following, not mutually independent, ways:

(1) They differ in the extent to which the reference they are used to make is dependent on the context of their utterance. Words like 'I' and 'it' stand at one end of this scale—the end of maximum dependence —and phrases like 'the author of *Waverley*' and 'the eighteenth king of France' at the other.

(2) They differ in the degree of 'descriptive meaning' they possess: by 'descriptive meaning' I intend 'conventional limitation, in application, to things of a certain general kind, or possessing certain general characteristics'. At one end of this scale stand the proper names we most commonly use in ordinary discourse; men, dogs, and motor-bicycles may be called 'Horace'. The pure name has no descriptive meaning (except such as it may acquire *as a result of* some one of its uses as a name). A word like 'he' has minimal descriptive meaning, but has some. Substantival phrases like 'the round table' have the maximum descriptive meaning. An interesting intermediate position is occupied by 'impure' proper names like 'The Round Table'—substantival phrases which have grown capital letters.

(3) Finally, they may be divided into the following two classes: (i) those of which the correct referring use is regulated by some *general* referring-cum-ascriptive conventions; (ii) those of which the correct referring use is regulated by no general conventions, either of the contextual or the ascriptive kind, but by conventions which are *ad hoc* for each particular use (though not for each particular utterance). To the first class belong both pronouns (which have the least descriptive meaning) and substantival phrases (which have the most). To the second class belong, roughly speaking, the most familiar kind

of proper names. Ignorance of a man's name is not ignorance of the language. This is why we do not speak of the meaning of proper names. (But it won't do to say they are meaningless.) Again an intermediate position is occupied by such phrases as 'The Old Pretender'. Only an old pretender may be so referred to; but to know which old pretender is not to know a general, but an *ad hoc*, convention.

In the case of phrases of the form 'the so-an-so' used referringly, the use of 'the' together with the position of the phrase in the sentence (*i.e.* at the beginning, or following a transitive verb or preposition) acts as a signal *that* a unique reference is being made; and the following noun, or noun and adjective, together with the context of utterance, shows *what* unique reference is being made. In general the functional difference between common nouns and adjectives is that the former are naturally and commonly used referringly, while the latter are not commonly, or so naturally, used in this way, except as qualifying nouns; though they can be, and are, so used alone. And of course this functional difference is not independent of the descriptive force peculiar to each word. In general we should expect the descriptive force of nouns to be such that they are more efficient tools for the job of showing what unique reference is intended when such a reference is signalized; and we should also expect the descriptive force of the words we naturally and commonly use to make unique references to mirror our interest in the salient, relatively permanent and behavioural characteristics of things. These two expectations are not independent of one another; and, if we look at the differences between the commoner sort of common nouns and the commoner sort of adjectives, we find them both fulfilled. These are differences of the kind that Locke quaintly reports, when he speaks of our ideas of substances being *collections* of simple ideas; when he says that 'powers make up a great part of our ideas of substances'; and when he goes on to contrast the identity of real and nominal essence in the case of simple ideas with their lack of identity and the shiftingness of the nominal essence in the case of substances. 'Substance' itself is the troublesome tribute Locke pays to his dim awareness of the difference in predominant linguistic function that lingered even when the noun had been expanded into a more or less indefinite string of adjectives. Russell repeats Locke's mistake with a difference when, admitting the inference from syntax to reality to the extent of feeling that he can get rid of this metaphysical unknown only if he can purify language of the referring function altogether, he draws up his programme for 'abolishing particulars'; a programme, in fact, for abolishing the distinction of logical use which I am here at pains to emphasize.

The contextual requirement for the referring use of pronouns may be stated with the greatest precision in some cases (*e.g.* 'I' and 'you') and only with the greatest vagueness in others ('it' and 'this'). I propose to say nothing further about pronouns, except to point to an additional symptom of the failure to recognize the uniquely referring use for what it is; the fact, namely, that certain logicians have actually sought to elucidate the nature of a variable by offering such *sentences* as 'he is sick', 'it is green', as examples of something in ordinary speech like a *sentential function*. Now of course it is true that the word 'he' may be used on different occasions to refer to different people or different animals: so may the word 'John' and the phrase 'the cat'. What deters such logicians from treating these two expressions as quasi-variables is, in the first case, the lingering superstition that a name is logically tied to a single individual, and, in the second case, the descriptive meaning of the word 'cat'. But 'he', which has a wide range of applications and minimal descriptive force, only acquires a use as a referring word. It is this fact, together with the failure to accord to expressions, used referringly, the place in logic which belongs to them (the place held open for the mythical logically proper name), that accounts for the misleading attempt to elucidate the nature of the variable by reference to such words as 'he', 'she', 'it'.

Of ordinary proper names it is sometimes said that they are essentially words each of which is used to refer to just one individual. This is obviously false. Many ordinary personal names—names *par excellence*—are correctly used to refer to numbers of people. An ordinary personal name is, roughly, a word, used referringly, of which the use is *not* dictated by any descriptive meaning the word may have, and is *not* prescribed by any such general rule for use as a referring expression (or a part of a referring expression) as we find in the case of such words as 'I', 'this' and 'the', but is governed by *ad hoc* conventions for each particular set of applications of the word to a given person. The important point is that the correctness of such applications does not follow from any *general* rule or convention for the use of the word as such. (The limit of absurdity and obvious circularity is reached in the attempt to treat names as disguised descriptions in Russell's sense; for what is in the special sense implied, but not entailed, by my now referring to someone by name is simply the existence of someone, *now being referred to*, who is *conventionally referred to* by that name.) Even this feature of names, however, is only a symptom of the purpose for which they are employed. At present our choice of names is partly arbitrary, partly dependent on legal and social observances. It would be perfectly possible to have a thorough-going *system* of names, based *e.g.* on dates of birth, or on a minute classification of physiological and anatomical differences. But the success of any such system would depend entirely on the convenience of the resulting name-allotments for the purpose of making unique references; and this would depend on the multiplicity of the classifications used and the degree to which they cut haphazard across normal social groupings. Given a sufficient degree of both, the selectivity supplied by context would do the rest; just as is the case with our present naming habits. Had we such a system, we could use name-words descriptively (as we do at present, to a limited extent and in a different way, with some famous names) as well as referringly. But it is by criteria derived from consideration of the requirements of the referring task that we should assess the adequacy of any system of naming. From the naming point of view, no kind of classification would be better or worse than any other simply because of the kind of classification—natal or anatomical —that it was.

I have already mentioned the class of quasi-names, of substantival phrases which grow capital letters, and of which such phrases as 'the Glorious Revolution', 'the Great War', 'the Annunciation', 'the Round Table' are examples. While the descriptive meaning of the words which follow the definite article is still relevant to their referring rôle, the capital letters are a sign of that extra-logical selectivity in their referring use, which is characteristic of pure names. Such phrases are found in print or in writing when one member of some class of events or things is of quite outstanding interest in a certain society. These phrases are embryonic names. A phrase may, for obvious reasons, pass into, and out of, this class (*e.g.* 'the Great War').

V

I want to conclude by considering, all too briefly, three further problems about referring uses.

(*a*) *Indefinite references.* Not all referring uses of singular expressions forestall the question 'What (who, which one) are you talking about?' There are some which either invite this question, or disclaim the intention or ability to answer it. Examples are such sentence-beginnings as 'A man told me that . . . .', 'Someone told me that . . . .' The orthodox (Russellian) doctrine is that such sentences are existential, but not uniquely existential. This seems wrong in several ways. It is ludicrous to suggest that part of what is asserted is that the class of men or persons is not empty. Certainly this is *implied* in the by now familiar sense of implication; but the implication is also as much an implication of the *uniqueness* of the particular object of reference as when I begin a sentence with such a phrase as 'the table'. The difference between the use of the definite and indefinite articles is, very roughly, as follows. We use 'the' either when a previous reference has been made, and when 'the' signalizes that the same reference is being made; or when, in the absence of a previous indefinite reference, the context (including the hearer's assumed knowledge) is expected to enable the hearer to tell *what* reference is being made. We use 'a' either when these conditions are not fulfilled, or when, although a definite reference *could* be made, we wish to keep dark the identity of the individual to whom, or to which, we are referring. This is the *arch* use of such a phrase as 'a certain person' or 'someone'; where it could be expanded, not into 'someone, but you wouldn't (or I don't) know who' but into 'someone, but I'm not telling you who'.

(*b*) *Identification statements.* By this label I intend statements like the following:

(i*a*) That is the man who swam the channel twice on one day.
(ii*a*) Napoleon was the man who ordered the execution of the Duc d'Enghien.

The puzzle about these statements is that their grammatical predicates do not seem to be used in a straightforwardly ascriptive way as are the grammatical predicates of the statements:

(i*b*) That man swam the channel twice in one day.
(ii*b*) Napoleon ordered the execution of the Duc d'Enghien.

But if, in order to avoid blurring the difference between (i*a*) and (i*b*) and (ii*a*) and (ii*b*), one says that the phrases which form the grammatical complements of (i*a*) and (ii*a*) are being used referringly, one becomes puzzled about what is being said in these sentences. We seem then to be referring to the same person twice over and either saying nothing about him and thus making no statement, or identifying him with himself and thus producing a trivial identity.

The bogy of triviality can be dismissed. This only arises for those who think of the object referred to by the use of an expression as its meaning, and thus think of the subject and complement of these sentences as meaning the same because they could be used to refer to the same person.

I think the differences between sentences in the (*a*) group and sentences in the (*b*) group can best be understood by considering the differences between the circumstances in which you would say (i*a*) and the circumstances in which you would say (i*b*). You would say (i*a*) instead of (i*b*) if you knew or believed that your hearer knew or believed that *someone* had swum the channel twice in one day. You say (i*a*) when you take your hearer to be in the position of one who can ask: 'Who swam the channel twice in one day?' (And in asking this, he is not saying that anyone did, though his asking it implies—in the relevant sense—that someone did.) Such sentences are like answers to such questions. They are better called 'identification-statements' than 'identities'. Sentence (i*a*) does not assert more or less than sentence (i*b*). It is just that you say (i*a*) to a man whom you take to know certain things that you take to be unknown to the man to whom you say (i*b*).

This is, in the barest essentials, the solution to Russell's puzzle about 'denoting phrases' joined by 'is'; one of the puzzles which he claims for the Theory of Descriptions the merit of solving.

(*c*) *The logic of subjects and predicates.* Much of what I have said of the uniquely referring use of expressions can be extended, with suitable modifications, to the non-uniquely referring use of expressions; *i.e.* to some uses of expressions consisting of 'the', 'all the', 'all', 'some', 'some of the', etc. followed by a noun, qualified or unqualified, in the *plural*; to some uses of 'they', 'them', 'those', 'these'; and to conjunctions of names. Expressions of the first kind have a special interest. Roughly speaking, orthodox modern criticism, inspired by mathematical logic, of such traditional doctrines as that of the Square of Opposition and of some of the forms of the syllogism traditionally recognized as valid, rests on the familiar failure to recognize the special sense in which existential assertions may be implied by the referring use of expressions. The universal propositions of the fourfold schedule, it is said, must *either* be given a negatively existential interpretation (*e.g.* for *A*, 'there are no Xs which are not *Y*s') *or* they must be interpreted as conjunctions of negatively and positively existential statements of, *e.g.*, the form (for *A*) 'there are no Xs which are not *Y*s, and there are Xs'. The *I* and *O* forms are normally given a positively existential interpretation. It is then seen that, whichever of the above alternatives is selected, some of the traditional laws have to be abandoned. The dilemma, however, is a bogus one. If we interpret the propositions of the schedule as neither positively, nor negatively, nor positively *and* negatively, existential, but as sentences such that *the question of whether they are being used to make true or false assertions does not arise except when the existential condition is fulfilled for the subject term*, then all the traditional laws hold good together. And this interpretation is far closer to the most common uses of expressions beginning with 'all' and 'some' than is any Russellian alternative. For these expressions are most commonly used in the referring way. A literal-minded and childless man asked whether all his children are asleep will certainly not answer 'Yes' on the ground that he has none; but nor will he answer 'No' on this ground. Since he has no children, the question does not arise. To say this is not to say that I may not use the sentence, 'All my children are asleep', with the intention of letting someone know that I have children, or of deceiving him into thinking that I have. Nor is it any weakening of my thesis to concede that singular phrases of the form 'the so-and-so' may sometimes be used with a similar purpose. Neither Aristotelian nor Russellian rules give the exact logic of any expression of ordinary language; for ordinary language has no exact logic.

9

Presupposing[1]

Wilfrid Sellars

I

In his paper "On Referring,"[2] and, more recently, in his book, *Introduction to Logical Theory*,[3] Strawson reopens, in a sense, the debate between the "old" and the "new" logics which raged in the early years of the present century. There are, however, important differences. In the first place, Strawson has a clear and incisive understanding of the contents and methods of contemporary mathematical logic. He knows what he is talking about. Secondly, the issues he raises are given a more precise location. He makes no blanket attack on the meaningfulness of logistic formalisms. Indeed, he agrees that they are both meaningful and important. His concern is with the claim of the logisticians to have captured in certain of their more elementary formulae the logical devices of ordinary discourse. And, in the third place, he brings to the evaluation of this claim that ability to make fresh, first-hand observations of living language which, cultivated by Moore and the later Wittgenstein, has recently come to full flower on the banks of the Isis. A discussion of basic issues in logical theory by someone with these qualifications was bound to throw light on venerable con-

Reprinted with the kind permission of the author and the editor from *The Philosophical Review*, 63 (1954): 197–215.

[1] A revision for publication of a paper read at the University of Chicago Philosophy Department Seminar, March 6, 1953.
[2] *Mind*, 59 (1950): 320–344.
[3] P. F. Strawson, *Introduction to Logical Theory* (New York, 1952).

troversies, and Strawson more than lives up to expectations. He not only gives us a brilliant critique of typical modern accounts of the relation of logistic formalisms to the logic of actual discourse but also builds an account of his own on concepts and distinctions which will find an abiding place, though perhaps not without a twist here and a touch there, in the logician's toolbox.

Now, I propose in this paper to examine Strawson's account of definite descriptions and the Square of Opposition, in an attempt to evaluate the outcome of his argument. The conclusion at which I shall arrive is, in general terms, that his critique of the logisticians is more successful than his own efforts at a positive analysis and, indeed, that the success of the critique and the shortcomings of the analysis spring alike from the clusters of ideas embodied in his notion of a "presupposition." On the other hand, I shall argue that the features of the give and take of everyday argument to which he calls attention, and which have indeed been neglected and misconstrued by modern logicians, do make possible a solution of his problem. And if this solution, which I shall attempt to sketch, turns out to be, in a sense, a vindication of the logisticians, it is also, in at least equal measure, a vindication of Strawson. Which leads me to hope that, if sound, it resolves at least one controversy between the "old" and the "new" logics by a settlement which, if without victory, is also without annihilation.

II

Let me begin by distinguishing between two of many (so-called) "types of ambiguity." The first and simplest of these is illustrated by the word "bank," concerning which I shall do no more than point out that we should be quite happy to say that the sound *bank* functions as *two* words, being governed by two different sets of rules. A second "type" of ambiguity is more directly related to our problem. Once called "systematic ambiguity," this is the ambiguity characteristic of "ego-centric particulars"—"this," "here," "now," "I," etc. Here we note that the word "this," for example, is "ambiguous" in spite of the fact that on each occasion of its use it is used according to the *same* rules. The point is that these rules enable it to refer to different items on different occasions.

Logicians have taken either of two steps with respect to the applicability of logical principles to statements involving ego-centric expressions. Some have made the claim that to every statement of an ego-centric character can be correlated a non-ego-centric statement which communicates the same information, and that it is, strictly speaking, to the latter that logical principles apply. This has seemed plausible because the demand that logical principles be *formal* (in Carnap's sense), i.e., be formulated as rules for manipulating symbols without peeking at the extralinguistic context in which these symbols are used, would seem to be incompatible with a recognition of logical rules concerning ego-centric expressions. After all, if one were confronted with the argument: *This* is red and *this* is square, therefore *this* is red and square, one could only know that "this" referred to the same object on the three occasions of its use in this argument by taking extralinguistic circumstances into account.

Clearly, however, this approach is mistaken on all counts. To begin with, it is by no means clear that we are able to correlate every statement of an ego-centric character with a non-ego-centric statement which communicates the same information. The decisive consideration, however, is that when correctly formulated the above argument becomes: *This* is red and *it* is square, therefore *it* is red and square, and this argument *is* valid on formally specifiable grounds. Strawson is therefore quite correct in his claim that logical principles can be so formulated as to apply directly to expressions of an ego-centric character.

It should be noticed in this connection that ego-centricity is a pervasive feature of ordinary discourse. Thus, in most cases, the tenses of verbs have an ego-centric significance. Where we are dealing with a slow march of events, we can argue, "*x is* red and *x is* square, therefore *x is* red and square." Where an object changes as quickly as we can talk, we have to use more complex locutions. Notice also that many words other than verbs contain an ego-centric component in their meaning, thus "the *present* king of France."

We have distinguished between "simple ambiguity" and "systematic ambiguity." We must now take into account a third "type" distinct from both. Consider the following exchanges between two mathematicians:

> Jones: Seven is divisible by three.
> Smith: Seven is not divisible by three.
> Jones: Seven is.

(later) Jones: Seven is divisible by four.
         Smith: Seven is not divisible by four.
         Jones: Seven is.

Now, each of these dialogues contains an utterance of "Seven is"; and it is clear that what is communicated by these utterances is a function of the contexts in which they are uttered. What I wish to make clear is that the way in which what they communicate depends on their context is *not* the same as in the case of two utterances of "This is red." Correctly made utterances of the latter sentence are *complete* even though they say what they do by virtue of their context. A context of a certain kind (e.g., the occurrence of a pointing gesture) is part and parcel of the grammar of the referring word "this." On the other hand, the two utterances of "Seven is" are as such *not* complete and are only made complete by the context in which they are uttered. That the context serves in this way to complete them is as much a matter of linguistic convention as is the role of ego-centric expressions. Let us call this type of ambiguity *ellipsis* and say that in ellipsis the context completes the utterance and enables it to say something which it otherwise would not, different contexts enabling it to say different things.

It is clearly sensible of logicians to take as what Strawson calls their "representative" statements, statements which are nonelliptical, i.e., do not depend on their contexts for their *completion*. One can do so without omitting from one's logic any form of valid argument in ordinary discourse. On the other hand, as we have seen, one would indeed impoverish one's logic if one left out of consideration statements which depend on their context in the manner characteristic of ego-centric expressions.

Once the distinction between ellipsis and ego-centricity is drawn, it should be clear that the sentence "The table is large" is ambiguous in *both* ways. In the first place, a given utterance of it is elliptical and states what would be nonelliptically stated, for example, by "The table *over here* is large." In the second place, it is clearly ego-centrically ambiguous (a) in that it contains the verb "is"; and (b) in that, as in our example, utterances of it are ellipses for statements involving ego-centric expressions ("over here," "beside me," etc.).

Now, as I see it, one of the radical defects of Strawson's account of definite descriptions lies in his failure to distinguish between these two ways in which a sentence can depend for what it says on its context of utterance. Clearly the expression "the table" in a use of "The table is large" mentions the table it does because of its context. But surely the context functions to give the statement the force, for example, of "The table *over here* is large." Thus, the fact that "the table" in such a sentence is ambiguous in that on different occasions it refers to different tables should not lead us, as it does Strawson,[4] to assimilate definite descriptions to ego-centric expressions. For "the table" is ambiguous not *qua* definite description, but *qua* ellipsis for an expression (also a definite description) which contains the ego-centric term "here."

The above, however, is but one prong of a more inclusive attack on Strawson's account of definite descriptions.

III

One more *leitmotiv* and we can turn to the development. It concerns the function in discourse of such statements as "That is true" and, more particularly, "That is false." It is only too easy to assume that if one believes a statement to be false, then—questions of manners aside—it is correct usage to say "That (statement) is false." Then, from the fact that it would obviously be inappropriate to say "That is false" to a storyteller who has just said, "Prince Edward exchanged his clothes for the rags of the beggar boy,"[5] even though one believes on good evidence that such an incident never occurred, one will be strongly tempted to conclude that the original statement *was not false*, and hence, since not true, *was neither true nor false*.

Surely, however, it can be argued that it would be *true* to say of the storyteller's statement that it was false, even though, given the function performed by utterances of "That is false" in human discourse, it would be *incorrect* to *say* "That is false" to the storyteller. After all, one says, "That is false," when one takes the other person's statement to be the expression of a belief, and one says it in order to institute a discussion or argument by which the other person can be shown that his belief is false. Clearly this situation does not normally obtain in

---

[4] See, for example, "On Referring," pp. 334, 336.
[5] The reference is to Mark Twain's *The Prince and the Pauper*. I am not discussing fiction *generally*, but fictional statements which, being "about real people," satisfy at least one prerequisite of "being true or false." Let me also emphasize that this discussion is designed to introduce a theme, rather than to be an independent and adequate account of the status of fictional statements.

the storytelling context. Fiction contains many devices to signalize that statements made in its course are not to be "taken seriously." We are warned not to infer from the fact that a statement is made that the speaker (or writer) holds the belief of which the statement would be, in serious discourse, the expression. Hence, to listen to a story as a story is to agree not to draw inferences as to the storyteller's beliefs and, a fortiori, not to challenge them. But while this entails that there is normally no point in *saying* "That is false" to a storyteller's statements, it by no means follows that the storyteller's statements may not *be* false. And surely if I later became convinced that the storyteller did believe that Prince Edward exchanged clothes with a beggar boy, I would find it appropriate to say that his statement was false. The statement itself, however, was false all along.

The above remarks are intended to pave the way for the idea that there are cases of central concern to logical theory in which it would be a mistake to infer from the fact that it would be incorrect to *say* of a statement that is obviously not true "That statement is false," that the statement in question is *neither true nor false*. But more of this in a moment.

IV

Consider, now, the sentence:

(S) Jones has stopped beating his grandmother.

An explication of this sentence on Strawsonian principles would run as follows: An utterance of S presupposes that Jones once beat his grandmother. If Jones never did beat his grandmother the utterance is *neither true nor false*. If Jones did once beat his grandmother, then if he does not now beat her, the utterance is true, otherwise false.

Now, the meaning of S has two components, one of which can be formulated by the sentence "Jones once beat his grandmother," the other by "Jones does not at present beat his grandmother." Let us therefore interpret the above as the claim that an utterance of S *presupposes* that Jones once beat his grandmother, and *asserts* both that Jones once beat his grandmother and that he does not now do so. Let me make it clear to begin with that I believe that in *some* sense this is both true and important. It is only if "presupposes" is given the force it has in Strawson's theory that I find myself forced to disagree.

For, according to Strawson, only if the presupposition of an utterance is satisfied is the utterance *either true or false*.

Now what could it mean to say that utterances of S "presuppose" that Jones once beat his grandmother? Strawson nowhere gives an explicit analysis of *x presupposes y*, so we shall have to strike out on our own. One is tempted to reply, "It means that it is incorrect to make such an utterance unless one *believes* that Jones once beat his grandmother." This, however, is clearly not enough for Strawson. For the speaker might believe *falsely* that Jones once beat his grandmother, and if presupposition were merely a matter of the speaker believing that Jones once beat his grandmother, the utterance would thereupon be *true-or-false*, even though the speaker's belief were false. And if the speaker falsely believed that Jones once beat his grandmother, then the utterance, asserting as it does that Jones once beat his grandmother and no longer does so, would itself be false. Yet Strawson's account was designed to rule out the possibility of a correctly made utterance of S being false on the ground that Jones never did beat his grandmother.

(It should be noted parenthetically that should it be claimed that an utterance of S presupposes that Jones once beat his grandmother but asserts *only* that he does not now do so, then if the presupposition in question were merely a matter of the speaker's believing *truly or falsely* that Jones once beat his grandmother, and if it were false that he ever did beat her, but true that he does not now do so, then the utterance would be true—which is absurd.)

Clearly, then, if the above account of presupposition is to have any promise, it must be added that for the presupposition to be satisfied, the speaker must not only believe, *but believe truly*, that Jones once beat his grandmother. If so, and granting for the moment that an utterance is neither true nor false unless its presupposition obtains, then the following cases arise:

(1) If the speaker believes that Jones once beat his grandmother, if this belief is true, and if Jones does not now beat his grandmother, then the utterance is *true*.

(2) If the speaker believes that Jones once beat his grandmother, if this belief is true, and if Jones continues to beat his grandmother, then the utterance is *false*.

(3) If the speaker believes that Jones once beat his grandmother, and if this belief is false, then the utterance is *neither true nor false*.

But what if (4) the speaker doesn't believe that Jones once beat his grandmother? Should we say that the utterance is neither true nor false? Yet if Jones once beat his grandmother and does not now do so, would we not be inclined to say that the speaker's utterance was true, even though it did not express a belief on his part that Jones once beat his grandmother? And, looking again at (3) as well, it is not paradoxical to suppose that the truth-or-falsity of what we say is a function of what we believe?

But perhaps Strawson would have it that presupposition requires merely that a certain state of affairs obtain whether or not the speaker believes it to obtain, in order for him to make correct use of the sentence having that presupposition. Thus, it might be claimed that an utterance of S is true-or-false if and only if Jones *in point of fact* once beat his grandmother, whether or not the speaker believes this to have been the case. Yet this seems to do violence to our preanalytic notion of presupposition. More important is the fact that if what the speaker believes is left out of account, then it is difficult to see how the utterance can involve Jones's having once beaten his grandmother in any other way than by asserting it, in which case the utterance would surely be false if Jones had never laid hands on his grandmother.

V

So much by way of an attempt to tease out of our preanalytic understanding of "presupposes" an analysis according to which utterances whose presuppositions do not obtain are neither true nor false. I shall now offer my own account, which drops the latter requirement while claiming to do justice to the considerations which led Strawson to adopt it. Consider the following dialogue:

> Tom: Harry has stopped beating his grandmother.
> Dick: That's not so (or, No, that's false).

If we ask under what circumstances Dick is likely to make the above reply, it soon emerges (for reasons which will be considered in a moment) that Dick will find it appropriate to *say* "That's false" only if he believes that Harry did once beat his grandmother. From this it appears proper to infer that Tom's utterance *was* false only on condition that Harry did once beat his grandmother. And once one has made this inference, something like the Strawson account is inevitable.

But such an inference would be based on the idea that if it is a mistake to *say* of an utterance that it is false, it must be a mistake to suppose that the utterance *is* false. This is questionable, to say the least. There can be many reasons why it might be a mistake to *say* something, even though it were true. Some of these reasons lie in ethics, some in manners. Some, however, concern the conventions governing discourse as a means of reaching agreement in discussion or argument and are, therefore, in a suitable sense, logical reasons.

To understand why Dick will find it appropriate to *say* "That's false" only if he believes that Harry did once beat his grandmother, consider the following dialogue, where "*p* and *q*" is, in the logistician's sense, a conjunctive proposition:

> Jones: *p* and *q*.
> Smith: No, that's false.

Now, might it not be a universal convention of human discourse that, other things being equal, points are to be made in the order in which they are to be questioned or defended? In this case it would be appropriate for Jones to say "*p* and *q*" only if (a) he believes *p* and (b) he believes that Smith shares this belief. Otherwise he would say not "*p* and *q*" but rather "*p*," raising it for discussion.

Knowing this, Smith would know that Jones would not have said "*p* and *q*" unless Jones believed that the two of them shared the belief that *p*. Smith would thus realize that if he were to say "That's false" Jones would assume that he did so because *accepting* *p* he rejects *q*. Consequently, Smith would realize that if he were to say "That's false" on the ground that *p* is false he would be misleading Jones. Presumably, therefore, if he were to say "That's false," he would say it on the ground that while *p* is true, *q* is false. We thus see how, even though Jones's utterance of "*p* and *q*" would be false if "*p*" were false, it would nevertheless be *incorrect* for Smith to *say* that it is false on the ground that "*p*" is false. Now, it is along these lines, as I see it, that the concept of presupposition is to be understood; if so, Strawson's account is based on a simple mistake.

The analogy of the grandmother case to the above artificially constructed (but not unfounded) example is straightforward and obvious. (a) When Tom says, "Harry has stopped beating his grandmother," he has in effect said, "Harry once beat his grandmother and Harry does not now beat his grandmother." (b) He is asserting both that Harry once beat his grandmother and that Harry does not now do so.

(c) His utterance is false if either of these situations fails to obtain. (d) It is *incorrect*, in terms of most useful conventions governing the orderly and unambiguous progression of discourse, for Tom to make this utterance (which packs both "Harry once beat his grandmother" and "Harry does not now beat his grandmother" into one verbal package) unless he believes that Harry once beat his grandmother and that Dick shares this belief. (e) It is *incorrect* in terms of these same conventions for Dick to say "That is false" unless he believes that Harry once beat his grandmother and thus has as his reason for saying "That's false" the belief that Harry continues his wicked ways.

I am now in a position to defend Russell's theory of descriptions against Strawson's attack, while admitting that Strawson calls attention to (even though he misinterprets) certain logical features of statements involving descriptive phrases. To begin with it will be remembered that the fact that an utterance of "The table is large" acquires reference to a particular table only by virtue of the context in which it is uttered, should not lead us to assimilate it (and other descriptive phrases) to expressions involving ego-centric expressions. Nonelliptical statements involving descriptive phrases have a meaning which depends on context not *qua* involving descriptive phrases, but *qua* involving ego-centric expressions.

According to the Russellian analysis, "The table over here is large" *asserts* (in part) that there is one and only one table "over here," and, consequently, is false if there is either no table or more than one table "over here." Strawson grants that there being one and only one table in a certain place is involved in an utterance of "The table is large." He argues, however, that it is involved by way of *presupposition*; only if this presupposition obtains is the utterance true-or-false. Indeed, it seems clear that he is claiming that there being one and only one table in that place is involved *only* by way of presupposition; that it is not *asserted* by the utterance.[6]

Now as in the grandmother case, the plausibility of Strawson's thesis (in so far as it does not rest on a confusion between the "elliptical ambiguity" of "the table" and the "systematic ambiguity" of ego-centric particulars) rests on the fact that if Jones were to say "The table is

---

[6] It is interesting to note that on Strawson's principles a person is not making a correct use of "The table over here is large" unless he holds the belief properly expressed by "There is one and only one table over here and all tables over here are large." In short our hearts beat (believe) with Russell even when our tongue wags (asserts) with Strawson.

large," it would be a mistake for Smith to *say* "No, that's false" unless he believes that the uniqueness condition is satisfied. If he doesn't, he should say rather, "There's no table over there," or, "There are seven tables over there, which one do you mean?" Strawson infers from this that the utterance is neither true nor false unless the uniqueness condition is satisfied.

The truth of the matter, of course, is that Russell's analysis is correct, but needs to be supplemented by an account of the conventions relating to the *dynamics* of discussion or argument, the order in which assertions should be made and challenged. An utterance of "The table over here is large" does indeed presuppose that there is one and only one table "over here." To say that the utterance presupposes this is to say that it is correct to make the utterance, which packs the information which could be conveyed by the joint use of "There is one and only one table over here" and "It is large" into one condensed verbal package, only if one believes there to be one and only one table "over here" and that this belief is shared by the listener. Furthermore, to say "That's false" when told that the table is large equally *presupposes* that the uniqueness condition is satisfied; where this in turn means that it is correct to say "That's false" only if one believes the uniqueness condition to be saisfied and that the original speaker shares this belief. But even though both the original utterance and the reply presuppose that the uniqueness condition is satisfied, the utterance is nevertheless *false* if the uniqueness condition is not satisfied. The utterance is false if the uniqueness condition is not satisfied, *even though it is not correct to say that it is false unless one believes that the condition is satisfied.*

VI

I come now to the square of opposition. Here, again, I shall argue that Strawson's account has the great merit of taking into account important considerations neglected or misinterpreted by "modern" treatments of this topic. Indeed, Strawson's account errs not so much by being downright mistaken as by failing to draw essential distinctions.

Let me begin by making the following points:

(1) It is a matter of general agreement that the structure of implications which traditional logic holds to obtain between A, E, I, and O propositions is a *consistent* structure. The latest and most complete

demonstration of this fact is contained in Łukasiewicz' incisive, if overpolemical, book, *Aristotle's Syllogistic*.

(2) It is equally agreed that this structure of implications does not hold within the functional and class calculi of propositions having the logical forms

$$(x)fx \supset gx \quad (x)fx \supset \text{-}gx \quad \text{or} \quad A \subset B \quad A \subset \bar{B}$$
$$(\exists x)fx \cdot gx \quad (\exists x)fx \cdot \text{-}gx \quad \phantom{\text{or}} \quad AB \neq O \quad A\bar{B} \neq O$$

(3) There is, as Strawson shows (and, in part, Lewis and Langford before him), no set of propositional forms belonging to the functional or class calculus which both stand in the implicative relations characteristic of the traditional *A, E, I,* and *O* propositions *and* can plausibly be interpreted as the logical forms of "universal" and "particular" statements in ordinary usage.

Now from these undeniable facts, Strawson concludes that we must choose between (a) taking universal and particular statements in ordinary usage to have the forms "$(x)fx \supset gx$," "$(\exists x)fx$ & gx," etc.—in which case we must reject the inferences from "All *A* is *B*" to "Some *A* is *B*" and from "Not (Some *A* is *B*)" to "Some *A* is not *B*," etc., and (b) retaining this pattern of inferences, in which case we must abandon the view that these statements can be interpreted in terms of forms belonging to the functional or class calculi.

After a careful exploration of ordinary usage, Strawson concludes that we *do* recognize the inferences enshrined in traditional logic to be sound. He concludes that universal and particular statements in ordinary usage are not to be interpreted in terms of the logical forms of the functional or class calculi. He then proceeds to offer the following positive account of the logical relations of these statements.

He notes, to begin with, that ordinary discourse *does* contain devices by the use of which we can make statements having the logical forms of affirmative and negative existential statements. Thus, we *can* say, "There are no philosopher kings," and, "There are (or exist) untamed elephants." These statements must not, however, be supposed to have the same logical forms as universal and particular statements "All (or No) *A* is *B*," "Some *A* is (not) *B*." The latter, he claims, unlike the former, are not correctly represented in the formalism of the functional or class calculus, and, which is more important, the latter, unlike the former, do stand in relations of logical implication and incompatibility which justify the traditional pattern of inferences.

Now (to continue with Strawson's account), when we make a statement of the form "All *A* is *B*," it *presupposes* as a condition of its *truth-or-falsity* that the subject class has members, and so do "Some *A* is *B*," "No *A* is *B*," and "Some *A* is not *B*." Once again it is not clear from his account whether he means by this that it is incorrect to make a statement of one of these forms unless one *believes* (truly) that the subject class has members, or that it is incorrect to make the statement unless the subject class has members *whether one believes it or not.* (A third interpretation, to the effect that it is incorrect to make such a statement unless one believes truly *or falsely* that the subject class has members is ruled out by the fact that if the presupposition obtained merely by virtue of the speaker's belief that the subject class has members, then the statement "All *A* is *B*" could be true or false even though there were no *A*'s, an eventuality Strawson clearly intends to exclude.)

To say, then, that an utterance of "All *A* is *B*" *presupposes* that there are *A*'s as a condition of its *truth-or-falsity* must, on Strawson's account, mean either (a) that it is incorrect to make such an utterance unless there are, in point of fact, *A*'s, or (b) that it is incorrect to make such an utterance unless one believes truly that there are *A*'s. I suspect that Strawson would have some difficulty in choosing between these two alternatives. On the one hand he would be tempted to say that if it is incorrect to say "All *A* is *B*" unless one *believes* that there are *A*'s, this must be because it is "objectively" incorrect to utter this sentence when there *are* no *A*'s—just as, according to many moralists, the wrongness of inflicting what one believes to be unnecessary pain rests on the "objective" wrongness of inflicting unnecessary pain. But do we recognize a basic or underived[7] rule not to say "All *A* is *B*" unless there are *A*'s?[8]

On the other hand, he would be tempted to agree that presupposition is a matter of what the speaker must believe in order to make correct use of the expression said to have the presupposition. But why, then, must the requisite belief of the speaker (in the present case, the belief that there are *A*'s) be *true*, in order for the presupposition to obtain? Strawson gives no indication of what he would say on this score

---

[7] If it were a derived obligation, surely it would be derived from the role of saying things in "rational discourse," that is, discourse designed to bring about reasoned agreement in belief. But what would be derived from such considerations would be rules to the effect that it is incorrect to say *x* unless *y* is *believed* to be the case (by oneself and/or by those to whom one is speaking).

[8] Notice that in applying this supposed rule, a speaker would find it correct to say "All *A* is *B*" when he believes there are no *A*'s; but the rule itself makes no reference to belief.

—the reason being, I suspect, that he has not clearly distinguished in his own mind between these two alternatives. Thus, the fact that the first alternative requires that there be A's has led him (when thinking along the lines of the second alternative) to suppose that the belief that there are A's required by this alternative must be true.

When it comes to telling us what A, E, I, and O statements *do* assert (as opposed to what they presuppose) Strawson is even less explicit. Consider, again, a statement of the form "All A is B"; it presupposes that there are A's and is *true-or-false* only if this presupposition obtains. Under what circumstances is it true? Surely if and only if the class of A's is included in the class of B's. But how can this be the condition of the truth of "All A is B" unless it is what is *asserted* by "All A is B"; and how can it be what is asserted by "All A is B" unless the latter has the logical form of a class inclusion proposition? And this, according to Strawson, it does not have—for the reason, once again, that class inclusion and class overlap statements do not have the logical properties of universal and particular statements in actual use.

Now, the truth of the matter is that the issue between Strawson and modern logic is a mislocated one. For while it must be admitted that the modern account does not do justice to the inferences which may properly be made from universal and particular statements in actual discourse, it must also be admitted that modern logicians are quite correct in claiming that these statements do assert relations of inclusion, exclusion, and overlapping among classes, and that in the sense of "logical" current among logisticians, the *logical* implications relating these statements do not constitute a basis for the inferences sanctioned by the traditional square of opposition.

Is there a way of combining the following theses?

(1) Universal and particular statements in ordinary discourse have the logical force of affirmative and negative existential propositions. Thus "All A is B" has the logical force of "$A \subset B$."

(2) Universal and particular statements in actual discourse have a logical force which is not *exhausted* by that of affirmative and negative existential propositions. Thus the logical force of "All A is B" is not exhausted by that of "$A \subset B$."

(3) The surplus logical force of universal and particular statements in actual discourse over and above that of affirmative and negative existential propositions cannot be located by representing them as conjunctions or disjunctions of positively or negatively existential propositions; thus, by representing "All A is B" by "$A \subset B . A \neq O$."

(4) The logical force of universal and particular statements in actual use (apart from their modal role) can be exhaustively accounted for in terms of the logic of classes.

I shall now sketch an account of the square of opposition in which all these four theses are reconciled and combined.

(1) Universal and particular statements *assert* exactly what is asserted by the corresponding affirmative and negative existentials and stand in the logical relations explained in the class calculus. *From the standpoint of what they assert*, then, they have the logical form of affirmative and negative existentials and are *not* related as are the *A*, *E*, *I*, and *O* propositions in the classical square of opposition.

(2) Universal and particular statements in ordinary usage differ from the corresponding affirmative and negative existentials in ordinary usage in that their *correct* usage *presupposes* that the subject class has at least one member. By this I mean that it is *correct* to make statements of this form *only if one believes that the subject class has members and that the listener shares this belief.* The distinctive language of universal and particular statements *signalizes* this presupposition. It is correct to use this language only where one believes that the subject class has members and that the listener shares this belief.

(3) Where either of these beliefs is absent, it is incorrect to use the language of universal and particular statements. Thus, instead of saying "All *A* is *B*," one should say, depending on what one wishes to establish, either "If anything were an *A* it would be a *B*" or, where one believes that the subject class has members but suspects that the listener would deny this, "There are *A*'s," going on to say "All *A* is *B*" only after one has gained the listener's assent to the former proposition.

(4) A rule of inference can be a sound rule, even though what is asserted by the premise does not *logically* entail what is asserted by the conclusion. Thus, I suppose that most philosophers would agree that inductive inference can be sound even though the premises do not logically entail the conclusion.

(5) Suppose, for the moment, that we did not have the distinctive language of universal and particular statements. Suppose that, in view of the practical function of discourse, we were concerned for the most part with classes which do have members, yet were understandably reluctant to prefix every statement of class inclusion or exclusion with an existential statement "There are *A*'s." Suppose, therefore, that simple statements of class inclusion or exclusion were usually made where they could properly have been prefixed by "There are *A*'s." Would it

not be *misleading* in such circumstances to say "$A \subset B$" where one's ground for saying this was the belief that the class A was empty, although one believed that the listener thought there were A's? Can we not imagine a convention to develop according to which it would be incorrect to say "$A \subset B$" unless one believed that there were A's and that this conviction was shared by the listener?

(6) And given the above convention, can we not imagine that the *moves* in discourse from stating "$A \subset B$" to stating "$AB \neq O$," etc., might come to be sanctioned even though the former statement does not entail the latter? The adoption of this further convention concerning legitimate moves in discourse would be justified on the ground that the statement "$A \subset B$" is made only where "There are A's" is taken to be a matter of agreement (unless it is explicitly repudiated or challenged) and "$A \subset B$" together with "There are A's" *does* logically imply "$AB \neq O$." This rule together with rules sanctioning other *moves* in the square of opposition which are not sanctioned by logical relations between what these statements assert could nevertheless be called "logical rules" in a broad sense, in that they sanction moves in argument which could be reconstructed as logically valid moves if the *presuppositions* of the argument were added as premises.

(7) How much stronger the justification for such rules would be if the very language used contained a *signal* that the speaker regarded them as operative! And, of course, the point at which I have been driving is that our language, containing as it does verbal forms for universal and particular statements distinct from the verbal forms of class inclusion, etc., does contain just such a signal that just such rules are operative.[9]

---

[9] The notion of a conventional signal of a dialectical commitment throws light on other philosophical issues. *Ethics:* "You ought to keep that promise" can be compared to "Keep thou that promise!" where the archaic form is a signal that the speaker is prepared to derive this from a universal imperative of the form "All men do ye . . . !" (in this case, "All men keep ye promises!") or from a universal imperative together with factual indicatives. *Philosophy of Science:* When I say, "This is soluble," or, "This caused that," I acknowledge the responsibility of backing up my statement by deriving it from properly established empirical laws. The latter, however, are not asserted by the statements. Thus, I might say, "This is sugar, and whenever sugar is put in water it dissolves." That the latter is not asserted by my original statement is shown by the fact that I can be led to abandon it in favor of a more sophisticated law and still be defending the original assertion. "This is soluble" asserts nothing about micro-structure; but a scientist who makes this statement may well be convinced that a defense immune from further challenge would take him to micro-theoretical considerations.

(8) We can even say if we wish that the inferences making up the square of opposition are valid *ex vi terminorum*, that is, by virtue of the meaning of the language of universal and particular statements. Yet, the fact remains that the validity of the move from "All A is B" to "Some A is B" rests ultimately on the validity of the move from "$A \subset B$" and "There are A's" to "$AB \neq O$" (as do *mutatis mutandis* the other moves in the square of opposition). Thus, even though it is an aspect of the *meaning* of universal and particular statements that they *signalize* existential presuppositions and the correctness of certain moves, nevertheless "All A is B" does not *assert* that there are A's, and the move from "All A is B" to "Some A is B" is not warranted by what "All A is B" *asserts*, even though it is warranted by what it, in a broader sense, *means*.

I have thus, I believe, sketched an account of universal and particular statements, according to which (a) they assert (considerations of modality aside) what modern logicians say they do even though (b) in a legitimate sense of "logical rule" they obey logical rules which do not belong to the calculus of classes, and which do belong to the rules of traditional logic. On the other hand (c) the justification of these rules rests ultimately on the logical rules of the calculus of classes, in combination with considerations relating to the reasonable presuppositions of effective and orderly everyday discourse about the inclusion, exclusion, and overlap of classes.

10

A Reply to Mr. Sellars

P. F. Strawson

M R. Sellars finds unclear and un-
satisfactory in various ways the account I have given of the relation
between statements which I called "presupposition." He undertakes to
clarify this notion by giving an alternative account of the relation, for
which he claims: (a) that it vindicates Russell's analysis both of statements containing definite descriptions and of universal and particular
statements of ordinary discourse, and (b) that at the same time it accommodates those facts of language to which I was seeking to draw
attention and which might seem incompatible with the correctness
of Russell's analyses. In what follows I shall first argue that the difficulties which Sellars finds in my account do not exist. Then I shall
draw attention to the fact that Sellars offers, not one alternative account of the relation between presupposed and presupposing statements, but two alternative and incompatible accounts, and that he
applies one of these accounts to one set of cases and the other to another set, without giving any reason for so discriminating between
them. I shall suggest that the *explanation* of his so discriminating is
simply a *parti pris* in favor of what is in question, namely the correctness of Russell's analyses, and, in general, that Sellars is animated by a
metaphysical belief that the symbolism of *Principia Mathematica*
somehow embodies the *real* logic of ordinary language. I shall then
discuss some minor points in Sellars' article and shall conclude with

Reprinted with the kind permission of the author and the editor from
The Philosophical Review, 63 (1954): 216–231.

certain qualifications of my own thesis as stated in the publications to which Sellars refers.

(1) Sellars says that I "nowhere give an explicit analysis of *x presup- poses y*" and that I leave various questions about this relation unan- swered. I think the answers to most of his questions are to be found on page 175 of *Introduction to Logical Theory* (cf. also p. 213). "*S* pre- supposes *S'*" is defined as follows: "The truth of *S'* is a necessary con- dition of the truth or falsity of *S*."[1] It will be noted that this definition has the consequence that *S'* is *not* in any ordinary sense a component of what is asserted by *S*. It will also be noted that the definition makes no reference at all to the beliefs of speakers or hearers. It does, how- ever, have the fairly obvious consequence that, where *S* presupposes *S'*, it would be incorrect (or deceitful—the cases are different) for a speaker to assert *S* unless he believed or took for granted that *S'*. But it certainly does not have the consequence that if it is for this reason in- correct for a given speaker to assert *S*, then *S* does not have a truth- value; nor does it follow that if it is not incorrect for a certain speaker to assert *S*, then *S* does have a truth-value. Whether or not *S* has a truth-value depends on one thing, viz., whether *S'* is true. Whether or not it is correct for a speaker to assert *S* depends on quite another thing (I do not mean, on this thing alone): viz., whether or not the speaker believes that *S'*. Sellars, in Section IV of his article, seems to think that I am committed to saying that the conditions under which *S* has a truth-value are the same as the conditions under which it is cor- rect for a speaker to assert *S*, or, perhaps, to think that I cannot regard the speaker's beliefs as relevant to the *correctness* of the assertion with- out making this identification. But this is simply a mistake; so none of the embarrassing consequences which Sellars draws from it holds. In fact, of course, as far as my definition and its consequences go, it is per- fectly possible both for *S* to lack a truth-value and for it to be a correct use of language for someone to assert *S*; and this will be so in the case where that person mistakenly believes that the presupposed statement *S'* is true.

In the same section, Sellars says that if what the speaker believes is left out of account then it is difficult to see how the presupposing state- ment can "involve" the presupposed statement in any other way than by asserting it. But the whole point of the relation of presupposition, as

---

[1] Strictly speaking, I should here write "the statement that *S*" instead of "*S*"; elsewhere, for example, I shall write the phrase "that *S*." But the risk of confusion here is small.

I conceive it, is just that this is possible—and familiar. Perhaps it will be easier to see how it is possible if we consider, not a statement, but a question (e.g., "Has Jones stopped beating his grandmother?") or a command (e.g., "Jones, you are to stop beating your grandmother!"). Neither the question nor the command *asserts* anything. But both may be said to involve (presuppose) the truth of the statement that Jones was in the habit of beating his grandmother: in that the question does not admit of a simple "Yes" or "No" answer, the command can be neither obeyed nor disobeyed, unless that statement is true. Similarly, when one statement presupposes another, the first does not admit of an assignment of a truth-value unless the second is true.

(2) The two alternative accounts given by Sellars of the relation between presupposed and presupposing statements emerge respectively in Sections V and VI of his article. They will be referred to as account A and account B. On account A, the relations between the presupposing statement (S) and the presupposed statement (S') are given by the propositions:

(i) S entails (or incorporates the assertion of) S', and hence if S' is false, S is false;

(ii) it is incorrect for a speaker either to assert S or to deny it (i.e., say that it is false) unless he believes that S' and believes that his hearer shares this belief.

On account B, the relations are as follows:

(i) S does not entail S', and the truth-value of S is in no way dependent on the truth-value of S';

(ii) it is incorrect for a speaker either to assert S or to deny it (i.e., say that it is false) unless he believes that S' and believes that his hearer shares this belief.

It will be noted that the second element in each account is identical. The difference lies in the first element. It will also be noted that the first element in neither account agrees with the definition given by me of "presupposition," but that the second element has affinities with one of the consequences of my definition. (I think Sellars would perhaps agree that, on *any* theory, his second element is a little too strong as it stands, and should be weakened, say, by the addition of the clause "or at least does not believe that his hearer believes that S' is false." But this is a minor point.)

Examples to which Sellars applies account A, in Section V, include the "grandmother case," and the case of statements containing definite descriptions. Thus, according to Sellars, a statement (S) made by the use of a sentence of the form "The so-and-so is such-and-such", contains three asserted components corresponding, with one minor modification, to the three components of Russell's original analysis. We may refer to these as respectively s_1 (which states that the existence-condition is satisfied), s_2 (which states that the uniqueness-condition is satisfied), and s_3 (which states that there is nothing which both answers to the description in question—duly expanded to get rid of Sellars' "ellipsis"—and lacks a certain predicate). The components s_1 and s_2 are presupposed, in the sense of account A, by the statement S as a whole. (Sellars in fact concentrates his attention on component s_2, but would, I take it, say that s_1 was similarly related to S.) Account B, on the other hand, is applied, in Section VI, to universal statements, of the forms "All f's are g" and "No f's are g." Here the entire assertion-content of the statements is said to be given by the forms "$\sim(\exists x)(fx.\sim gx)$" and "$\sim(\exists x)(fx.gx)$" respectively. The presupposed statement in each case is the statement that the subject-class is not empty. Since these cases fall under account B, the actual truth-value of the universal statements is quite independent of the truth-value of the presupposed statement, though it is incorrect to assert or deny the universal statement unless the presupposed statement is believed to be true.

Now there is surely no reason whatever, except a determination to adhere at all costs to orthodox modern analyses, for simultaneously adopting account A in the case of statements containing definite descriptions and account B in the case of universal statements. What is there, except a partiality for the Theory of Descriptions, to stop Sellars from adopting account B for the first case; from saying, that is, that the whole assertion-content of a statement containing a definite description is given by s_3, so that its truth-value is quite independent of the truth-values of the presupposed statements, although it is incorrect to assert it or call it false unless etc.? Alternatively, what is there, except a partiality for the class-inclusion and -exclusion forms, to stop Sellars from adopting account A for the case of universal statements and declaring that the statement that the subject-class is not empty is one of the asserted components of these statements? I ask these questions, because the reasons which seem to me good reasons against adopting either these or any other analyses in terms of accounts A and B are not reasons which it is open to Sellars to give; for they involve acceptance of precisely the idea which he repudiates, viz., the idea that a presupposing statement lacks a truth-value if the presupposed statement is false.

But the capriciousness with which Sellars now associates, now refuses to associate, a presupposition-relation with dependence of the truth-value of the presupposing statement on that of the presupposed statement is greater than I have so far indicated. For his program requires that in the case of particular, as opposed to universal, statements, the presupposed statement (that the subject-class is not empty) *is* a part of the assertion-content of the presupposing statement. Account B applies to the top two propositional forms of the fourfold schedule, account A to the bottom two. Who, if he had never seen a bound variable, would have supposed that the difference between saying that all his shirts were at the laundry, and that some of them were, involved *this* difference?

The situation is this. Sellars can reconcile himself to the logical force which universal and particular propositions have in ordinary discourse only if he can somehow explain these facts to himself *in terms of* the negatively and positively existential forms of *Principia Mathematica*. For (he thinks) it is *these* forms and *their* logical relations which show the ultimate logical structure of language. But why should language have just one ultimate logical structure? And why, if it had one, should it be *this* one? How very extraordinary, if the *real* structure of natural ways of talking should be found to lie in artificial ways of writing! Sellars says, for example, that "the fact remains that the validity of the move from 'All A is B' to 'Some A is B' rests ultimately on the validity of the move from '$A \subset B$' and 'There are A's' to '$AB \neq O$'." But how does he know that the one "rests ultimately" on the other? Why should it rest on anything? Perhaps it does not need anything to rest on. Again Sellars says: "When it comes to telling us what A, E, I, and O statements *do* assert . . . Strawson is even less explicit." But what is there to be explicit about here? There is no mystery about it. When I assert that all the fuses have blown, *that* is what I assert. Of course what Sellars is asking is: What do I think they assert in terms of the negatively and positively existential forms of *Principia Mathematica*? But this question does not arise. For they do not assert anything in terms of these forms. They are *different* (though not unrelated) forms.

(3) In preparing the ground for his own accounts (especially account A) of the relations between presupposing and presupposed state-

ments, Sellars seeks to show in Section III of his article that, "questions of manners aside," it may be incorrect usage to say of a statement that it is false even though (a) it is false and (b) one believes it is false. He illustrates his point from the case of fictional narrations about historical persons. If we overlook his point, he says, we may draw mistaken conclusions about this case. Thus "from the fact that it would be obviously inappropriate to say 'That is false' to a storyteller who has just said, 'Prince Edward exchanged his clothes for the rags of the beggar boy,' even though one believes on good evidence that such an incident never occurred, one would be strongly tempted to conclude that the original statement *was not false*, and hence, since not true, *was neither true nor false*"; and this would be wrong. But what does Sellars mean by "the original statement" here? The statement that Prince Edward exchanged his clothes, etc.? But the storyteller made no such statement. Of course the storyteller *uttered the words* "Prince Edward exchanged his clothes," etc. But—someone might object—aren't these words *what he said*? and aren't they the same words as an historian might have used? and so isn't *what he said* false? Of course, one could say, if one liked, that what he said was false, meaning by this that anyone who uttered those words and *was also making a statement* would be making a false statement. But it does not follow from this that the storyteller, in uttering these words, was making a false statement. The point is that the words "true" and "false" and the word "statement" belong together to one way, or class of ways, of using language; but telling stories is a way of using language which falls outside this class. Sellars also writes: "Fiction contains many devices to signalize that statements made in its course are not to be 'taken seriously'." But he ought rather to write: "Fiction contains many devices to signalize that sentences used in its course are not to be taken as being used to make statements." He writes as if the word "statement" and the words "true" and "false" contained no reference at all to a certain way of using language, as if you could decide whether a group of words in use constituted a statement or not without considering the use that was being made of them.

Suppose a company commander gives his sergeant-major the order "The men will spend the morning cleaning their equipment" and then countermands the order. Would this be the right description of the situation: "What the company commander said in fact turned out to be false, though it would be incorrect to say so"? This description could be right only as a philosophical joke. Yet the same words uttered in another context, by another person, might well be used to say something which turned out to be false.

One further comment. Sellars writes: "One says 'That is false' when one takes the other person's statement to be the expression of a belief." These particular words are surely at least as naturally used when one takes it to be a lie.

(4) In Section II of his article, Sellars distinguishes between (among others) two kinds of "ambiguity." The first is manifested by sentences containing certain words, among them the word "this." Sentences such as "This hat is yours," "This wine is good," "This room is airy," "This solution is elegant" may be uttered in many different situations, and in each case the context or setting of the utterance will be an essential element in the determination of the reference made by the use of the phrases "This hat," "This wine," etc. Contrasted with these are sentences which manifest a different kind of "ambiguity" and which Sellars calls "incomplete" or "elliptical." Examples analogous with his own would be the sentence "James is," which might be uttered as an answer to the question "Who is going to drive?" or to the question "Who is going to walk?"; or the sentence "Castor oil *is*," which might be uttered as a rejoinder to the assertion "Castor oil isn't harmful" or to the assertion "Castor oil isn't horrible." Now it is clear that there are many differences between the two classes of sentences here contrasted by Sellars, and many differences between his two sorts of ambiguity. It also seems very reasonable to call the second set of sentences, as opposed to the first, incomplete or elliptical. If one had to justify these phrases, I think one would be inclined to say that the sentences were *formally*, *linguistically* deficient, that they did not come up to a certain standard of how a nonconversational English sentence should be composed; and one would point out that in their conversational setting, the deficiency is remedied by the *linguistic* context, that the surrounding *remarks* supply the missing words.

But Sellars' next suggestion I find utterly puzzling. For he says that such a sentence as "The table is large" is incomplete or elliptical in the same sense as sentences of his second class; that *this* sentence has *this* kind of ambiguity (in addition to the first kind). I fail to see any reason whatever for saying this. Suppose I am writing an account of a certain house and gardens, and in my account there occur the following two sentences: "In the center of the park is a pond. This pond is used by children for sailing boats on. . . . " Now, according to Sellars, if in revising my account, I were to replace the words "This pond" by the words "The pond," I should be replacing a complete and nonelliptical sentence by an incomplete and elliptical sentence! How would Sellars in this case make good the ellipsis and supply the missing words? Would the nonelliptical version run: "The pond referred to in the sentence before this one"?

In general, Sellars thinks that a sentence containing a singular "the"-phrase can be rendered nonelliptical only by supplementing the "the"-phrase by some phrase containing what he calls an "ego-centric" expression. But as far as the actual working of language goes, this is just a dogma without any foundation in fact. (I do not say that, deep in the metaphysical problem of individuation, there may not be a *point* in saying what he says, only that it does not advance the present topic and, if taken as relevant to the present topic, is false.) Of course there are differences between "the" and "this." But there are also close resemblances between the ways in which context, in the widest sense, helps to determine the reference of many "the"-phrases and the ways in which context helps to determine the reference of many "this"-phrases. And there are no ways peculiar to the former, as opposed to the latter, in which their contextual dependence resembles the contextual dependence of incomplete or elliptical sentences.

It does not seem, however, that the contentions of Section II are of major importance for the rest of Sellars' thesis.

(5) I wish now to make certain qualifications of my own thesis as stated in the publications referred to by Sellars. In view of Sellars' approach to the problem, I must first make a remark about the relation between two questions: the question whether a statement has a truth-value and the question whether it is linguistically correct to assign it one.

When a man says "p" in an ordinary statement-making context (i.e., is not telling a story or practicing his pronunciation or acting a part in a play, etc.), his hearers are entitled to assume that he believes that p.[2] This is a tautology. If he says "p" in such circumstances but does not believe that p, there are at least two possibilities: he may be using language incorrectly or he may be intending to deceive. We may, if we choose, count the second as a special case of the first. Whether or not we choose to do this, we can say that at least sometimes when a man says "p" and does not believe that p, he is using language incor-

[2] This goes also for the presuppositions, if any, of the statement that p. Cf. Sec. (1) of this article.

rectly, whether or not it is the case that *p*. This will apply as much to saying that a statement is false as to saying anything else. So I will agree with Sellars that a statement's being false is not the same as its being linguistically correct for anyone to say that it is false. But this lack of identity is perfectly general and has no special relevance to the case of saying that a statement is false as opposed to saying anything else. So in what follows I shall set it aside; and in default of any cogent reason for distinguishing further between the cases in which a statement is false and the cases in which it is linguistically correct to say that it is false, I shall make no such distinction.

Roughly speaking, the thesis I maintained was as follows: (a) that a statement containing [3] a definite singular description was neither true nor false unless there existed something to which the speaker was referring and which answered to the description; (b) that many statements of the kinds traditionally called universal and particular also lacked a truth-value unless there existed members of the subject-class. I shall make my qualifications mainly with reference to (a); the application to (b), where appropriate, is not difficult. The main qualification that I want to make is to admit that *in certain cases and circumstances* it may be quite natural and correct to assign a truth-value to a statement of one of these kinds (to say that it is false or even that it is true), even though the condition referred to is not satisfied. I shall begin by considering two sorts of case in which it may be correct to say that a statement of one of the kinds in question is false, even though the existence-condition is not satisfied.

(A1) Suppose I make a remark of the form "The *S* is *P*," knowing that there is no *S*, with the deliberate intention of deceiving my hearer.[4] Suppose, for example, that I am trying to sell something and say to a prospective purchaser, "The lodger next door has offered me twice that sum," when there is no lodger next door and I know this. It would seem perfectly correct for the prospective purchaser to reply, "That's false," and to give as his reason the fact that there was no lodger next door. And it would indeed be a lame defense for me to say, "Well, it's not actually false, because, you see, since there's no such person, the question of truth or falsity doesn't arise." Both the speaker, in his attempt to deceive, and the hearer, in rejecting the speaker's assertion for the reason he gives, are relying on the fact that

[3] Strictly, here and elsewhere, "a statement made by the use of a sentence containing . . . ."
[4] I am indebted to Mr. Stuart Hampshire for pointing this case out to me.

the speaker, by using the form of words he does, commits himself[5] to the existence of a lodger next door. The speaker exploits this logical feature of that form of words to induce a belief which he (and, as it happens, his hearer too) knows to be false. The word "false" has to a pre-eminent degree the ring of an accusation of intended deception. The hearer applies it to the speaker's assertion. What the speaker says is false, is a lie.

Clearly, then, this case calls for some modification of my thesis.

(A2) Let us now consider another kind of case of a statement containing a definite description, where nothing answers to the description. This kind of case could be characterized by saying that the statement in question would be said to be about (in one use of "about") something or someone other than the nonexistent item to which the descriptive phrase in question refers or purports to refer.[6] Suppose I am ignorantly boasting about my friend's visit to Rome and mention the king of France as one among the distinguished people he had seen there. I might say, "He had lunch with the prime minister, had an audience of the pope, and then went for a drive with the king of France." Someone might say, "Well, at least it's false (not true) that he went for a drive with the king of France—for there's no such person." Now it is important to note that in this case, where I would be said to be talking about my friend rather than about the king of France, it would also be permissible simply to *negate* the subject-predicate proposition in the ordinary way, on the strength of the nonexistence of the king of France; whereas it would not be permissible to do so in the classical case in which one is taken to be talking *about* the king of France. That is, one could say, "Well, at least he didn't go for a drive with the king of France—for there's no such person"; but one could not normally say, "The king of France isn't wise—for there's no such person." I shall refer later to this remark.

Now, to offset these concessions, I want first to make three points:

(B1) In a large number of imaginable cases in which there is nothing answering to the descriptive phrase, one would be very reluctant indeed to say either that the statement in question was true or that it was false. I have given examples elsewhere, and Sellars does not dispute their existence, so I shall not recapitulate them here.

(B2) Even in the case of deliberate deceit, as in (A1) above, where

---

[5] Cf. P. F. Strawson, *Introduction to Logical Theory* (New York, 1952), p. 175.
[6] Messrs. H. P. Grice and G. J. Warnock have both drawn my attention to this case.

it might be *natural* to call the statement false, it might also be highly *misleading*, unless the full circumstances, and, in particular, one's reason for calling it false, were made known. And it would be misleading because we are strongly inclined to treat the singular form "It is false that S is P" as logically equivalent to the singular form "S is not P"; and "S is not P" resembles "S is P" in that he who utters a statement of this form commits himself to the existence of S. From "It is false (untrue) that the lodger next door has offered him twice that sum" or "The statement that the lodger next door has offered him twice that sum is untrue (false)," one would be justified in concluding, "The lodger next door has not offered him twice that sum," *unless* the special circumstances, the special way, in which "false" is being used here, were made plain.

(B3) Finally, in some of the cases of the sort we are concerned with, it seems to me that, if forced to choose between calling what was said true or false, we shall be more inclined to say that it was true. Thus if, in Oxford, I declared, "The Waynflete Professor of Logic is older than I am," it would be natural to describe the situation by saying that I had confused the titles of two Oxford professors,[7] but, whichever one I had meant, what I had said about him was true. Here it may be remarked that it is the phrase "what I said" rather than the word "true" which acquires a slightly specialized use. If it is insisted that *what I actually said* rather than *what I meant* should be characterized, then resistance to applying either "true" or "false" once more becomes very strong. Similarly, perhaps, if I say, "The United States Chamber of Deputies contains representatives of two major parties," I shall be allowed to have said something true even though I have used the wrong title, a title, in fact, which applies to nothing. If "two" is replaced by "three," what I said may be called false; and the appropriateness of "false" here rests on the fact that what I was talking about (though misnaming or misdescribing) does not have the property I ascribed to it.

The points made so far in this section and the arguments of previous sections, may, I think, be drawn together into the following conclusions.

(i) There exists, in our ordinary use of language, a strong tendency (though not a rigid rule) for the words "true" and "false" to be used in certain ways in application to large classes of singular, universal, and

---

[7] The Waynflete Professor of Metaphysics and the Wykeham Professor of Logic.

particular statements, and for certain logical relationships, associated by way of mutual dependence with these ways of applying "true" and "false," to be acknowledged in our ordinary transitions and arguments. Some of the crucial relationships and applications concerned are the following:

(a) The singular form "It is false that the so-and-so is such-and-such (the S is P)" tends to be treated as logically equivalent to "The so-and-so is not such-and-such (the S is not P)."

(b) The singular form "The S is P" tends to be treated as the contradictory of "The S is not P." The universal form "All S are P," tends to be treated as the contradictory of the particular form, "Some S are not P."

(c) The two traditional universal forms tend to be treated as contraries, the two traditional particular forms as subcontraries.

(d) There is a tendency to withhold the words "true" and "false" from statements of all three kinds when, in the one case, the singular description fails to apply to anything or, in the others, the subject-class lacks members.

The point of the utmost importance here is that all these tendencies go together, are part of one and the same logical-linguistic phenomenon. They are not—to anticipate my next point—to be separately and *differently* explained and justified, as, on Sellars' thesis, they have to be.

(ii) Now it is true that Sellars' account can be held *in a sense* to give an explanation of these facts—in the sense, namely, that all these facts are covered, allowed for, by his explanation. But (1) his explanation turns on a distinction between a statement's being true or false and its being correct to say that it is true or false, the very existence of which (except as a special case of something quite general) is inadequately supported by the arguments he uses, while its applicability to the cases in question is not supported by any arguments at all, but only by the suggestion of an analogy with specially constructed cases. Moreover, (2) there is a suspicious capriciousness about the way in which the distinction works out in application to the facts agreed between us. He, as it were, takes for granted the correctness of the analyses "$(\exists x)[fx.(y)(fy \supset x=y).gx]$," "$(x)(fx \supset gx)$," "$(\exists x)(fg.gx)$" for the cases of singular descriptions, affirmative universal, and particular propositions respectively, and applies his explanation just as and when it is necessary to *adjust* the actually observed tendencies to these analyses. For example, *he does not have to explain at all*, in terms of his account, the tendency for "All *S* are *P*" and "Some *S* are not *P*" to be treated as contradictories, because this relation happens to be already assured by the analysis he favors. His apparatus has to be applied now in this way, now in that, and sometimes not at all, to a set of phenomena which are surely systematically connected manifestations of one and the same linguistic tendency. I conclude that it is not enough for Sellars just to fit his explanation on in such a way that it reconciles the logical facts of (i) above with the requirements of his chosen analyses. There should also be, as there are not, independent reasons for accepting the chosen analyses and for accepting his various applications of the doctrine of the distinction between a statement's being true or false and its being correctly said to be so.

(iii) My own opposite error, in the first expositions of my thesis, was to *canonize* the tendencies noted in (i) and make them into fixed and rigid rules, whereas we see they have exceptions. I think the truer account of the matter would run as follows: Those uses of "true" and "false" and of the associated logical relation words which were canonized in my unqualified doctrine of presupposition are reasonably to be regarded as the *primary* uses of these words in application to statements of the kinds in question. (On Sellars' view, these uses of these words will be in some, but not in all,[8] cases secondary.) They yield the standard and customary logic of these statements. Discussion of the truth or falsity of these statements, and comment on their logical relations, are customarily carried on against a certain background of unquestioned assumption and commitment. When these background assumptions and commitments *are* called into question, that discussion is, in general, stultified: questions of truth or falsity no longer arise, etc.[9] But *sometimes*, as in the case (A1) of deliberate deception, where the background assumption is forcibly thrust forward in a way which points accusingly at the speaker, the word "false" may acquire a *secondary* use, which collides with the primary one; and the customary logical relations, too, are involved in this collision. (I do not say that the case of deliberate deception is the only one in which this happens.) I am not sure that the other apparent exceptions mentioned above are genuine exceptions at all. What we do in cases, (B3) for example, where the speaker's *intended* reference is pretty clear, is simply

---

[8] Cf. (ii) above on the case of "All *S* are *P*" and "Some *S* are not *P*" as contradictories.

[9] Cf. *Introduction to Logical Theory*, p. 18.

to amend his statement in accordance with his guessed intentions and assess the *amended* statement for truth or falsity; we are not awarding a truth-value at all to the original statement. Case (A2) is an interesting one and merits fuller discussion than I shall give it. Clearly, however, the existence of a king of France is not, in this example, a presupposition of the whole discussion, as is the existence of the friend whose exploits I am recounting. The informal indication of this is that in no sense could the king of France be said to be the *theme* of my remarks. The formal indication is that the phrase purporting to refer to him does not figure as a grammatical subject and can be regarded as simply a *part* of a grammatical *predicate* which lacks application. But we should not find this formal indication in every such case.

(iv) It should now be clear that the dispute between Sellars and myself could disappear completely if he would agree—to use a phrase of Professor Ryle's—that we are not producing competing solutions to the same problem but noncompeting solutions to different problems. That is to say, I should represent myself as trying to describe the actual logical features of ordinary speech in this region; and he might perhaps agree to regard himself as offering a theoretical construction designed to answer the following theoretical question: Assuming that there existed a language having the structure of the skeleton language of the elementary parts of *Principia Mathematica*, how might there be developed from it a language having the logical features which we both agree to note in our own?

(v) Finally, in order to avoid misunderstanding, I must recall a point about my use of such expressions as "contradictories," "logically equivalent," "subcontraries," etc.[10] It might be thought, for example, that in saying that "All S are P" and "Some S are not P" are contradictories, I am saying that it must be the case that, of two statements of these forms with the same fillings and the same intended reference, one is true and the other false, and thus that I am saying something inconsistent with the claim that both statements may lack a truth-value. Similarly in saying that "It is false that the S is P" and "The S is not P" are logically equivalent forms, I might be thought to be saying that two statements of these forms with the same filling and the same intended reference must both be true or both be false and thus again to be contradicting my own thesis. But a very simple amendment re-

[10] Cf. *Ibid.*, pp. 176–177.

moves all such worries. All that is required is the insertion into such definitions of these terms of the proviso that both statements have a truth-value; thus, e.g., to say that two statements are logically equivalent is to say that *if* both have a truth-value, then both must have the same truth-value.

I I

Descriptions, Scope and Identity

Herbert Hochberg

IN *Principia Mathematica* White-
head and Russell (A) define '$x=y$' as '$(\phi) : \phi x . \supset . \phi y$'[1]; (B) treat (1)
'$(\imath x)(\phi x) = (\imath x)(\phi x)$' as analytical equivalent to (2) '$(\exists b) : \phi x . \equiv_x$
$. x=b : b=b$'; and (C) adopt as a notational convention the omission
of a scope operator for a description when the scope intended is the
smallest sentence in which the description in question occurs. However, the definition in (A) cannot be applied to the '$=$' of (1), since
descriptions cannot be treated as arguments, without an additional
premise. This prevents us from arriving at (3) '$(\imath x)(\phi x) = (\imath x)(\phi x)$.
$\equiv : . (\psi) : \psi(\imath x)(\phi x) . \supset \psi(\imath x)(\phi x)$' where the left hand side of the
equivalence is not, by (B), analytic, while the right hand side is, by
(C). Since both '$=$' and the incomplete symbol '$(\imath x)(\phi x)$' are defined
signs in *PM*, we may conclude that the order of replacement of defined signs makes a difference or, even, that the definition of '$=$' and
the "rules" for handling descriptions *require* a specific order of replacement. Or, since '$=$' is not directly replaceable in contexts involving descriptions, one might even suggest that it operates, in some sense,
as an undefined sign in those contexts.

If, however, we forget (C) and write (1) as (1') '$[(\imath x)(\phi x)]$.

Reprinted with the kind permission of the author, the editor, and the
publisher from *Analysis*, 18 (1958): 20–22.

[1] I omit '!' from the definition (of '$=$') where that sign is supposed to indicate
"predicative contexts", *i.e.*, the defining phrase, as it occurs in *PM*, is '$(\phi):\phi ! x . \supset$
$. \phi ! y$'.

$(\imath x)(\phi x) = (\imath x)(\phi x)$', we note two things: (a) the identity sign in ($1'$) is now directly replaceable without giving rise to (3), and, consequently, (b) the order of replacement in ($1'$) no longer matters. For, replacing '=' in ($1'$), assuming for the moment that we may, we get (4) '$[(\imath x)(\phi x)] : . (\psi) : \psi(\imath x)(\phi x) . \supset . \psi(\imath x)(\phi x)$', from which, by expanding the description, one gets (5) '$(\exists b) :: \phi x . \equiv_x . x = b : . (\psi) : \psi b . \supset . \psi b$'. (5) is not analytic, and, moreover, it is just what one gets by expanding the description *before* the identity sign in ($1'$). Hence, instead of (3), one can now only prove the equivalence of ($1'$) and (4). The use of the scope operator preserves the "existence condition" that prevents (3). Thus, if we abandon the notational convention stated in (C), we may be said to have, due to (a) and (b), a more general treatment of identity, since we can now afford to alter (A) in order to allow '=' to be directly replaceable in contexts involving descriptions. A rather minor alteration in the conventions of *PM* thus results, I believe, in an improvement in the theory of descriptions presented there.

Mr. Geach has pointed out[2] that in the case of a context like (1) the Russell-Whitehead definition of '$[(\imath x)(\phi x)] . \psi(\imath x)(\phi x)$' by '$(\exists b) : \phi x . \equiv_x . x = b : \psi b$' leads to an ambiguity. For, it is not determined which of

$(a_1) \quad b = (\imath x)(\phi x)$
$(a_2) \quad (\imath x)(\phi x) = b$
$(a_3) \quad b = b$

would replace 'ψb'. Mr. Geach argues that (C) does not prevent this ambiguity since (1) contains no part that is a sentence. Actually an analogue of Mr. Geach's point can be raised about contexts that do contain sentences as parts. Consider (4). It is analytically equivalent to (5), but we could consider typographically different expressions as its expansion. (5) would be one of these. Another would be ($5'$) '$(\exists b) :: \phi x . \equiv_x . x = b :: (\exists c) : . \phi x . \equiv_x . x = c : . (\psi)\psi b . \supset . \psi c$'. The point is simply that the *PM* conventions are stipulated for descriptions rather than for *occurrences* of descriptions. Thus, where more than one occurrence of the same description falls under a scope operator we face the ambiguity in question. In keeping with the illustrations, (5) and ($5'$), we can see two alternative solutions.

---

2 P. T. Geach, "Russell's Theory of Descriptions," *Analysis*, 10 (March, 1950): 4. One should note that to speak of an "ambiguity" overstates the case, since (a1), (a2), and (a3) are logically equivalent.

First, taking a hint from the treatment of '$(\imath x)(\phi x) = (\imath x)(\psi x)$' in *PM*, where the description occurring first typographically is to have the larger scope, we may introduce the following convention. (I) Where two or more occurrences of a description are *bound* by an occurrence of a scope operator then the first occurrence (typographically) has the larger scope, the second occurrence the next largest scope, etc. In stating (I) I used the term 'bound'. This is to prevent a problem arising from an occurrence of a description which lies within the scopes of two occurrences of the same scope operator. For example, consider '$[\imath x)(\phi x)] \mathbf{:} \cdot \psi(\imath x)(\phi x) \cdot \supset \mathbf{:} [(\imath x)(\phi x)] \cdot \psi(\imath x)(\phi x).$' The scope of the occurrence of '$(\imath x)(\phi x)$' in the clause to the right of the conditional is intended to be determined by the second occurrence of the scope operator and not by the first. We must thus indicate which occurrence of the description is "determined" by which occurrence of the scope operator. Since speaking in terms of occurrences of descriptions and scope operators bears an evident analogy to quantified variables and quantifiers,[3] the term 'bound' is suggestive. An occurrence, a, of a description will be said to be bound by an occurrence, β, of a scope operator if:

(b_1) a lies within the scope of β;

(b_2) β contains an occurrence of the description;

(b_3) a does not lie within the scope of another occurrence, β', of the scope operator such that β' lies within the scope of β. We may notice that in accordance with the proposal to drop (C) no well-formed expression would contain a "free" description.

According to (I), ($5'$) is the result of replacing the descriptions (the two occurrences of the same description) or the identity sign first in ($1'$). The same result is achieved even if one replaces one occurrence first, the identity sign second, and the other occurrence last. In this latter case one simply has to keep an occurrence of a scope operator to indicate the scope of the remaining occurrence of the description. Likewise, (I) specifies the replacement of 'ψb' by (a_1) in Mr. Geach's illustration.

A second and typographically simpler alternative is to adopt the following convention. (II) '$[(\imath x)(\phi x)] \cdot \psi(\imath x)(\phi x)$' is defined by '$(\exists b) \mathbf{:} \phi x \cdot \equiv_x \cdot x = b \mathbf{:} \psi b$' where (with '$\beta$' standing for the occurrence of the scope operator in the definiendum) 'ψb' is like '$\psi(\imath x)(\phi x)$' except for containing a free occurrence of 'b' at each place that '$[(\imath x)(\phi x)] \cdot$

[3] Cf. W. V. Quine, *Mathematical Logic* (1951), pp. 74–78.

$\psi(\imath x)(\phi x)$' contains an occurrence of '$(\imath x)(\phi x)$' bound by β.[4] By (II), (5) is the result of replacing either the descriptions (occurrences) or the identity sign first (1'). In this case, however, both occurrences must be replaced simultaneously. (II) likewise provides for an unambiguous replacement of 'ψb', this time by (a₃) in Mr. Geach's illustration.

4 (II), as well as (I), must also require that replacing descriptions does not involve one in problems (similar to those occurring in illicit substitutions) by permitting an introduced quantifier to "catch" free variables. See Quine, *Methods of Logic* (1950), pp. 133–134.

12

Russell on Meaning and Denoting

P. T. Geach

IN a recent article[1] Mr. Searle has shown the odd irrelevance of Russell's criticism of Frege in the famous paper *On Denoting*. I here offer an explanation of the oddity: Russell had excusably, but wrongly, conflated Frege's distinction between *Sinn* and *Bedeutung* with his own distinction between what an expression 'means' and what it 'denotes', as expounded in *The Principles of Mathematics* (hereafter *PM*). The occurrence of this conflation is clear from Russell's explicit statement that the two theories are 'very nearly the same'[2]; and also from a fact remarked by Mr. Searle—that in expounding Frege's alleged theory Russell uses the term "denoting complex", which is not Frege's term at all but is a technicality of the *PM* theory. Church apparently supposes that all Russell was doing was to recommend certain translations of Frege's "*Sinn*" and "*Bedeutung*", since he professes to be just following Russell in rendering "*bedeuten, Bedeutung*" as "denote, denotation"[3]; this is likely to give

Reprinted with the kind permission of the author and the editor from *Analysis*, 19 (1958–1959): 69–72.

[1] *Analysis*, 18 (June, 1958), 6:137 ff.

[2] Cf. the reprint of "On Denoting," in *Logic and Knowledge*, ed. R. C. Marsh (Allen & Unwin, 1956): first footnote on p. 42.

[3] This way of rendering Frege's terms is anyhow undesirable; what the general term "man" denotes would ordinarily be taken to be men, whereas for Frege the *Bedeutung* of "man" is not men but a concept.

the confusion longer life. It is high time the record were set straight.

As I said, Russell's conflation of Frege's theory with the *PM* theory was excusable. In many contexts, "meaning" would be the natural English for "*Sinn*"; and again, what the definite description "*the King of England in* 1905" would be said by Russell to 'denote' is the same as what Frege would say is the *Bedeutung* of the description—*viz.* Edward VII. The apparent parallelism between Frege's theory and the *PM* theory may be succinctly expressed as follows: A proposition (*Gedanke*) that corresponds to a sentence with a definite description in it will have the meaning (*Sinn*) of that description as a constituent part, but will not be *about* that meaning, but *about* the object that the description denotes (*bedeutet*).

We get, however, a more fruitful and less misleading comparison of the two theories if we rather set beside each other Russell's *PM* use of "mean, meaning" and Frege's use of "*bedeuten, Bedeutung*". We then get the following results: The 'meaning' (*Bedeutung*) of a sentence has as parts the 'meanings' (*Bedeutungen*) of the significant bits of the sentence.[4] For Frege, an indicative sentence is always *about* these *Bedeutungen* of the significant bits of the sentence; Russell in *PM* says the same thing concerning the 'meanings' of the significant bits of sentences—*with the exception of* '*denoting*' *phrases*, a 'denoting' phrase being a general term prefaced with "the", "a", "every", "any", "some", or "all".[5] The 'meaning' (*Bedeutung*) of a proper name is its bearer; the 'meaning' of a general term is a predicative entity—a concept; the 'meaning' of a relative term is a relation. These similarities justify us in rejecting Russell's later equation of his "denote" to Frege's "*bedeuten*"; on the contrary, it is clear that when Frege enquires what the *Bedeutung* of an expression is, and when Russell in *PM* asks what its 'meaning' is, the question is essentially the same, and the answers they give are often the same. The fact that to these questions Russell (in

---

4 Cf. *Philosophical Writings of Gottlob Frege*, ed. Geach and Black (Blackwell, 1952), p. 65.

5 Russell's use of 'about' is, however, further complicated by the following restriction: A sentence is not to be regarded as being 'about' the concept 'meant' by its predicate or the relation 'meant' by its verb, e.g. "Socrates is wise" is not 'about' the concept *wise*, and "Socrates excels Plato" is not 'about' the relation *excels*. But in any such case there will be a logically equivalent sentence—e.g. "*wise* is an attribute of Socrates", "*excels* relates Socrates to Plato"—which *is* 'about' the concept or relation in question. (*PM* §48) For present purposes the restriction is unimportant.

PM) and Frege *sometimes* gave divergent answers[6] is not of itself proof that the questions were different.

Frege's distinction between *Sinn* and *Bedeutung* was largely (I think entirely) derived from puzzles about indirect-speech clauses; no such considerations are used in *PM* to justify the distinction between meaning and denoting. The sort of argument we do find is that in "I met a man" the phrase 'a man' does not 'mean' the man I met—'an actual man with a tailor and a bank-account and a public-house and a drunken wife' (*PM* §56); and no such argument is to be found in Frege. In fact, if we equate Russell's 'meaning' and Frege's *Bedeutung*, then nothing in Frege's theory will correspond to Russell's 'denoting'. Russell's motive for his own distinction was clearly his 'robust sense of reality'—his laudable dislike of such Meinongian monstrosities as the round square and the indefinite man.

If we confine our attention to definite descriptions, the *PM* theory of denoting may be stated as follows:

(1) The general term following the "the" has a concept as its 'meaning', and so the sentence containing the definite description is in any event analysable as making an assertion about this concept. Thus it never happens that a sentence fails to be about anything at all, because it contains a definite description (or other denoting phrase) that denotes nothing. (Russell says, however, that sentences containing vacuous denoting phrases must be 'rejected', apparently as false: *PM* §73).

(2) The concept *A* is however not the 'meaning' of the whole phrase "the *A*"; the 'meaning' of "the *A*" is a peculiar sort of entity—a *denoting concept* or *denoting complex*.

(3) A denoting complex is always part of the 'meaning' of a sentence that contains the corresponding definite description; but the sentence is not in general *about* the denoting complex.

(4) There are, however, contexts in which a definite description is so used that the assertion made is about the denoting complex 'meant' by the definite description; in these contexts there is no 'denoting'. An example would be: "*the even prime* is not a number but a denoting complex". Clearly, though, this is not the ordinary use of definite descriptions.

(5) With the ordinary use of a definite description, we are talking

[6] Apart from the divergence here discussed, about denoting phrases, there is a divergence as to when two sentences have the same 'meaning': in *PM*, it is when they convey the same assertion; for Frege, it is when both are true or both false.

not about the denoting complex that it 'means', but about the object it describes (supposing it is not vacuous): e.g. "the King of England in 1905 was bearded" is about Edward VII.

(6) The fundamental denoting-relation holds between a non-linguistic denoting complex and an object, e.g. between the denoting complex *the even prime* and the number 2; a denoting *phrase* 'denotes' an object secondarily, by having as its 'meaning' the denoting complex that primarily 'denotes' the object.

This historical background enables us to understand Russell's later statements that definite descriptions are 'incomplete symbols' with no 'meaning'. The opinion seems to prevail in some quarters that Russell thought, or half thought, that his Theory of Descriptions reduced the entities described to mere 'logical fictions', and that this was why he said descriptions had no 'meaning'. It would be admitted that this involves a gross confusion; but some people are willing to ascribe confusion as gross as this to Russell, rather than suspect it is their own.

What Russell was in fact doing was to hark back to his own *PM* theory. Definite descriptions have no 'meaning' in the sense that we need not postulate a piece of meaning, a logical unit, answering to a definite description in the way the denoting complex was supposed to. In fact, when

"The King of England in 1905 was bearded"

is analysed as

"For some *x*, *x*, and nobody other than *x*, reigned over England in 1905, and *x* was bearded",

the sentence-fragment that is left when the predicate "was bearded" is removed no longer forms a syntactical unity, as "The King of England" did; so the temptation to postulate a unified piece of meaning that should correspond to this sentence-fragment no longer arises.

Considered as criticisms not of Frege, but of Russell's own *PM* theory, the arguments in *On Denoting* take on quite a different force and relevance. Whether they are valid I shall not here try to determine. It is unfortunate that Russell, like Aristotle, so often distorts others' thought into his own mould; readers of *On Denoting* will find it best simply to ignore his use of Frege's name.

13

Strawson on Referring

C. E. Caton

IN his paper "On Referring,"[1]
P. F. Strawson argues that what Russell gave as an analysis of propositions involving definite descriptions is actually not part of what is
asserted in these propositions, but rather part of what they imply in a
special sense of 'imply'. This sense of 'imply' is what Strawson also
calls presupposing; it is that p implies or presupposes q when p would
be neither true nor false, the question of its truth or falsity would not
arise, unless q were true. (*Cf.* p. 34 and Strawson's "A Reply to Mr.
Sellars," *The Philosophical Review*, 63 (1954), p. 216.) Thus Strawson says, for example, that the referring use of a definite description
implies, in this sense, "that we are, or intend to be, referring to one particular individual of the species 'such-and-such'," *i.e.* of the sort indicated by the expression following the word 'the' (p. 36). In other
words, as he says, Strawson takes such a use of a definite description
to imply that "the existential conditions described by Russell are
fulfilled" (*ibid.*).

In the original version of the paper, Strawson also held that one can
intend to refer to or mention something but fail to do so. He talks

Reprinted with the kind permission of the author and the editor from
Mind, 68 (1959): 539-544.

[1] Originally in *Mind*, New Series, 59 (1950): 320-344; reprinted, with additional footnotes, in *Essays in Conceptual Analysis*, ed. Antony Flew (New York:
St. Martin's Press, 1956), pp. 21-52. All subsequent references are to the latter,
unless otherwise indicated.

about "spurious uses" of uniquely referring expressions; he says, for example,

> ... when we utter the sentence without in fact mentioning anybody by the use of the phrase, 'The King of France', the sentence does not cease to be significant: we simply *fail* to say anything true or false because we simply fail to mention anybody by this particular use of that perfectly significant phrase. It is, if you like, a spurious use of the sentence, and a spurious use of the expression ... (p. 35; Strawson's italics).

Strawson also talks about "succeeding in mentioning somebody or something" (p. 36). However, to the reprinted paper Strawson added some footnotes indicating that there was an error in this. After discussing make-believe or fictional uses of uniquely referring expressions, he concludes, "Hence we can, using significant expressions, pretend to refer, in make-believe or fiction, or mistakenly think that we are referring when we are not referring to anything" (p. 40).

To this he now attaches as a qualification the following footnote:

> This sentence now seems to me objectionable in a number of ways, notably because of an unexplicitly restrictive use of the word 'refer'. It could be more exactly phrased as follows: 'Hence we can, using significant expressions, refer in secondary ways, as in make-believe or in fiction, or mistakenly think we are referring to something in the primary way when we are not, in that way, referring to anything' (*ibid.*).

What I wish to suggest in this paper is that both of Strawson's accounts have gone wrong because he has made too little change in Russell's theory regarded as an account of the ordinary use of this sort of referring expression. The defects of Strawson's account are, first, that the ordinary distinction between failing to refer to or to mention something and referring to or mentioning something is not the distinction that Strawson draws, and, second, that the suggestion of ordinary usage is that referring is the same sort of thing whether the thing referred to exists or does not exist or is fictional or make-believe or whatever else it may be. Finally, I will offer some suggestions toward an account which would avoid the difficulties caused by regarding it as important to the question of whether or not something was referred to or referred to in some primary way, whether or not the thing referred to exists.

The first defect of Strawson's account in its original version is that he thought that it was possible to intend to refer to or to mention something and, presumably, although he does not actually use this phrase, to try to refer to something, and then either to fail or succeed in referring to or in mentioning that something. Now I think it is possible to do these things, *i.e.* these phrases do have a use, but that the ordinary use of these phrases is not the use that Strawson suggests that they have. Thus the only way in which one can fail to refer to or to mention something is either through (1) omitting to refer to or to mention the thing at all, or (2) mis-speaking, being interrupted, or not getting the words out. In the first case, one has not even tried to refer to or to mention the thing in question and there is no correlative success in mentioning or referring to the thing: what is opposed to failing to mention something is actually mentioning it or remembering to mention it or coming near to mentioning it without actually doing so, etc. But as Strawson originally viewed the matter, one could fail to refer to something by using some expression which could be used to refer to that thing if it existed but which failed to do so, since that thing actually did not exist, although one thought that it did. Now this situation sometimes obtains, but it is worth nothing that when it does, we do not say that the person has failed to refer but rather we point out to the person that the thing does not exist. In the second case, one can fail to refer to or to mention something, but not because the thing does not exist, although one thought it did; rather, one fails because one does not even succeed in uttering the referring expression, a minimal condition for using it to refer to something. Here the existence of the thing one would have referred to is obviously irrelevant.

Now it is clear that these ordinary meanings of the phrase 'fail to refer' are not what Strawson has in mind. The usual phrase for what he does have in mind is 'referring to something that does not exist, thinking it does'. This he would express in his terminology as 'intending to refer to something, but failing to do so' or as 'mistakenly thinking that one is referring when one is not referring to anything'. In the revised version of his account, he would express this by 'mistakenly thinking one is referring to something in the primary way when one is not, in that way, referring to anything'. But clearly this would differ from the ordinary phrase in the same way: if one says 'The King of France is bald', one is not corrected by the remark that one is not referring to anything but by the remark that there is no such person. In other words, Strawson's revised account still seems to imply that one can think that one is referring in the primary way to something when one is not. However, as 'refer' is ordinarily used, it seems that all one can do is to refer to something thinking it exists when it does not: but this nowise commits us to saying that one has not referred at all and it even looks as though one must have, if one referred to something which did not exist.

In connection with this, it may be noted that we would ordinarily talk about someone's *succeeding* in referring to something only if he managed to do so despite some obstacle or hindrance. But this again is independent of whether or not the person thinks the thing he refers to exists and of whether or not it does exist.

The feature of our ordinary use of 'refer' which Strawson seems not to have noticed and which he has certainly omitted from his account or from his use of 'refer' is that referring is ordinarily regarded as the same whether or not the thing referred to exists, is fictional, pretended, dreamt, or whatever. This can be seen from the fact that whenever any substantive is used to refer to something, it may be unclear what thing is referred to and a question intended to remove the ambiguity can be phrased with the word 'refer'. Ambiguous uses of substantives can occur in straightforward talk about things known or thought to exist, in jokes, in overtly fictional accounts, in relations of dreams, and indeed anywhere. And the question 'Which one are you referring to?' and similar questions involving the word 'refer' can be and are asked in all such cases. The only possible inference, it seems to me, is that there is no necessary connection between the existence of what is referred to and one's referring to it. That is, referring is the same sort of linguistic performance in all these cases.

This is not to say, of course, that whether 'John loves Mary' is said on the street, in a joke, in a play, in a novel, etc., there will be no difference in the implications that it has regarding the existence of John and Mary. It is only to say that these differences in context of utterance and in the corresponding implications do not affect the question of whether or not John and Mary were referred to. If the sentence was used to make a statement or report and perhaps in some cases even if such a sentence was taken as an example, the substantives can fail to identify the persons referred to and the question of which John or Mary was referred to will arise. Indeed, one can even ask to whom a fictional character was referring when he used a certain substantive in a fictional conversation. In other words, not even the substantive which is used as the subject of the verb 'to refer' itself need refer to something which exists.

There is obviously raised here the question of whether Strawson's account could be revised in order to accord more closely with the ordinary use of 'refer' which is in question in these examples. I think it probably could and that this might be done along lines some of which are adumbrated by Strawson. In discussing the uniqueness condition of the non-fictional use of uniquely referring phrases, Strawson suggests that the presupposition of uniqueness should be stated in terms of referring, *i.e.* that the notion of referring should be used in stating the presupposition itself. In connection with distinguishing what is asserted from what is implied by a uniquely referring use, and referring to the use of the phrase 'the table' in the sentence 'The table is covered with books', Strawson says,

> It is . . . tautologically true that, in such a use, the phrase will have application only in the event of there being one table and no more *which is being referred to.* . . . To use the sentence is not to assert, but it is (in the special sense discussed) to imply, that there is only one thing which is *both* of the kind specified (*i.e.* a table) *and is being referred to* by the speaker. (p. 37; Strawson's italics).

Now in the discussion of the presuppositions of a uniquely referring use of an expression given earlier in the article, there is no mention of the presupposition that there is only one thing which is both of the kind specified and is being referred to; but it is said there that what is presupposed is that there is one and only one thing of the kind specified. But, as Strawson states in this later passage, it is obviously the former fact which is presupposed.

Now if we were to use 'refer' in the ordinary way, then we would get, I believe, an account of these presuppositions of the use of uniquely referring expressions which is what Strawson ought to have said, but without his altered use of 'refer' and without the difficulties about the existence of what is referred to. Thus anyone who asserts that the King of France is bald, using the sentence 'The King of France is bald', will be said to have referred to the King of France, as indeed he would ordinarily be said to have.

Then a rough sketch of what the relations between referring and existence are would be the following. To begin with, our ordinary language can be and is used to discuss real people, things, and occurrences, but it is also used to discuss the people, things, and occurrences in novels and plays and in jokes and dreams. The same language can be and is used in discussing all of these—exactly the same expressions— so long as it is understood by everyone concerned what sort of thing, *e.g.* real people, people in a novel, or people in a dream, is being discussed. When what sort of thing is being discussed is *not* understood, an indefiniteness or ambiguity in the use of all the language prevails and it is impolite or something verging on lying not to inform a listener who is not aware of or does not understand what the subject-matter is. Such information is regularly given when it is thought that someone may not understand and there are many ways of giving it. In some cases of discourse shifted from the straightforward employment special sorts of language are used, *e.g.* the historical present tense in the verbs of stage directions; but in other cases the same language is used, *e.g.* the imperative mood of verbs in recipes and other sorts of directions. The difficulties in connection with the relation between referring and existence seem to me to be caused mainly by the fact that when discussing other sorts of thing than the real world we use largely the same language and that we use it in closely similar ways.

Now as the discourse shifts, the implications of the utterances may and usually do change, though the expressions uttered may remain the same. These implications shift systematically, so that by finding out the sort of discourse that is occurring one is able to take the utterances as they ought to be taken, *i.e.* as they are meant. Thus when we find out, for example, that it was in a dream, in a novel, in a story or lie told, or in a fairy tale that a certain person received a large sum of money, we would not seek to verify the fact by checking with his bank. But the same expression, 'He was given a large sum of money', say, may be used in all these cases.

One sort of implication that changes is, of course, the implication of the use of referring expressions. This fact is no doubt what Strawson has in mind when he speaks of the distinction between primary and secondary uses of referring expressions, which in my terms would be the distinction between the use of referring expressions in straightforward discourse about the real world and their use in shifted discourse about fictional, dreamt, lied-about, fairy persons and things, as well as those in directions, recipes, jokes, and the like. But it is a noteworthy fact that the phrases 'to refer to', 'to mean', 'there is', 'there are', 'to exist', etc., are used in all sorts of discourse and the implications of their use and of the use of referring expressions in connection with them change just as do those of any other expressions. That is, whether it is the real world, a dream, a joke, a novel, directions, or a recipe that is under discussion, we are prepared to and do talk about what there is, whether there is a thing of a certain kind or a person called so-and-so, that someone, real or not, was referring to, etc. For example, the implications of the use of the referring phrase 'the table' are the same in 'I was referring to the table in the corner' as they are in 'The table is covered with books', whatever the sort of discourse is in which both are uttered. If it is understood in the one case that no particular table is being referred to, *e.g.* in discussing the properties for a play to be performed, this would also be understood in the other—provided that it is clear what sort of discourse is being conducted.

What I wish to suggest, then, is that the locus of the problem about the relation between the use of referring expressions, whether uniquely referring expressions or some other kind, and the existence of the things referred to—where this problem lies is not in the account of referring, if the ordinary use of the verb 'to refer' is to be any guide, but rather in that of the shifting of discourse from the normal straightforward sort to discourse about things dreamt, joked about, in novels, etc. That is, to take the case of unique reference, if one uses the sentence 'The table is covered with books', it is always presupposed that there is one table that one is referring to—though it may be a table so far unspecified which is to be used on stage, an imagined table, etc., as well as some real table. In short, the use of 'to refer' and 'to exist' and similar expressions changes just as the use of other expressions changes when the sort of discourse which is being conducted shifts. If, then, the ordinary use of these expressions is to be the guide, the account of the connection between the use of these expressions should be given in terms independent of what sort of discourse they are employed in—for this connection *is* independent of the latter, as is shown by the way we ordinarily employ 'refer' and 'there is'.

14

Reference and Referents

Leonard Linsky

I

In discussing the topics of definite descriptions, referring expressions, and proper names, mistakes are made due to a failure to distinguish referring and making a reference, in the ordinary meanings of these terms, from what philosophers call "denoting", and "referring". Of first importance here is the consideration that it is the users of language who refer and make references and not, except in a derivative sense, the expressions which they use in so doing. Ryle, for example, says, "A descriptive phrase is not a proper name, and the way in which the subject of attributes which it denotes is denoted by it is not in that subject's being *called* 'the so-and-so', but in its possessing and being *ipso facto* the sole possessor of the idiosyncratic attribute which is what the descriptive phrase signifies."[1] I do not wish to deny that what Ryle says here is true, in his technical sense of "denote". The example is chosen only to bring out how different this sense is from what we ordinarily understand by referring. I might, for example, refer to someone as "the old man with grey hair". Still, the phrase "the old

Reprinted with the kind permission of the author and the publisher from C. E. Caton, ed., *Philosophy and Ordinary Language* (Urbana: University of Illinois Press, 1962), pp. 74–89.

[1] "Systematically Misleading Expressions," reprinted in *Essays on Logic and Language*, ed. Antony Flew (New York, 1951), p. 23.

man with grey hair" does not "signify" an "idiosyncratic attribute", if what is meant by this is an attribute belonging to just *one* person. It is equally obvious that I might refer to a person as "the so-and-so" even though that person did not possess the attribute (idiosyncratic or not) "signified" by that phrase. I might, for example, refer to someone as "the old man with grey hair", even though that person was not old but prematurely grey. In both cases I would be referring to someone not "denoted" (in Ryle's sense) by the expression used in so doing. But these *expressions* do not refer to that person, I do. The question "To whom does the phrase 'the so-and-so' refer?" is, in general, an odd question. What might be asked is "Who is the president of the United States?" or "To whom are you referring?" not "To whom does the phrase 'the president of the United States' refer?"

The question "To whom (what) does the phrase 'the so-and-so' refer?" is generally odd. It is not always odd. Certainly it sounds odder in some cases than in others. I think one might ask, "To what does the phrase 'the morning star' refer?" or, pointing to a written text, I might ask, "To whom is the author referring with the phrase 'the most influential man in Lincoln's cabinet'?" But, in speaking about referring, philosophers have written as though one might sensibly ask such questions in an unlimited number of cases. What else could have caused Russell to say in "On Denoting," "A phrase may denote ambiguously; e.g., 'a man' denotes not many men, but an ambiguous man"?[2]

It is of course perfectly true that one can ask, "To whom does the pronoun 'he' refer?" if one is oneself referring to a particular passage in a text, or to something which has just been said. But it does not follow that one can ask this question *apart* from such a context. Clearly, the question "To whom does 'he' refer?" is a senseless question unless such a context is indicated. The same is true of Russell's example, "a man". It is senseless to ask, "To whom does 'a man' refer?" or (using Russell's term) "Whom does 'a man' denote?" But even when the context is clearly indicated this question does not *always* make sense. If, for example, I tell you that I need a wife, you can hardly ask me, "To whom are you referring?"

Failure clearly to mark these distinctions leads to confusions about uniqueness of reference. Russell says that a definite description "will

[2] "On Denoting," reprinted in *Readings in Philosophical Analysis*, ed. H. Feigl and W. Sellars (New York, 1949), p. 103.

only have an application in the event of there being one so-and-so and no more."[3] But can I not refer to someone as "the old madman" even though he is not mad and more than one man is? Does my phrase not have "application" to the one to whom I am referring? Certainly I was speaking of him. What is usually said here is that uniqueness of reference is secured by making the description more determinate, for example by saying, "The old man who lives next door". But this attempt to secure uniqueness of reference through increased determination of the "referring expression" is otiose, for what secures uniqueness is the user of the expression and the context in which it is used *together* with the expression.

We may now notice Ryle's futile attempt to get uniqueness of reference somehow guaranteed by the words themselves. "Tommy Jones is not the same person as the king of England" means, Ryle says, what is meant by: "(1) Somebody, and—of an unspecified circle—one person only is called Tommy Jones; (2) Somebody, and one person only has royal power in England; and (3) No one both is called Tommy Jones and is king of England." But surely when I say "Tommy Jones is not king of England" I am not claiming that exactly one person of any circle is named "Tommy Jones". What is indeed necessary, if I am to make a definite assertion, is not that one person only be named "Tommy Jones", but that I be referring to just one person, however many others there may be with the same name as his. It is a mistake to think that the "referring expression" itself can secure and guarantee this uniqueness. This is obvious in the case of proper names, for here we cannot appeal to meaning. "Tommy Jones" does not have a meaning, and many people share it. Proper names are usually (rather) common names.

Ryle's account makes it appear that it is an intrinsic characteristic of certain groups of words that they denote something or other. They possess this characteristic in virtue of their "signifying an idiosyncratic attribute". Perhaps he is thinking of such an expression as "the oldest American university". It is a matter of fact that the oldest American university is Harvard. But nothing prevents one from referring to another school (by mistake, or in jest) with these words.

Perhaps Ryle has confused referring to something with referring to it correctly as this or that. I might, for example, refer to L. W. in say-

3 *Principia Mathematica*, I (Cambridge, 1910), p. 30.

ing, "He is the president of the bank." Still, I would have referred to him incorrectly as the president of the bank, because he is not the president of the bank, but the vice-president. Some of what Ryle says will be correct if we interpret his comments about denoting as giving an account of what it is to refer to something *correctly* as such-and-such. But it is, after all, possible to refer to something incorrectly as such-and-such, and that is still to refer to it. Furthermore, for one to refer correctly to something as "the such-and-such" it is not necessary that the thing referred to be the sole possessor of the "property signified" by the phrase, though it must certainly have that property. Conversely we can say that it is not necessary that the property "signified" by a phrase of the form "the such-and-such" be "idiosyncratic" if one is to refer to something correctly as "the such-and-such".

II

The question "To whom (what) does the phrase 'the so-and-so' refer?" is generally odd. But it is not always odd. I am arguing that the sense in which expressions (as opposed to speakers) can be said to refer to things is derivative. I mean by this that the question "To whom (what) does the phrase 'the so-and-so' refer?" means the same as the question with regard to some person, "To whom (what) is that person referring with the phrase 'the so-and-so'?" Where the question cannot be so rephrased, it cannot be asked at all, for example, "To whom does the pronoun 'he' refer?", "To whom does the phrase 'the old man' refer?"

Much of the philosophical discussion of this topic has assumed that this was not so. Russell says that a denoting phrase is such "solely in virtue of its form". Thus we should be able to ask, "To whom does the phrase 'the tallest man in the prison' refer?" for the denoting phrase here is of the same form as "The Sultan of Swat" and this phrase can be said to refer to someone, namely Babe Ruth. But the first question cannot be asked. The second question, "To whom does the phrase 'The Sultan of Swat' refer?", does not require a special context and is not the same question as the one which asks with regard to some person, "To whom was he referring with that phrase?" For clearly this last question might receive a different answer than the first. This would occur if the speaker in question had erroneously been referring to Mickey Mantle. So the question "To whom does 'the so-and-so' refer?" seems not always to be the same question as the one with regard to some person, "To whom was he referring with the phrase 'the so-and-so'?"

I am claiming that the counter examples are only apparent and that the general thesis is still true. There is a class of expressions which (to use Strawson's happy description) have grown capital letters. Some examples are "The Sultan of Swat", "The Morning Star", "The City of the Angels". One can ask, "To what city does the phrase 'The City of Angels' refer?" The answer is, "Los Angeles". Such expressions are on their way to becoming names, for example "The Beast of Belsen". They are what a thing or person is called often and repeatedly, and that is why one can ask to what they refer. Philosophers were perhaps concentrating on such examples as these when they said or implied that the question "To whom (what) does the 'so-and-so' refer?" can always be asked. But it cannot.

Perhaps another source of this mistake derives from a confusion between meaning and referring. One can ask both "What does this phrase mean?" and "Whom do you mean?" Also, "I referred to so-and-so" and "I meant so-and-so" seem very close indeed. But these verbs are radically different, as can be seen from the following considerations. One can ask, "Why did you refer to him?" but not "Why did you mean him?" One can say, "Don't refer to him!" but not "Don't mean him!" "How often did you refer to him?" is a sensible question, but "How often did you mean him?" is not. One can ask, "Why do you refer to him as the such-and-such?" but not "Why do you mean him as the such-and-such?" I can ask why you refer to him at all, but not why you mean him at all. The verb "to mean" has noncontinuous present tense forms, for example, "I mean you", but it lacks the present progressive tense form, "I am meaning you". The verb "to refer" has a present progressive form, "I am referring to you", as well as a noncontinuous present form, "I refer to Adlai Stevenson".

What these grammatical considerations show is that referring to someone is an action; meaning someone is not an action. As an action it can be right or wrong for one to perform. Thus it can be wrong of you to refer to someone, but not wrong of you to mean someone. It can be important or necessary that you should refer to someone, but not important or necessary that you should mean someone. One can intend to refer to someone, but not intend to mean him.

III

In discussions of statements such as "Edward VII is the king of England", it is sometimes said that in making them one is referring to the same person twice. Frege would say that the person is referred to in different ways each time. This way of looking at them leads to their interpretation as identities. But consider the following conversation to see how odd it is to talk of referring twice to the same person in such contexts:

> A: He is the king of England.
> B: To whom are you referring?
> A: That man behind the flag.
> B: How many times did you refer to him?

Referring to someone several times during the course of a speech would be a rather different sort of thing. If I mention a man's name, I would not ordinarily be said to have referred to him in so doing. Using a man's name is in some ways opposed to referring to him rather than an instance of it.

If we assume that whenever in an assertion something is mentioned by name by a speaker, he is referring to that thing, certain very paradoxical conclusions can be deduced. It would follow that when I write in my paper "I am not, of course, referring to Ludwig Wittgenstein", I would be referring to Ludwig Wittgenstein. But if someone were asked to show where in my paper I had referred to Ludwig Wittgenstein, it would be absurd for him to point to the statement in which I say, "I am not referring to Ludwig Wittgenstein". The same would be true of the statement in which I say, "I am referring to Ludwig Wittgenstein". If it were asked where in my paper I had referred to Ludwig Wittgenstein, it would be absurd to point to the statement in which I say, "I am referring to Ludwig Wittgenstein". In both cases I would have used Wittgenstein's name. Therefore, to mention someone by name is not necessarily to refer to him. And consider this example. Suppose the porter at Magdalen College asks me whom I am looking for. I answer, "Gilbert Ryle". Would anyone say I had referred to Gilbert Ryle? But if I say, in the course of a talk, "I am not referring to the most important of present-day philosophers", I would then and there be referring to Ludwig Wittgenstein; though in saying, as I just did, "I would then and there be referring to Ludwig Wittgenstein", I could not be said to have referred to Ludwig Wittgenstein. And this is so notwithstanding the fact that Ludwig Wittgenstein is the most important of present-day philosophers. This then is the paradox of reference. In saying "I am referring to Ludwig Wittgenstein" I am not referring to Ludwig Wittgenstein.[4]

Some of the statements which have been counted as identities cannot be interpreted as such. Suppose I explain to my confused son, "Charles de Gaulle is *not* the king of France". That this statement is not an identity can be shown as follows. From $a \neq b$, it follows that $b \neq a$, but from "Charles de Gaulle is *not* the king of France" it does not follow that "The king of France is *not* Charles de Gaulle". The first of these statements is true while the second is neither true nor false. The reason for this is not, as is sometimes said, that I have failed to refer in saying, "The king of France . . .". The reason is that France is not a monarchy and there is no king of France. Just so, and said of a spinster that "Her husband is kind to her" is neither true nor false. But a speaker might very well be referring to someone in using these words, for he may think that someone is the husband of the lady (who in fact is a spinster). Still, the statement is neither true nor false, for it presupposes that the lady has a husband, which she has not. This last refutes Strawson's thesis that if the presupposition of existence is not satisfied, the speaker has failed to refer. For here that presupposition is false, but still the speaker has referred to someone, namely, the man mistakenly taken to be her husband.

Of course a man may "fail to refer", but not as Strawson uses this expression. For example, in your article you may fail to refer to my article.

IV

Now it is, of course, the case that on the analysis of propositions containing descriptive phrases proposed by Russell, the proposition "The king of France is not Charles de Gaulle" is not an identity. The reason he gives for this is entirely different from the reason which I have just given. According to Russell, this proposition is an existential generalization which, however, contains an identity proposition as a part. In

---

[4] Philosophical tradition sanctions the production of such paradoxes. I am thinking of Meinong's paradox about Objects of which it is true to say that no such objects exist; and Frege's paradox that the concept *horse* is not a concept.

fact, on Russell's view, our proposition has two possible interpretations according as the descriptive phrase is considered to have what he calls "primary occurrence" or "secondary occurrence" in the whole proposition of which it is a part. Another way of putting this is to say that "The king of France is not Charles de Gaulle" has two analyses on Russell's view, depending upon whether the negation in the proposition is viewed as being an inner negation or an outer negation. In the first interpretation it would be of the form:

$$(1) \qquad [(\imath x)(\phi x)]\{\sim\psi(\imath x)(\phi x)\}.$$

On the second interpretation our proposition would be of the form:

$$(2) \qquad \sim\{[(\imath x)(\phi x)](\psi(\imath x)(\phi x))\}.$$

On either interpretation, and against Strawson, the proposition "The king of France is not Charles de Gaulle" has a truth-value. On the first interpretation (1) it is false and on the second interpretation (2) it is true.

For this reason I find both interpretations objectionable. But I should now like to present reasons in support of the claim that Russell's analysis of propositions containing definite descriptions is mistaken and that in fact it cannot at all do the job it was designed to do. It does not provide a solution for Russell's famous puzzle about George IV and the author of *Waverley*. What puzzled Russell was why one could not conclude from the premise that George IV wished to know whether Scott was the author of *Waverley* that George IV wished to know whether Scott was Scott, since Scott was the author of *Waverley*. The solution proposed by Russell says that the inference to "George IV wished to know whether Scott was Scott" from "George IV wished to know whether Scott was the author of *Waverley*" is not warranted because this latter proposition, when properly analyzed, contains no constituent definite description for which we may substitute "Scott".

Now there are two ways (and only two ways) in which a descriptive phrase may be eliminated from a proposition and there are good reasons against accepting either of the resulting interpretations. In the first way we interpret "George IV wished to know whether Scott was the author of *Waverley*" as being of the form:

$$(3) \qquad [(\imath x)(\phi x)]\{\psi(\imath x)(\phi x)\},$$

and the result of the elimination of the descriptive phrase is:

(4) $\qquad (\exists c)[(x)((\phi x) \equiv (x=c)) \,\&\, (\psi c)].$

In the second way we interpret our proposition as being of the form:

(5) $\qquad X\{\psi(\imath x)(\phi x)\},$

and the result of the elimination is:

(6) $\qquad X\{(\exists c)[(x)((\phi x) \equiv (x=c)) \,\&\, (\psi c)]\}.$

Interpreted as (4) our proposition would be:

(7) One and only one person wrote *Waverley* and George IV wished to know whether that individual was Scott.

Interpreted as (6) our proposition reads:

(8) George IV wished to know whether one and only one individual wrote *Waverley* and whether that individual was Scott.

And now for the reasons for rejecting *both* interpretations. First let us consider (7). This is the interpretation which accords the definite description a primary occurrence. The trouble with this is that on this interpretation it really does follow from the other premises that George IV wished to know whether Scott was Scott. This last is of the form ψb. The proposition that Scott is the author of *Waverley* is of the form $b=(\imath x)(\phi x)$. From this, together with the other premise which is of the form $\psi(\imath x)(\phi x)$, we get our unwanted conclusion. The argument on this interpretation becomes a straightforward substitution instance of a theorem of *Principia Mathematica*:

14.15 $\qquad \{(\imath x)(\phi x)=b\} \to \{\psi(\imath x)(\phi x) \equiv \psi b\}.$

Another queer consequence of the interpretation (7) is that if "George IV wished to know whether Scott was the author of *Waverley*" is given that analysis, it follows from it that *Waverley* was not co-authored. But it is obvious that this does not in fact follow and therefore the interpretation (7) is unsatisfactory. But what is the proof that this queer consequence does thus follow from this interpretation? (7) is of the form (4). (4) is an existentially generalized conjunction so that we can distribute the existential quantifier to each of the conjuncts. Now simplifying we get:

(9) $\qquad (\exists c)\{(x)[(\phi x) \equiv (x=c)]\}.$

But (9) by the definition 14.02 of *Principia* is:

(10) $E!(\imath x)(\phi x).$

Consistently with the interpretation we have supplied for the variables above, this says,

(11) One and only one person wrote *Waverley*.

From (11) it follows that *Waverley* was not co-authored.

Let us now turn to the alternative interpretation, which accords a secondary occurrence to "the author of *Waverley*" in the proposition "George IV wished to know whether Scott was the author of *Waverley*". This is our (8). But it is obvious that (8) does not mean the same as our proposition, for what (8) says is that George IV wanted to know both whether one and only one individual wrote *Waverley and* whether, if so, Scott was that individual. But surely from the proposition that George IV wished to know whether Scott was the author of *Waverley* it does not follow that George IV wished to know whether or not *Waverley* was either not written at all or written by more than one person. It is entirely possible that George IV knew very well that *Waverley* was written by one and only one man, even though he did not know who that man was. Nor can I see that any other English version of (6) can avoid this unwanted result. It follows that neither (6) nor (4) is a possible form of the proposition in question.

V

Referring does not have the omnipresence accorded to it in the philosophical literature. It sounds odd to say that when I say "Santa Claus lives at the North Pole" I am referring to Santa Claus, or that when I say "The round square does not exist" I am referring to the round square. Must I be referring to something? Philosophers ask, "How is it possible to refer to something which does not exist?" But often the examples produced in which we are supposed to do this ("Hamlet was a prince of Denmark", "Pegasus was captured by Bellerophon", "The golden mountain does not exist") are such that the question "To whom (what) are you referring?" simply cannot sensibly arise in connection with them. In these cases, anyway, there is nothing to be explained.

How is it possible to make a true statement about a nonexistent object? For if a statement is to be about something, that thing must exist, otherwise how could the statement mention *it*, or refer to *it*? One cannot refer to or mention nothing, and if a statement cannot be about nothing it must always be about something. Hence, this ancient line of reasoning concludes, it is not possible to say anything true or false about a nonexistent object. It is not even possible to say that it does not exist.

It is this hoary line of argument which, beginning with Plato, has made the topic of referring a problem for philosophers. Still, ancient or not, the reasoning is outrageously bad. Surely here is a case where philosophers really have been seduced and led astray by misleading analogies. I cannot hang a nonexistent man. I can only hang a man. To hang a nonexistent man is not to do any hanging at all. So, by parity of reasoning, to refer to a nonexistent man is not to refer at all. Hence, I cannot say anything about a nonexistent man. One might as well argue that I cannot hunt for deer in a forest where there are no deer, for that would be to hunt for *nothing*.

It must have been philosophical reflections of this genre which prompted Wittgenstein to say in his *Remarks*, "We pay attention to the expressions we use concerning these things; we do not understand them, however, but misinterpret them. When we do philosophy we are like savages, primitive people, who hear the expressions of civilized men, put a false interpretation on them, and then draw queer conclusions from it."[5]

Let us look a bit closer at what it is to talk about things which do not exist. Of course there are a variety of different cases here. If we stick to the kind of case which has figured prominently in philosophy however, this variety can be reduced. What we now have to consider are characters in fiction like Mr. Pickwick; mythological figures like Pegasus; legendary figures like Paul Bunyan; make-believe figures like Santa Claus, and fairy tale figures like Snow White. (And why not add comic strip figures like Pogo?) And do not these characters really exist? Mr. Pickwick really is a character in fiction; Mr. Ryle is not. There really is a figure in Greek mythology whose name is "Pegasus", but none whose name is "Socrates"; and there really is a comic strip character named "Pogo". In talking about these characters I may say things which are true and I may also say things which are not. If I say, for example, that Pogo is a talking elephant, that is just not true. Neither is Pegasus a duck. In talking about these things there is this

5 *Remarks on the Foundations of Mathematics* (Oxford, 1956), p. 39.

matter of getting the facts straight. This is a problem for me; it is not a problem for Dickens or for Walt Kelly. What Dickens says about Mr. Pickwick in *The Pickwick Papers* cannot be false, though it can be not true to character; and in the comic strip, Walk Kelly does not say anything about his possum Pogo, for Pogo talks for himself. Still, Pogo could say something about Walt Kelly (or Charles de Gaulle) and that might not be true.

There is, however, another group of cases discussed by philosophers, and this group has the important characteristic that in talking about its members there is no such thing as getting the facts straight. Here we find Russell's famous example, the present king of France; and Meinong's equally famous example of the golden mountain. What are they supposed to be examples of? Well, just things that do not exist. But in saying this we must keep in mind how different they are from Mr. Pickwick, Santa Claus, Snow White, etc. Keeping this difference in mind we can see that though it makes perfectly good sense to ask whether Mr. Pickwick ran a bookstore, or whether Santa Claus lives at the North Pole, it makes no sense whatever to ask whether the golden mountain is in California. Similarly, though we can ask whether Mr. Pickwick was married or not, *we* cannot sensibly ask whether the present king of France is bald or not.

If the question is "How can we talk about objects which do not exist?" then it is wrong to use the examples of the golden mountain and the present king of France. These famous philosophical examples, the round square, the golden mountain, are just things we do *not* talk about (except in telling a story or a fairy tale or something of the kind). Meinong, Russell, and Ryle all puzzle over sentences such as "The golden mountain is in California", as though one just had to make up one's mind whether to put it in the box with all the other true propositions, or into the box with the other false propositions. They fail to see that one would only utter it in the course of telling a story or the like. It does not occur in isolation from some such larger context. If it did so occur, if someone were just to come up to us and say, "The golden mountain is in California," we would not concern ourselves with truth or falsity, but with this man. What is wrong with him? When the sentence occurs in a fairy tale it would never occur to us to raise the question of its truth. And if we are asked to consider whether it is true or false outside of such a context, we can only say that it does not so occur, we just do not say it.

Of course we may sometimes in error, or by mistake, talk about nonexistent things, for example Hemingway's autobiography. So here is *one* way in which it can occur that we speak of nonexistent objects. As a result of a mistake!

VI

It is said to be an astronomical fact of some importance that

(1)   the morning star = the evening star.

This was not always known but the identification was early made by the Greeks. Frege said that it was because the two expressions, "the morning star" and "the evening star", had the same reference that (1) was true, and because these two had different senses that (1) was not a trivial thing to say.

Frege's way of putting the matter seems to invite the objection that the two expressions, "the morning star" and "the evening star", do not refer to the same thing. For the first refers to the planet Venus when seen in the morning before sunrise. The second refers to the same planet when it appears in the heavens after sunset. Do they refer then to the same "thing"? Is it, as Carnap says,[6] a matter of "astronomical fact" that they do? One wants to protest that it is a matter of "linguistic fact" that they do not.

Perhaps Frege's view is better put if we think of the two expressions as names, that is, "The Morning Star" and "The Evening Star". Thus Quine,[7] in repeating Frege's example but adding capital letters, speaks of the expressions "Evening Star" and "Morning Star" as names. Quine would say that what the astronomers had discovered was that

(2)   The Morning Star = The Evening Star.

This is better, for (1) implies (or presupposes) what (2) does not, that there is only one star in the sky both in the morning and in the evening. Also, a purist might object that it cannot be taken as ground for (1) that Venus is both the morning star and the evening star. Venus is not a star but a planet. It would be wrong to say that what the astronomers discovered was that the morning planet is the evening planet.

[6] *Meaning and Necessity* (Chicago, 1947), p. 119.
[7] *From a Logical Point of View* (Cambridge, Mass., 1953), p. 21.

(2) is free from these criticisms, but still the same protest is in order as was made against (1). The name "The Morning Star" does not refer *simpliciter* to the planet Venus. It does not refer to the planet in the way in which the demonstrative "that" might be used to refer to the planet on some occasion. The names "The Morning Star" and "The Evening Star" are not that sort of "referring expression".

It would be incorrect for me to say to my son as he awakens, "Look to the place where the sun is rising and you will see The Evening Star", for that is not what the star is called when seen in the east before sunrise. Again, the proposal that we stay up until we see The Evening Star is quite a different proposal from the proposal that we stay up until we see The Morning Star. In dealing with failures of substitutivity in some ways like these, Frege developed his concept of "oblique" (*ungerade*) discourse, and Quine has talked about "referential opacity". Names in oblique contexts, according to Frege, do not have their "ordinary" referents but an oblique referent which is the same as their ordinary sense. But it would be absurd to suggest that when I tell my boy that if he looks to the east on arising he will see The Evening Star, I am not referring to a planet but to a "sense", whatever that might be. Using Quine's notion of referential opacity, one might suggest that the reason why the proposal to wait up until we see The Evening Star is a different proposal from the proposal to wait up until we see The Morning Star is that here the context is referentially opaque, so that the two names in these contexts do not refer to anything at all. But surely this result is too paradoxical to be taken seriously, and in any case no one has yet told us how to understand the view that a proposal can be referentially opaque.

Under the entry on "Venus" in the *Encyclopaedia Britannica* we are given the following information: "When seen in the western sky in the evenings, i.e., at its eastern elongations, it was called by the ancients 'Hesperus', and when visible in the mornings, i.e., at its western elongations, 'Phosphorus'." Did the astronomers than discover that

(3)   Hesperus = Phosphorus?

In the entry under "Hesperus" in Smith's *Smaller Classical Dictionary* we read, "Hesperus, the evening star, son of Astraeus and Eos, of Cephalus and Eos, or of Atlas." From this, together with (3), we are able to get by Leibniz's Law,

(4)   Phosphorus is the evening star.

And avoiding unnecessary complications, let us interpret this as meaning

(5)   Phosphorus is The Evening Star.

Any competent classicist knows that this is not true.

Under the entry on "Phosphorus" in Smith's *Smaller Classical Dictionary* we find, "Lucifer or Phosphorus ('bringer of light'), is the name of the planet Venus, when seen in the morning before sunrise. The same planet was called Hesperus, Vespergo, Vesper, Noctifer, or Nocturnus, when it appeared in the heavens after sunset. Lucifer as a personification is called a son of Astraeus and Aurora or Eos; of Cephalus and Aurora, or of Atlas." So the stars were personified, and it seems to be a matter of mythology that

(6)   Hesperus is not Phosphorus.

Then did the astronomers discover that the mythologists were wrong?

Of course (3) is false and no astronomical research could have established it. What could we make of the contention that the Greeks mistakenly believed that Hesperus was not Phosphorus? According to the *Encyclopaedia Britannica* (under "Hesperus"), "... the two stars were early identified by the Greeks." But once identification was made, what was left to be mistaken about here?

Could not one mistake The Evening Star for The Morning Star? Certainly one could. This would involve mistaking evening for morning. One could do this. In the morning it is just getting light and in the evening it is just getting dark. Imagine someone awaking from a sleep induced by a soporific. "But there aren't *two* stars so how *could* one be mistaken for the other?"

Hence, though it is sometimes made to look as though the Greeks were victims of a mistaken astronomical belief, this is not so. And Quine suggests that the true situation was "probably first established by some observant Babylonian." If that is the case, a knowing Greek would not have said

(7)   The Morning Star is not The Evening Star

unless, of course, he were in the process of teaching his child the *use* of these words. And, drawing on his unwillingness to say (7) (except in special circumstances when he might want to say just that), we might push him into saying that The Morning Star is The Evening

Star, and even that Hesperus is Phosphorus, though now he would begin to feel that these sayings were queer.

The moral is that if we allow ourselves no more apparatus than the apparatus of proper names and descriptions, sense and reference, and the propositional function "$x=y$", we just cannot give an undistorted account of what the astronomers discovered, or about Hesperus and Phosphorus. Only the logician's interest in formulas of the kind "$x=y$" could lead him to construct such sentences as "The Morning Star = The Evening Star" or "Hesperus = Phosphorus". Astronomers and mythologists don't put it that way.[8]

[8] The whole of Part VI of this essay has previously been published under the title "Hesperus and Phosphorus," in *The Philosophical Review*, 68 (October, 1959): 4.

15

Identifying Reference and Truth-Values

P. F. Strawson

THE materials for this paper are: one familiar and fundamental speech-function; one controversy in philosophical logic; and two or three platitudes.

We are to be concerned with statements in which, at least ostensibly, some particular historical fact or event or state of affairs, past or present, notable or trivial, is reported: as that the emperor has lost a battle or the baby has lost its rattle or the emperor is dying or the baby is crying. More exactly, we are to be concerned with an important subclass of such statements, viz. those in which the task of specifying just the historical state of affairs which is being reported includes, as an essential part, the sub-task of designating some particular historical item or items which the state of affairs involves. Not all performances of the reporting task include the performance of this sub-task—the task, I shall call it, of identifying reference to a particular item. Thus, the report that it is raining now, or the report that it was raining here an hour ago, do not. But the statement that Caesar is dying, besides specifying the historical fact or situation which it is the function of the statement as a whole to report, has, as a part of this function, the sub-function of designating a particular historical item, viz. Caesar, which that situation essentially involves. And this part of the function of the

Reprinted with the kind permission of the author and the editor from *Theoria*, 30 (1964): 96–118.

whole statement is the whole of the function of part of the statement, viz. of the name 'Caesar'.

The speech-function we are to be concerned with, then, is the function of *identifying reference* to a particular historical item, when such reference occurs as a sub-function of statement. We are to be concerned with it in relation to a particular point of philosophical controversy, viz. the question whether a radical failure in the performance of this function results in a special case of falsity in statement or, rather, in what Quine calls a truth-value gap. The hope is not to show that one party to this dispute is quite right and the other quite wrong. The hope is to exhibit speech-function, controversy and one or two platitudes in a mutually illuminating way.

I introduce now my first pair, a complementary pair, of platitudes. One, perhaps the primary, but not of course the only, purpose of assertive discourse is to give information to an audience of some kind, viz. one's listener or listeners or reader or readers. Since there is no point in, or perhaps one should say no possibility of, informing somebody of something of which he is already apprised, the making of an assertive utterance or statement—where such an utterance has in view this primary purpose of assertion—implies a presumption (on the part of the speaker) of ignorance (on the part of the audience) of some point to be imparted in the utterance. This platitude might be called the Principle of the Presumption of Ignorance. It is honoured to excess in some philosophical proposals for analysis or reconstruction of ordinary language, proposals which might appear to be based on the different and mistaken Principle of the Presumption of Total Ignorance. To guard against such excess, we need to emphasise a platitude complementary to the first. It might be called the Principle of the Presumption of Knowledge. The substance of this complementary platitude, loosely expressed, is that when an empirically assertive utterance is made with an informative intention, there is usually or at least often a presumption (on the part of the speaker) of knowledge (in the possession of the audience) of empirical facts relevant to the particular point to be imparted in the utterance. This is *too* loosely expressed. The connexion between the presumption of knowledge and the intention to impart just such-and-such a particular point of information may be closer than that of customary association; the connexion between the *identity* of the particular point it is intended to impart and the kind of knowledge presumed may be closer than that of relevance. Just as we might say that it could not be true of a speaker that he intended to *inform* an audience of some particular point unless he presumed their ignorance of that point, so we might often say that it could not be true of a speaker that he intended to inform the audience of just *that* particular point unless he presumed in his audience certain empirical knowledge. So the second principle, in which I am mainly interested, is truly complementary to the first.

Now this may sound a little mysterious. But at least there will be no difficulty felt in conceding the general and vague point that we do constantly presume knowledge as well as ignorance on the part of those who are the audiences of our assertive utterances, and that the first kind of presumption, as well as the second, bears importantly on our choice of what we say. The particular application that I want to make of this general point is to the case of identifying reference. To make it, I must introduce the not very abstruse notion of identifying knowledge of particulars.

Everyone has knowledge of the existence of various particular things each of which he is able, in one sense or another, though not necessarily in every sense, to distinguish from all other things. Thus a person may be able to pick a thing out in his current field of perception. Or he may know there is a thing (not in his current field of perception) to which a certain description applies which applies to no other thing: such a description I shall call an *identifying description*. Or he may know the name of a thing and be able to recognise it when he encounters it, even if he can normally give no identifying description of it other than one which incorporates its own name. If a man satisfies any one of these conditions in respect of a certain particular, I shall say he has identifying knowledge of that particular. One is bound to define such a notion in terms of its outlying cases, cases, here, of minimal and relatively isolated identifying knowledge. So it is worth emphasizing that, in contrast with cases of minimal and relatively isolated identifying knowledge, there are hosts of cases of very rich and full identifying knowledge, and that, in general, our identifying knowledge of particulars forms an immensely complex web of connexions and relations—the web, one might say, of our historical and geographical knowledge in general, granted that these adjectives are not to be construed as qualifying academic subjects alone, but also knowledge of the most unpretentious kind about the particular things and people which enter into our minute-to-minute or day-to-day transactions with the world.

The notion of identifying reference is to be understood in close relation to the notion of identifying knowledge. When people talk to each other they commonly and rightly assume a large community of identifying knowledge of particular items. Very often a speaker knows or assumes that a thing of which he has such knowledge is also a thing of which his audience has such knowledge. Knowing or assuming this, he may wish to state some particular fact regarding such a thing, e.g. that it is thus-and-so; and he will then normally include in this utterance an expression which he regards as adequate, in the circumstances of utterance, to indicate to the audience *which* thing it is, of all the things in the scope of the audience's identifying knowledge, that he is declaring to be thus-and-so. The language contains expressions of several celebrated kinds which are peculiarly well adapted, in different ways, for use with this purpose. These kinds include proper names, definite and possessive and demonstrative descriptions, demonstrative and personal pronouns. I do not say that *all* expressions of these kinds are well adapted for use with this purpose; nor do I say, of those that are, that they are not regularly used in other ways, with other purposes.

When an expression of one of these classes *is* used in this way, I shall say that it is used to *invoke* identifying knowledge known or presumed to be in possession of an audience. It would now be easy to define identifying reference so that only when an expression is used to invoke identifying knowledge is it used to perform the function of identifying reference. But though it would simplify exposition thus to restrict attention to what we shall in any case count as the central cases of identifying reference, it would not be wholly desirable. For there are cases which cannot exactly be described as cases of invoking identifying knowledge, but which are nevertheless sufficiently like cases which *can* be so described to be worth classifying with them as cases of identifying reference. For instance, there may be within a man's current field of possible perception something which he has not noticed and cannot be said actually to have discriminated there, but to which his attention may be intentionally drawn simply by the use, on the part of a speaker, of an expression of one of the kinds I mentioned, as part of a statement of some fact regarding the particular item in question. In so far as the speaker's intention, in using the expression in question, is not so much to *inform* the audience of the existence of some particular item unique in a certain respect as to bring it about that the audience *sees for itself* that there is such an item, we may think this case worth classifying with the central cases of identifying reference. Again, there are cases in which an audience cannot exactly be credited wih *knowledge* of the existence of a certain item unique in a certain respect, but can be credited with a strong *presumption* to this effect, can be credited, we might say, with *identifying presumption* rather than identifying knowledge. Such presumed presumption can be invoked in the same style as such knowledge can be invoked.

So we may allow the notion of identifying reference to a particular item to extend beyond the cases of invoking identifying knowledge. We must then face the unsurprising consequence that if, as we do, we wish to contrast cases in which a speaker uses an expression to perform the function of identifying reference with cases in which the intention and effect of a speaker's use of an expression is to inform the audience of the existence of a particular item unique in a certain respect, then we shall encounter some cases which do not *clearly* belong to either of these contrasting classes, which seem more or less dubious candidates for both. But this is not a situation which should cause us embarrassment, in philosophy; and, having made the point, I shall for simplicity's sake speak in what follows as if all cases of identifying reference were, at least in intention, cases of invoking identifying knowledge.

What I have said so far, in describing the function of identifying reference is, I think, uncontroversial in the sense that the description has proceeded without my having to take up a position on any well-worn point of controversy. It has a consequence, just alluded to, which should be equally uncontroversial, and which I shall labour a little now, partly in order to distinguish it from any *prise de position* on a matter which is undoubtedly one of controversy.

I have explained identifying reference—or the central case of identifying reference—as essentially involving a presumption, on the speaker's part, of the possession by the audience of identifying knowledge of a particular item. Identifying knowledge is knowledge of the existence of a particular item distinguished, in one or another sense, by the audience from any other. The appropriate stretch of identifying knowledge is to be invoked by the use of an expression deemed adequate by the speaker, in the total circumstances of utterance, to indicate to the audience which, of all the items within the scope of the audience's identifying knowledge, is being declared, in the utterance as a whole, to be thus-and-so. Depending upon the nature of the item and the situation of utterance, the expression used may be a name or a pronoun or a definite or demonstrative description; and it is of course not necessary that either name or description should in general be *uniquely* applicable to the item in question, so long as its choice, in the total circumstances of utterance, is deemed adequate to indicate to the audience which, of all the particular items within the scope of his identifying knowledge, is being declared, in the utterance as a whole, to be thus-and-so.

Now one thing that is absolutely clear is that it can be no part of the speaker's intention in the case of such utterances to *inform* the audience of the *existence* of a particular item bearing the name or answering to the description and distinguished by that fact, or by that fact plus something else known to the audience, from any other. On the contrary, the very task of identifying reference, as described, can be undertaken only by a speaker who knows or presumes his audience to be already in possession of such knowledge of existence and uniqueness as this. The task of identifying reference is *defined* in terms of a type of speaker-intention which *rules out* ascription to the speaker of the intention to impart the existence-and-uniqueness information in question. All this can be put, perfectly naturally, in other ways. Thus, that there exists a particular item to which the name or description is applicable and which, if not unique in this respect, satisfies some uniqueness-condition known to the hearer (*and* satisfies some uniqueness-condition known to the speaker) is no part of what the speaker *asserts* in an utterance in which the name or description is used to perform the function of identifying reference; it is, rather, a *presupposition* of his asserting what he asserts.

This way of putting it is still uncontroversial. For it is a natural way of putting what is itself uncontroversial. But it introduces a contrast, between the *asserted* and the *presupposed*, in words which are associated with an issue of controversy.

We can come at this issue by considering some of the ways in which an attempt to perform the function of identifying reference can either fail altogether or at least fall short of complete success and satisfactoriness. There are several ways in which such an attempt can fail or be flawed. For instance, it may be that though the speaker possesses, the audience does not possess, identifying knowledge of the particular historical item to which the speaker intends to make an identifying reference; that the speaker credits the audience with identifying knowledge the audience does not possess. It may be that though the audience possesses identifying knowledge of the particular item in question, the expression chosen by the speaker fails to invoke the appropriate stretch of identifying knowledge and leaves the audience uncertain, or even misleads the audience, as to who or what is meant. Failures of this kind may be, though they need not be, due to flaws of another kind. For it may be that the speaker's choice of expression reflects mistakes of fact or language on his part; and such mistake-reflecting choices are still flaws, even where they do not mislead, as, for example, references to Great Britain as 'England' or to President Kennedy as 'the U. S. Premier' are not likely to mislead.

Though these are all cases of flawed or failed reference, they are not cases of the most radical possible kind of failure. For my descriptions of these cases imply that at least one fundamental condition of success is fulfilled, even if others are not fulfilled. They imply at least that there *is* a particular historical item within the scope of the speaker's identifying knowledge—even if not all his beliefs about it are true—such that he intends, by suitable choice of expression, to invoke identifying knowledge, presumed by him to be in possession of the audience, of that item. But this condition might fail too; and that in various ways. It might be that there just is no such particular item at all as the speaker takes himself to be referring to, that what he, and perhaps the audience too, take to be identifying knowledge of a particular item is not knowledge at all, but completely false belief. This is but one case of what might uncontroversially be called radical failure of the existence presupposition of identifying reference. It involves no moral turpitude on the part of the speaker. Different would be the case in which the speaker uses an expression, by the way of apparently intended identifying reference, to invoke what he knows or thinks the audience thinks to be identifying knowledge, though he, the speaker, knows it to be false belief. The speaker in this case can have no intention actually to refer to a particular historical item, and so cannot strictly fail to carry out *that* intention. He can have the intention to be *taken* to have the former intention; and in *this* intention he may succeed. A full treatment of the subject would call for careful consideration of such differences. For simplicity's sake, I shall ignore the case of pretence, and concentrate on that case of radical reference-failure in which the failure is not a moral one.

Our point of controversy concerns the following question: given an utterance which suffers from radical reference-failure, are we to say that what we have here is just one special case of false statement or are we to say that our statement suffers from a deficiency so radical as to deprive it of the chance of being either true or false? Of philosophers who have discussed this question in recent years some have plumped uncompromisingly for the first answer, some uncompromisingly for the second; some have been eclectic about it, choosing the first answer for some cases and the second for others; and some have simply contented themselves with sniping at any doctrine that was offered, while wisely refraining from exposing any target themselves. In virtue of his Theory of Descriptions and his views on ordinary proper names as being condensed descriptions, Russell might be said to be the patron of the first party—the "special case of false statement" party. One recent explicit adherent of that party is Mr. Dummett in his interesting article on *Truth* (*P.A.S.* 58–59). The second party—the "neither true nor false" party—might be said, with some reservations, to have included Quine, Austin and myself. Quine invented the excellent phrase 'truth-value gap' to characterise what we have in these cases (See *Word and Object*). Austin (see *Performative Utterances* and *How to Do Things with Words*) contrasts this sort of deficiency or, as he calls it, 'infelicity' in statement with straightforward falsity and prefers to say that a statement suffering from this sort of deficiency is void—'void for lack of reference'.

Let us ignore the eclectics and the snipers and confine our attention, at least for the moment, to the two uncompromising parties. I do not think there is any question of demonstrating that one party is quite right and the other quite wrong. What we have here is the familiar philosophical situation of one party being attracted by one simplified, theoretical—or 'straightened out'—concept of truth and falsity, and the other by another. It might be asked: How does ordinary usage speak on the point? And this, as always, is a question which it is instructive to ask. But ordinary usage does not deliver a clear verdict for one party or the other. Why should it? The interests which ordinary usage reflects are too complicated and various for it to provide overwhelming support for either way of *simplifying* the picture. The fact that ordinary usage does not deliver a clear verdict does not mean, of course, that there can be no other way of demonstrating, at least, that one view is quite wrong. It might be shown, for example, to be inconsistent, or incoherent in some other way. But this is not the case with either of these views. Each would have a certain amount of explaining and adjusting to do, but each could perfectly consistently be carried through. More important, each is *reasonable*. Instead of trying to demonstrate that one is quite right and the other quite wrong, it is more instructive to see how both are reasonable, how both represent different ways of being impressed by the facts.

As a point of departure here, it is reasonable to take related cases of what are indisputably false statements and then set beside them the disputed case, so that we can see how one party is more impressed by the resemblances, the other by the differences, between the disputed case and the undisputed cases. The relevant undisputed cases are obviously of two kinds. One is that of an utterance in which an identifying reference is successfully made, and all the conditions of a satisfactory or all-round successful act of empirical assertion are fulfilled except that the particular item identifyingly referred to and declared to be thus-and-so is, as a matter of fact, *not* thus-and-so. It is said of Mr. Smith, the new tenant of the Grange, that he is single, when he is in fact married: a statement satisfactory in all respects except that it is, indisputably, false. The other relevant case is that in which an explicit assertion of existence and uniqueness is made. It is said, say, that there is one and not more than one island in Beatitude Bay. And this is false because there is none at all or because there are several.

Now, it might be said on the one side, how vastly different from the ways in which things go wrong in either of these undisputed cases of falsity is the way in which things go wrong in the case of radical reference-failure. A judgment as to truth or falsity is a judgment on what the speaker asserts. But we have already noted the uncontroversial point that the existence-condition which fails in the case of radical reference-failure is not something asserted, but something presupposed, by the speaker's utterance. So his statement cannot be judged as a false existential assertion. Nor, evidently, can it be judged as an assertion false in the same way as the first undisputed example, i.e. false as being a *mis*characterisation of the particular item referred to. For there is no such item for it to be a mischaracterisation of. In general, where there *is* such an item as the speaker refers to, and the speaker asserts, with regard to that item, that it is thus-and-so, his assertion is rightly assessed as true if the item is thus-and-so, as false if it is not. In the case of radical reference-failure, the speaker, speaking in good faith, *means* his statement to be up for assessment in this way; he takes himself similarly to be asserting, with regard to a particular item, that it is thus-and-so. But in fact the conditions of his making an assertion such as he takes himself to be making are not fulfilled. We can acknowledge the character of his intentions and the nature of his speech-performance by saying that he makes a statement; but we must acknowledge, too, the radical character of the way in which his intentions are frustrated by saying that his statement does not qualify as such an assertion as he takes it to be, and hence does not qualify for assessment as such an assertion. But then it does not qualify for truth-or-falsity assessment at all. The whole assertive enterprise is wrecked by the failure of its presupposition.

But now, on the other side, it could be said that what the disputed case has in common with the undisputed cases of falsity is far more important than the differences between them. In all the cases alike, we may take it a genuine empirical statement is made; a form of words is used such that if there were as a matter of fact in the world (in Space and Time) a certain item, or certain items, with certain characteristics —if, to put it differently, certain complex circumstances did as a matter of fact obtain in the world (in Space and Time)—then the statement would be true. The important distinction is between the case in which those complex circumstances do obtain and the case in which they don't. This distinction is the distinction we *should* use the words 'true' and 'false' (of statements) to mark, even if we do not consistently do so. And this distinction can be drawn equally in the disputed and the undisputed cases. A false empirical statement is simply any empirical statement whatever which fails for *factual* reasons, i.e. on account of circumstances in the world being as they are and not otherwise, to be a true one. Cases of radical reference-failure are simply one class of false statements.

It no longer seems to me important to come down on one side or the other in this dispute. Both conceptions are tailored, in the ways I have just indicated, to emphasise different kinds of interest in statement; and each has its own merits. My motives in bringing up the issue are three, two of which have already partially shown themselves. First, I want to disentangle this issue of controversy from other questions with which it is sometimes confused. Second, I want to dispel the illusion that the issue of controversy can be speedily settled, one way or the other, by a brisk little formal argument. Third, I want to indicate one way—no doubt there are more—in which, without positive commitment to either rival theory, we may find the issues they raise worth pursuing and refining. I shall say something on all three points, though most on the third.

First, then, the issue between the truth-value gap theory and the falsity theory, which has loomed so large in this whole area of discussion, has done so in a way which might be misleading, which might give a false impression. The impression might be given that the issue between these two theoretical accounts was the *crucial* issue in the whole area—the key, as it were, to all positions. Thus it might be supposed that anyone who rejected the view that the Theory of Descriptions gives an adequate general analysis, or account of the functioning, of definite descriptions was committed, by that rejection, to uncompromising adherence to the truth-value gap theory and uncompromising rejection of the falsity theory for the case of radical reference-failure. But this is not so at all. The distinction between identifying reference and uniquely existential assertion is something quite undeniable. The sense in which the existence of something answering to a definite description used for the purpose of identifying reference, and its distinguishability by an audience from anything else, is presupposed and not asserted in an utterance containing such an expression, so used, stands absolutely firm, whether or not one opts for the view that radical failure of the presupposition would deprive the statement of a truth-value. It remains a decisive objection to the Theory of Descriptions, regarded as embodying a generally correct analysis of statements containing definite descriptions, that, so regarded, it amounts to a denial of these undeniable distinctions. I feel bound to labour the point a little, since I may be partly responsible for the confusion of these two issues by making the word 'presupposition' carry simultaneously the burden both of the functional distinction and of the truth-value gap theory. Only, at most, partly responsible; for the lineup is natural enough, though not inevitable; and though there is no logical compulsion one way, there is logical compulsion the other. One who accepts the Theory of Descriptions as a correct analysis is bound to accept the falsity theory for certain cases and reject the truth-value gap theory. One who accepts the truth-value gap theory is bound to reject the Theory of Descriptions as a generally correct analysis. But it is perfectly consistent to reject the view that the Theory of Descriptions is a generally correct analysis, on the grounds I have indicated, and also to withhold assent to the truth-value gap theory.

Now for my second point. I have denied that either of the two theories can be decisively refuted by short arguments, and I shall support this by citing and commenting on some specimen arguments which are sometimes thought to have this power. First, some arguments for the truth-value gap theory and against the falsity theory:

A (1) Let *Fa* represent a statement of the kind in question. If the falsity theory is correct, then the contradictory of *Fa* is not -*Fa*, but the disjunction of -*Fa* with a negative existential statement. But the contradictory of *Fa* is -*Fa*. Therefore the falsity theory is false.

(2) If 'false' is used normally, then from *It is false that S is P* it is correct to infer *S is not P*. But it is agreed on both theories that *S is not P* is true only if there is such a thing as *S*. Hence, if 'false' is used normally, *It is false that S is P* is true only if there is such a thing as *S*. Hence, if 'false' is used normally in the statement of the falsity theory, that theory is false.

(3) The question *Is S P?* and the command *Bring it about that S is P* may suffer from exactly the same radical reference-failure as the statement *S is P*. But if an utterance which suffers from this radical reference-failure is thereby rendered false, the question and command must be said to be false. But this is absurd. So the falsity theory is false. Now arguments on the other side:

B (1) Let *Fa* represent a statement of the kind in question (e.g. *The king of France is bald*). Then there may be an equivalent statement, *Gb*, (e.g. *France has a bald king*) which is obviously false if there is no such thing as *a*. But the two statements are equivalent. So *Fa* is false if there is no such thing as *a*. So the truth-value gap theory is false.

(2) Let *P* be a statement which, on the truth-value gap theory, is neither true nor false. Then the statement that *P* is true is itself false. But if it is false that *P* is true, then *P* is false. In the same way we can derive from the hypothesis the conclusion that *P* is true, hence the conclusion that *P* is both true and false. This is self-contradictory, hence the original hypothesis is so too.

The defender of either view will have little difficulty in countering these arguments against it. Thus to B2 the reply is that if a statement lacks a truth-value, any statement assessing it as true *simpliciter* or as false *simpliciter* similarly lacks a truth-value. So no contradiction is derivable. To B1 the reply is that the argument is either inconclusive or question-begging. If 'equivalent' means simply 'such that if either is true, then necessarily the other is true', it is inconclusive. If it also means 'such that if either is false, then necessarily the other is false', it is question-begging. To A3 the reply is that there is no reason why what holds for statements should hold also for questions and commands. To A2 the reply is that the inference is not strictly correct, though it is perfectly natural that we should normally make it. To A1 the reply is that it is question-begging, though again it is perfectly intelligible that we should be prone to think of contradictories in this way.

It is just an illusion to think that either side's position can be carried by such swift little sallies as these. What we have, in the enthusiastic defence of one theory or the other, is a symptom of difference of direction of interest. One who has an interest in actual speech-situations, in the part that stating plays in communication between human beings, will tend to find the simpler falsity theory inadequate and feel sympathy with—though, as I say, he is under no compulsion, exclusively or at all, to embrace—its rival. One who takes a more impersonal view of statement, who has a picture in which the actual needs, purposes and presumptions of speakers and hearers are of slight significance—in which, as it were, there are just statements on the one side and, on the other, the world they should reflect—he will naturally tend to brush aside the truth-value gap theory and embrace *its* simpler rival. For him, one might say, the subject of every statement is just the world in general. For his opponent, it is now this item, now that; and perhaps sometimes—rarely and disconcertingly enough—nothing at all.

And now for the third matter, which we shall find not unconnected with this last thought. It seems to be a fact which advocates of either, or of neither, theory can equally safely acknowledge, that the intuitive appeal, or prima facie plausibility, of the truth-value gap theory is not constant for all example-cases of radical reference-failure which can be produced or imagined. We can, without commitment to either theory, set ourselves to explain this variation in the intuitive appeal of one of them—which is also an inverse variation in the intuitive appeal of the other. The attempt to explain this fact may bring into prominence other facts which bear in interesting ways upon speech-situations in general, and those involving identifying reference in particular. I shall draw attention to but one factor—no doubt there are more—which may contribute to the explanation of this fact in some cases. In doing so, I shall invoke another platitude to set beside, and connect with, the platitudes we already have.

First, we may note that the truth-value gap theory can be expressed, in terms of the familiar idea of predication, in such a way as to secure for it a certain flexibility in application. Let us call an expression *as and when used in a statement with the role of identifying reference*— whether or not it suffers in that use from radical reference-failure—a *referring expression*. Then any statement containing a referring expression, E, can be regarded as consisting of two expression-parts, one the expression E itself, to be called the subject-expression or subject-term, and the other the remainder of the statement, to be called the predicate-expression or predicate-term. In the case of a statement containing more than one, say two, referring expressions, it is to be open to us to cast one of these for the role of subject-expression, while the other is regarded as absorbed into the predicate-term which is attached to the subject-term to yield the statement as a whole. The adherent of the truth-value gap view can then state his view as follows.[1] The statement or predication as a whole is true just in the case in which the predicate-term does in fact apply to (is in fact 'true of') the object which the subject-term (identifyingly) refers to. The statement or predication as a whole is false just in the case where the negation of the predicate-term applies to that object, i.e. the case where the predicate-term can be truthfully denied of that object. The case of radical reference-failure on the part of the subject-term is of neither of these two kinds. It is the case of the truth-value gap.

Now consider a statement consisting of two referring expressions one of which is guilty of reference-failure while the other is not. Then it is open to us to carve up the statement in two different ways; and different decisions as to carving-up procedure may be allowed to result in different assessments of the statement for truth-value. Thus (1) we can see the guilty referring expression as absorbed into a predicate-term which is attached to the innocent referring expression to make up the statement as a whole; or (2) we can see the innocent referring expression as absorbed into a predicate-expression which is attached to the guilty referring expression to make up the statement as a whole. Now if we carve up the statement in the second way, we must say—according to our current statement of the truth-value gap theory —that the statement lacks a truth-value. But if we carve it up in the first way, we *may* say that it is false (or, sometimes—when negative in form—that it is true). For to carve it up in the first way is to think of the statement as made up of the satisfactory or innocent referring expression together with one general term or predicate into which the guilty referring expression has been absorbed. The question whether that predicate does or does not apply to the object referred to by the satisfactory referring expression remains a perfectly answerable question; and the fact that the predicate has absorbed a guilty re-

---

[1] This way of stating it is in fact implicit in the fundamental definition of predication which Quine gives in *Word and Object*, p. 96.

ferring expression will, for most predicates affirmative in form, merely have the consequence that the right answer is 'No'. Thus, if we look at such a statement in this way, we can naturally enough declare it false or untrue, and naturally enough affirm its *negation* as true, on the strength of the reference-failure of the guilty referring expression.

In this way, it might seem, the truth-value gap theory can readily modify itself to take account of certain examples which may seem intuitively unfavourable to it. For example, there is no king of France; and there is, let us say, no swimming-pool locally. But there is, let us say, an Exhibition in town; and there is, let us say, no doubt of Jones' existence. If we consider the statements

(1) that Jones spent the morning at the local swimming-pool and
(2) that the Exhibition was visited yesterday by the king of France

it may seem natural enough to say (1) that it is quite untrue, or is false, that Jones spent the morning at the local swimming-pool, since there isn't one; that, however Jones spent the morning, he did *not* spend it at the local swimming-pool, since there's no such place; and similarly (2) that it is quite untrue, or is false, that the Exhibition was visited yesterday by the king of France; that, whoever the Exhibition was visited by yesterday, it was *not* visited by the king of France, since there is no such person. And the modified truth-value gap theory accommodates these intuitions by allowing the guilty referring expressions, 'the local swimming-pool', 'the king of France', to be absorbed into the predicate in each case.

This modification to the truth-value gap theory, though easy and graceful, will scarcely seem adequate. For one thing, it will not be available for all intuitively unfavourable examples, but only for those which contain more than one referring expression. For another, it will remain incomplete inside its own domain unless some *principle of choice* between alternative ways of carving up a statement is supplied. The theory might resolve the latter question self-sacrificially, by declaring that the carving-up operation was always to be so conducted as to permit the assignment of a truth-value whenever possible. But this move might be too self-sacrificial, turning friends into enemies, turning intuitively favourable cases into unfavourable ones.

So let us consider further. Confronted with the classical example, "The king of France is bald", we may well feel it natural to say, straight off, that the question whether the statement is true or false doesn't arise because there is no king of France. But suppose the statement occurring in the context of a set of answers to the question: "What examples, if any, are there of famous contemporary figures who are *bald?*" Or think of someone compiling a list in answer to the question, "Who has died recently?" and including in it the term "the king of France". Or think of someone including the statement "The king of France married again" in a set of statements compiled in reply to the question: "What outstanding events, if any, have occurred recently in the social and political fields?" In the first two cases the king of France appears to be cited as an *instance* or example of an *antecedently introduced class*. In the last case the statement as a whole claims to report an event as an instance of an *antecedently introduced class*. The question in each case represents the antecedent centre of interest as a certain class—the class of bald notables, the class of recently deceased notables, the class of notable recent events in a certain field— and the question is as to what items, if any, the classes include. Since it is certainly false that the classes, in each case, include any such items as our answers claim they do, those answers can, without too much squeamishness, be simply marked as wrong answers. So to mark them is not to reject them as answers to questions which don't arise, but to reject them as wrong answers to questions which do arise. Yet the answers need include only *one* referring expression for a particular item, viz. the one guilty of reference failure; and the questions need not contain any at all.

This suggests a direction in which we might look for the missing principle of choice in the case of our previous examples, those about the swimming-pool and the Exhibition, which contained two referring expressions. The point was not, or was not solely, that each contained an extra and satisfactory referring expression. It was rather that we could easily see the centre of interest in each case as being the question, e.g. *how Jones spent the morning* or *what notable visitors the Exhibition has had*, or *how the Exhibition is getting on*. And the naturalness of taking them in this way was increased by the device of putting the satisfactory referring expression *first*, as grammatical subject of the sentence, and the unsatisfactory one last. We might, for example, have felt a shade more squeamish if we had written "The king of France visited the Exhibition yesterday" instead of "The Exhibition was visited yesterday by the king of France". We feel very squeamish indeed about "The king of France is bald" presented abruptly, out of context, just because we don't naturally and immediately think of a context in which interest is centred, say, on the question *What bald notables are there?* rather than on the question *What is the king of France like?* or *Is the king of France bald?* Of course, to either of *these* two questions the statement would not be just an incorrect answer. *These* questions have no correct answer and hence, in a sense, no incorrect answer either. They *are* questions which do not arise. This does not mean there is no correct *reply* to them. The correct reply is: "There is no king of France". But this reply is not an answer to, but a rejection of, the question. The question about bald notables, on the other hand, *can* be answered, rightly or wrongly. Any answer which purports to mention someone included in the class, and fails to do so, is wrong; and it is still wrong even if there is no such person at all as it purports to mention.

I should like to state the considerations I have been hinting at a little more generally, and with less dependence upon the notion of a question. Summarily my suggestions are as follows.

(1) First comes the additional platitude I promised. Statements, or the pieces of discourse to which they belong, have subjects, not only in the relatively precise senses of logic and grammar, but in a vaguer sense with which I shall associate the words 'topic' and 'about'. Just now I used the hypothesis of a *question* to bring out, with somewhat unnatural sharpness, the idea of the topic or centre of interest of a statement, the idea of what a statement could be said, in this sense, to be about. But even where there is no actual first-order question to pinpoint for us with this degree of sharpness the answer to the higher-order question, 'What is the statement, in this sense, about?', it may nevertheless often be possible to give a fairly definite answer to this question. For stating is not a gratuitous and random human activity. We do not, except in social desperation, direct isolated and unconnected pieces of information at each other, but on the contrary intend in general to give or add information about what is a matter of standing or current interest or concern. There is a great variety of possible types of answers to the question what the topic of a statement is, what a statement is 'about'—about baldness, about what great men are bald, about which countries have bad rulers, about France, about the king, etc.—and not every such answer excludes every other in a given case. This platitude we might dignify with the title, the Principle of Relevance.

(2) It comes to stand beside that other general platitude which I

announced earlier under the title, the Principle of the Presumption of Knowledge. This principle, it will be remembered, is that statements, in respect of their informativeness, are not generally self-sufficient units, free of any reliance upon what the audience is assumed to know or to assume already, but commonly depend for their effect upon knowledge assumed to be already in the audience's possession. The particular application I made of this principle was to the case of identifying reference, in so far as the performance of this function rests on the presumption of identifying knowledge in the possession of the audience. When I say that the new platitude comes to stand beside the old one, I mean that the spheres of (a) what a statement addressed to an audience is *about* and (b) what, in the making of that statement, the audience is assumed to have some knowledge of already, are spheres that will often, and naturally, overlap.

But (3) they need not be co-extensive. Thus, given a statement which contains a referring expression, the specification of that statement's topic, what it is about, would very often involve mentioning, or seeming to mention, the object which that expression was intended to refer to; but sometimes the topic of a statement containing such an expression could be specified without mentioning such an object. Let us call the first type of case Type 1 and the second type of case Type 2. (Evidently a statement could be of Type 1 relative to one referring expression it contained and of Type 2 relative to another).

Now (4) assessments of statements as true or untrue are commonly, though not only, topic-centred in the same way as the statements assessed; and when, as commonly, this is so, we may say that the statement is assessed *as* putative information *about its topic*.

Hence (5), given a case of radical reference-failure on the part of a referring expression, the truth-value gap account of the consequences of this failure will seem more naturally applicable if the statement in question is of Type 1 (relative to that referring expression) than if it is of Type 2. For if it is of Type 2, the failure of reference does not affect the topic of the statement, it merely affects what purports to be information *about its topic*. We may still judge the statement as putative information *about its topic* and say, perhaps, that the failure of reference has the consequence that it is *mis*informative *about its topic*. But we cannot say this if it is a case of Type 1. If it is a case of Type 1, the failure of reference affects the topic itself and not merely the putative information about the topic. If we know of the reference-failure, we know that the statement cannot really have the topic it is intended to have and hence cannot be assessed as putative information about that topic. It can be seen neither as correct, nor as incorrect, information *about its topic*.

But, it might be said, this account is self-contradictory. For it implies that in a Type 1 case of radical reference-failure the statement does not really *have* the topic which by hypothesis it does have; it implies that a statement which, by hypothesis, is *about* something is really about nothing. To this objection we must reply with a distinction. If I believe that the legend of King Arthur is historical truth, when there was in fact no such person, I may in one sense make statements *about* King Arthur, *describe* King Arthur and make king Arthur my *topic*. But there is another sense in which I cannot make statements about King Arthur, describe him or make him my topic. This second sense is stronger than the first. I may suppose myself to be making statements about him in the second, stronger sense; but I am really only making statements about him in the first and weaker sense. If, however, my belief in King Arthur were true and I really was making statements about him in the second sense, it would still be true that I was making statements about him in the first sense. This is why the first is a weaker (i.e. more comprehensive) sense than the second and not merely different from it.

Bearing this distinction of sense in mind, we can now frame a recipe for distinguishing those cases of reference-failure which are relatively favourable to the truth-value gap theory from those cases which are relatively unfavourable to it. The recipe is as follows. Consider in its context the statement suffering from reference-failure and frame a certain kind of description of the speech-episode of making it. The description is to begin with some phrase like 'He (i.e. the speaker) was saying (describing). . . .' and is to continue with an interrogative pronoun, adjective or adverb, introducing a dependent clause. The clause, with its introductory conjunction, specifies the topic of the statement, what it can be said (at least in the weaker, and, if there is no reference-failure, also in the stronger, sense) to be *about*; while *what is said about its topic* is eliminated from the description in favour of the interrogative expression. Examples of such descriptions based on cases already mentioned would be:

> He was describing *how Jones spent the morning*
> He was saying *which notable contemporaries are bald*
> He was saying *what the king of France is like*.

If the peccant referring expression survives in the clause introduced by the interrogative, the clause which specifies what the original statement was about, then we have a case relatively favourable to the truth-value gap theory. If the peccant referring expression is eliminated, and thus belongs to what purports to be information about the topic of the original statement, then we have a case relatively unfavourable to the truth-value gap theory. There can be no true or false, right or wrong, descriptions-of-what-the-king-of-France-is-like, because there is no king of France. But there can be right or wrong descriptions-of-how-Jones-spent-the-morning, and the description of him as having spent it at the local swimming-pool is wrong because there is no such place.

It is easy to see why the relevance of these factors should have been overlooked by those philosophers, including myself, who, considering a few example sentences in isolation from possible contexts of their use, have been tempted to embrace, and to generalise, the truth-value gap theory. For, first, it often is the case that the topic of a statement is, or includes, something referred to by a referring expression; for such an expression invokes the knowledge or current perceptions of an audience, and what is of concern to an audience is often what it already knows something about or is currently perceiving. And, second, it often is the case that the placing of an expression at the beginning of a sentence, in the position of grammatical subject, serves, as it were, to announce the statement's topic. The philosopher, thinking about reference-failure in terms of one or two short and isolated example sentences beginning with referring expressions, will tend to be influenced by these facts without noticing *all* of what is influencing him. So he will tend to attribute his sense of something more radically wrong than falsity to the presence alone of what is alone obvious, viz. a referring expression which fails of reference; and thus will overlook altogether these considerations about aboutness or topic which I have been discussing.

Let me remark that I do not claim to have done more than mention one factor which may sometimes bear on the fact that a truth-value gap theory for the case of radical reference-failure is apt to seem more intuitively attractive in some instances than it does in others.

16

Russell's Discussion of Meaning and Denotation: A Re-examination

Chrystine E. Cassin

Previous discussions[1] of Russell's objections to Frege's theory of sense and reference have concentrated on the relevant sections of "On Denoting."[2] This approach ignores Russell's much longer discussion in his appendix to the *Principles of Mathematics*,[3] which I maintain is essential for a clear understanding of the 1905 discussion. In order to show this, I shall present a brief summary of the relevant parts of Russell's 1903 theory of denoting. This will then be used to clarify Russell's treatment of Frege in the *Principles*. Finally, I shall use the results of this examination as the basis for a new interpretation of the 1905 discussion of meaning and denotation. This interpretation, if correct, clears Russell of some of the charges which have been levelled against him, and provides an

[1] For example, R. J. Butler, "The Scaffolding of the Theory of Descriptions," *Philosophical Review*, 64 (1954): 350-366 (henceforth referred to as "Scaffolding"), and J. R. Searle, "Russell's Objections to Frege's Theory of Sense and Reference," *Analysis*, 18 (1958): 137-142 (henceforth referred to as "Russell's Objections").

[2] In *Logic and Knowledge*, ed. R. C. Marsh (London: Macmillan & Co., 1956). Henceforth referred to as "OD."

[3] 2nd ed. (New York: W. W. Norton & Co., 1950). Appendix A, pp. 501-522. Henceforth referred to as *POM*.

essential link between his 1903 and 1905 theories. With these aims, I limit myself chiefly to exposition, rather than criticism, and do not attempt any general comparison of Russell's and Frege's theories as a whole.

Synopsis of Russell's 1903 Theory of Denoting[4]

A denoting phrase, such as 'the present Queen of England', indicates a denoting concept, the present Queen of England. This concept denotes "a term," which, in this case, is Elizabeth II. So, in 1903, denoting is *not* a relation between words and entities, but between concepts and terms. Russell states this quite clearly. "The fact that description is possible—that we are able, by the employment of concepts, to designate a thing which is not a concept—is due to a logical relation between some concepts and some terms, in virtue of which such concepts inherently and logically denote such terms. It is this sense of denoting which is here in question."[5] As is well known, in 1903 Russell held that every word in a significant sentence must have a meaning, and that there must be something that it means.[6] Although he is not consistent, Russell uses "indication" for the relation between words and the entities that they mean, and I shall follow this usage. Thus, 'the present Queen of England' indicates, i.e., means, the denoting concept, the present Queen of England.

Russell calls this kind of meaning "linguistic," and he explicitly contrasts it with a second type of meaning, which he calls "logical" meaning. Logical meaning is, in fact, denotation. Thus, the denoting concept, the present Queen of England, denotes, i.e., means, the term, Elizabeth II.[7] All words have meaning in the sense of indication, but only denoting concepts have meaning in the sense of denotation. In order to avoid any confusion over which sense of 'meaning' is being used, I shall use 'meaning$_i$' for indication, and 'meaning$_d$' for denotation. Russell himself frequently uses 'meaning' without being clear as to which sense of 'meaning' is being employed, and this ambiguity

---

[4] This is based chiefly on Chapters 4 and 5 of *POM*. My exposition is brief, because of limitations of space here, but a fuller exposition may be found in my dissertation, *Bertrand Russell's Theory of Descriptions (1903–1919)*, 1968.

[5] *POM*, p. 53.

[6] *Ibid.*, p. 47.

[7] *Ibid.*

must be recognized when examining his discussion of Frege. The term 'reference' should not be applied to Russell's 1903 theory without making it clear that 'reference' covers both indication and denotation.

Now, words mean$_i$ either terms or concepts for Russell, and a term is "whatever may be an object of thought, or may occur in any true or false proposition."[8] Examples of terms which he lists are: Socrates, men, a chimaera, a class, and all terms have being of some kind.[9] Thus, terms are *not* words, but the entities which some words indicate. Furthermore, Russell clearly states that "a proposition, unless it happens to be linguistic, does not itself contain words: it contains the entities indicated by words."[10] So, terms, concepts, and propositions are all entities which have being of some kind. They are what is symbolized, not the symbols themselves. Strange though this view sounds today, it is the theory which Russell held in 1903.

For my purpose here, the last relevant point is the relation between sentences and propositions. Russell is not explicit about this in the *Principles*, although his theory clearly implies that the relation is one of indication. However, in his discussion of Meinong,[11] Russell first identifies Meinong's Objectives with his propositions,[12] and then states that a sentence indicates an Objective. Thus, a sentence indicates a proposition, which is the meaning$_i$ of the sentence. These are the vital points of Russell's 1903 theory, which must be employed in understanding his discussion of Frege.

The 1903 Discussion of Sense and Reference[13]

Russell begins his discussion of Frege with the statement that "the distinction between meaning (*Sinn*) and indication (*Bedeutung*) is roughly, though not exactly, equivalent to my distinction between a concept as such and what the concept denotes."[14] In a footnote to this

8 *Ibid.*, p. 43.
9 *Ibid.*, pp. 43, 45.
10 *Ibid.*, p. 47.
11 Russell, "Meinong's Theory of Complexes and Assumptions," *Mind*, New Series, 13 (1904), 1:204–219; *ibid.*, 2:336–354; *ibid.*, 3:509–524.
12 *Ibid.*, 2:350. This identification is based on Russell's misunderstanding of Meinong's Objectives, but that does not concern us here.
13 'Sense' and 'reference' will be used only for Frege, reserving 'meaning', 'indication', and 'denotation' for Russell.
14 *POM*, p. 502.

passage, he recognizes that his use of 'denotation' prohibits using it for Frege's '*Bedeutung*', but it is still difficult to see exactly what Russell meant by the above remark. If 'indication' is used for the relation between words and their referents, then Russell can use this for Frege's reference and so there is no difficulty here. The problem arises when Russell claims that Frege's distinction between sense and reference is analogous to his own distinction between a concept and the denotation of that concept. The difference between these two distinctions can be shown quite clearly.

First, as has been seen, the relationship between a denoting concept and its denotation holds between two nonlinguistic entities. Secondly, the denotation, which is a term, is the meaning$_d$ of that denoting concept. Thirdly, both the denoting concept and its denotation are constituents of that strange nonlinguistic entity, a proposition, which is indicated by the sentence as a whole. On the other hand, Frege speaks of his own distinction between sense and reference in the following way: "It is natural . . . to think of there being connected with a sign (name, combination of words, letter), besides that to which the sign refers, which may be called the reference of the sign, also what I should like to call the *sense* of the sign, wherein the mode of presentation is contained."[15] The contrast between Frege's and Russell's views is obvious. Frege's referring-relation is a relation holding between a linguistic symbol and the entity which is symbolized; Russell's denoting-relation is a relation which holds between two nonlinguistic entities. For Frege, the sense of a symbol is never its referent, but, for Russell, the meaning$_i$ of a symbol is its indication, and the meaning$_d$ of a denoting concept is its denotation. Finally, in Frege's theory, a sentence does not have a proposition as its referent, but a truth-value.[16]

These differences make it tempting to simply dismiss Russell's remark as yet another instance of his misunderstanding of Frege, and so totally worthless. Now, there is no doubt that Russell did misunderstand Frege, but an explanation of his remark can be found by examining Russell's notion of meaning. Such an explanation will throw light on both his disagreements with Frege, and on his discussion of meaning and denotation in the 1905 article. It has been pointed out that Russell recognized two senses of 'meaning'. In the first sense, meaning is what a word indicates, while in the second sense, viz., meaning$_d$,

[15] "On Sense and Reference," *The Philosophical Writings of Gottlob Frege*, ed. P. Geach and M. Black (Oxford: Blackwell, 1952), p. 57.
[16] *Ibid.*, p. 63.

meaning is what is denoted by a denoting concept. If this distinction beween indication and denotation is used, then it can be seen that Russell takes Frege's sense as his denoting concept, which is the meaning$_i$ of the denoting phrase. A denoting concept also has a meaning$_d$, which is the term which it denotes. Thus, the term Elizabeth II is the meaning$_d$ of the denoting concept, the present Queen of England, but it is also the meaning$_i$ of the name 'Elizabeth II'.

Russell had to find some kind of conceptual equivalent for Frege's sense, and the only possible candidate was his denoting concept. Now, Russell translates Frege's '*Bedeutung*' as indication, but he states that Frege's distinction between *Sinn* and *Bedeutung* is roughly equivalent to his distinction between a denoting concept and what it denotes. This means that *Bedeutung* cannot be indication, because Russell uses 'indication' for what a word symbolizes, not for what a denoting concept denotes. On the other hand, a denoting phrase does mean$_i$ a denoting concept. Thus, in fact, Russell regards Frege's sense as his indication and Frege's reference (*Bedeutung*) as his denotation. Unfortunately, this destroyed Frege's distinction, because the denoting concept is both the meaning and the indication of the denoting expression. Furthermore, in cases such as the above example, the term Elizabeth II is both the meaning$_i$ of 'Elizabeth II', and the meaning$_d$ of the denoting concept. Thus, Frege's distinction becomes, for Russell, the distinction between indication and denotation with the result that Russell retained the identification of meaning and reference, which Frege rejected.

Since this interpretation explicitly rejects Russell's own stipulation concerning his translation of '*Bedeutung*', further evidence for it is necessary, and this is found in Russell's remarks concerning proper names. Russell denied that Frege's distinction between sense and reference could be applied to all proper names, claiming that "only such proper names as are derived from concepts by means of 'the' can be said to have meaning, and that such words as 'John' merely indicate without meaning."[17] This passage is another example of the careless way in which Russell frequently expressed himself, because he held throughout the *Principles* that every word must have some meaning. 'John' does have meaning$_i$ because 'John' indicates a term, but 'John' does not have meaning$_d$ because the term John does not denote. Thus, as Russell interprets Frege, names such as 'John' do not have a sense,

---

[17] *POM*, p. 502 [quotation marks added].

i.e., do not have meaning$_d$, but only have a referent, i.e., they indicate a term.[18]

Russell could not agree with Frege that every proper name has both sense and reference, because he took this to mean that every proper name both indicates and denotes, and this obviated his whole distinction between terms and denoting concepts. For Russell, some proper names simply indicate a term, which is the logical subject of the proposition in which it occurs.[19] Other proper names, that is, denoting expressions, indicate a denoting concept, which is not the logical subject of the proposition in which it occurs.[20] Such expressions are a special class of proper names, and are related to terms only through their denoting concepts.

The remainder of Russell's appendix contains valuable material for a general comparison of Frege's views and his own, but nothing more which is relevant for the 1905 discussion.[21] So, the hypothesis that Russell understood Frege's sense-reference distinction as his indication-denotation distinction will now be applied to that article.

The 1905 Discussion of Meaning and Denotation

Russell's 1905 arguments concerning meaning and denotation are obscure, and have been subjected to much criticism on the grounds that he ignored the use-mention distinction, and that he completely misunderstood Frege.[22] These arguments will be reexamined in the light of the preceding material, with the aim of showing that one of the most commonly accepted criticisms of Russell is based on certain questionable assumptions. Furthermore, it will be argued that it is possible to interpret Russell's arguments in such a way that they provide the fundamental link between the 1903 theory and the revised theory of definite descriptions.

The core of Russell's argument is contained in the following notorious passage:

[18] *Ibid.*, p. 47.
[19] *Ibid.*, p. 53.
[20] *Ibid.*, pp. 47, 53.
[21] Russell does discuss the sense-reference distinction with respect to sentences (pp. 502–505), but the whole discussion simply illustrates his inability to understand the distinction because of his theory of propositions.
[22] Cf. Searle, "Russell's Objections," and Butler, "Scaffolding."

The one phrase C was to have both meaning and denotation. But if we speak of 'the meaning of C', that gives us the meaning (if any) of the denotation. [1]

'The meaning of the first line of Gray's Elegy' is the same as 'The meaning of "the curfew tolls the knell of parting day",' and is not the same as 'the meaning of "the first line of Gray's Elegy".' [2]

Thus in order to get the meaning we want, we must speak not of 'the meaning of C', but of 'the meaning of "C",' which is the same as 'C' itself. [3]

Similarly 'the denotation of C' does not mean the denotation we want, but means something, which, if it denotes at all, denotes what is denoted by the denotation we want. [4]

For example, let 'C' be 'the denoting complex occurring in the second of the above instances'. Then C = 'the first line of Gray's Elegy', and the denotation of C = The curfew tolls the knell of parting day. [5]

But what we *meant* to have as the denotation was 'the first line of Gray's Elegy'. Thus we have failed to get what we wanted. [6][23]

Russell states that he is using quotation marks to show when he is speaking about meaning, as opposed to denotation.[24] This convention led Church to claim that all the difficulties which Russell found in Frege's theory "are traceable merely to confusion between use and mention of expressions of a sort which Frege is careful to avoid by the use of quotation marks. Russell applies quotation marks to distinguish the sense of an expression from its denotation, but leaves himself without any notation for the expression itself; upon introduction of, say, a second kind of quotation mark to signalise names of expressions, Russell's objections to Frege completely vanish."[25] For the moment, it should simply be noted that Church assumes that Russell's use of 'meaning' is the same as Frege's use of 'sense'. This is an assumption which should obviously be doubted in view of the preceding discussion.

If Church's claim is correct, then a reformulation of Russell's arguments, using an adequate notational device, will obviate his criticisms of Frege. Butler provides such a device.

23 "OD," p. 49. The numbers, which refer to the sentence immediately preceding them, are used for the purpose of future reference to these sentences.

24 *Ibid.*, p. 48.

25 Alonzo Church, "Carnap's Introduction to Semantics," *Philosophical Review*, 52 (1943): 302.

Let us suppose that whenever we mean the sense of "*C*" we write
* *C* *. Then the sense of the sign "The first line of Gray's Elegy" is
* The first line of Gray's Elegy *, and this refers to the first line of
Gray's Elegy which . . . is "The curfew tolls the knell of parting day."
Now, on Frege's theory, "The curfew tolls the knell of parting day"
is not the sense of "The first line of Gray's Elegy" but its referent, and
neither is *its* sense the sense of "The first line of Gray's Elegy." We can
tabulate Frege's distinctions in the following way:

(a) Significant expression A: "The first line of Gray Elegy."

(b) Sense of A: * The first line of Gray's Elegy *.

(c) Referent of A: "The curfew tolls the knell of parting day."

(d) Significant expression B: "The curfew tolls the knell of parting
day."

(e) Sense of B: * The curfew tolls the knell of parting day *.

(f) Referent of B: Truth (or Falsehood).[26]

These distinctions are correct for Frege, provided that in (d) B is
actually used, rather than mentioned as the referent of A. Butler goes
on to point out that Russell makes the following identifications: (a)
with (e); (e) with (d); (d) with (c). Since (b) is the sense of A,
Russell then concluded that (b) was the same as (c), thus destroying
the distinction between sense and reference.[27]

This is a clear exposition of the argument, but it depends on several
assumptions. First, it assumes that Russell did misuse quotation marks;
secondly, that Russell's use of 'meaning and denotation' exactly paral-
lels Frege's use of 'sense and reference'; and, thirdly, that 'denoting
complex' is simply another name for a denoting phrase. Each one of
these assumptions can be challenged and shown to be doubtful, if not
completely mistaken.

First, it is difficult to determine whether or not Russell has retained
his 1903 notion of a proposition as a nonlinguistic entity. He does distinguish between a proposition and its verbal expression when he states
that denoting phrases occur in the verbal expression of propositions.[28]
Also, "things" are still constituents of propositions.[29] So, if the 1903
distinction between sentences and propositions does still hold, then
names or signs of referents will occur only in sentences, but not in

[26] Butler, "Scaffolding," p. 362.
[27] *Ibid.*, pp. 362–363.
[28] "OD," p. 56.
[29] *Ibid.*

propositions. However, once again Russell is not consistent in his use of 'proposition', since he also speaks of denoting phrases as occurring in propositions. Since Russell did not explicitly discuss the nature of propositions again until 1919, it is almost impossible to determine exactly what he meant by 'proposition' in the years between 1903 and 1919. For our purposes, this simply means that in the 1905 article, the possibility that Russell still uses 'proposition' for a complex, nonlinguistic entity is a feasible one. Thus, using the 1903 notion of a proposition may throw light on some aspects of Russell's discussion.

Secondly, it has been shown that for Russell, 'meaning' can be either indication or denotation and it has been claimed that, as regards denoting expressions, he treated Frege's sense as his indication. So, whenever Russell speaks of 'meaning', the way in which he is using it must be determined. Thirdly, the introduction of the notion of a denoting complex involves further problems. The phrase is not used before 1905, and so the question arises whether it is used for a new notion, or is simply a new name for an old notion. If the latter, then it names either a denoting concept, or is an alternative expression for a denoting phrase. All of these problems are vital for understanding exactly what Russell meant by these arguments concerning meaning and denotation, and whether he was criticising Frege alone, or a combination of Frege's ideas and his own 1903 theory, as has been suggested.[30]

Before reexamining Russell's arguments it is necessary to adopt certain notation devices. It is inadvisable to use quotation marks for reference to meaning, since these are now used for expressions themselves. Consequently, single quotation marks will indicate that the expressions are mentioned, while double quotation marks will be reserved for quotations from Russell. Wherever Russell uses single quotation marks, as in (1), the expression within the quotation marks will be italicized. Wherever he uses double quotation marks, asterisks will be used. Thus, (2) will be written as

The meaning of the first line of Grey's Elegy is the same as *The meaning of* * *The curfew tolls the knell of parting day* *, and is not the same as *The meaning of* * *the first line of Grey's Elegy* *.

Unless explicitly stated otherwise, the use of these conventions will correspond exactly to Russell's usage of quotation marks.

In the whole argument, Russell is concerned with the relation be-

---

30 R. Jager, "Russell's Denoting Complex," *Analysis*, 20 (1960): 53–62.

tween meaning and denotation, with respect to denoting phrases, and he introduces these notions as though they were equivalent to Frege's sense and reference.[31] However, the discussion of his appendix on Frege, in the *Principles*, has suggested that these notions are not equivalent. Since there are no intervening works on this topic between 1903 and 1905, it seems reasonable to consider whether, when Russell contrasts meaning and denotation, he is contrasting his own indication and denotation with respect to denoting phrases, rather than Frege's sense and reference. Similarly, there is no reason to suppose that Russell is considering denoting as a different relation from that used in the 1903 theory. So, for the purposes of discussion, it will be assumed that Russell is examining the relation between indication and denotation. It will be remembered that indication holds between the denoting expression and the denoting concept, while denotation holds between the denoting concept and a certain term, or terms.

Russell's own statement of the problem becomes clearer when these suggestions are adopted. "Now the relation of meaning and denoting is not merely linguistic through the phrase: there must be a logical relation involved, which we express by saying the meaning denotes the denotation. But the difficulty which confronts us is that we cannot succeed in both preserving the connexion of meaning and denotation and preventing them from being one and the same; also that meaning cannot be got at except by means of denoting phrases."[32] The contrast between a linguistic relation and a logical relation is obviously reminiscent of Russell's earlier contrast between linguistic meaning (indication) and logical meaning (denotation).[33] If the relation between meaning and denotation is not linguistic, Russell has only one possible candidate for the logical relation which he demands, and that is denoting. He provides no explanation of what he means by this relation, and this strongly suggests that it is not a new notion, but the one used in the *Principles*. Since only two years have elapsed, it is not surprising that Russell presupposed knowledge of this work when writing "On Denoting." Russell expresses this relation by saying that ". . . the meaning denotes the denotation . . . ," and so he must be using 'meaning' here for the denoting concept. In which case, the denoting phrase means$_i$ the denoting concept, which, I have suggested, Russell identifies with Frege's sense. On this interpretation, Russell's problem

[31] "OD," p. 45.
[32] *Ibid.*, p. 49.
[33] *POM*, p. 47.

is to preserve the connexion between the denoting concept and its denotation, without identifying them.

This interpretation also clarifies the notion of a denoting complex. Russell gives as examples of a denoting complex: "... the centre of mass of the solar system is a denoting complex not a point ...," and "the first line of Gray's Elegy does not state a proposition."[34] The identification of this complex with a denoting phrase seems impossible. First, Russell introduces these examples to illustrate his notational device for talking about meaning, and it is scarcely feasible to suggest that he misused this device in the very place where he is demonstrating its use. Secondly, he states immediately afterwards that where C is a denoting phrase, C is its meaning. Thus, denoting phrase is contrasted with meaning, and the same device is used to indicate both meaning and a denoting complex.

Moreover, in his first discussion of Frege, it is possible to trace Russell's use of 'denoting', 'complex', and 'meaning' so that using the first two words for the latter is a natural step. A long denoting phrase, such as 'the centre of mass of the solar system at the beginning of the twentieth century', has a complex meaning, which is composed of the meanings of its constituent words.[35] Similarly, "... if we say 'the King of England is bald', that is, it would seem, not a statement about the complex meaning of the King of England, but about the actual man denoted by the meaning."[36] This statement not only shows Russell combining 'complex' and 'meaning', but also supports the proposed interpretation. As in the *Principles*, 'the King of England' means$_i$ the denoting concept, the King of England (complex meaning). This concept is not the logical subject of a proposition in which it occurs. Instead, the logical subject is the term, the actual man, which is denoted by the denoting concept. These examples show that since the meaning$_i$ of a denoting phrase is distinguished by the properties of being complex and denoting, it is an easy step to actually calling the meaning$_i$ a denoting complex. On this view, of course, a denoting complex is the same as a denoting concept. This is the view which I shall adopt here for the rest of the paper.[37]

---

34 "OD," pp. 48–49.

35 *Ibid.*, p. 45.

36 *Ibid.*, p. 46.

37 For further evidence in support of this identification see P. T. Geach, "Russell on Meaning and Denotation," *Analysis*, 19 (1958): 70–71, and for further discussion see Jager, "Russell's Denoting Complex."

If these suggestions concerning Russell's use of 'meaning', 'denotation', and 'denoting complex' are correct, then it is obvious that Russell's detailed arguments are directed not so much against Frege as against his own 1903 theory. In fact, Russell's whole problem becomes clearer when it is expressed in 1903 terminology. Denoting concepts and their terms are supposedly separate entities, but related in an inexplicable manner by the relation of denoting. Thus, Russell ought to be able to talk about a denoting concept as the meaning$_i$ of a denoting phrase without talking about its denotation, and he should be able to preserve the relation of denoting without identifying terms and their denoting concepts. Taking 'the first line of Gray's Elegy' as an example, this phrase indicates the denoting concept, the first line of Gray's Elegy, which is its meaning$_i$, and which Russell wants to be able to talk about. The first line of Gray's Elegy denotes a term, which in this case is, the curfew tolls to knell of parting day. Russell also wants to be able to talk about this denotation, separately from the denoting concept and from the denoting phrase, in order to show that terms and their denoting concepts are different, and are related logically rather than linguistically. By showing that this cannot be done he will show that the relation between meaning and denotation has been wrongly conceived.

If this approach is followed, a radically different impression of Russell's detailed arguments can be gained. For the sake of convenience the following conventions will be adopted:

'A' = 'the first line of Gray's Elegy'.
A = *the first line of Gray's Elegy.*
'B' = 'the curfew tolls the knell of parting day'.
B = the curfew tolls the knell of parting day.

'A' and 'B' are phrases, while *A* is a denoting concept, i.e., denoting complex, which is 'A' 's meaning. B is the term, which is indicated by 'B', and denoted by *A*.

First, this interpretation explains why Russell says that whenever a denoting phrase occurs, the denotation is being talked about.[38] By the 1903 theory, a sentence containing 'A', indicates a proposition of which the logical subject is not *A*, but B. Thus, any occurrence of 'A' involves *A* as its meaning$_i$, and B as *A*'s denotation. This explains why Russell used 'C' for both a denoting phrase and its denotation, because

[38] "OD," p. 49.

on his view it is impossible to use the phrase without speaking about its denotation. Since Russell's aim is to talk about the denoting concept alone, he needs a phrase which will indicate this alone. His first candidate for this is the *meaning of C*, but he claims that whenever this is used, it gives the meaning$_d$ (if any) of the denotation, whereas what we wanted was the meaning$_i$ of the phrase (1). Russell then states, "The *meaning of A* is the same as the *meaning of * B *, and is not the same as the *meaning of * A **," (2). This is the first identification to which Butler objected, but on Russell's early theory this identification is correct.[39]

First, Russell's use of single quotation marks is consistent so far, because in each case he is talking about a denoting concept, that is, the meaning$_i$ of a denoting phrase. Secondly, his use of double quotation marks (i.e., '*') is also correct, if these are taken as indicating phrases. * B * only has meaning in the sense of indication, and it indicates the term, which is denoted by A. So the meaning$_d$ of A is the same as the meaning$_i$ of * B *. Russell has not shifted his use of quotation marks, but his use of 'meaning' from meaning$_d$ to meaning$_i$. Similarly, * A * means$_i$ A, so that * A * does not mean the same as A. If Russell's use of double quotation marks here is regarded as mistaken, then the statement involves the senseless assertion that the *meaning of A* is not the same as the *meaning of A*. Butler's claim that Russell identified the meaning of 'B' with B[40] depends on regarding Russell's use of double quotation marks as mistaken, but this claim now seems doubtful.

The suggestion that Russell uses these double quotes to refer to an expression is supported by (3), where Russell states that in order to get at the denoting concept "... we must speak not of the meaning of C, but of the *meaning of * C *....*" Here, his double quotes are clearly used for the name of the denoting concept C. The name is introduced as a device for talking about C, without talking about its denotation. Obviously, Russell is approaching here the distinction between use and mention, which he needs. By means of * C *, C is mentioned, but not its denotation. Unfortunately, Russell could not use this device, because * C *'s meaning$_i$ is C itself, and thus Russell regarded * C * and C as the same (3). In this sense the criticism that Russell confused a sign with its referent is correct, but the confusion is not due to carelessness. It is rather an integral part of Russell's whole 1903 theory. Talking about something always involves a nonlinguistic entity for

39 Butler, "Scaffolding," pp. 362–363.
40 *Ibid.*

Russell, and so he cannot mention words as opposed to using them.

So far, it has been shown that, by using certain fundamental characteristics of the 1903 theory, Russell can be considered to be consistent in his use of quotation marks. This in turn shows that he made certain correct identifications for his own theory, at least with respect to denoting phrases and denoting concepts. These identifications show that Russell was unable to talk about a denoting concept, without talking about its denotation, and he should have been able to do this. The second stage of his argument raises the same problem with respect to denotations, and this must be examined also. The first task is to clarify exactly what Russell is looking for. In (6) he states "... what we meant to have as the denotation was *the first line of Gray's Elegy.*" So, he is looking for something which denotes A, which is itself a denoting concept. This seems to be a continuation of the problem of the relation of $*C*$ to C. The phrase which indicates C, where C is a denoting concept, will itself be a denoting phrase, because its form will be 'the denoting concept C'. So, the phrase must indicate a denoting concept, which denotes C. Thus, Russell has moved the problem to another level, in the sense that denoting concepts$_1$, which denote denoting concepts$_0$, are required.

Russell begins this stage of the problem by asking what the *denotation of A* means (4). If, as Butler[41] maintains, this is a misuse of quotation marks, then Russell is simply asking for the denotation of A, which is B. However, Butler cannot be correct, because Russell explicitly rejects B as the required denotation (5), and states that A is the required denotation (6). It seems clear that Russell did not realize that he required two levels of denoting concepts here, and so did not provide the notational device he needed. In (5) he takes A as his denoting complex, when he should have taken the *denotation of A_1*, where A_1 is the denoting concept, which denotes A. Since A is a denoting concept itself and is the required denotation, then there must be a denoting concept, which denotes it. It is then correct to write *the denotation of A_1*, because this denotation is a denoting concept and so the same notational device can be used for this as was used for A.

Even with the introduction of an adequate notational device Russell's early theory is in serious difficulties here. Originally, it was maintained that only terms could be denoted, but, with the introduction of another level, denoting concepts themselves must be denoted. Also,

[41] *Ibid.*

Russell's arguments concerning denotations do not show that it is impossible to talk about all denotations. They only show that, when a denoting concept of the first level is to serve as the denotation of a concept of the second level, talking about the denoting concept involves its denotation, which is not what was wanted. This arises again because, on Russell's view, if A occurs then its denotation B must also occur. So, saying that A_1 denoted A does not avoid the occurrence of B.

This lengthy and complicated discussion of Russell's treatment of meaning and denotation has been necessary, not simply to absolve him from the charges of misusing quotation marks and misunderstanding Frege. It has been presented because it offers a reassessment of Russell's arguments, which makes them highly significant for the development of his 1905 theory. Their chief purpose can be seen as showing that denoting concepts cannot be talked about apart from their denotations, which reveals serious defects in the 1903 theory. A denoting concept was an entity indicated by a denoting phrase, but if it cannot be talked about without its denotation, then it seems the two cannot be as distinct as Russell thought they were. Furthermore, the denoting concept was supposed to be the meaning$_i$ of the denoting phrase, and, as such, it should be possible to talk about it. If this cannot be done, then it seems likely that it is not the meaning$_i$ of the phrase; in fact, it may not be a distinct entity at all. Thus, Russell subjects his own early theory to criticisms designed to show that his whole conception of a denoting concept, and of the relation of denoting was misconceived.

Once this was done, the distinction between indication and denotation could be dropped, and denoting phrases no longer need to indicate. Thus, Russell states that in his revised theory denoting phrases have no meaning and only sometimes a denotation.[42] Moreover, the rejection of denoting concepts meant that there was no longer any intermediary entity between the denoting phrase and its term. Denoting becomes a relation between a phrase and a term, so that Scott is now denoted by 'the author of *Waverley*'.[43] Thus, Russell abolished his mysterious relation of denoting together with denoting concepts. The passages, which have been discussed, provide the only source for Russell's reasons for making this vital change. In the *Principles*, denot-

[42] "OD," p. 46.
[43] *Ibid.*, p. 51.

ing clearly holds between a concept and a term, but, in the 1905 theory, it clearly holds between a phrase and a term. Such a radical change requires explanation which has not been provided, because these arguments have been regarded solely in the light of controversy between Russell and Frege.

These claims are so important for an understanding of Russell that they will certainly raise the objection that if Russell meant his arguments to be criticisms of his own 1903 theory, then he would have said so explicitly. Obviously, only general suggestions can be made to answer this objection but some of these have textual support. First, as is well known, "On Denoting" was originally written as an article, and thus was subject to limitation in length. This is obvious from the fact that the extremely important principle of acquaintance is simply mentioned without exposition.[44] Secondly, Russell obviously presupposed knowledge of the *Principles*, or at least a willingness to consult it. This is clearly shown by the footnotes on pages 42, 46, and 48, as well as by his cursory treatment of the original analysis of 'the present King of France is bald'.[45]

Finally, the assumption that Russell's arguments on pages 48 to 51 are directed against Frege has no *direct* textual support. Russell introduces Frege's thesis before these arguments, and his direct criticism of Frege on the problem of denoting phrases involves only those which have no denotation. He simply states that Frege's claim that 'the present King of France' denotes the null class ". . . is plainly artificial and does not give an exact analysis of the matter."[46] Nowhere in his detailed arguments about meaning and denotation does Russell mention Frege by name. Thus, the sole textual basis for treating these arguments as criticisms of Frege lies in his use of 'meaning and denotation', which is assumed to be same as Frege's use of 'sense and reference'. If this assumption is not granted, then the purpose of his arguments is open to question. The *Principles* clearly shows that Russell recognised a difference in usage between Frege's terminology and his own, and it seems strange that he should have either forgotten this by 1905, or carelessly misrepresented a philosopher for whom he had great respect. Given the importance of the 1905 article, an attempt to explain these arguments by some other means should at least be made.

[44] *Ibid.*, pp. 41, 56.
[45] *Ibid.*, p. 46.
[46] *Ibid.*, p. 47.

The preceding interpretation represents such an attempt and, while no claim is made for absolute correctness, it does make sense of many of Russell's arguments, which have hitherto been regarded as mistaken or inexplicable. Moreover, the value of this interpretation can be demonstrated further by an examination of Russell's revised theory as a whole, but that is beyond the scope of this particular paper.

17

Russell's Distinction between the Primary and Secondary Occurrence of Definite Descriptions[1]

Chrystine E. Cassin

MY chief purpose in this paper is to clarify Russell's distinction between the primary and secondary occurrence of definite descriptions. I shall show first that Russell's own presentation of this distinction is inadequate, because it does not provide an adequate criterion for deciding whether a definite description has a primary or secondary occurrence. However, I maintain that a careful examination of the relevant parts of Section 14 in *Principia Mathematica*[2] does provide the required criterion. Finally, I use this criterion to clarify part of Russell's analysis of sentences of the form 'C (the author of *Waverley*)', as well as his proposed solution to one of the puzzles which he presents in "On Denoting."[3]

As is well known, Russell introduces the distinction to solve two

[1] A shorter version of this paper was read at the Florida Philosophical Association annual meeting in November, 1968.

[2] A. N. Whitehead and B. Russell, *Principia Mathematica* (Cambridge: The University Press, 1910–1913). Henceforth referred to as *PM*.

[3] "On Denoting," *Mind*, New Series, XIV (1905): 479–493, reprinted in *Logic and Knowledge*, ed. R. C. Marsh (London: Macmillan & Co., 1956). All references are to this edition which is referred to as "OD."

problems, the first of which is to prevent such inferences as the following.

(1) George IV wished to know whether Scott was the author of *Waverley*.

(2) Scott = Scott.

(3) George IV wished to know whether Scott was Scott.

Russell points out that (1) is ambiguous, because it may mean either

(1a) George IV wished to know whether one and one only man wrote *Waverley* and Scott was that man.

or

(1b) One and one only man wrote *Waverley* and George IV wished to know whether Scott was that man.[4]

In (1a), 'the author of *Waverley*', or more accurately, 'one and one only man wrote *Waverley*' has secondary occurrence, but in (1b), it has primary occurrence. Russell then defines the secondary occurrence of a definite description as "one in which the phrase occurs in a proposition [sentence] p which is a mere constituent of the proposition [sentence] we are considering, and the substitution is to be affected in p, not in the whole proposition [sentence] concerned."[5] Thus, substitution of 'Scott' for 'the author of *Waverley*' is restricted to cases where the latter has primary occurrence, and so, provided (1) is interpreted as (1a), the inference of (3) is prevented.

Russell also used the distinction between primary and secondary occurrence to deal with the question of whether the present King of France is bald, or not bald. By the law of the excluded middle, he must be one or the other, but, as Russell points out, he is not to be found either in the class of bald people or in the class of people who are not bald. Like (1),

(4)   The present King of France is not bald.

is ambiguous. It may mean either

4 "OD," p. 52.

5 *Ibid.* I prefer to use 'sentence' rather than 'proposition', because Russell changed his conception of a proposition sometime between 1903 and 1919, and I want to avoid any confusion between his 1903 conception of a proposition and his later one, as well as any confusion between sentence and proposition. For a full discussion of this problem, see my dissertation *Bertrand Russell's Theory of Descriptions* (Tallahassee: Florida State University, 1968).

(4a) There is an entity which is now King of France and is not bald.

or

(4b) It is false that there is an entity which is now King of France and bald.

In (4a), 'the King of France' has primary occurrence, and (4a) is false, but 'the King of France' has secondary occurrence in (4b), and (4b) is true. "Thus all propositions [sentences] in which 'the King of France' has primary occurrence are false; the denials of such propositions [sentences] are true, but in them 'the King of France' has a secondary occurrence. Thus we escape the conclusion that the King of France has a wig."[6]

These two problems clearly show the importance of Russell's distinction. In the first one, the distinction is used to restrict the principle of substitutivity, as based on the identity of indiscernibles. The second problem shows that whether a descriptive phrase has a primary or a secondary occurrence affects the truth value of the sentence in which it occurs, at least in cases where the phrase is not a denoting phrase. Consequently, it is important that there should be a clear criterion for deciding whether a descriptive phrase has primary or secondary occurrence. Unfortunately, Russell's various definitions of his distinction do not provide such a criterion. His most common attempt to clarify the distinction involves treating the sentence in which the description occurs as part of a larger sentence. For example, in *Principia*, Russell states that when '$f(\imath x)(\phi x)$' forms part of some other sentence, then '$(\imath x)(\phi x)$' has secondary occurrence.[7] Similarly, in *Introduction to Mathematical Philosophy*, "a description has a 'primary' occurrence when the proposition [sentence] in which it occurs results from substituting the description for 'x' in some propositional [sentential] function ϕx; a description has a 'secondary' occurrence when the result of substituting the description for 'x' in ϕx gives only *part* of the proposition [sentence] concerned."[8]

The first peculiarity about the distinction is that, while Russell speaks of a description occurring in a subordinate sentence, the description itself does not occur at all when the sentence is analysed. The

---

[6] *Ibid.*, p. 53.

[7] *PM*, p. 68.

[8] *Introduction to Mathematical Philosophy* (London: Allen & Unwin, 1940), p. 179. Henceforth referred to as *IMP*.

generalised form of (4), as expressed in the iota notation, is

(5) $\qquad \sim\psi(\imath x)(\phi x)$

Now (5) exhibits the same ambiguity as (4). This can be seen from the fact that (5) has two analysed forms, which is shown clearly in *Principia*[9]

(5a) $\qquad (\exists x)(y)[(\phi x \equiv y = x) . \sim\psi x]$
(5b) $\qquad \sim\langle(\exists x)(y)[(\phi x \equiv y = x) . \psi x]\rangle$

No description occurs in either (5a) or (5b), despite the fact that it is only by analysing (5) that primary or secondary occurrence can be determined. It is here that appeal must be made to 14.02 of *Principia*.

14.02 $\qquad E!(\imath x)(\phi x) = (\exists x)(y)[\phi x \equiv (y = x)]$[10]

If 14.02 is kept in mind, then it can be seen that what does occur in (5a) and (5b) is the definition of

(6) $\qquad E!(\imath x)(\phi x)$

That is

(6a) $\qquad (\exists x)(y)[\phi x \equiv y = x]$

Thus, the analysis of (5) reveals an existence assertion, and it seems clear that it is (6a) which will have primary or secondary occurrence.

Now, (5a) is supposed to be an example of primary occurrence, and (5b) of secondary occurrence, so that (6a) should occur as a part of a larger sentence in (5b), but not in (5a). However, both (5a) and (5b) involve a conjunction, and so it seems that (6a) could be regarded as a constituent sentence in both cases. Moreover, if

(7) $\qquad \psi(\imath x)(\phi x)$

is analysed, it should be a clear case of primary occurrence. Yet, in its analysed form,

(7a) $\qquad (\exists x)(y)[(\phi x \equiv y = x) . \psi x]$

(6a) still appears as part of a larger sentence formed by conjunction. Finally, the rule of addition can be used to effect a reductio.

(8) $\qquad \psi(\imath x)(\phi x) \vee \psi(\imath x)(\phi x)$

9 *PM*, p. 68.
10 *Ibid.*, p. 31.

can be derived from (7), and its analysed form is

(8a) $(\exists x)(y)[(\phi x \equiv y = x) . \psi x] \vee$
$(\exists x)(y)[\phi x \equiv y = x) . \psi x]$

In (8a), (6a) is a part of a larger sentence and so it has secondary occurrence, which means that (8a) could be true. However, if (7) is regarded as an example of primary occurrence, then the situation arises where (7) may be false, while (8) could be true. In which case, a true disjunction has been derived, but both of its disjuncts are false!

Now, it may be objected that these arguments are unfair to Russell because they involve using compound sentences formed by logical connectives. In contrast to this, Russell's examples are always either oblique contexts, such as belief sentences, or negative assertions. This point is quite correct, but it does not damage my arguments. Russell persists in speaking of *parts* of sentences in a completely general manner, and so conjuncts cannot be excluded. Consequently, the notion of a definite description being part of a sentence does not provide an adequate criterion for distinguishing between primary and secondary occurrence.

Russell also discusses the distinction in terms of the scope of '$(\imath x)$ (ϕx)'. So, this may clarify the notion of occurring as part of a constituent sentence. "When $(\imath x)(\phi x)$ does not exist, there are still true propositions [sentences] in which '$(\imath x)(\phi x)$' occurs, but it has, in such propositions [sentences], a secondary occurrence . . . i.e., the asserted proposition [sentence] concerned is not of the form $\psi(\imath x)$ (ϕx), but of the form $f\{(\imath x)(\phi x)\}$, in other words the proposition [sentence] which is the scope of $(\imath x)(\phi x)$ is only part of the asserted proposition [sentence]."[11] For example,

(9) $\psi(\imath x)(\phi x) \supset p$

may be analysed as

(9a) $(\exists x)(y)[(\phi y \equiv y = x) . \psi x] \supset p$

or

(9b) $(\exists x)(y)[(\phi y \equiv y = x) . (\psi x \supset p)]$[12]

Obviously, (9a) and (9b) do show a difference in the scope of the

[11] *PM*, p. 182.
[12] *Ibid.*, p. 69.

quantifiers, but they do not clarify the notion of (6a) occurring as part of a constituent sentence. In both cases, (6a) is part of a conjunction. Thus, the difference in scope of '$(\imath x)(\phi x)$' does not clarify the distinction between primary and secondary occurrence.

This leaves only one possibility for extracting an adequate criterion for primary occurrence. It is clear that the question of the existence of $(\imath x)(\phi x)$ is closely related to the distinction between primary and secondary occurrence. If $(\imath x)(\phi x)$ does not exist, i.e., if (6) 'E!$(\imath x)$ (ϕx)' is false, then (9a) may be true, but (9b) is false. This is exactly analogous to (5a) and (5b), since the truth of the former is dependent on the truth of 'E!$(\imath x)(\phi x)$', but the truth of the latter is not. In fact, the ambiguity of sentences such as (5) and (9) is only important when 'E!$(\imath x)(\phi x)$' is false. "When $(\imath x)(\phi x)$ exists, the two interpretations of ambiguity give equivalent results, but when $(\imath x)(\phi x)$ does not exist, one interpretation is true and one false."[13] An examination of the relation of 'E!$(\imath x)(\phi x)$' to such sentences as (5) and (9) may provide the required criterion for primary occurrence.

It is obvious that the ambiguity of

(5) $\sim\psi(\imath x)(\phi x)$

could be avoided easily by the use of brackets. Thus, (5) can be considered the unanalysed form of

(5a) $(\exists x)(y)[(\phi x \equiv y=x) \cdot \sim\psi x]$

and

(5′) $\sim[\psi(\imath x)(\phi x)]$

the unanalysed form of

(5b) $\sim\langle(\exists x)(y)[(\phi x \equiv y=x) \cdot \psi x]\rangle$

In fact, Russell uses this device in connection with the identity sign, when he distinguishes between '$a \neq (\imath x)(\phi x)$' and '$\sim\{a = (\imath x)(\phi x)\}$'.[14] However, Russell does not employ this distinction, for the simple reason that sentences such as (5) and (5′) are sometimes equivalent.

14.32   E!$(\imath x)(\phi x) \equiv \langle\{[(\imath x)(\phi x)] \cdot [\sim\chi(\imath x)(\phi x)]\} \equiv$
         $\sim\{[(\imath x)(\phi x)] \cdot [\chi(\imath x)(\phi x)]\}\rangle$[15]

13 *Ibid.*
14 *Ibid.*, p. 185.
15 *Ibid.*

Russell remarks concerning 14.32 that "the equivalence asserted here fails when $\sim E!(\imath x)(\phi x)$. Thus, for example, let ϕy be 'y is the King of France'. Then $(\imath x)(\phi x) =$ the King of France. Let χy be 'y is bald'. Then $\{[(\imath x)(\phi x)] \cdot \sim\chi(\imath x)(\phi x)\} =$ the King of France exists and is not bald; but $\sim\{[(\imath x)(\phi x)] \cdot \chi(\imath x)(\phi x)\} =$ it is false that the King of France exists and is bald. Of these the first is false, the second is true."[16] On the other hand, when $(\imath x)(\phi x)$ does exist, i.e., when '$E!(\cdot x)(\phi x)$' is true, then the equivalence does hold. Thus, (5) is equivalent to (5') if and only if $E!(\imath x)(\phi x)$. Consequently, Russell retained the ambiguous form of (5), because it is an extra-logical consideration that determines whether this ambiguity affects truth values. The truth or falsity of '$E!(\imath x)(\phi x)$' can be decided only by empirical investigation, i.e., by determining whether there is a constant, which can be said to satisfy 'x' in

(6a)
$$(\exists x)(y)[\phi x \equiv y = x]$$

If '$E!(\imath x)(\phi x)$', (6), is false, then (5a) will be false, but (5b) may be true. If (6) is true, then (5a) and (5b) will be equivalent.

Similarly, when (6) is true, the scope of '$(\imath x)(\phi x)$' becomes irrelevant to the truth value of a truth functional sentence. Russell makes this clear in *Principia*. If '$\chi(\imath x)(\phi x)$' occurs in a truth functional sentence, then provided $E!(\imath x)(\phi x)$, the truth value of '$f\{[(\imath x)(\phi x)] \cdot \chi(\imath x)(\phi x)\}$' is the same as the truth value of '$\{[(\imath x)(\phi x)] \cdot f[\chi(\imath x)(\phi x)]\}$'.[17] "It will be seen that when $(\imath x)(\phi x)$ has the whole of the proposition [sentence] concerned for its scope, the proposition [sentence] cannot be true unless $E!(\imath x)(\phi x)$; but when $(\imath x)(\phi x)$ has only part of the proposition [sentence] concerned for its scope, it may often be true even when $(\imath x)(\phi x)$ does not exist."[18]

The relation between '$E!(\imath x)(\phi x)$' and sentences containing '$(\imath x)(\phi x)$' as a constituent can be summarised as follows. If '$E!(\imath x)(\phi x)$' is true, then the distinction between primary and secondary occurrence does not affect the truth values of the sentences in which '$(\imath x)(\phi x)$' occurs. In such a case, a sentence such as

(7)
$$\psi(\imath x)(\phi x)$$

when true, will imply '$E!(\imath x)(\phi x)$'. This is stated by Russell as

16 *Ibid.*
17 *Ibid.*, p. 184.
18 *Ibid.*, p. 70.

14.21 $\psi(\imath x)(\phi x) \supset E!(\imath x)(\phi x)$[19]

Similarly, when '$E!(\imath x)(\phi x)$' is true, then

(5) $\sim\psi(\imath x)(\phi x)$

                                   and

(5') $\sim[\psi(\imath x)(\phi x)]$

are equivalent sentences. On the other hand, when '$E!(\imath x)(\phi x)$' is not true, then (5) and (5') are not equivalent sentences, since (5) will be false, while (5') may be true. Also, sentences such as (5b) and (9a) do not imply $E!(\imath x)(\phi x)$, and the falsity of '$E!(\imath x)(\phi x)$' does not imply that (5b) and (9a) are false. Thus, the relation between (6) and the sentences in which its definiendum has primary occurrence is different from its relation to those sentences in which its definiendum has secondary occurrence.

This contrast is stated explicitly by Russell when he discusses

(10) $[a \neq (\imath x)(\phi x)] = (\exists x)(y)[(\phi x \equiv y = x) \cdot (a \neq x)]$

(11) $\sim\{a = (\imath x)(\phi x)\} = \sim\{(\exists x)(y)[(\phi x \equiv y = x) \cdot$
                                              $(a = x)]\}$[20]

According to Russell, (10) "necessarily implies" (6a), and this can be interpreted as stating not only that (6a) must be true if (10) is true but also that (6a) is *deducible* from (10). In fact, (6a) is *deducible* from *each* of the examples of *primary* occurrence, which have been discussed, i.e., (5a), (7), (9b), and (10). On the other hand, (6a) is *not deducible* from the instances of secondary occurrence, i.e., (5b), (9a), and (11). Thus, the required criterion for distinguishing between primary and secondary occurrence can finally be given. A definite description, δ, has primary occurrence in a sentence S_1 if and only if a sentence S_2, consisting of the analysed form of δ, is deducible from the analysed form of S_1. Correspondingly, δ has secondary occurrence in a sentence S_1 if and only if S_2 is not deducible from the analysed form of S_1. In every case, S_2 will be a sentence of the form of (6a).

This criterion seems to be very different from Russell's own definition of secondary occurrences, which, as you remember, read:

[19] *Ibid.*, p. 181.
[20] *Ibid.*, pp. 173–174.

one in which the phrase occurs in a sentence p which is a mere constituent of the sentence we are considering.

However, the criterion which I have formulated is Russellian in content, if not in expression. It is based solely on Russell's Section 14 of *Principia* and is a clarification, rather than an improvement, of Russell's own remarks. I shall now use this criterion to clarify a part of Russell's analysis which puzzled G. E. Moore.

By Russell's analysis, 'the author of *Waverley* was Scotch' means

(12) x wrote *Waverley* is sometimes true.
(13) if y wrote *Waverley*, then y is identical with x, is always true of y.
(14) if x wrote *Waverley*, x was Scotch, is always true.[21]

Furthermore, Russell states that "all these three together are implied by 'the author of *Waverley* was Scotch'. Conversely, the three together (but no two of them) imply that the author of *Waverley* was Scotch."[22] Moore correctly pointed out that if Russell is using "implies" for material implication, then any one of (12)–(14) would materially imply that the author of *Waverley* was Scotch. Consequently, Moore maintained that Russell must be using "implies" so that "a *necessary* condition for its being true that p implies q is that it shall be *self-contradictory* to assert that p is true but q is false."[23] In other words, where p is 'the author of *Waverley* was Scotch', and q is (12), (13) and (14), p entails q, i.e., p and q are logically equivalent.[24]

Moore's point seems to be correct for the logical relation between 'the author of *Waverley* was Scotch' and its entire analysis, i.e., (12)–(14). However, it cannot hold for (12) alone, which Russell claims is "implied" by any sentence of the form 'C(the author of *Waverley*)'.[25] It is obvious that (12) is not logically equivalent to 'the author of *Waverley* was Scotch', and so this relationship still needs clarification. It is clear that (12) is simply an alternative version of

(6a) $$(\exists x)(y)[\phi y \equiv y = x]$$

---

[21] *IMP*, pp. 176–177.
[22] *Ibid.*
[23] "Russell's Theory of Descriptions," *The Philosophy of Bertrand Russell*, ed. P. A. Schilpp (New York: Harper & Row, 1963), p. 181.
[24] *Ibid.*
[25] "OD," p. 51.

and also that sentences of the form 'C(the author of $Waverley$)' are
symbolised by

(7a) $(\exists x)(y)\langle[\phi y \equiv y=x] \cdot \psi x\rangle$

So, Russell is maintaining that all sentences of the form of (7a) "imply" (6a). The first step in clarifying this claim is made by Russell
himself.

> If I say that the author of $Waverley$ was human, or a poet, or a Scots-
> man, or whatever I say about the author of $Waverley$ in the way of
> primary occurrence, always this statement of his existence is part of the
> proposition [sentence]. In that sense all the propositions [sentences]
> that I make about the author of $Waverley$ imply that the author of
> $Waverley$ exists. So that any statement in which a description has a
> primary occurrence implies that the object described exists.[26]

Thus, (6a) will be implied only by those sentences in which a definite
description has primary occurrence.

Now, it has been shown that (6a) is deducible from the analysed
form of any sentence which contains a primary occurrence of a definite description. So, I suggest that when Russell states that 'C(the author of $Waverley$)' "implies" (12), this should be interpreted as
meaning that (6a), or some equivalent form, is deducible from all
sentences of the form of (7a). Russell is undoubtedly either misleading
or inconsistent in his use of "implies" because he states this relation in

14.21 $\psi(\imath x)(\phi x) \supset E!(\imath x)(\phi x)$

This suggests that the relation is one of either material or logical implication, but it is neither. The relation is rather one of necessary implication or deducibility. I turn now to Russell's treatment of the George
IV puzzle.

In order to clarify Russell's proposed solution to this puzzle, it is
necessary to appeal to one more definition in *Principia*.

14.28 $E!(\imath x)(\phi x) \equiv [(\imath x)(\phi x) = (\imath x)(\phi x)].$[27]

Russell states that '$(\imath x)(\phi x)$' obeys all the same logical rules as those
symbols which directly represent objects, with the exception of the
reflexivity of identity. Symbols directly representing objects must be

---

[26] "Philosophy of Logical Atomism," reprinted in *Logic and Knowledge*, ed.
R. C. Marsh (Allen & Unwin, 1956), pp. 250–251.

[27] *PM*, p. 175.

logically proper names, which are symbolised by individual variables in *Principia*. Thus, in 14.28 Russell states that reflexivity of identity holds for a definite description, if and only if that description is a denoting phrase.

It is clear that 14.28 imposes a restriction on substitution which could be made using

13.15 $(x)(x=x)$

and the rule of specification, which enables the deduction of 'fy' from '$(x)fx$'. This restriction is necessary, because otherwise it would be possible to deduce '$(\imath x)fx = (\imath x)fx$' from 13.15.[28] According to Russell's analysis, this could be the deduction of a false conclusion from a true premise, if $(\imath x)\ fx$ did not exist. Pap believes that Russell probably intends to avoid such inferences by using 14.28 to prevent definite descriptions being substituted for individual variables.[29] However, it seems more likely that Russell is restricting substitution to those descriptions which are denoting phrases. Whenever '$E!(\imath x)(\phi x)$' is true, then there is one and only one entity, a, which is denoted by '$(\imath x)(\phi x)$', and '$(\imath x)(\phi x) = (\imath x)(\phi x)$'. Thus, reflexivity of identity holds for denoting phrases, but not for all definite descriptions. This restriction does prevent the deduction of factually false sentences, because, unless $E!(\imath x)(\phi x)$, 'fx' is not substitutable for 'x' in 13.15.

Now, as Russell presented his solution to the puzzle of (1)–(3), it consisted of analysing (1) and then appealing to the notion of the secondary occurrence of a definite description. Thus, provided (1) was interpreted as (1a) substitution of 'Scott' for 'the author of *Waverley*', or, more accurately, for 'one and one only man', is prohibited because (1a) is an example of secondary occurrence. It is now clear why (1a) is an example of secondary occurrence, but Russell does not provide any justification for this restriction on substitutivity. So, it appears to be simply an *ad hoc* device designed to prevent such inferences. However, Russell's restriction can be justified in the following manner. A sentence, with a primary occurrence of '$(\imath x)(\phi x)$', can be true only if '$E!(\imath x)(\phi x)$' is true. When $E!(\imath x)(\phi x)$, then $(\imath x)(\phi x) = (\imath x)(\phi x)$, by 14.28. Furthermore, when $E!(\imath x)(\phi x)$, then there is an entity, a, which '$(\imath x)(\phi x)$' describes and this entity can be named. So, $a = (\imath x)(\phi x)$; where 'a' is a logically proper name, and 'a'

[28] A. Pap, "Logic, Existence, and the Theory of Descriptions," *Analysis*, 13 (1953): 97.

[29] *Ibid.*, p. 98.

can be substituted for '$(\imath x)(\phi x)$'. On the other hand, a sentence with a secondary occurrence of '$(\imath x)(\phi x)$', may be true even if $\sim E!(\imath x)$ (ϕx). If $\sim E!(\imath x)(\phi x)$, then $(\imath x)(\phi x) \neq (\imath x)(\phi x)$, and $a \neq (\imath x)(\phi x)$. So, '$a$' is not substitutable for '$(\imath x)(\phi x)$'. However, this justification reveals obvious defects in Russell's "solution." It shows that Russell imposes *two* restrictions on substitution. The first is imposed by 14.28, and the second demands that the denoting phrase have secondary occurrence. Now, in (1b) the denoting phrase does not have secondary occurrence, and so 'Scott' could be substituted. Thus, Russell's "solution" will work only if (1) is interpreted as (1b). Furthermore, it is quite clear that Russell does not have a formal rule of substitution. Before '$(\imath x)(\phi x)$' can be substituted for a variable or vice versa, it is necessary to determine whether '$E!(\imath x)(\phi x)$' is true.[30] This is an empirical question not a syntactical one.

Finally, it is clear that while the distinction between primary and secondary occurrence of definite descriptions can be formulated syntactically, its application demands empirical investigation. Given a sentence such as (4a), it must be seen first whether (6a) is deducible. If (6a) is deducible, then it must be determined whether (6a) is true or false, and this can be done only by empirical investigation. If (6a) is false, then (4a) is false. In other words, the distinction between primary and secondary occurrence affects the truth values of sentences, in which definite descriptions occur, only when those definite descriptions are *not* denoting phrases. Thus, application of the distinction is determined by an empirical investigation, not syntactical rules.

Throughout this paper my purpose has been exegesis rather than polemics, and so I have carefully avoided any discussion of the controversial aspects of Russell's analysis. To the best of my knowledge, while the distinction between primary and secondary occurrence is usually referred to in any discussion of the Theory of Descriptions, it has never been clarified. I hope that my criterion provides the type of clarification which is a necessary basis for fruitful discussion.

[30] Cf. *Ibid.*, p. 100 for a slightly different expression of this point.

18

Russell and Strawson on Referring

Arthur Jacobson

RUSSELL'S Theory of Descriptions is properly regarded as one of the major achievements in philosophy in the twentieth century. The theory underwent one rather major change as Russell's thought developed. He gave up the notion of the 'denoting concept', which he defended in *Principles of Mathematics*, in favor of the interpretation of descriptions as incomplete symbols which characterizes all subsequent statements of the theory. I intend to say no more about denoting concepts here, or about the early stages of Russell's analysis of descriptions, except to make one comment. A particular conception of the philosophical undertaking is common to both the developing and the developed theory. Philosophy is taken to be concerned with the analysis of the language (sentences) with which we describe the world. A correct philosophical analysis of this language (these sentences) will reveal what it really means, what it is really about. The analysis is required because much of the language we use to describe the world is intrinsically misleading with respect to the *kinds* of things there are. The obscurity arises not from the fact that we make some particular claim about the world on insufficient grounds but, rather, from the fact that the grammatical and logical forms of our language (sentences) are frequently incongruent. It is the logical structure of our language and not its grammatical structure that reveals the most general features of reality.

When we are insufficiently aware of at just what points these diverge we run the risk of assimilating grammatical categories to logical categories, and these in turn to ontological ones. The consequences of such an assimilation may frequently be disastrous, leading us, for instance, to posit the being of subsistent entities.

I

Our language contains many phrases of the form 'the so-and-so' which are constituents of sentences used to refer to some one definite object, person, or event. Among Russell's own examples of sentences containing such definite descriptions are the following:

(1) Scott is the author of *Waverley*.
(2) The present king of France is wise.
(3) The square root of minus one is half the square root of minus four.

In the first example the descriptive phrase, 'the author of *Waverley*', occurs in an identity statement, and the 'is' is the 'is' of identity. In the second sentence the descriptive phrase, 'the present king of France', occupies the subject place of a subject-predicate sentence, and the 'is' is the 'is' of predication. Russell holds not only that the 'is' of identity is ordinarily discriminated from the 'is' of predication in common speech, but that the latter is not as a matter of logic reducible to the former. Hence any analysis of descriptive phrases must offer an account of the way they function in both sorts of sentences. I include both of these examples in the list I have given because it is precisely one of Russell's criticisms of Strawson that he has failed to discuss the issues attendant upon an analysis of 'Scott is the author of *Waverley*' in the article "On Referring."[1] Russell also implies that Strawson can give no adequate account of sentences like example three. I will return to these points in Section III of this paper, where I will take up in some detail the burden of Russell's reply.[2]

Consider the first example, 'Scott is the author of *Waverley*'. What is the proper analysis of this sentence and sentences like it? How and

[1] P. F. Strawson, "On Referring," originally in *Mind*, 59 (1950): 320–344, reprinted in *Philosophy and Ordinary Language*, ed. Charles E. Caton (Urbana: University of Illinois Press, 1963), pp. 162–193, and in this volume.
[2] Bertrand Russell, "Mr. Strawson on Referring," *Mind*, 66 (1957): 385–389.

what do they mean? Our most naively direct response to this question would be to say that descriptive phrases like 'the author of *Waverley*' are names and that they mean in the same way that names mean, by denoting some object. The sentence in question would then be taken as asserting the synonymy of two names. Russell's objections to the treatment of descriptions as names is succinctly stated in "The Philosophy of Logical Atomism." If 'the author of *Waverley*' is another name for Scott, then the sentence 'Scott is the author of *Waverley*' means no more than 'Scott is Scott', which is a tautology. On the other hand suppose you try to substitute any other name for 'the author of *Waverley*'; then if the name is the name of someone who is *not* Scott the sentence is false. Under any substitution instance of a name for 'the author of *Waverley*', the sentence 'Scott is the author of *Waverley*' is either tautologous or false. Since it is neither, 'the author of *Waverley*' is not a name.

A second argument against the treatment of descriptive phrases as proper names is the following. Names are arbitrary, so if 'the author of *Waverley*' is treated as a name synonymous with 'Scott', then whether or not 'Scott' is identical with 'the author of *Waverley*' is a nomenclatural decision. But, "You cannot settle by choice of nomenclature whether he is or not the author of *Waverley* because in actual fact he chose to write and you cannot help yourself."[3]

Over and above these arguments one might object to the attempted analysis of descriptive phrases as names on the grounds that it obliterates an obvious and important difference between the two. Descriptions refer by mentioning properties possessed by some individual object, event, or person. Such phrases are meaningful even when there is no object, event, or person having just the complex of properties referred to. We can speak significantly about an instance of a certain property or complex of properties even when such a complex is not or could not be given. The reason for this is that we are already acquainted with those properties from other experiential contexts. The case of proper names is altogether different. When I use a name to refer to some object I tell you nothing about it that would assist in classifying it as like or unlike some other object. The object denoted by the name simply is the meaning of the name. A name having no referent, now or in the past, would simply be a meaningless noise.

To object to the treatment of descriptions in identity statements as

[3] Bertrand Russell, "The Philosophy of Logical Atomism," reprinted by the Department of Philosophy, University of Minnesota, p. 42.

proper names is to deny that descriptions mean by denotation. Whether the descriptive phrase occurs in an identity statement or in the subject or predicate place of a subject-predicate sentence, it is not the case that there is anything which directly and unambiguously corresponds to it. Russell suggests that it might at first occur to you to say that the proper analysis of 'The king of France is wise' or 'Scott is the author of *Waverley*' is that these sentences are really about three things. The three things being what are referred to by 'the king of France', 'is' and 'wise', or 'Scott', 'is' and 'the author of *Waverley*'. But this is clearly false since there are many perfectly significant assertions which explicitly deny that certain things exist. Such sentences, for instance, as 'The unicorn does not exist'. If the expression 'the unicorn' named a fact about the world in any sense whatever, then in order to significantly assert the nonexistence of unicorns there would in some sense have to *be* unicorns and the sentence in question would imply a contradiction.

It should be noted in passing that Russell is here cutting the ground from under a possible alternate analysis. We might try to treat sentences which are identity statements as if they were predication statements. We might, that is, suggest that the proper analysis of 'Scott is the author of *Waverley*' is that it says that there is a man named 'Scott' who has the property to which we give the name 'the author of *Waverley*'. The arguments against treating 'the author of *Waverley*' as a name bear also against this suggestion. Set them aside for a moment and try to treat the descriptive phrase in question as a name. If it *is* a name it must directly denote something, in this case a property, with which we are or could be directly acquainted. But there is no such property. No property, that is, of being the author of *Waverley*. And in that case the expression, lacking a referent, would not be a name but simply a nonsignificant noise.

In its final form Russell's Theory of Descriptions satisfied a number of philosophical requirements. It allowed him to offer an analysis of sentences containing descriptions without transforming them into proper names, without assimilating the 'is' of identity to the 'is' of predication, and without positing the being of subsistent entities. The theory is consonant with his basic sense of reality and maintains the distinction between logical and empirical truths.

When there are sentences in which descriptive phrases occur, such phrases can be replaced by equivalent statements in which no descriptive phrases occur. As in the case of 'The present king of France is wise', where the analysis would be as follows:

(1) There is a king of France.
(2) There is not more than one king of France.
(3) There is nothing which is not the king of France and not wise.

The analysis shows that it is possible to treat significant sentences in which descriptive phrases occur in such a manner as not to imply the existence or subsistence of some object referred to by that phrase. One final point is, I take it, crucial, and bears on a major detail of the Strawson-Russell debate. I judge it to be Russell's view that sentences (1)–(3), although an expression in ordinary English sentences of what would be expressed this way

$$(\exists x)[\phi x . (y)(\phi y \supset y = x) . \psi x]$$

in formal notation, are not actually a philosophically unambiguous linguistic formulation. Only in the appropriate formal notation do we remove all possibility of ambiguity. We not only express what we mean but reveal, by the structure of the expression itself, the structure of the world about which we speak. We say something that may be either true or false, in this case something about the king of France. The notation in which we express what we say, *whether what we say is true or false*, reveals the kinds of things and relations having ontological status that there must be for the statement to *be* either true or false. The notation is not merely a pragmatically useful device but a condition of carrying the philosophical project forward. It is a language in which we not only do not but quite literally cannot assert anything which is either ambiguous or paradoxical.

II

The Theory of Descriptions has not been without its commentators and critics, but a prominent feature of that criticism has been that Russell and his critics have always held one philosophically very important piece of common ground. Even in the face of relatively serious disagreements Russell and his critics have shared, in a very general way, a common theory of meaning. If not the whole at least a significant part of the story of meaning was to be sought in the notion of denotation or reference. They shared the denotationist theory of meaning. Both the significance of the Strawson-Russell debate and the curiously indecisive character of that exchange are to be found in the fact that precisely this bit of common ground is missing. Indeed that is exactly the point of Strawson's criticism. In Russell's thought the Theory of Descriptions assumes a theory of meaning and offers itself as the only philosophically adequate account of what, in particular cases, is meant. Strawson's attack takes the form of denying in toto the theory of meaning presupposed by the Theory of Descriptions so that the burden of the argument between them rests *there*, rather than on any details of Russell's analysis of definite descriptions.

The heart of Strawson's position can be put, as indeed Strawson himself does put it, in a single sentence: "There are no logically proper names, and there are no descriptions (in this sense)."[4] The denial that there are logically proper names is the denial that there are names of a logical character such that they alone can be candidates for the subject place of genuine subject-predicate sentences. A word or expression which is a logically proper name designates an individual object, person, or event and that object, person, or event is what such a name means. The object is the meaning. What the denial of descriptions '(in this sense)' means it is less easy to state succinctly. First it means that there are no translations of sentences containing descriptive phrases of the form 'the so-and-so' into a set of propositions which *asserts* the unique existence of some object, event, or person. The offered translation pattern for sentences containing expressions of the form 'the so-and-so' is wrong because in fact sentences like 'The king of France is wise' do not themselves make any existential assertions at all. It is not even the case that a speaker, seriously using such sentences to refer, would be asserting that such a person existed. He would, in a special sense of the word 'imply', be implying that such a person existed. Or, alternatively, a speaker's serious use of such a sentence to refer would in a sense presuppose that there was a king of France. Secondly, Strawson takes Russell to hold that sentences containing definite descriptions, if such sentences are significant, must be either true or false. It is Strawson's view that the issue of whether or not such sentences are truly *used* to refer in some particular context is different from the

4 Strawson, "On Referring," p. 167.

question of whether and what such sentences mean. I truly or falsely use sentences to refer. The sentences or expressions themselves do not refer. A consequence of this is that the sentence 'The king of France is wise' is significant although neither true nor false. My detailed comments on the debate begin with Strawson's article.

Let's begin by asking what it was that Strawson took Russell to be doing, and what he thought Russell's philosophical motives and intentions were in doing it. He understands Russell to have been attempting to give "a correct account of the use of such expressions in ordinary language."[5] That is, a correct account of the use of such expressions as 'the so-and-so' as they occur in daily speech. And it is his claim that the Theory of Descriptions does not in fact give the correct account. The phrase 'a correct account of the use of such expressions in ordinary language' is sufficiently ambiguous as to obscure the debate between the two philosophers to some degree. In particular the ambiguity permits one to raise the question of whether Strawson in his criticism and Russell in his reply don't each beg the central point at issue. There are three loci of obscurity in the quoted expression:

(1) The idea of 'use' or linguistic usage.
(2) The conception of what a 'correct account' in philosophy would be.
(3) The importance of 'ordinary language' in and for philosophy.

These three notions are, of course, intimately connected. The most important one is the idea of 'use'. It is also the most in need of clarification. For Strawson, and within the context of philosophical discussion, it is synonymous with 'meaning' so that to give an account of the use of a word or expression is to give an account of its meaning. How I use a word is what *it* means but not, of course, what *I* mean (mention, refer to). "For to talk about the meaning of an expression or sentence is not to talk about its use on a particular occasion, but about the rules, habits, conventions governing its correct use, on all occasions, to refer or to assert."[6] It turns out that the use of 'use' in the phrase 'a correct account of the use of such expressions in ordinary language' is not itself an ordinary use of 'use'. It is a technical or spe-

[5] *Ibid.*, p. 163.
[6] *Ibid.*, pp. 171–172.

cialist's use, which comes freighted with a philosophical theory of meaning. Now if 'use' is taken in this technical sense, then it will of course turn out that Russell's Theory of Descriptions is seriously misguided (or wholly false). Because if that theory is taken as an account of the use of certain expressions in Strawson's sense of 'use', and if Russell's view depends on an altogether different theory of meaning, then the Theory of Descriptions is misplaced from the outset.

If 'use' is not taken in this technical sense then Russell could quite properly object that he is not trying to give an account of the way expressions of the sort 'the so-and-so' are used at all. Such an account would properly belong to some field like the sociology of language, and while this field *may* have something to say which is important for philosophy it is not really what Russell has in mind when he offers an explanation of what such phrases really mean. To give an account of descriptions is to give an analysis of what sentences containing descriptive expressions mean. And what they mean are certain facts in the world. Knowing how to use certain expressions or sentences correctly is parasitic upon being acquainted with the sorts of things they do or could denote.

Both Russell and Strawson would agree that the philosopher is rightly concerned with the meanings of ordinary expressions or ordinary language, but the significance for each of them of such language is different. Russell will argue that what the philosopher says neither is nor could be itself a piece of ordinary speech. It is rather a piece of specialist's speech, with a vocabulary and syntax all its own and a context of use that is far from ordinary. I do not wish to argue that Russell's view of what has come to be called an ideal language is necessarily very clear. Only that he has a conception of such a language, that it is different from ordinary language, and that philosophical work would either be impossible or incredibly difficult without it.

There is agreement, or at least ought to be, on one point. Strawson would hardly deny that philosophy requires a specialized vocabulary of its own. He introduces such a vocabulary in the article, "On Referring." That paper abounds with words or terms like the following: 'use', 'spurious use', 'uniquely referring use', 'uniquely existential sentences', 'identification statement'; all of which are given carefully specified meanings. Of course these are not parts of the common speech of English-speaking people. But Russell takes Strawson to task for holding that "common speech is good enough not only for daily life but also for philosophy" when in fact he ought to recognize that any "attempt to be precise and accurate requires modification of common speech both as regards vocabulary and syntax."[7]

The issue between them concerns not vocabulary, but syntax. To say that the syntax of ordinary language is in need of modification is to claim that it is in some way wrong or misleading, inefficient or inelegant. It is not really easy to understand what such a claim might mean. The charge of inelegance might be dismissed as nothing more than the expression of an esthetic preference. There are natural languages in which the syntactical rules are very complicated, and one can imagine wishing they might be simplified after the model of invented languages like Esperanto. There are languages in which the syntactical rules are not clear or easily grasped, or which make it more difficult to execute what we take to be nice twists of style. But it is not clear that any of these complications would make a substantive difference to the philosophical enterprise. They might make the job of philosophy harder without in any way making it more likely that that more difficult job was being done wrong.

In what sense can the syntax of a language be "wrong" or "misleading"? Upon the most common understanding of what is meant by the syntax of a natural language that syntactical structure simply can't be wrong. We can *get* it wrong, or make mistakes in classifying its various grammatical rules, but the grammatical form of a language is simply what it is. It (the form) is neither "right" nor "wrong." Here when we talk about the form of a language we are talking, in the first instance, of what is frequently called its grammatical syntax as opposed to its logical syntax. Many philosophers would find nothing exceptionable in such a distinction, even though it is a dangerously misleading and indistinct sort of a distinction. I wish to suggest that the word 'grammatical' introduced as a modifier of the word 'syntax' in the expression 'grammatical syntax' is strictly speaking a redundancy. The form of a language is given in that set of rules for constructing well formed sentences in that language. These are the rules according to which 'The cat is on the mat' is a properly constructed English sentence while "Cat mat on is the' is not a properly constructed English sentence. No one who violated these rules could be said to be uttering significant English sentences, although they would of course be giving voice to English words.

In order to make reasonable the claim that there is something wrong

[7] Russell, "Mr. Strawson on Referring," p. 387.

or misleading about the syntax of ordinary language it is necessary to oppose it to the conception of the logical syntax of the language. The claim can then be made that for some particular natural language its grammatical form (syntax) is not isomorphic with its logical form (logical syntax) and that the former cannot be taken as an index of the latter. The addition of the prefix 'logical', however, obscures more than it clarifies. At the very least it hides the fact that the expression 'grammatical syntax' is a redundancy. In the strict sense the syntax of a language is given in that part of the set of grammatical rules for the language governing the construction of well formed sentences. The only syntactical rules a language exhibits *are* its 'grammatical' ones. But by introducing the notion of logical syntax and juxtaposing it to grammatical syntax we seem to suggest that the expression 'grammatical syntax' is not after all redundant. The notion of syntax has now become the notion of a genus within which there are two species, the logical and the grammatical, and somehow natural languages have both. The great approbative force of the term 'logical' reinforces any tendency we might have on other grounds to think the logical syntax of greater significance than the grammatical syntax. But this dangerous illusion depends on our continuing to suppose that in this context we can still say what the word 'syntax' means, that in using it we are referring to some formation rules for the language, but logical ones rather than grammatical ones. But in this context the word 'syntax' no longer has any meaning. What are the logical rules for the forming of proper English sentences which are different from the grammatical ones? There are none. The distinction is empty.

The objection might surely be raised at this point that a great number of important philosophers have spoken of the logical syntax of language and that they have taken it to be a significant expression specifying a crucial philosophical distinction. Am I to be taken as asserting out of hand that they are wrong? Not entirely, but in part. Specifically in the exchange between Strawson and Russell I am holding that Russell's charge that the syntax of ordinary language needs to be modified is a mistake. The mistake lies in thinking that there is somehow a second, less problematical, syntax of ordinary language which the grammatical syntax obscures. The substitution of a formal language, such as the language of *Principia*, for English is not to modify the syntax of English. The clearest meaning that could be given to the expression 'logical syntax' would be to treat it as an ellipsis for the expression 'the syntax of a formal logical system'. Since natural or ordinary languages are not formal systems there is no logical syntax of them in this sense.

What underlies the notion that there is something wrong with the syntax of ordinary language is the assimilation of all linguistic rules to those of formal systems at the same time one treats the formation rules of a language as reflecting what there is. This is the burden of Russell's position. One can see the fatal ease with which it is possible to fall into this view. Beginning with the expression 'logical syntax' our attention is directed upon the term 'syntax'. On the model of grammatical syntax we assume ourselves to be talking about the rules for the production of well formed sentences. Or about rules analogous to such. Turning to the 'logical' part of the expression the meaning of this 'logical' is loosened and transformed. To speak of the "logical" syntax is now somehow to speak of the "real" syntax of language, as opposed to its "merely" grammatical syntax. It is tempting to say that now 'logical' is being covertly used in this context as a substitute for 'ontological'. So the logical syntax of a language is a set of rules conceived of after the model of rules for formal logical systems governing the formation of well formed sentences, such that sentences constructed in accord with these rules will successfully express or mean the most general ontological features of reality. That is, the rules say what types of words are to be connected, and in what patterns, and the kinds of words and the relations in which they stand in well formed sentences reflect or express or mean the kinds of things there are and the relations in which they stand in reality.

In any natural language it is possible to distinguish the grammatical rules of that language from its semantical rules. The distinction may not be absolutely rigid and clear cut, although by and large it would be true to say that only grammatically correct sentences or sentence fragments (expressions) can be used meaningfully. The distinction is one between the rules for successfully constructing a sentence, and the rules for using such sentences in significant ways. To confuse these two kinds of rules is something like confusing the rules for well formed formulae with the rules or conventions for interpreting the variables of a formal system, and assimilating the latter to the former. If it is at all correct to hold that any rules of language reflect what there is, then it is the semantical rules of the language and not the syntactical rules that do this. But it is important to keep clearly in mind the difference between these two kinds of rules, and it is one of Strawson's major criticisms of Russell that Russell has failed to do this.

Grammatical rules (syntactical rules properly so called) cover the construction of sentences; semantical rules govern the use of sentences, and hence what we can mean with them.

The importance of ordinary language for Strawson is twofold. First, it reflects the same common sense view of reality that prompts Russell to reject subsistent entities because they offend against "that feeling for reality which ought to be preserved even in the most abstract studies."[8] This way of describing Strawson's view of ordinary language is not strictly correct, but a close enough approximation for purposes of comparison with Russell. It would be more strictly correct to say that for Strawson or, better, someone maintaining a Strawsonian view it is not the language itself which in the appropriate sense "reflects" the general features of reality but rather the semantical rules governing the significant employment of sentences or expressions to make successful references. And even here we should feel a certain reticence about the word 'reflects'. These rules do not even in some straightforward *metaphorical* way mirror reality. Rather, to the degree in which thought about the world is discourse about that world, they condition our thought and hence the world *about* which we think. Second, a proper account of how expressions like 'The present king of France' come to be significantly employed in our ordinary speech, an account distinguishing grammatical rules from semantical rules, can explain why it is we have that "feeling" for reality which rejects subsistent entities. It offers a line of defense or explanation that needs no recourse to feeling or to some (in the extremest case) faculty of metaphysical intuition.

Russell and Strawson are agreed on preserving what Russell calls "that feeling for reality." And they are agreed on what the deliverances of that feeling are, the most important of which is, in this case, the denial that there are subsistent entities. It is against this sense of the world that Russell in part measures the adequacy or inadequacy of accounts of the meaning of sentences containing descriptions. One reason for judging his own account acceptable is that it is consistent with a principle of direct acquaintance and neither asserts, nor entails, nor misleads us by its form to assert the being of subsistents. But this appeal to one's feeling or to one's sense of the real is a dangerously two-edged philosophical weapon. There is no proving that one's "sense" or "feeling" is correct if that feeling is the final court of appeal.

[8] *Ibid.*

One could confess to it and ask others if they didn't have it too, but beyond that no defense could be given. By itself this state of affairs might be considered one of the acceptable risks of any philosophical undertaking since, it could be suggested, there is always some point beyond which no further explanation or justification can be given. In the case of the claim that there are, or are not, subsistent entities this would be a mistake since such a claim is part of the ontology being defended. I take it that it is at least strategically desirable that the principles or grounds or starting assumptions of a developing ontological view be not themselves distinctively ontological claims. Why would anyone think that the sense of reality which proscribes subsistent entities is correct? He can hardly claim that it is obvious that this sense is epistemologically privileged. Are we to say that we know our sense is correct because, after all, that is the way the world is? Then this begs the question and leaves us with no response to the counter-assertion that after all some other philosopher's sense of reality reveals to him subsistent entities, bare particulars, or what have you.

Fortunately there is no need to counter one claim with another. The matter is not one which needs to be settled by appeal to senses for reality at all. We don't feel there are no subsistent entities, we *know* there are none, although what we know when we know this is not so much a proposition about the world as it is a proposition about the conditions of meaningful discourse. Russell felt he must offer an analysis of the meaning of sentences like 'The king of France is bald' which does not lead to the assertion of subsistent entities because he has a theory of meaning which makes it extremely easy to fall into the claim that there are such things. If that theory of meaning is incorrect, as Strawson points out that it is, then no ontological questions arise in the first place. There are no ontological traps to be avoided. The resolution of the problem takes the form now so familiar in much of the philosophy of the twentieth century. The way to resolve the problem is to show that it need never to have arisen in the first place. (Let me say, parenthetically, that to say this of the case in hand does not entail that there are no legitimate ontological questions at all, or that all of them are linguistically induced neuroses or illusions.) Further, the way in which we show that the question need never have arisen does not entail our assuming some *other* ontological principle or appealing to any special faculty or sense for the real.

It does, however, entail certain assumptions about language. Or perhaps it would be more nearly correct to say that it entails a willingness to refuse to continue asking certain questions. We must accept the semantical rules of natural languages for what they are. We may of course ask *what* they are and there is room for dispute about this. But there are public procedures for resolving such disputes. The question that it seems we cannot ask is *why* the semantical or grammatical rules are what they are. If this is taken to be some sort of historical question, then the origins of language are lost to us in a past so distant that all that is left is conjecture. The same would be true if the question were taken to be a request for a psychogenetic account of the origins of language, although we might be able to extrapolate from the language learning behaviour of children some interesting hypotheses.

I have said that we must accept the semantical rules of natural languages for what they are and *as* what they are. To say that we must accept them for what they are is to say that any suggestion that they may be wrong can be seen upon reflection to have no substantive meaning. Although the word 'assumption' suggests a degree of choice and voluntary acceptance of the rules which is not, as a matter of fact, characteristic of them, it is still helpful to speak of them as the most primitive assumptions of our philosophical thinking. The word 'assumption' is used as a reminder of the fact that no justification of the rules could be given and 'primitive' to suggest that where there are different semantical rules or levels of rules, one rule or level of rule is not reducible to another. (The semantical rules for categorical utterances are not reducible to the rules for indefinite references, for instance.)

Still there is a residual tendency to return constantly to the question, "Yes, but why are the rules just what they are rather than something else?" The questioner has in mind something like the following. Since it has been suggested that what there is is in some way reflected by the semantical rules of the language, might it not be the case that they overlook some feature of reality? Might they not be "wrong" in the sense of not properly reflecting its most general features and the relations between them? The answer is that this suggestion is without meaning. To see this let us try to talk about the ontological structure of the world and the semantical structure of language as if they were independent. I have already said that the latter reflects the former in no straightforward way. Not even in some straightforward metaphorical way. If the structure of my language is such that I can adequately speak about all the discoverable features of the world in which I live, then I have no problem. Now try to imagine what would obtain if this were *not* the case. It is suggested that there is some feature of the real which I have neglected because of the misleading or incomplete semantical structures of my language. I then ask what that feature is. If the objector can successfully identify that feature for me, that is if he can explain what it is he is talking about and point me in the right direction to find it, then he must do it in a language I can understand. That is, he must do it in a language the semantical rules of which I understand. (In this case English.) If he can do this, however, then there can have been nothing either incomplete or misleading about the language in the first place. On the other hand, if there *were* something intrinsically incomplete or misleading about the semantical rules, so that they were inadequate to the ontological structure of the world, then he could never successfully say in just what way this was true. The suggestion that the semantical rules of a language might be wrong is grounded then in the mistake of supposing that the semantical structure of language and the ontological structure of the world are separable; on the assumption that the ontological structure is what it is independent of the semantical structure of the language in which we think about that world. But we do not first become acquainted with, or intuit, or grasp, or come to know this ontological structure and then proceed to describe or talk or think about it. If we *did* then it might be significant to suggest that for whatever reason our language was inadequate to the world being described. The fact of the matter is that language simply *is the medium through which we come to know what the most general features of reality are.* To know one is to know the other. To ask why the semantical rules are the way they are is simply to ask why reality in its most general features is the way it is. And that from the nature of the case is a question which is not possible to answer. (If what we are trying to talk about are the most general features of reality, then there are by definition no more general features that can be the ground, reason, cause of them.)

It is now possible to deal in a fairly direct fashion with Strawson's attack on Russell's treatment of descriptions. It is Strawson's position that the Theory of Descriptions is intended to avoid the consequences of two arguments that could or might be employed by philosophers concerning such expressions as 'The king of France is wise'. Because expressions such as 'the king of France' are employed as the subjects of significant sentences there must be, in some sense of 'be', an existing or subsisting king of France. Since if the sentence is significant there must be something it is about. If there is nothing it is about, then it is not literally significant. The second argument is that if such sentences are significant, as they clearly are, then they must be either true or false. But they could be neither true nor false save upon the condition that there was some king of France of which it could be truly or falsely asserted that he was wise.

Strawson here correctly identifies the underlying ontological motive for the Theory of Descriptions. It enables us to avoid the positing of subsistent entities. Of course the ordinary speaker never, in his stock use of such expression takes himself to be positing, supposing, or implying the existence of such a realm or of such a kind of entity. (This is characteristically a philosopher's supposition when he talks about or analyzes these sorts of expressions.) It is not, of course, that the ordinary speaker disbelieves in subsistent entities. He is neither saying that there is or is not such a realm; he is neither implying or not implying that there is such a realm. In this sense ordinary speech reflects the same firmly commonsensical view of what there is that Russell embraces. The important feature of the Theory of Descriptions at this point (although Strawson does not make this comment) is not that the formulation of the theory reveals that there are no realms of subsistent entities but that it allows us to recapture the core of meaning of ordinary speech and at the same time does justice to our prior sense of what sorts of things should be included in a proper ontology. We want to avoid any account of the meaning of such expressions that might mislead us into asserting that there are subsistent entities because the view that there are such entities is simply false. This means that in no sense could the Theory of Descriptions prove that there were no subsistents. It is merely an elegant expression of an Occamite resolve to simplify our ontology.

Strawson recognizes that Russell rejects the arguments that might lead one to assert the being of subsistent entities, and agrees that Russell's "feeling for the real" is at least correct insofar as it leads him to do so. But although the Theory of Descriptions rejects the principle of an over-blown ontology and presents a logical reconstruction of such problematic assertions as 'The king of France is wise', what it accepts is more important than what it rejects. What it accepts is the basic presupposition of the two spurious arguments that Russell is eager to avoid. Russell is intent on distinguishing the ordinary grammar of a sentence from its logical grammar. It is not always the case (and here sentences containing descriptions are what Russell has in mind) that a grammatically proper name is a logically proper one. The fact that a phrase or expression occupies the subject place of a subject-predicate sentence is no guarantee that the logical form of that sentence is that of a subject-predicate assertion, or that the phrase in question is a logical subject. The arguments that Russell is interested in avoiding, however, all assume the essential isomorphism of logical and grammatical form. In effect they hold that these are always the same, that all grammatically proper names are logically proper names. Russell has to deal with these arguments, regardless of how good they may be judged to be, because he himself wants to hold the following propositions:

(1) There are some sentences which are, both with respect to ordinary grammar and with respect to logical grammar, of the subject-predicate form.

(2) Where the grammatical subject does not refer then the sentence is either meaningless or not logically of the subject-predicate form.

(3) For any sentences logically of the subject-predicate form, if they are significant, then there is something referred to by the logical subject of the sentence.[9]

Strawson then goes on to enter a reminder of Russell's views on logically proper names which is that only they can be the subjects of genuinely subject-predicate form sentences and that the things they designate are their meanings. Where names *seem* to designate something but there is nothing in fact which they do designate, then they are meaningless. The burden of the view attributed to Russell is the following:

Generally, we may say that Russell recognizes only two ways in which sentences which seem, from their grammatical structure, to be about some particular person or individual object or event, can be significant:

(1) The first is that their grammatical form should be misleading as to their logical form, and that they should be analysable, like S (The king of France is wise), as a special kind of existential sentence.

(2) The second is that their grammatical subject should be a logically

[9] Quoted by Strawson in "On Referring."

proper name, of which the meaning is the individual thing it designates.[10]

Strawson argues that there are neither logically proper names nor descriptions in the sense specified. There are no logically proper names because *no* word or expression has as its meaning some designated object, meanings not being things denoted by words. Meaning is an activity of language users, not the entities that they use language to refer to. There are no descriptions in the requisite sense because no one employing sentences like 'The king of France is wise' is asserting that there is a king of France. With respect to this last point Strawson asserts that Russell fails to distinguish between

(1) Using an expression to make a unique reference; and
(2) Asserting that there is one and only one individual which has certain characteristics (e.g. is of a certain kind, or stands in a certain relation to the speaker, or both.)[11]

Sentences used to make assertions of this sort Strawson calls "uniquely existential sentences."

There are three lines of attack against the Theory of Descriptions. All three are dependent, to different degrees, upon the acceptance of a theory of meaning which identifies the meaning of expressions like 'The king of France' with the rules for using such expressions to refer or mention. The first argument is simply that the Theory of Descriptions is *de trop*. It is constructed to avoid difficulties that are fancied rather than real, and which owe their existence to the fact that Russell holds a denotationist or reference theory of meaning. If he didn't hold that there were logically proper names, he would not have to guard against the interpretation of expressions like 'The king of France' as such a name. Since there are no logically proper names, the Theory of Descriptions is unnecessary. Accepting this argument of course requires that we accept the Strawsonian view that "To give the meaning of an expression . . . is to give *general directions* for its use to refer or mention particular objects or persons; to give the meaning of a sentence is to give *general directions* for its use in making true or false assertions."[12]

The second argument against the Theory of Descriptions is less de-

10 Strawson, "On Referring," pp. 165–166.
11 *Ibid.*, p. 166.
12 *Ibid.*, p. 179.

pendent upon the theory of meaning that Strawson proposes, since it is at least possible to run the argument without committing oneself to the theory of meaning in question. This argument simply says that to analyze the meaning of sentences like 'The king of France is wise' in terms of the conjunction of three sentences which together assert the unique existence of something is an error. To use an expression like 'The king of France' to begin a sentence is not to assert that there *is* a king of France, nor does the sentence, or my use of it, entail some other sentence or conjunction of sentences making a uniquely existential assertion. Strawson says that while it would be wrong to say that I assert the existence of (in this case) the king of France, or that my sentence entails some other sentence making a uniquely existential assertion, I do just the same 'imply' or presuppose, or signal my belief in the existence of such a unique individual. One of the functions of the definite article in sentences beginning 'the such-and-such' is that it "shows but does not state, that we are, or intend to be, referring to one particular individual of the species 'such-and-such'."[13]

In the final analysis it is the third argument against the Theory of Descriptions which is crucial. It is crucial for two reasons. First, the other arguments or analyses rest wholly or in part upon it, and secondly because the subject matter of that argument is the real issue between Russell and Strawson, that is, *theory of meaning*. The Theory of Descriptions constitutes no more than the occasion on which the semantical question is raised. To argue against the Theory of Descriptions is to argue against the theory of meaning upon which the Theory of Descriptions depends. According to Strawson this is what I have called the denotationist theory of meaning. The suggested alternative to this theory is one which identifies the meanings of expressions with their use. Upon the assumption that these two accounts of meaning are incompatible one with the other, and the whole mutually exclusive story about meaning, then an argument for meaning as use will be an argument, by extension, against the Theory of Descriptions. And this constitutes the crucial third argument.

The major fault with Strawson's paper is that in the body of the paper itself we are given very little in the way of argument to support the notion that "to give the meaning . . . is to give general directions" and so forth. No matter how sympathetic one might be to this view, it is hardly self-evident. Merely explaining it is not an argument that in

[13] *Ibid.*, p. 171.

itself persuades us that this is the one true account of meaning or even a large part of the true account. At the very least one must admit that it falls strangely upon 'the ordinary ear' to say that the meaning of either an expression or a sentence is a set of general directions for its use. In particular one can imagine the Russellian critic of Strawson arguing that in addition to its sounding very odd to speak of the meaning of an expression as a set of directions, any attempt to explain what it would be to *give* general directions of this sort would show that the concept of giving general directions covertly entails the very denotative theory of meaning being denied.

If the directions are *really* general, then they would be the directions for using *any* expression of a given type to mention or refer. Such directions would be equally appropriate for 'the king of France' or 'the motorcycle in the garage'. But if equally appropriate, then they are insufficient to explain the difference in meaning between these two expressions (or my use of them). Directions for using words to mention or refer must include an explanation of their meaning in a sense sufficiently like denotation not to be worth quibbling about. Giving a set of directions for using an expression to refer is not unlike giving a set of directions for using a hammer to drive nails. The person receiving directions for the use of a hammer will be at a complete loss to understand what it is he is being directed to do unless he understands the meaning of 'hammer'. Teaching someone how to recognize a hammer when he sees one is certainly not like teaching him to use the one he has successfully identified. And furthermore, only if you have done the former can you proceed to do the latter.

Similarly it would hardly seem possible to give general directions for the use of a term or expression to mention or refer to something unless both the teacher and the student had some way of determining that the term had been used correctly. But knowing how to use a term or expression, it might be argued, is *parasitic* upon understanding what it means, rather than being the same thing.

III

Russell's reply to Strawson, "Mr. Strawson on Referring,"[14] is interesting primarily for the way in which Russell failed to grasp

[14] Russell, "Mr. Strawson on Referring," *Mind*, 66 (1957): 385–389.

Strawson's main argument against the Theory of Descriptions. It seems to me that although Russell properly recognized that he and Strawson disagreed in a most profound way on the issue of philosophical semantics his reply never did full justice to the fact that the burden of Strawson's argument is carried by his attack on denotationist theories of meaning. The result is that Russell's counter-arguments seem somehow always off center.

Nowhere is this clearer than in Russell's understanding of Strawson's argument. And what he thinks that argument is can best be judged by his defense. Russell thinks that Strawson's objections center on the occurrence of what Russell has called "ego-centric" words in the description. He takes Strawson to be saying something like the following.

Russell has failed to note that words like 'present' in sentences like,

(a)   The present king of France is bald.

are such that specification of their referents depends upon the temporal (and in appropriate cases the spatial) location of the speaker. So no straightforward translation of such sentences as (a) in terms of a conjunction of assertions can be given.

Clearly Russell thinks that Strawson holds the problems occasioned by the analysis of sentences containing expressions of the form 'the so-and-so' are the result of their containing "ego-centric" words and that Russell's analysis hasn't done justice to this, or to words of this sort. That this is the correct version of Russell's understanding of Strawson can be seen from the things Russell says in his own defense. First, he is at pains to point out that in *Inquiry into Meaning and Truth* and in *Human Knowledge* he did in fact discuss the role of context in determining the meanings of words. And Russell says, speaking of Strawson, "The gist of what he says about such words is the entirely correct statement that what they refer to depends upon what and where they are used."[15] Second, Russell reminds Strawson that in his original discussions of descriptions he had cited, in addition to

(a)   The present king of France is bald.

sentences like

(b)   Scott is the author of *Waverley*.

and he accuses Strawson of ignoring sentences like (b) while missing

[15] *Ibid.*, p. 386.

the point of the problems presented by (a) because it contains the 'ego-centric' word 'present'. He suggests that Strawson's argument would have collapsed if instead of 'present' Russell had substituted the words 'in 1905'. That Russell takes Strawson to be worried about descriptive sentences only *when* they contain, and *because* they contain, ego-centric words is evident from the challenge to Strawson to apply "his doctrine" to the following:

(c) The square root of minus one is half the square root of minus four.

Russell concludes that even though there is no ego-centric word in that sentence "the problem of interpreting the descriptive phrases is exactly the same as if there were."[16]

It is extremely interesting that Russell's reply could come at once so close to the mark and at the same time fly so wide of it. Of course Strawson understands both the general and the particular aims of the Theory of Descriptions. He is at great pains to point out the motives underlying its formulation. He is not simple-mindedly worried about the occurrence of the word 'present' in descriptions of the king of France. (As a matter of fact Strawson, in using the king of France example, uses as his paradigm, "The king of France is wise" in which no ego-centric word appears.) On the other hand, in discussing what he takes to be Strawson's treatment of 'ego-centric' words he comes tantalizingly close to a full appreciation of the application of Strawson's theory of meaning. Russell said, "The gist of what he says about such words is the entirely correct statement that what they refer to depends upon what and where they are used." But this persists in missing one of the main points of Strawson's argument, and of confusing exactly what Strawson *claimed* Russell confused—the difference between what I mean when I use a certain referring expression and the meaning of the expression. Clearly Russell implies that it is *words* which denote or refer. While it is the Strawsonian position that words or expressions are *used* to refer. And he fails either to see or appreciate the degree to which the motive for, and the development of, the Theory of Descriptions is grounded in a reference theory of meaning.

When Russell turns to deal with Strawson's denial that there are any logically proper names we come to the culminating point of the

16 *Ibid.*, p. 385.

debate. Russell is perfectly clear that there is disagreement and what it is. Strawson's denial that there are logically proper names is the denial "that there are words which are only significant because there is something they mean and that if there were not this something they would be empty noises."[17] Russell, of course, holds that the passage just quoted is true. In support of this claim, and as counters to Strawson's denial, Russell says two things:

(1) We cannot know what the words 'red' and 'blue' mean if we have not seen red and blue.

(2) I defy Mr. Strawson to give the usual meaning to the word 'red' unless there is something which the word designates.[18]

Concerning sentence (1) we might note first that it is so ambiguous as to admit of an interpretation perfectly consistent with Strawson's position. Of course we cannot know what the words 'red' and 'blue' mean unless we have seen or could see red and blue. But the reason for this is not that these experienced colors are the *meanings* of 'red' and 'blue'. Knowing what these words mean is knowing how to employ them on appropriate occasions to say something about the world, to give a description of that world. The occurrence of red and blue is one of the criteria for the correct use of the words 'red' and 'blue'. We could not come to know what 'red' and 'blue' mean if there were no experiences of red and blue. Not because these experiences are the 'meanings' of the words but because the occurrence of red and blue is one of the primary checks available to us (but not the only one) for determining that we do understand the words in question.

In the case of sentence (2) note that the word 'red' designates. And note also that this sentence, which is supposed to be an argument against Strawson is nothing in fact but an instance of question-begging. The force of 'I defy Mr. Strawson' in this context is simply that of 'it is logically impossible'. What sentence (2) comes to then is the claim that it is logically impossible for the word 'red' to have meaning unless there is something that it designates. But whether this is true, or the correct account of meaning, is precisely the point at dispute. Sentence (2) like sentence (1) is loose enough to accept an interpretation consistent with Strawson's position. After all, we might ask, what is it to give the meaning of a word? Does it literally mean to give, exhibit, or show the thing referred to? Of course not. As Strawson points out,

[17] *Ibid.*, p. 387.
[18] *Ibid.*

my handkerchief is not the meaning of the expression 'my hand-kerchief'. To give someone the meaning of 'handerkerchief' is not to hand them a piece of cloth. Again, we can say here what we said in connection with sentence (1), of course there must be handkerchiefs, or instances of red and blue, if we are going to give or explain the meanings of the words 'handkerchief', 'red' and 'blue'. If there were not contexts, real or imaginable, within which the terms could be used, and checks made that they were used correctly, we could not know that we or anyone else knew what the terms in question meant. But it follows from none of this that the things I refer to are the *meanings* of the words I use to refer.

I have called the argument over whether there are or not logically proper names the culminating point of the Strawson-Russell exchange. Yet it is curiously unsatisfactory. Russell's arguments that there must be such things seem no more than disguised assertions that there are such things. If there were not objects which were the designata of words, words could have no meaning. But this supposes that things *are* the meanings of words. On the other hand Strawson's denial that there are *any* logically proper names must strike us as in some ways equally arbitrary. There are no logically proper names because "words don't mean, people *use* words to mean." This is of course true only if there are no logically proper names. Besides it does a curious sort of injustice to Russellians. No one ever thought that people's use of words made no difference to language. Of course 'red' doesn't mean red by some power of its own. It has been tied to a certain quality of experience such that to explain it to anyone you *would* have to exhibit that quality to the person. I am not myself sure that there is as great a significant difference between saying that the occurrence of a red patch is the (or a) criterion for correctly saying 'red', and saying that the patch is what 'red' means as denotationists and use-theorists sometimes maintain. The truth in this matter probably lies, as is so frequently the case, not at the simple extremes but somewhere in the extraordinarily complex region in between.

19

Strawson, Russell, and the King of France

Herbert Hochberg

STRAWSON'S attack on Russell's theory of descriptions is also an attack on Russell's view of proper names and their function as referring signs.[1] In this paper I shall consider both of Strawson's critiques and shall attempt to show that they are misleading and unfounded. I shall also attempt to show that Strawson's alternative view is philosophically more problematic than Russell's and that attempts to justify it as closer to ordinary usage are mistaken. First, I shall take up the question of names and reference and then turn to descriptions.

I. Naming and Referring

The issue between Russell and Strawson can be seen in terms of a simple artificial situation. Consider the signs 'a', 'b', 'F_1', and 'F_2'. Assume we have not provided any interpretation for them in the sense of specifying what objects or properties they may be used to refer to. But, assume that we have specified grammatical rules determining that 'F_1a' is well-formed, that 'F_1' and 'F_2' are predicates that may be used

---

[1] P. F. Strawson, "On Referring," originally in *Mind*, 59 (1950), reprinted in *Essays in Conceptual Analysis*, ed. Anthony G. N. Flew (New York: St. Martins, 1960), pp. 21–52, and in this volume.

to refer to properties, and that '*a*' and '*b*' are to be used as proper names of individuals, as opposed to properties or characteristics. Here 'name' may be used synonymously with 'zero-level constant' and, hence, a sign is a name only in that it belongs to a certain grammatical category and not in virtue of its referring to some object. In this sense names need not name. Knowing that the sign is a name and knowing the grammatical rules of our simple system, we may say that we know how to use the signs. Since we know what kind of sign it is and, perhaps, what sort of things we will use signs of that kind to refer to, even without knowing what specific references, if any, we will make, we may say we know the meaning of the sign. Suppose we then use the sign '*a*' to refer to various objects on different occasions. One might then believe that the sign has been used to name them all and, hence, that the name, as such, does not name one thing, but may be used to name several different things at different times or even at the same time. We can distinguish between the sign, as a physical mark (or class of such), and the sign together with its interpretation in a particular use. To use it to refer to an object is to give it a specific interpretation. The sign, taken as a type as opposed to a token, can also be said to have several interpretations. We might then consider *it* to be a different name on the different occasions on which *it* is used to refer to different objects. This emphasizes the different senses of 'name' that are involved. First, we have a sign type being a name in the sense of belonging to a category of signs whose members are used to refer to objects. Second, there is the sense in which the sign type is a name of something in that it is used to refer to a specific object. This latter sense gives rise to the idea that the name is the sign *as an* interpreted sign or as a sign with a specific referential use. Thus a sign type, used to refer to different objects at different times, may be taken as being a different name on each occasion. Or, perhaps better, some tokens of *the* sign type would be different names while some tokens would be *the same* name. If we then raise questions as to whether a sign can be a name if it is not interpreted or as to whether two objects designated by the same sign type have the same name, we can give either affirmative or negative answers, depending on which sense of 'name' we use. In turn, these different senses of 'name' can give rise to different senses of 'meaning'. One may say he knows the meaning of a sign if he knows its grammatical category, the rules applying to it, and the kind of object it could be used to refer to. In this sense the meaning has nothing to do with the actual referent, on a given occasion, or even with the question of whether there is one. Alternatively, one may hold that he knows the meaning only if he knows the referent of the sign. The first sense of 'name' and 'meaning' sums up Strawson's view. Russell takes the second to be philosophically significant.

Strawson holds that Russell's view of meaning is confused. But it is, I think, clear that Russell did not confuse the two senses of meaning just noted. What one might claim is that speaking of 'meaning', 'referring', and 'names' as Strawson does fits better with the way we commonly speak of such matters. One could then claim that Russell would be confused or wrong if he thought that his view recorded or reflected common usage of the relevant expressions. But Russell did not seem to think that he was recording such usage, in spite of the fact that he sometimes speaks as if he is. Rather, what Russell seems to have been concerned with were certain problems that arise in connection with such ordinary usage, and what he proposed was a solution to those philosophical problems. Consider one apparent problem about names. Let 'a' and 'F_1' refer, respectively, to a white square patch and to the color white. Given appropriate syntactical or grammatical rules, we may then use the sign sequence 'F_1a' to assert that the object designated by 'a' has the color indicated by 'F_1'. If it were asked what was said or meant by uttering or writing a token of that sentence type, a reply could be made in just that manner. If the questioner knew the interpretation of the signs, he wouldn't have to ask. Suppose the sequence is uttered without an interpretation being made of the name 'a'. It is clear that we would not then say anything in the sense in which something was said the first time. Both Strawson and Russell agree about this. The former holds that the sentence is significant and meaningful but that an assertion was not made. The latter denies the sentence to be significant or meaningful. One motive for the disagreement could be Russell's desire to avoid introducing assertions, the propositions of earlier writers, in addition to interpreted sentences. Russell, aware of the ontological issues, would recognize that something, in addition to the signs and their reference, is being implicitly appealed to in order to account for meaning and the connection between language and what it is about. In short, talk of assertions along Strawsonian lines involves, for Russell, the introduction of assertions as entities in one's ontology in spite of what Strawson may say to the contrary. This issue aside, it might seem that there is only a terminological dispute about 'meaning'. Russell speaks of 'meaning' and 'names' in one way, Strawson in another. But, in addition to avoiding propositional entities,

Russell was pointing to a distinctive feature of signs used simply as labels or referring signs. In the case of a name which names, we *are not forced* to use descriptions to "indicate" what we are speaking about. We *need not* explain our use by employing descriptions. By contrast, where we use names that do not name, we *are forced* to use descriptions to indicate what we are talking "about." This seemingly trivial difference between names that name and names that do not has significant consequences, if one takes metaphysical or ontological questions seriously. We can get into those questions by noting another set of problems that arise with names that do not name. These are questions of the truth and falsity of sentences, and the validity of inferences involving sentences, containing nondesignating names. Suppose 'a' is a nondesignating zero level constant. A question then arises about '$F_1a \lor \sim F_1a$' as an instance of a logical truth. To accept it as logically true in the standard sense is to accept either 'F_1a' or '$\sim F_1a$' as true. But to retain existential generalization as a valid inference pattern is to derive either '$(\exists x)F_1x$' or '$(\exists x)\sim F_1x$' on the basis of a being F_1 or $\sim F_1$ where a doesn't exist. This is unpalatable. Several alternative solutions are open. Russell, in effect, refused to acknowledge '$F_1a \lor \sim F_1a$', 'F_1a', and '$\sim F_1a$' as sentences when 'a' did not designate. For a sign to be a name "presupposed" that it did designate. Here 'presuppose' is used in a quite straightforward and clear manner. To say that 'a' is a name presupposes that 'a' designates is simply to say that the latter statement logically follows from the former, by the requirements for a sign's being a name; *i.e.*, by the meaning of 'name'. Russell rules out the problematic sentences by a metalinguistic requirement. Alternatively, if one allows such signs and sentences into a language then something else must be done. One may complicate the logical machinery by permitting existential generalization only if the sign 'a', in the above example, does designate.[2] Along this line one could syntactically distinguish two kinds of zero-level constants and require that only signs of the one kind designate. The problematic inferences could then be avoided by restricting existential generalization to sentences containing signs of that kind. In such a language we would have names, in one sense, that did not name.

Another alternative would be to stipulate that sentences like 'F_1a', '$\sim F_1a$', and '$F_1a \lor \sim F_1a$' are neither true nor false, and hence no prob-

---

2 On Quine's use of this pattern see H. Hochberg, "The Ontological Operator," *Philosophy of Science*, 23 (1956): 250–259, and "Professor Quine, Pegasus, and Dr. Cartwright," *Philosophy of Science*, 24 (1957): 191–203.

lem of an inference to either '$(\exists x)F_1x$' or $(\exists x)\sim F_1x$' arises. In effect Strawson adopts this alternative via his distinction between sentences and assertions and the claim that the sentences 'F_1a' and '$\sim F_1a$' can be used to make true or false assertions only if 'a' does in fact designate. The use of either sentence to make either a true or false assertion is said to "presuppose" that 'a' does designate. In his way, by speaking of "presupposing," Strawson does something that amounts to what Russell does; he neutralizes the troublesome sentences. Only he does it not by banning the troublesome terms, and hence the sentences, but by holding that the sentences containing such terms cannot be used to make true or false assertions. The problematic inferences are avoided, since even if one allows logical inference patterns to apply to sentences, rather than assertions, we could still not infer that either existential sentence was true (or, perhaps, was used to make a true assertion), since neither 'F_1a' nor '$\sim F_1a$' is true or is used to make a true assertion. This would be so irrespective of whether or not we allowed the inferences from 'F_1a' and '$\sim F_1a$' to their existential generalizations. Thus Strawson's solution, like Russell's, avoids the problematic inferences. Russell does so by specifying a metalinguistic criterion for a term's being a name of a problem-free language, and from that criterion it logically follows that if 'a' is a name then 'a' designates. A Russellian's claim that being a name presupposes that something be designated is then a tautology. As we noted above, 'presupposes' here only means 'logically entails'. Strawson holds, in effect, that 'F_1a' being either true or false presupposes that 'a' designates. But this is not a tautological consequence of a criterion for a term's being a name. It is, for him, a logical truth of a different kind. Just what kind locates a problem in Strawson's analysis. It appears as if Strawson is laying down a generalization about language and its use. Being neither an empirical generalization nor the consequence of a stipulation or definition, it may be characterized as a "conceptual" or "logical" truth. Thus Strawson is, in effect, led to introduce both an unanalyzed notion of "implies" or "presupposes" and of "conceptual" or "logical truth," for there does not seem to be any explication available for these notions as there is for the standard formal notion of logical truth and inference. Even if one specified a set of axioms governing Strawson's notion of "presupposes" this would only correspond, for example, to an axiomatization of propositional logic without any reference to the explicative device of the truth tables. We would then have an axiomatization without any explication.

Whatever explicatory problems there are about Strawson's notion of "presupposes," it may be held that Strawson's view is closer to and supported by our ordinary use of language, while Russell violates such usage, since we commonly use names that do not name. Unlike Strawson, Russell apparently refuses to allow such signs into a logically proper language. This implies that our ordinary language is not logically proper and hence mistaken. But the point that Russell was concerned to make can be made even if we allow nondesignating zero-level constants, so long as we preserve a syntactical distinction between names that name and names that do not. One could, as noted above, avoid the problematic inferences to existential statments in such a system. But there is another question regarding the truth and falsity of subject-predicate sentences containing nondesignating names. If one wishes, unlike Strawson, to adhere to the twofold claim that all (indicative) sentences are either true or false and that a sentence is true if and only if its negation is false, he could introduce a further stipulation that atomic sentences of the form 'ϕa' are false, where 'a' stands for any name that does not name, while the negations of such sentences are true. Strawson, by his doctrine of assertions, denies that all indicative sentences are true or false but reflects the second claim that a sentence is true if and only if its negation is false. I say "reflects" since, on his view, one may hold *an assertion* is true if and only if its negation is false. This shows that there are different kinds of assertions in two senses: in the sense of true and false and in the sense of positive and negative. Consequently, we see how close Strawson's doctrine of assertions is to an earlier metaphysical claim that there are propositions. For Strawson, as on the earlier view, negation is properly a characteristic of assertions, not of sentences. This brings us to a peculiarity of the treatment of negation on the doctrine of assertions. In an early form of the view, Strawson seems to have held that assertions were either true or false, but he later holds that some assertions may be neither.[3] On this later view, we could have two assertions such that one is the negation of the other with neither being true or false. This means that negation, in some contexts, is not truth-functional. Moreover, on either the earlier or the later view, one would recognize that sentences containing negation signs were meaningful but not used to make assertions. Such uses of negation are also not truth-functional. It would not do to reply that such uses are truth-functional since if contradictory

---

[3] P. F. Strawson, "Identifying Reference and Truth-values," *Theoria*, 30 (1964): 103, 105, 106.

sentences[4] *were* to be used to make assertions with truth values then one assertion *would be* true and the other false. For the use of the negation sign on such occasions is still not quite the same; *i.e.* once it is used to make a true or false assertion and once it is not. The latter use is then clearly not truth-functional. Thus we have a correlate to Strawson's unexplicated notion of "presupposes"—an unexplicated notion of "negation." We can consider one feature of Strawson's talk about assertions, sentences, truth and falsity to be reflected by a three-valued logic that applied to sentences.[5] A sentence 'Wa' could take one of three values T, F or N. If 'a' designated then 'Wa' would be either T or F, otherwise N. Then '$\sim$' would have the following truth table:

P	$\sim P$
F	T
T	F
N	N

This shows in what sense Strawson does and in what sense he does not abandon the standard truth table for negation.

All this is just another way of pointing out that Strawson denies the claim, (I_1), that every indicative sentence is either true or false. His denial is put in terms of the doctrine of assertions and presuppositions. But we may ignore the question of assertions in getting at his difference with Russell. If we allow atomic sentences like 'F_1a' where 'a' is a nondesignating constant, we face, as noted above, a question about its truth value. In effect, Strawson's solution is that neither 'F_1a' nor '$\sim F_1a$' is either true or false. Whether we withhold a truth value or introduce a third value N makes no real difference. Another alternative we noted earlier is to adhere to (I_1) and stipulate that 'F_1a' is false and, hence, its negation true. A third alternative might be to stipulate that both 'F_1a' and '$\sim F_1a$' are false and thus not only give up (I_1) but also hold that for such sentences we alter the rules about negation and con-

---

[4] Contradictory sentences would be pairs of sentences of a certain form, i.e. involving the negation sign. Even if one wishes to insist that a notion like "contradictory" applies properly to assertions, not sentences, there is still a precise sense in which we can talk of contradictory sentences, especially if we avoid the issues that arise from the possibility of interpreting one sign in several ways and hence using "one" sentence design to say several things on different occasions.

[5] To get at several different themes in Strawson's views we can and shall consider his view, at times, to claim that a sentence can take one of three values; rather than that a sentence is not properly said to have a truth value, since some sentences are neither true nor false.

tradiction. This last alternative thus gives up the further claim, (I_2), that an indicative sentence is true if and only if its negation is false. This third alternative may seem extreme. I mention it to point to a similarity it has with Strawson's alternative. Both abandon the uniform use of the standard truth table for negation and both hold that a conjunction of a *sentence* and its negation need not be or reflect a contradiction. For the moment, let us consider the second alternative, which "stipulates" that 'F_1a' is false and its negation true, to be Russell's.

Supposedly Strawson's view is closer to ordinary usage than Russell's and to preserve this fit he is willing to pay the philosophical price of introducing assertions, secondary referents, an unexplicated notion of presupposes, and a nontruth-functional use of negation. But the one supposed strength of Strawson's view, and weakness of Russell's, the match with ordinary usage, is specious. Consider the sign 'b' as belonging to a certain grammatical category, which we call that of zero-level constants or proper names. To separate issues let us forget about the possibility of the sign being used on many occasions to refer to many things and simply say, if it refers at all, it refers to one and only one thing. If it does so refer we will call it a referring name. We may establish this reference relation in many ways: by a gesture, a coordination procedure as in mathematics, or by giving a definite description, say '$(\imath x)(\phi x)$'. The gesture and the description do the same job. But there is a radical difference. We can assert '$b = (\imath x)(\phi x)$' but not that the gesture is identical with b or '$b = $ this'. This last sentence would be useless without being accompanied by the gesture (or an appropriate context). Given that '$(\imath x)(\phi x)$' serves to connect 'b' to its referent, the sentence '$b = (\imath x)(\phi x)$' is peculiar. It plays exactly the role of the assertion 'Let "b" stand for this', where that statement is accompanied by an appropriate context or gesture, or of 'Let "b" refer to a', where we know what 'a' refers to. In short, we are dealing with a conventional assignment of a sign to an object. Thus '$b = (\imath x)(\phi x)$' is perhaps better expressed by the rule (R_1) 'Let "b" stand for $(\imath x)(\phi x)$'. The identity statement may then be taken as a consequence of (R_1). The peculiarity arises simply because '$b = (\imath x)(\phi x)$' reflects or is a consequence of the rule of interpretation for 'b' and is thus not an ordinary statement of identity like "Descartes is the most significant French philosopher." The role of the descriptive phrase '$(\imath x)(\phi x)$' is to connect 'b' to some object, just as a gesture or coordination procedure may do. Assume that there actually is such an object and that the sign '*b*' is then connected with it. Let us call the object the "referent-meaning" of the sign '*b*'. This notion may then be contrasted with that of the "grammatical-meaning," which we may construe as being provided by the implicit or explicit rules governing the use of the sign, including those specifying what sort of referent-meaning it may have. Let us further call the descriptive phrase '$(\imath x)(\phi x)$' the "semantical-meaning" of the sign '*b*'.[6] Thus the object, $(\imath x)(\phi x)$, is the referent-meaning while the sign '$(\imath x)(\phi x)$' is the semantical-meaning of the sign '*b*'. Suppose, however, there is no referent of '*b*' since $(\imath x)(\phi x)$ does not exist. We then have a grammatical-meaning and a semantical-meaning for '*b*' but no referent-meaning. This merely points out that, aside from the rules specifying the use of '*b*', we have only the sign '$(\imath x)(\phi x)$' and not the object $(\imath x)(\phi x)$ to provide "meaning" for '*b*'. To put it another way, aside from '*b*' and its grammar, we have only the descriptive phrase. Since there is no object, a Russellian may claim that the descriptive phrase gives *the meaning* of '*b*'. However, since there are the grammatical rules a Strawsonian may claim *they* provide *the meaning*. By contrast, since we have only the sign '$(\imath x)(\phi x)$', and not the object, to provide more than grammatical meaning, the Russellian may insist that '*b*' is defined by '$(\imath x)(\phi x)$'. A definition is often characterized as the specification of meaning for a sign solely in terms of other signs; and (R_1), or '$b = (\imath x)(\phi x)$', which introduces '*b*' into the language, is remarkably like a definition in that respect. Consider a predicate 'F_1' defined by '$F_1 = (\imath F)(x)(Fx \equiv (G_1 x \,\&\, H_1 x))$'. Such a sentence may be said to introduce 'F_1' into the language by description, just as '*b*' is introduced. The similarity may reinforce the idea that '$b = (\imath x)(\phi x)$' defines '*b*'. The distinctions we have made between grammatical, semantical, and referential meaning should enable us to see what is reasonable in the claim. For, given the distinctions, one need not deny that the descriptive phrase provides a definition, and hence semantical meaning, since the sign already has "meaning"— *grammatical* meaning. Likewise, one need not deny that a definition is provided if the sign has a referent and, hence, has *referential* meaning. If there is a referent, a Russellian may rightly insist that the sign has *the same meaning* it would have if the referent did not exist, just as a sentence means the same thing whether it is true or false. What he has in mind is clearly semantical meaning, and, possibly, grammatical meaning as well. Thus, he may well hold that '$(\imath x)(\phi x)$' defines

---

[6] I apologize for the jargon, but it will be helpful.

'b', whether there is a referent or not, since '$b = (\imath x)(\phi x)$' *introduces* 'b' into the language. This merely reflects the difference between 'b' and a sign, say 'a', which is not introduced by a definite description as 'b' is. In the case of 'a' there must be a referent, if the sign is to have more than merely grammatical meaning. Given referents for both 'a' and 'b', they differ only in that 'b' has '$(\imath x)(\phi x)$' as its semantical meaning while 'a' has, associated with it, an interpretation, expressed metalinguistically or ostensively, in lieu of any semantical meaning. Such an interpretation plays the same role for 'a' as the sentence '$b = (\imath x)(\phi x)$' does for 'b': to connect the zero-level constant to its referent. Hence one can understandably come to hold that 'b' is *really* an *abbreviation* for a definite description and not a proper name like 'a'. Yet, it is also understandable why one might balk at holding that '$(\imath x)(\phi x)$' defines 'b', for, although it is quite natural to say that an interpretation provides or gives meaning to a sign, it is awkward to assert that the sign is an abbreviation for the interpretation. In a way there is nothing to argue about. If we recognize (1) that terms like 'a' and 'b' can be distinguished and, in fact, must be with respect to certain logical inferences, (2) that a sentence like '$b = (\imath x)(\phi x)$' is quite different from a true sentence like '$a = (\imath x)(\psi x)$' where the latter does not introduce 'a' into the language, and (3) that an ostensive definition can only be given where there is an object to be associated with the sign, then the points made by Russell's theory of names are granted. The distinctions pointed at by the terms *semantical*, *grammatical*, and *referential* meaning reveal that disputes about whether "names" are *really* proper names if they do not name, about *the* meaning of 'b', and about whether 'b' is really a name if it is introduced by (R_1) or '$b = (\imath x)(\phi x)$' are specious.

When $(\imath x)(\phi x)$ does not exist the identity statement '$b = (\imath x)(\phi x)$' poses a problem that I have avoided in the above discussion. For, even though that sentence is taken as a stipulation introducing 'b' into the language schema, it will be false if $(\imath x)(\phi x)$ does not exist and that sentence is treated in accordance with Russell's theory of descriptions. If $(\imath x)(\phi x)$ does not exist, then, in one obvious sense, 'b' cannot stand for or refer to it. Hence, instead of R_1 or the identity statement, one should, strictly speaking, use something like R_1': Let 'b' abbreviate '$(\imath x)(\phi x)$'. Thus, 'b' may replace '$(\imath x)(\phi x)$' wherever the latter occurs, but then '$b = (\imath x)(\phi x)$' would not be a consequence of R_1', since '$(\imath x)(\phi x) = (\imath x)(\phi x)$' is false when $(\imath x)(\phi x)$ does not exist. However, this does not affect the difference between '$b = (\imath x)(\phi x)$' and '$a =$

$(\imath x)(\psi x)$', on which my discussion depends. The crucial difference remains since the identity '$b = (\imath x)(\phi x)$' is a consequence of 'E!$(\imath x)$ (ϕx)' and a stipulated rule or definition, R_1', while '$a = (\imath x)(\psi x)$' is not a consequence of 'E!$(\imath x)(\psi x)$' together with any such rule or definition.

There are other, more complex ways, of making the same point. Thus, one could introduce 'b' by a stipulation like '$(F)(Fb \equiv F(\imath x)$ $(\phi x))$', which also avoids the problem of having the sentence introducing 'b' into the schema be false under certain conditions. Likewise, one could introduce 'b' by a pair of sentences which copy Russell's introduction of descriptive phrases:

(1) $$E!b \equiv E!(\imath x)(\phi x);$$

(2) $$\psi b \equiv \psi(\imath x)(\phi x).$$

Or, one could introduce the sign by '$b = (\imath x)(\phi x) \equiv (\imath x)(\phi x) = (\imath x)(\phi x)$' or by '$b = df.(\imath x)(\phi x)$' where '$= df.$' is taken, unlike '$=$', to hold even when the description is not fulfilled. In effect this use of '$= df.$' amounts to another way of putting R_1'. None of these alternatives affects the issue. For, as we just noted, the fundamental difference between '$b = (\imath x)(\phi x)$' and '$a = (\imath x)(\psi x)$' would be preserved whether $(\imath x)(\phi x)$ exists or not.

Just as the above mentioned issues are specious so is the one regarding Russell's supposed unfaithfulness to ordinary language. Consider the ordinary language name 'Pegasus'. At one level of discussion no problem arises, since for a Russellian the term 'Pegasus' would not occur in an idealized language, call it L, used solely for purposes of describing the world and reproducing the truths of logic and mathematics. It would be misleading to say that 'Pegasus' is really a descriptive phrase in L. Rather, what one should say is that on Russell's program a sentence of ordinary language, such as 'Pegasus does not exist', would correspond to a sentence of L which contains a description rather than a proper name or zero-level constant of L. This is one thing that can be meant by the claim that the term 'Pegasus' is really a description. But this does not mean that alternative approaches, like Strawson's, are more faithful to ordinary language. Suppose one holds that the context of the Greek myths and ordinary grammar (Greek or English) provide *the meaning* of the term 'Pegasus'. A Russellian need not argue. Given the above distinctions, it is clear that grammatical and semantical meaning are involved and not referential meaning.

This is another point behind the insistence that the term 'Pegasus' is really a disguised description and not a proper name. By so insisting the Russellian seeks to point up the distinction between zero-level constant signs that would have to be introduced into L by sentences involving descriptions, and hence need not have referents, and constant signs that are not so introduced but are interpreted, and which, therefore, do have referents. The distinction is crucial for Russell's solution to the standard puzzles surrounding names that do not name. This involves both the question of existential inferences from sentences containing the term 'Pegasus' as well as the question about the truth value of such sentences. The point is that Strawson also seeks to deal with these puzzles, while the ordinary user of ordinary language does not. It is thus not at all clear that the paraphernalia of assertions and presuppositions is any closer to ordinary usage or ordinary language than Russell's solution. To merely note that the term 'Pegasus' is held to be a proper name on Strawson's account, as it is in ordinary language, is too simple. For, Strawson's solution involves recognizing a distinction between names that name and names that do not with respect to existential inferences, presuppositions, and assertions that are taken as true or false. In short, Strawson's claim that the term 'Pegasus' is a name is made against a contextual background of philosophical puzzles and proposed solutions: the ordinary use of the term as a name is not. Thus, there is a crucial difference between Strawson's notion of a proper name and the ordinary concept of a proper name. This becomes apparent, in one way, when Strawson speaks of the "secondary reference" of terms like 'Pegasus' and 'Hamlet'.[7] What lies behind the notion of secondary reference is that in an obvious sense we do speak *about* Hamlet and we also speak truly and falsely about him. Some even attempt to prove that Hamlet loved his mother too well or hesitated too long. But all this is easily explained without taking 'Hamlet' as a referring term. One treats the play "as if" it were about someone or, to put it less metaphorically, the evidence for Hamlet's having an Oedipus complex must consist solely of sentences in a manuscript. Perhaps this is all Strawson intends by the notion of secondary reference. But then it is misleading to introduce the term 'reference' at all in such contexts, even with the modifying adjective. For, to speak of a sign referring to an object is to speak of two things we have connected in a special way. In the case of secondary reference

---

[7] Strawson speaks of secondary reference in notes added to "On Referring," pp. 35, 40.

we do not have two things and hence no connection is established. To keep reference as a connection or relation, one would have to reintroduce the possible or fictional entities that Russell sought to avoid. Even if we neglect the problems raised by speaking of "secondary reference," the point remains that by means of such a notion and his views regarding assertions, inference, and truth, Strawson distinguishes between names like 'Pegasus' and names that refer in an ordinary way. With this distinction he seeks to avoid the same puzzles Russell dealt with. Since Strawson considers both kinds of signs to be names, while Russell does not, and since we speak of both as names in ordinary usage, it appears that Strawson's view jibes better with ordinary usage. But it should be clear that both kinds of signs are names in ordinary usage only in the sense of grammatical names. That is, in ordinary usage 'Pegasus', 'Hamlet', and 'Peter Strawson' are all treated as belonging to a certain grammatical category. Similarly, as we noted earlier, one could consider L to contain two kinds of zero-level constants, names that name and names that do not. Thus, a Russellian type ideal language could also reflect the grammatical kinship of referring and nonreferring zero-level constants. Moreover, in keeping with the earlier discussion of the sentence '$b = (\imath x)(\phi x)$', when $(\imath x)(\phi x)$ does not exist, we may consider the constants that do not refer to be abbreviations of descriptions in L. The names which do not name are then, of course, different from those that do, not only in that they do not name but in that they are "connected" with a defining definite description. They will also function differently in certain contexts: existential generalization for example. But Strawson's non-naming names also function differently, for, secondary reference aside, one does not use them to make true or false assertions. Actually we need not bother with introducing abbreviations for descriptions in L. We could simply consider a general sense of name whereby we called zero-level constants, as well as definite descriptions, names. It will not do to object that in ordinary usage we do not have different grammatical rules for the two kinds of names whereas in L we would have different rules. For the difference in L between zero-level descriptions and zero-level constants can be taken to amount to restrictions on the inference and transformation rules. Such rules are not grammatical rules in the sense of 'grammatical' which we use when we speak of ordinary usage. That both nondesignating descriptions like '$(\imath x)(\phi x)$' and referring zero-level constants are zero-level terms in L reflects that they are of the same grammatical category. The logical differences between them, as reflected in the rules of L, are merely the correlates of Strawson's distinctions regarding which terms are and which are not used to make true or false assertions on certain occasions. In short, if we are careful about the various senses of 'name' involved in these issues, there is no cogency to the claim that Strawson's analysis jibes with ordinary language better than Russell's does. Nevertheless, there are three key objections the Strawsonian can raise.

First, he may claim that in ordinary language a term like 'Pegasus' is undefined, just as a referring name is, and, hence, it does not function as an abbreviation for a description. Consequently, second, the sentence 'Pegasus is white' is not logically equivalent to an existential statement. And, third, where the sign 'a' does not refer and we have no context to provide a secondary reference, the sentence 'a is ϕ' is neither true nor false. These points hold about both ordinary usage and Strawson's analysis but are not reflected by Russell's analysis and L.

For the moment we will discuss only the first point, since the second and third can be taken as objections to the theory of descriptions and may be more profitably discussed in connection with that theory in the next section. The answer to the first objection is simple. Either there is some context for the sign 'Pegasus' or not. If there is no context for the use of a name, it is then like 'b' in L without either an interpretation or a sentence that serves to introduce it. As such it is a completely useless sign. But, if one insists, L could admit a class of signs, as we noted, that are neither abbreviations of descriptions nor referring names. Atomic sentences containing such signs could be stipulated to be false. This could not be taken as being unfaithful to ordinary usage, since one does not employ such totally useless signs in ordinary language. For this issue they can then safely be ignored. However, if there is a context for the sign, then the context plays exactly the same logical role as '$(\imath x)(\phi x)$' did for 'b', when the sentence '$b = (\imath x)(\phi x)$' was taken to introduce the sign 'b' into the language. Once one sees that, there is no force left to the claim that 'b' (or 'Pegasus') is primitive. Or, perhaps, to put it in a more conciliatory manner, in view of the discussion of the sentence '$b = (\imath x)(\phi x)$', I cannot see that there is really any issue about whether 'b' is or is not an abbreviation for '$(\imath x)(\phi x)$'. The identity sentence clearly functions as a linguistic stipulation. The Greek myths, I submit, play exactly the same *logical role* for the term 'Pegasus'. But even if I have not convinced the Strawsonian of that, for him to argue that it is not so would necessitate his bringing in the apparatus of presuppositions and assertions. His critique of Russell on the ground that Russell is unfaithful to ordinary usage would then collapse, or, at best, be circular. For he would have to argue that his view involving presuppositions, assertions, and secondary reference fits ordinary usage better since 'Pegasus' is not taken as an abbreviation in ordinary usage. But to show that it is not so taken in ordinary usage, it would not do to point to the absence, in the myths, of an explicit stipulation of the form 'Pegasus $= (\imath x)(\phi x)$'. Rather, one would have to argue that it is not an abbreviation, since it really functions as a name with secondary reference. Hence, one ultimately appeals to Strawson's theory. To make the point clear, all we need note is that it would do no good to ask ordinary readers of the Greek myths if the term 'Pegasus' is used as a name in the stories. For, clearly, no one would deny that it is used as a grammatical name, and a careful Russellian can hold that a definite description is, in a corresponding sense, a name in *L*. The simple, perhaps trivial, point is that to elicit a relevant response would necessitate explaining what is at issue. The question of whether the term 'Pegasus' is *really a name* or not must be asked in the context of the philosophical dispute between Strawson and Russell. To raise the question is thus to ask which philosophical analysis, Strawson's or Russell's, is preferred; it is not to ask the trivial question of whether the term 'Pegasus' functions as a grammatical name in ordinary usage. This latter sense, in which the term is unproblematically and trivially a "name" in ordinary usage, is thus neutral with respect to the opposed analyses. As such, it cannot serve as a means of deciding between them, and it is therefore mistaken to think that because Strawson holds 'Pegasus' to be a "name" his analysis is closer to ordinary usage. Perhaps the point can be emphasized if we consider another example where Strawson's approach may be taken to fit better with ordinary usage but where to do so also involves oversimplifying the issue.

Consider the sentence 'This is red' used on different occasions to speak about two different objects, one that is red and one that is not. A Strawsonian might argue that such a feature of ordinary usage presupposes that assertions, not sentences, are what is true and false. For the same sentence would otherwise be both true and false. But one might hold that if we distinguish the sign-design type from its token, we can hold that one token is true while the other is false. Or, better yet, we must distinguish between sign-design types, sign-design tokens, and sentences. Different tokens of the same sign-design type can be used as different sentences. For, if we are concerned with more than the grammatical meaning of the sign, we must take into account not only the sign-design and the grammatical rules but the interpretation, in order to determine or understand or know *the meaning* and the truth value of the sentence. While it is true that anyone who knows English understands, in one sense, what is said if he overhears someone say "This is red," there is a further clear sense in which he doesn't quite know what is being said, if he doesn't know what is being referred to. But, again, there is no point quibbling about how to use the terms 'understand' and 'meaning'. All we need note is that our ordinary usage does not dictate the answer that assertions, not sentences, are the subjects of ascriptions of truth and falsehood. The questions we are raising about sentences, sign-designs, tokens, types, meaning, interpretations, and assertions do not arise in ordinary contexts. In such contexts we might well be satisfied with noting that *the* sentence 'This is red' is sometimes true, sometimes false, and, perhaps, sometimes unclear. Strawson attempts to offer one solution to certain puzzles that can be raised about sentences, terms, etc. Russell offers another. Strawson seems to retain the ordinary notion that on the two occasions mentioned above the same sentence is used, while on Russell's solution *it* is not the same sentence. But the context of the ordinary use of the notion of "same" and the context surrounding Strawson's, or Russell's, use are quite different. The notion of "sentence" is not determinate for certain issues in its ordinary use as it is, or ought to be, on both Strawson's and Russell's extraordinary use. Consider a Russellian language where we allow a proper name to have various referents at different times, and, hence, where it has different interpretations at different times. If by the "same sentence" of the language one means the sign-design type, without consideration of the interpretation, then the same sentence may have many interpretations. If one includes in the notion of sentence the interpretation of the sign-design, then one does not have one and the same sentence with many interpretations. But our ordinary use of the notion of the "same sentence" has nothing to do with a context in which the above distinctions are made. Such usage cannot then be held to favor either Strawson or Russell, and certainly not to presuppose Strawson's assertions or propositions. In short, the fact that on Strawson's view one holds that on two occasions the "same sentence" was uttered does not mean that Strawson is reproducing an ordinary observation that the "same sentence" was uttered. The phrase 'same sentence' doesn't mean the same thing in its first and second use in my previous sentence. The issues between Strawson and Russell on this point cannot then be settled by holding that Strawson preserves our ordinary usage while Russell does not. It can only be settled by noting such things as: (1) Strawson's ontology includes assertions, while Russell's does not;[8] (2) Strawson's problematic use of presuppose and negation; (3) the inclusion of fictional characters in one's ontology or, if not, the problematic use of the concept of "secondary reference" on Strawson's account, as opposed to Russell's attempt to exclude fictional entities while using only a straight-forward relational notion of reference. The issue between them, being a philosophical one, must be resolved by considering the ontological and logical features of their respective solutions to the problems that arise in the attempt to state what there is and how language can be used to refer to and truly describe the world. To believe that Strawson's doctrines about names and assertions are more viable in that they are more faithful to ordinary usage is, if my argument is correct, to depend on oversimplified and unanalyzed uses of 'name' and 'sentence'.

II. Descriptions

Strawson's argument against Russell's theory of descriptions involves four related claims; (s_1) ascriptions of a property to a described object are not existential statements but "presuppose" the truth of an existential claim; (s_2) a sentence ascribing a predicate by means of a description is not used to make a true or false assertion unless the described object exists; (s_3) descriptions are referring expressions like names; (s_4) sentences like 'the ϕ is ψ' are subject-predicate in form. To avoid the issue of assertions, which is not directly relevant here, (s_2) may be put as denying that sentences containing unfulfilled descriptions are either true or false, while other sentences may be spoken of as true or false (ignoring existential statements).

As we noted earlier, since a proper name for Russell must be co-ordinated with an object, names will not suffice to enable us to speak

[8] I have argued in detail that Strawson introduces the classical propositional entities into his ontology in "On Referring and Asserting," *Philosophical Studies*, 20 (1969), 81–88. In that paper I also attempt to show that Strawson's critique of Russell, which leads to the doctrine of assertions, is based on a basic misunderstanding of Russell's notion of "sentence."

"about" what is not. To do so we require a way of indicating, where "indicating" unlike "referring" is not a relational notion. Descriptions, for Russell, took on this function. Because of this we may say that a description is not a referring sign in the sense that a name is. Even if the description is fulfilled, there is a difference. For though we may say it refers to the object which fulfills it, the object does not provide an interpretation for the description as it would for a label or name. If a description were tied to a referent, as a name is, it would then function as a simple (as opposed to complex) sign or mere label, which it is not. Thus, the very use of a name involves the existence of its referent where the use of a description does not. This difference between descriptions and names (labels) serves a further, philosophical, purpose, in addition to allowing us to speak unproblematically about nonexistent "things" like Pegasus. It enables us to separate those signs in a language which *must* be tied to objects from those which need not be in order to reproduce, in principle, the ordinary truths of fact, logic, and mathematics. Assume a definite description is fulfilled. On Russell's account such a description, not being a label, is not a referring sign. But, ignoring Russell, we may take it as having a referent, since the crucial difference remains. For, the sign is not one which *requires* an interpretation or referent as a label requires one. In the case of the sign 'Pegasus', we *cannot* take it as a label; in the case of a fulfilled description we *need not* take it as a label. Just as the former case is crucial for ontological issues, the latter is also, but in a different way. The latter point enables us to separate those signs which *must be interpreted*, or connected with objects, from those signs which need not be. And this allows us to separate those objects which we *must* hold to exist, for the language to fulfill its descriptive use, from those objects whose existence *merely* provides the conditions for certain sentences being true. Consequently, we may distinguish two senses of 'exist': a special sense applying only to the objects that are the referents of the undefined constants or labels, and a more general sense applying to such objects and to the referents of fulfilled descriptions. The basic entities or, if you will, the *ontology*, of the user of the language is given by the former alone. Thus, one may speak "about" or "indicate" numbers via descriptions, rather than labels, without recognizing them as entities in one's ontology. Such objects are "logical fictions" or constructs. All this, of course, reflects the idea that ontology is a search for simple, as opposed to complex or constructed, entities. Descriptions are thus ontologically neutral. They are neutral in two senses.

First, the proposition '$\psi(\imath x)(\phi x)$' does not commit its user to the existence of something indicated by '$(\imath x)(\phi x)$' if the proposition is false. Second, even if the proposition is true one need not take $(\imath x)(\phi x)$ to be an entity in one's ontology since the sign '$(\imath x)(\phi x)$' is not an undefined constant.

In opposition to Russell, Strawson holds that the use of a descriptive phrase to make a true assertion presupposes, but does not entail, that something fulfills the description. As in the case of names, two points are involved. First, there is the denial that truth or falsity can be attributed to the sentence '$\psi(\imath x)(\phi x)$', if $(\imath x)(\phi x)$ does not exist. Second, there is the claim that a "logical" relation, i.e. *presupposes*, holds between '$\psi(\imath x)(\phi x)$' and '$(\exists x)[\phi x \ \& \ (y)(\phi y \supset y = x)]$', but this relation is not logical entailment. Putting the matter this way, we can consider these claims separately, as well as considering them apart from the problem about assertions. While we do not then literally deal with Strawson's view, we do, I believe, get at what is involved in his dispute with Russell, as well as gain in clarity from the separation of the different strands of Strawson's position. Let us then take Strawson to be holding that

$$(\text{S}_1) \qquad \psi(\imath x)(\phi x) \to (\exists x)[\phi x \ \& \ (y)(\phi y \supset y = x)]$$

is an axiom of a calculus, call it S, whereas Russell holds that

$$(\text{R}_1) \qquad \psi(\imath x)(\phi x) \supset (\exists x)[\phi x \ \& \ (y)(\phi y \supset y = x)]$$

is a theorem of *PM*. The use of '$\to$' indicates that Strawson's notion of *presupposes* is not the same as Russell's use of "implies" and that Strawson's logical connectives are not the ordinary truth-functional ones. (S_1)'s being an axiom of S reflects Strawson's notion that it is a necessary or conceptual truth that the left side of (S_1) being true presupposes that the right side is true. (R_1) being a theorem of *PM* reflects the idea that the left side logically implies the right side.[9]

For Russell, to assert that '$\psi(\imath x)(\phi x)$' implies that there is one and

[9] What is involved here is that (S_1) is really a metalinguistic statement since the arrow corresponds to Strawson's notion of 'presuppose.' Alternatively, the standard use of 'implies' corresponds to a statement, containing '$\supset$', being a logical truth. For the arrow there is, apparently, no corresponding truth functional notion of 'if-then' as there is for 'implies' or 'entails'. Thus if we were to replace (R_1) by (R_1')

$$\psi(\imath x)(\phi x) \dashv (\exists x)[\phi x \ \& \ (y)(\phi y \supset y = x)]$$

with '$\dashv$' for the metalinguistic 'entails', the difference would lie in the explication that is available for '$\dashv$' but not for '$\to$'.

only one ϕ means that (R_1) is a logical truth in exactly the same sense that '$(x)(Fx \supset Fx)$' is a logical truth. This notion of logical truth is not what is involved in Strawson's use of the term 'presuppose'. For Strawson, (S_1) expresses an axiom of his scheme, but '$\rightarrow$' differs from 'entails' and '$\supset$'. There is no truth table, in the ordinary sense, associated with '$\rightarrow$', and hence no explication of 'presupposes', in the sense in which there is a standard explication for 'logically implies' (in terms of truth tables, tautologies, and identical formulae).[10] This goes along with a second difference between Strawson and Russell. For Strawson '$\psi(\imath x)(\phi x)$' can take one of the three values T, F, or N. But even then '$\rightarrow$' is not associated with a three-valued truth function, for (S_1) holds as an axiom (conceptual truth) without any regard for the truth values of its constituents. The point is easily seen if we recall Strawson's usual way of putting what (S_1) expresses as (S_1'): '$\psi(\imath x)(\phi x)$' being (used to make a) true (assertion) presupposes that $(\imath x)(\phi x)$ exists. (S_1') holds not because ' '$\psi(\imath x)(\phi x)$' is (used to make a) true (assertion) $\supset (\imath x)(\phi x)$ exists' cannot be falsified in the sense in which (R_1) cannot be falsified, due to the definitions involved. Rather, *it*, (S_1') or (S_1), is (or reflects or expresses) a "conceptual truth." To put it another way, (R_1) is a consequence of certain definitions in *PM* while (S_1) or (S_1') is Strawson's rule governing the use of descriptions and of 'presupposes'. It functions with respect to '$\rightarrow$' and 'presupposes' in the way some speak of axioms as providing *implicit definitions* of primitive notions they contain. The two calculi, S and *PM*, have different basic logical signs as well as different axioms. Also, while *PM* is two-valued, S has some sentences that take three values. I say some sentences since there would seem to be a fundamental difference between subject-predicate sentences and existential sentences in S, where '$\psi(\imath x)(\phi x)$' is a subject-predicate sentence. Thus, if there is one and only one ϕ, the claim that it has ψ is either true or false, while, if the former claim is false, the latter is neither true nor false, but N. However, there seems to be no need to consider N being a possible value of the existential sentence. The latter's being true or false does not presuppose the existence of something in the sense that '$\psi(\imath x)(\phi x)$' being true or false does. Rather, the existential statement states that something exists, and hence may be said to "presuppose" the existence of something in the straightforward sense of logical implication. Existential sentences are then two-valued. S may thus be said to be only

10 That is, '$\rightarrow$' is neither a truth-functional notion itself nor connected with one as 'entails' is connected with '$\supset$'.

partly three-valued. We will return to this peculiar feature later. S would contain further axioms like

(S_2) $\quad \psi(\imath x)(\phi x) \rightarrow (\exists x)[\phi x \And (y)(\phi y \supset y = x) \And \psi x]$

(S_3) $\quad (\exists x)[\phi x \And (y)(\phi y \supset y = x) \And \psi x] \rightarrow \psi(\imath x)(\phi x)$

for it must be a further pair of conceptual truths that if the left sides of (S_2) and (S_3) hold (are true) so must the right sides. In S we should then have the theorem

(S_4) $\quad \psi(\imath x)(\phi x) \leftrightarrow (\exists x)[\phi x \And (y)(\phi y \supset y = x) \And \psi x].$

This correlates with *PM*'s

(R_2) $\quad \psi(\imath x)(\phi x) \equiv (\exists x)[\phi x \And (y)(\phi y \supset y = x) \And \psi x].$

Yet, (S_4)'s being a theorem does not mean its left and right sides are truth-functionally equivalent, for '$\rightarrow$' and '$\leftrightarrow$' are not truth-functional notions.[11] Moreover, the left side of (S_4) may take the value N, while the right side may not. All this just reflects the fact that, as Strawson uses the notion, if 'p' *presupposes* 'q', it does not "follow" that 'not q' *presupposes* 'not p', whereas the standard use of 'entails' does involve 'not q' entailing 'not p', if 'p' entails 'q'.

Strawson has recently insisted that the basic difference between himself and Russell is that on Russell's view a statement like '*the ϕ is ψ*' is only apparently a subject-predicate statement and really an existential statement. On Strawson's view, however, such statements are subject-predicate statements, not existential statements, but their being true or false presupposes existential statements holding. (R_2) being an analytic truth and theorem of *PM* expresses what it means to say that '$\psi(\imath x)(\phi x)$' is an existential statement. What is involved is that (R_2) either is one of the, or follows from, axioms of Russell's system, and that system employs the standard truth-functional notions. Russell's axioms embody definitions or rules for definite descriptions. As such they are among the "linguistic" truths or rules of the system. But as (S_1), (S_2) and (S_3) reflect logical or conceptual truths for Strawson, one might wonder what the difference amounts to. Since (R_2) is a theorem of *PM*, '$\psi(\imath x)(\phi x)$' is held to be an existential statement in *PM*, but it is not held to be an existential statement in S even though (S_4) is a theorem. One difference is that (R_2) states or is a consequence of a definition. (S_4) is not. But it is precisely because of this

---

[11] Again, in the two-fold sense of note 9.

that (R_1) and (R_2) may be held to be theorems in *PM* without introducing an unexplicated notion of *presupposes* and an extended notion of logical truth. It is because the theorems of *S* are not consequences of definitions that '→' is a problematic (unexplicated) sign. Even so, (S_1), (S_2) and (S_3) hold as axioms or conceptual truths. A definition in *PM* is, in effect, a further axiom. Why do not (S_1), (S_2), (S_3), and (S_4), taken as axioms (theorems), imply that '$\psi(\imath x)(\phi x)$' is an existential statement in *S*? One obvious part of the answer lies in the difference between '→' and '↔', on the one hand, and 'entails', '⊃', and '≡', on the other, and, consequently, between *S* and *PM*. Since '↔' differs from logical equivalence and '≡', (S_4) holds in *S* even though its left and right sides may take different truth values: *N* for the left when the right side is false. The left and right sides not being truth-functionally equivalent would naturally involve the claim that they do not (or are not used to) state the same thing. For, it would seem awkward to hold that two sentences state the same thing if they are not, at least, truth-functionally equivalent. But this is not all that is involved. Let us modify the treatment of descriptions in *S* in a way that resembles Russell's treatment of proper names. Russell, recall, holds, as a metalinguistic requirement, that names name. Suppose we treat Strawson's use of 'presupposes' in a similar manner. Consider *S* to be a calculus all of whose sentences are either true or false, due to a metalinguistic requirement that all admissible descriptions do in fact designate. Descriptions now function in *S* as names would in a Russellian ideal language. The comparison is especially suggestive if we note that descriptions are not defined signs in *S*, just as names would not be abbreviations for Russell. Call this modified system *S'*. In *S'* we could still have (S_1), (S_2), (S_3) and (S_4) as axioms or theorems. But what they state could be reflected in two other ways. On the one hand what they would state for *S'* could be reflected in the metalinguistic criterion for a definite description being a sign of *S'*. Alternatively, one could add an axiom '$(\exists x)[\phi x \;\&\; (y)(\phi y \supset y=x)]$' for every predicate like 'ϕ' used to build a description. Thus '$(\exists y)[y=(\imath x)(\phi x)]$' would function in *S'* like '$(\exists y)(y=a)$' functions in *PM* with 'a' as a name. Just as the latter is a theorem of *PM* (with constants) if 'a' is a name, so the former is a theorem or axiom of *S'* if '$(\imath x)(\phi x)$' is a description. Strawson's notion of presupposes is now reflected in *S'* by the metalinguistic criterion or the list of axioms of the form '$(\exists x)[\phi x \;\&\; (y)(\phi y \supset y=x)]$'. In *S'* we need no longer consider *N* as a third value of sentences.[12] We may then inquire as to whether or not '$\psi(\imath x)(\phi x)$' is an existential statement in S', as it is in *PM*. If a Strawsonian would say that it is, then it is clear that his critique of Russell reduces to his two-fold claim that some sentences (statements) can take one of three values and, consequently, that logical notions like negation and pre-supposition cannot be construed or explicated in the standard truth-functional manner. The notion of "presupposition" would then be necessarily tied to the claim that some sentences can take one of three values. If he holds that the sentence in question is still not an existential statement in S', then he may have some further points in mind. He might claim that even though the two statements '$\psi(\imath x)(\phi x)$' and '$(\exists x)[\phi x \& (y)(\phi y \supset y = x) \& \psi x]$' are truth-functionally equivalent in S' this is due to a "logical" connection (other than mutual entail-ment) and not the consequence of a definition, for descriptions are not defined signs in S'. Thus even though the two sides of (S_4) are truth-functionally equivalent in S', the ground of that "equivalence" is a unique logical connection reflected by '$\leftrightarrow$'. The double arrow is then not to be taken as the sign for either the biconditional or logical equiv-alence, even though the statements it connects are stipulated to be truth-functionally equivalent. Thus, while (R_2) is an analytic proposi-tion in a *PM* type schema under the standard interpretation, (S_4) is a conceptual truth of S', where "conceptual truth" does not mean ana-lytic in the standard sense. Thus, the issue of the meaning of "logical truth" arises *even* if we consider a schema in which all sentences are either true or false. One is forced to hold that (S_1), etc., in S', reflects a different kind of logical truth in order to hold that S' significantly differs from *PM*.[13] For, if (S_4), as an axiom of S', expresses an ordinary logical equivalence, it, like (R_2), may be taken as logically equivalent (in the ordinary sense) to a formula of the form '$p \equiv p$'. That the relevant axiom of *PM* is called a definition, while the corresponding one of S' is not, is merely a verbal difference. What is crucial is

---

[12] I am speaking only of the issues relevant here. That Strawson also has a non-truth-functional use of 'if-then', so that 'if p then q' is neither true nor false in some cases where 'p' is false or irrelevant to 'q' is not our concern in this paper; though it is, of course, a related question.

[13] If, instead of (S_1), etc., one employed the rule that for every $\ulcorner \phi \urcorner$ used to build a definite description in S' there was a theorem '$(\exists x)[\phi x \& (y)(\phi y \supset y = x)]$' the difference from *PM* would come out in that the use of this rule would not be held to make statements with descriptions abbreviations for the corresponding existential statements.

that in both (S_4) and (R_2) the left and right sides are stipulated to have identical truth values. To differ significantly from *PM*, the statement of *S'* must then be taken as other than an ordinary logical equivalence. One ultimate point of difference between the advocates of *PM* and *S'* would then be that the different schemas reflect different conceptions of logical truth, and this has nothing essentially to do with the possibility of some sentences being neither true nor false. Thus the Strawsonian critique would ultimately rest, in part, on the claim that Russell does not recognize that there is a unique and unexplicated logical connection other than ordinary entailment, which is quite different from the claim that Russell's analysis does not fit ordinary usage of descriptive phrases.

A further point could be involved. Consider '$p \supset q$' as an abbreviation for '$\sim p \vee q$'. Is '$p \supset q$' then a disjunction, really? In view of the definition of '$\supset$' one may reply in the affirmative; in view of the use of '$\supset$' and the problems of intentionality one may also reply in the negative. For, the sentence with the defined sign is not literally the same (or of the same form) as its defining sentence, and, when we use the defined sign, we may not intend or have in mind the definition of '$\supset$' in terms of disjunction and negation. Perhaps, Strawson's critique of Russell reflects, in part, this point.[14] Thus, on a given use of a description one might not *intend* or *have in mind* an existential statement, and, hence, should not be said to *mean* one by definition. But the problems of intentionality affect Russell's theory only in so far as they are involved in any definition or analysis whatsoever. Once we have distinguished the different senses of meaning involved (defining as opposed to intending, for example) one can only object to definitions and analyses as such, and not just to Russell's theory of descriptions.

The question of meaning is at the heart of Strawson's critique. He is claiming that Russell is mistaken, since sentences containing descriptions do not, in general, mean the same thing as existential statements. But the crucial question is, what can be taken to support his claim? The answer seems to lie in ordinary usage. Consider the sentence (I) 'The present king of France is bald'. Strawson seems to claim that, in ordinary usage, in the year 1969 we would consider neither that sentence nor its negation to be either true or false. But the evidence of

---

14 For example, in *Introduction to Logical Theory* (London: Methuen, 1964), pp. 191–192, Strawson says "From the fact that a statement is equivalent to another statement of a certain form, it does not follow that it itself is a statement of that form."

ordinary usage is surely not the explicit claim, by ordinary people, to the effect that Russell is wrong, since the sentences are neither true nor false. Rather, it would seem that the sentences in question create puzzlement, *if one raises a question about their respective truth values.* The evidence of ordinary usage is precisely this state of puzzlement, which, *prima facie*, supports neither Strawson nor Russell. Strawson accounts for the puzzlement in one way, Russell in another. A Russellian may point to two features of Russell's solution. First, there is Russell's treatment of the negative sentence, 'The present king of France is not bald', in two ways: one as the denial of (I) and the other as the existential claim that there is one and only one nonbald present king of France. Since one is true and the other false and yet both can be taken to correspond to the ordinary statement on his theory, Russell's analysis reflects the puzzlement that arises. That is, the ordinary negative statement can be taken as either true or false, depending on which way we transcribe it into Russell's symbolism. Moreover, the same thing is true of the affirmative statement (I). The straightforward transcription of (I), on Russell's account, is as the assertion that there is one and only one present king of France and that he is bald. But consider the sentence '$(y)[y = (\imath x)(PKx) \supset By]$', i.e. "Anything which is the present king of France is bald." This may also serve to transcribe the ordinary statement into a *PM* type ideal language. Just as the *ordinary* negative sentence is ambiguous, we may consider the affirmative one to be so too. And, just as in the case of the negation, one of the transcriptions of the ordinary statement is true, while the other is false. This is how the puzzlement of the ordinary user is reflected by Russell's theory. In a way this involves a slight modification of Russell's theory of descriptions, or, perhaps, a clarification of it. The definition of '$\psi(\imath x)(\phi x)$' as '$(\exists x)(\phi x \& (y)(\phi y \supset y = x) \& \psi x)$' occurs *in a clarified or ideal language.* One is not offering a definition for an ordinary English phrase like 'the present king of France' in context. Rather, what should be meant by the misleading claim that the ordinary English phrase is defined, or that the phrase in context is an existential statement, is that the English phrase is coordinated to, or transcribed by, a certain expression in a clarified language which is contextually defined in a certain way. The point can then be made that the English phrase, in use, lends itself to alternative transcriptions—one of which is true, the other false. It is this feature of Russell's theory that corresponds to the fact that puzzlement arises, if we raise a question about the truth value of certain sentences with unfulfilled descriptions. In a way closure is achieved when we recall that, where the description is fulfilled, the alternative transcriptions are equivalent, in both the affirmative and the negative cases. That is,

$$E! (\imath x)(\phi x) . \supset : (\exists x)[\phi x \ \& \ (y)(\phi y \supset y = x) \ \& \ \sim\psi x] . \equiv .$$
$$\sim(\exists x)[\phi x \ \& \ (y)(\phi y \supset y = x) \ \& \ \psi x]$$

and

$$E! (\imath x)(\phi x) . \supset : \psi(\imath x)(\phi x) . \equiv . (y)[y = (\imath x)(\phi x) . \supset \psi y]$$

are theorems of *PM*.

Strawson, too, seeks to deal with the puzzlement that arises in the case of unfulfilled descriptions. He does so by holding that the relevant sentences either do not make assertions or are not used to make assertions that are true or false, since their use presupposes an unfulfilled condition. In short, he introduces the neutral value and the unexplicated notion of presupposes to reflect the ordinary bewilderment. The fundamental point is that to settle the dispute between Russell and Strawson we cannot appeal to the situation they seek to account for: the puzzle that arises in ordinary contexts. One can only hope to settle the issue by appealing to other features of the competing views, such as that Strawson must introduce an unanalyzed notion of presupposes, that he give up the standard use of the truth-functional connectives, etc. One must, in short, seek philosophical reasons for resolving a philosophical dispute, which should not be surprising.

There is a further relevant, if peculiar, feature of Strawson's solution. While holding that sentences like '*the* ϕ *is* ψ' are subject-predicate in form, Strawson holds that sentences like '*the* ϕ *exists*' are not. The latter type of sentence is used to make an existential statement and, hence, does not presuppose one. It is obvious that he must hold something like this. If he did not, then the assertion that *the* ϕ *did not exist* would pose an obvious problem. Thus, in effect, both Strawson and Russell treat the apparent subject-predicate sentence of ordinary language 'the ϕ exists' as the existential statement that 'there is one and only one ϕ'. Interestingly enough, Strawson holds that this difference between 'the ϕ exists' and 'the ϕ is ψ' reveals that 'exists' is not *really* a predicate. To ascribe a predicate to a subject is to presuppose, but not assert, that the subject exists. But it is awkward to insist on this condition holding for sentences like 'the ϕ exists' and 'the ϕ does not exist'. Hence, Strawson believes he has found a ground for distinguishing existential statements from subject-predicate ones.[15] It seems as if Strawson here "clarifies" ordinary usage by appeal to his analysis, rather than attempting to justify his analysis by appeal to ordinary usage. (Is 'exists' really a predicate in ordinary usage?) This point aside, we made note that Strawson has two uses of descriptions: with predicates and in existential statements. Russell, too, we recall, had two axioms about descriptions: one for the use of a description with predicates and one with 'E!'. (But Russell did not argue, on such feeble ground, that 'exists' is not a predicate.) In a way Russell's distinction between the two contextual uses of a description also reflects Strawson's notion of *presupposition*. For Russell,

$$E!(\imath x)(\phi x) . \supset . (x)\psi x \supset \psi(\imath x)(\phi x)$$

is a theorem of *PM*. Thus, given that *the* ϕ exists, the description '$(\imath x)(\phi x)$' can, in effect, be treated like a proper name that names. That a name names is, we recall, a "presupposition" of a Russellian ideal language. Strawson, by insisting that '$(\imath x)(\phi x)$' is a simple subject sign, like a name, cannot consider a sentence like '*the ϕ is not ψ*' to be ambiguous, as Russell does. Hence, if he were to preserve the claims that every indicative sentence is true or false and that the negation of a sentence takes the opposite truth value of the sentence (in a two-valued calculus), he would face the problems Russell starts from. Russell, to solve the familiar problems, gives up the idea that the phrase 'the ϕ' is a simple sign and, consequently, does not consider a sentence like 'the ϕ is not ψ' to be unambiguous. Strawson retains the simplicity of the phrase and the claim that the sentence is not ambiguous. Hence, he must reject Russell's views about truth, falsity, and negation, as well as reintroduce the classical propositional entities in the new dress of "statements" or "assertions." But, again, there is no warrant from ordinary usage that a description is a simple label, like a name, or that a sentence like '*the ϕ is not ψ*' is not ambiguous. At most, one could claim that descriptive phrases are used, ordinarily, as grammatically proper names, in the specific sense of 'grammatical' that I mentioned in the previous section on names. With respect to ordinary usage, we might consider the following three sentences: (1) 'The present king of France is bald'; (2) 'The one and only present king of France is bald'; (3) 'The one and only existent present king of France is bald'.

[15] *Ibid*, pp. 191 ff. There is a further awkwardness posed by 'Pegasus does not exist'.

One might reasonably hold that (2) merely makes explicit and emphatic what is implicit in (1). But does *making explicit* mean that what is stated in (2) is only "presupposed" by (1) or that it is "implicitly stated" in (1)? If one does not appeal to the problems responsible for the introduction of Russell's theory of descriptions and Strawson's theory of presuppositions, how could one hope to make clear what the question is all about? Further, if one does not appeal to the problems of intentionality mentioned above, how could one hope to argue that (1) only presupposes, and does not implicitly state, (2) on the basis of ordinary usage? Again what we may take ordinary usage to provide is the fact that (2) does make explicit something implicit in (1). But, both Russell and Strawson have ways of fitting their respective views to this fact or feature of usage. With respect to (3), we may well feel puzzled, since one does not ordinarily talk about the nonexistent so-and-so (forgetting stories and the issue of secondary reference). Thus, (3) may be puzzling in that it expresses an even more obvious *condition* implicit in (1). But, again, how is 'implicit' to be taken here? Strawson is claiming that our ordinary usage presupposes (or entails?) that his sense of 'presuppose' is involved and not Russell's analysis. What I am suggesting is that ordinary usage neither "presupposes" nor entails either view.

There is an instructive corollary to Strawson's attack on Russell. In his original article, Strawson also castigates "logicians" for holding that a sentence like 'All mermaids are blond' is true, since there are no mermaids.[16] For Strawson, the use of such a sentence to make a true assertion also presupposes that there are mermaids. Such an assertion being true presupposes a "subject" just as the assertion "about" the present king of France presupposes a "subject." Forgetting the issue of assertions, we may note that, for the logicians Strawson castigates, the sentence 'All mermaids are not blond' is also true, since there are no mermaids. Thus, the unfortunate logician claims that '$(x)(Fx \supset Gx)$' and '$(x)(Fx \supset {\sim}Gx)$' both hold. But, for the same logician, the conjunction of '$(x)(Fx \supset Gx)$' and '$(x)(Fx \supset {\sim}Gx)$' is logically equivalent to '$(x){\sim}Fx$', which, in turn, is logically equivalent to '${\sim}(\exists x)Fx$'. Hence, all the logician is claiming is that there are no mermaids, when he holds that both universal conditionals are true. And this is not surprising, as he holds them both to be true, in the first place, since there are no mermaids. In short, all that is being asserted by the

16 Strawson, "On Referring," p. 52. Also see his discussion of 'if-then' in *Introduction to Logical Theory*, p. 85.

logician is that '~$(\exists x)(Fx)$' is logically equivalent to the conjunction of '$(x)(Fx \supset Gx)$' and '$(x)(Fx \supset \sim Gx)$'. This equivalence is, of course, based on the logicians' treatment of '$\supset$'. Thus, what Strawson may really be objecting to *is* the logicians' truth table for 'if-then'. This would jibe with his introduction of the notion of presupposes, which we saw, forces him to abandon the standard logical connectives, to be content with unexplicated uses of "presuppose," "negation," "conceptual truth," etc. and, in effect, to give up a two-valued logic. In reintroducing the classical propositional entities under the name of assertions, Strawson is thus doing more than asking us to recognize additional entities, entities which Russell sought to avoid. He is also asking us to give up the one coherent analysis of logical truth and inference that the tradition has produced.

Perhaps there is another point behind Strawson's attack on Russell and formal logic. Strawson's claim that existence is not a predicate leads him to hold that when we say that a class exists it is not clear what we mean if we do not mean that the class has members.[17] He must say something like this, since we cannot transform the apparent subject-predicate sentence 'the class ϕ exists' on the model of the transformation of 'the ϕ exists' into 'there is one and only one ϕ'. Hence his analysis of existential statements forces him to adopt or, perhaps, reflects his commitment to, an extreme form of nominalism. For, on his view, we cannot even say 'the class ϕ exists' in anything like the Platonist's sense. Strawson's analysis must then lead to his rejection of the null class, not only as a Platonic entity, but as a legitimate notion. Perhaps this is another strand in his rejection of 'all ϕ's are ψ's' as true, if there are no ϕ's. Be that as it may, we may note that Strawson's analysis is made to clear up a problematic area of usage and is not presupposed or justified by such usage. By contrast, he implicitly claims that a sentence like 'The present king of France is bald' is unproblematic and unambiguous in his critique of Russell; for he dismisses Russell's transcription of such a statement as unfaithful to ordinary usage. What he in effect does is deny that there is a problem about descriptive phrases which Russell undertook to solve. It is then not surprising that Strawson must end with unexplicated notions, like "presuppose," for he has merely wrapped the problem in ordinary usage and offered it as a solution.

[17] *Introduction to Logical Theory*, pp. 191 ff.

PART THREE

Philosophy of Logic
and Mathematics

20

The Logicist Foundations
of Mathematics

Rudolf Carnap

THE problem of the logical and epistemological foundations of mathematics has not yet been completely solved. This problem vitally concerns both mathematicians and philosophers, for any uncertainty in the foundations of the "most certain of all the sciences" is extremely disconcerting. Of the various attempts already made to solve the problem none can be said to have resolved every difficulty. These efforts have taken essentially three directions: *Logicism*, the chief proponent of which is Russell; *Intuitionism*, advocated by Brouwer; and Hilbert's *Formalism*.

Since I wish to draw you a rough sketch of the salient features of the logicist construction of mathematics, I think I should not only point out those areas in which the logicist program has been completely or at least partly successful but also call attention to the difficulties peculiar to this approach. One of the most important questions for the foundations of mathematics is that of the relation between mathematics and logic. *Logicism* is the thesis that mathematics is reducible to logic, hence nothing but a part of logic. Frege was the first to espouse this view (1884). In their great work, *Principia Mathe-*

Translated by Erne Putnam and Gerald J. Massey in *Philosophy of Mathematics: Selected Readings* ed. Paul Benacerraf and Hilary Putnam, © 1964. Reprinted with the kind permission of Prentice-Hall, Inc., Englewood Cliffs, New Jersey.

matica, the English mathematicians A. N. Whitehead and B. Russell produced a systematization of logic from which they constructed mathematics.

We will split the logicist thesis into two parts for separate discussion:

1. The *concepts* of mathematics can be derived from logical concepts through explicit definitions.
2. The *theorems* of mathematics can be derived from logical axioms through purely logical deduction.

I. The Derivation of Mathematical Concepts

To make precise the thesis that the concepts of mathematics are derivable from logical concepts, we must specify the logical concepts to be employed in the derivation. They are the following. In propositional calculus, which deals with the relations between unanalyzed sentences, the most important concepts are: the negation of a sentence p, 'not-p' (symbolized '$\sim p$'); the disjunction of two sentences, 'p or q' ('$p \vee q$'); the conjunction, 'p and q' ('$p \cdot q$'); and the implication, 'if p, then q' ('$p \supset q$'). The concepts of functional calculus are given in the form of functions, e.g., '$f(a)$' (read 'f of a') signifies that the property f belongs to the object a. The most important concepts of functional calculus are universality and existence: '$(x)f(x)$' (read 'for every x, f of x') means that the property f belongs to every object; '$(\exists x)f(x)$' (read 'there is an x such that f of x') means that f belongs to at least one object. Finally there is the concept of identity: '$a = b$' means that 'a' and 'b' are names of the same object.

Not all these concepts need be taken as undefined or primitive, for some of them are reducible to others. For example, '$p \vee q$' can be defined as '$\sim(\sim p \cdot \sim q)$' and '$(\exists x)f(x)$' as '$\sim(x)\sim f(x)$'. It is the logicist thesis, then, that the logical concepts just given suffice to define all mathematical concepts, that over and above them no specifically mathematical concepts are required for the construction of mathematics.

Already before Frege, mathematicians in their investigations of the interdependence of mathematical concepts had shown, though often without being able to provide precise definitions, that all the concepts of arithmetic are reducible to the natural numbers (i.e., the numbers 1, 2, 3, ... which are used in ordinary counting). Accordingly, the *main problem* which remained for logicism was to derive the natural numbers from logical concepts. Although Frege had already found a solution to this problem, Russell and Whitehead reached the same results independently of him and were subsequently the first to recognize the agreement of their work with Frege's. The crux of this solution is the correct recognition of the logical status of the natural numbers; they are logical attributes which belong, not to things, but to concepts. That a certain number, say 3, is the number of a concept means that three objects fall under it. We can express the very same thing with the help of the logical concepts previously given. For example, let '$2_m(f)$' mean that at least two objects fall under the concept f. Then we can define this concept as follows (where '$=_{Df}$' is the symbol for definition, read as "means by definition"):

$$2_m(f) =_{Df} (\exists x)(\exists y)[\sim(x=y) \cdot f(x) \cdot f(y)]$$

or in words: there is an x and there is a y such that x is not identical with y and f belongs to x and f belongs to y. In like manner, we define 3_m, 4_m, and so on. Then we define the number two itself thus:

$$2(f) =_{Df} 2_m(f) \cdot \sim 3_m(f)$$

or in words: at least two, but not at least three, objects fall under f. We can also define arithmetical operations quite easily. For example, we can define addition with the help of the disjunction of two mutually exclusive concepts. Furthermore, we can define the concept of natural number itself.

The derivation of the other kinds of numbers—i.e., the positive and negative numbers, the fractions, the real and the complex numbers—is accomplished, not in the usual way by adding to the domain of the natural numbers, but by the construction of a completely new domain. The natural numbers do not constitute a subset of the fractions but are merely correlated in obvious fashion with certain fractions. Thus the natural number 3 and the fraction $\frac{3}{1}$ are not identical but merely correlated with one another. Similarly we must distinguish the fraction $\frac{1}{2}$ from the real number correlated with it. In this paper, we will treat only the definition of the real numbers. Unlike the derivations of the other kinds of numbers which encounter no great difficulties, the derivation of the real numbers presents problems which, it must be admitted, neither logicism, intuitionism, nor formalism has altogether overcome.

Let us assume that we have already constructed the series of fractions (ordered according to magnitude). Our task, then, is to supply definitions of the real numbers based on this series. Some of the real numbers, the rationals, correspond in obvious fashion to fractions; the rest, the irrationals, correspond as Dedekind showed (1872) to "gaps" in the series of fractions. Suppose, for example, that we divide the (positive) fractions into two classes, the class of all whose square is less than 2, and the class comprising all the rest of the fractions. This division forms a "cut" in the series of fractions which corresponds to the irrational real number $\sqrt{2}$. This cut is called a "gap" since there is no fraction correlated with it. As there is no fraction whose square is two, the first or "lower" class contains no greatest member, and the second or "upper" class contains no least member. Hence, to every real number there corresponds a cut in the series of fractions, each irrational real number being correlated with a gap.

Russell developed further Dedekind's line of thought. Since a cut is uniquely determined by its "lower" class, Russell defined a real number as the lower class of the corresponding cut in the series of fractions. For example, $\sqrt{2}$ is defined as the class (or property) of those fractions whose square is less than two, and the rational real number $\frac{1}{3}$ is defined as the class of all fractions smaller than the fraction $\frac{1}{3}$. On the basis of these definitions, the entire arithmetic of the real numbers can be developed. This development, however, runs up against certain difficulties connected with so-called "impredicative definition," which we will discuss shortly.

The essential point of this method of introducing the real numbers is that they are *not postulated but constructed*. The logicist does not establish the existence of structures which have the properties of the real numbers by laying down axioms or postulates; rather, through explicit definitions, he produces logical constructions that have, by virtue of these definitions, the usual properties of the real numbers. As there are no "creative definitions," definition is not creation but only name-giving to something whose existence has already been established.

In similarly constructivistic fashion, the logicist introduces the rest of the concepts of mathematics, those of analysis (e.g., convergence, limit, continuity, differential, quotient, integral, etc.) and also those of set theory (notably the concepts of the transfinite cardinal and ordinal numbers). This "constructivistic" method forms part of the very texture of logicism.

II. The Derivation of the Theorems of Mathematics

The second thesis of logicism is that the *theorems of mathematics* are derivable from logical axioms through logical deduction. The requisite system of logical axioms, obtained by simplifying Russell's system, contains four axioms of propositional calculus and two of functional calculus. The rules of inference are a rule of substitution and a rule of implication (the *modus ponens* of ancient logic). Hilbert and Ackermann have used these same axioms and rules of inference in their system.

Mathematical predicates are introduced by explicit definitions. Since an explicit definition is nothing but a convention to employ a new, usually much shorter, way of writing something, the *definiens* or the new way of writing it can always be eliminated. Therefore, as every sentence of mathematics can be translated into a sentence which contains only the primitive logical predicates already mentioned, this second thesis can be restated thus: Every provable mathematical sentence is translatable into a sentence which contains only primitive logical symbols and which is provable in logic.

But the derivation of the theorems of mathematics poses certain difficulties for logicism. In the first place it turns out that some theorems of arithmetic and set theory, if interpreted in the usual way, require for their proof besides the logical axioms still other special axioms known as the *axiom of infinity* and the *axiom of choice* (or multiplicative axiom). The axiom of infinity states that for every natural number there is a greater one. The axiom of choice states that for every set of disjoint non-empty sets, there is (at least) one selection-set, i.e., a set that has exactly one member in common with each of the member sets. But we are not concerned here with the content of these axioms but with their logical character. Both are existential sentences. Hence, Russell was right in hesitating to present them as logical axioms, for logic deals only with possible entities and cannot make assertions about whether something does or does not exist. Russell found a way out of this difficulty. He reasoned that since mathematics was also a purely formal science, it too could make only conditional, not categorical, statements about existence: if certain structures exist, then there also exist certain other structures whose existence follows logically from the existence of the former. For this reason he transformed a mathematical sentence, say S, the proof of which required the axiom of infinity, I, or the axiom of choice, C, into a conditional sentence; hence S is taken to assert not S, but $I \supset S$ or $C \supset S$, respectively. This conditional sentence is then derivable from the axioms of logic.

A greater difficulty, perhaps the greatest difficulty, in the construction of mathematics has to do with another axiom posited by Russell, the so-called *axiom of reducibility*, which has justly become the main bone of contention for the critics of the system of *Principia Mathematica*. We agree with the opponents of logicism that it is inadmissible to take it as an axiom. As we will discuss more fully later, the gap created by the removal of this axiom has certainly not yet been filled in an entirely satisfactory way. This difficulty is bound up with Russell's *theory of types* which we shall now briefly discuss.

We must distinguish between a "simple theory of types" and a "ramified theory of types." The latter was developed by Russell but later recognized by Ramsey to be an unnecessary complication of the former. If, for the sake of simplicity, we restrict our attention to one-place functions (properties) and abstract from many-place functions (relations), then type theory consists in the following classification of expressions into different "types": To type o belong the names of the objects ("individuals") of the domain of discourse (e.g., $a, b, \ldots$). To type 1 belong the properties of these objects (e.g., $f(a), g(a), \ldots$). To type 2 belong the properties of these properties (e.g., $F(f), G(f), \ldots$); for example, the concept $2(f)$ defined above belongs to this type. To type 3 belong the properties of properties of properties, and so on. The basic rule of type theory is that every predicate belongs to a determinate type and can be meaningfully applied only to expressions of the next lower type. Accordingly, sentences of the form $f(a), F(f), 2(f)$ are always meaningful, i.e., either true or false; on the other hand combinations like $f(g)$ and $f(F)$ are neither true nor false but meaningless. In particular, expressions like $f(f)$ or $\sim f(f)$ are meaningless, i.e., we cannot meaningfully say of a property either that it belongs to itself or that it does not. As we shall see, this last result is important for the elimination of the antinomies.

This completes our outline of the simple theory of types, which most proponents of modern logic consider legitimate and necessary. In his system, Russell introduced the ramified theory of types, which has not found much acceptance. In this theory the properties of each type are further subdivided into "orders." This division is based, not on the kind of objects to which the property belongs, but on the form of the definition which introduces it. Later we shall consider the reasons why Russell believed this further ramification necessary. Because of the introduction of the ramified theory of types, certain difficulties arose in the construction of mathematics, especially in the theory of real numbers. Many fundamental theorems not only could not be proved but could not even be expressed. To overcome this difficulty, Russell had to use brute force; i.e., he introduced the axiom of reducibility by means of which the different orders of a type could be reduced in certain respects to the lowest order of the type. The sole justification for this axiom was the fact that there seemed to be no other way out of this particular difficulty engendered by the ramified theory of types. Later Russell himself, influenced by Wittgenstein's sharp criticism, abandoned the axiom of reducibility in the second edition of *Principia Mathematica* (1925). But, as he still believed that one could not get along without the ramified theory of types, he despaired of the situation. Thus we see how important it would be, not only for logicism but for any attempt to solve the problems of the foundations of mathematics, to show that the simple theory of types is sufficient for the construction of mathematics out of logic. A young English mathematician and pupil of Russell, Ramsey (who unfortunately died this year, i.e., 1930), in 1926 made some efforts in this direction which we will discuss later.

III. The Problem of Impredicative Definition

To ascertain whether the simple theory of types is sufficient or must be further ramified, we must first of all examine the reasons which induced Russell to adopt this ramification in spite of its most undesirable consequences. There were two closely connected reasons: the necessity of eliminating the logical antinomies and the so-called "vicious circle" principle. We call "logical antinomies" the contradictions which first appeared in set theory (as so-called "paradoxes") but which Russell showed to be common to all logic. It can be shown that these contradictions arise in logic if the theory of types is not presupposed. The simplest antinomy is that of the concept "impredicable." By definition a property is "impredicable" if it does not belong to itself. Now is the property "impredicable" itself impredicable? If we assume that it is, then since it belongs to itself it would be, according to the definition of "impredicable," not impredicable. If we assume that it is not impredicable, then it does not belong to itself and hence, according to the definition of "impredicable," is impredicable. According to the law of excluded middle, it is either impredicable or not, but both alternatives lead to a contradiction. Another example is Grelling's antinomy of the concept "heterological." Except that it concerns predicates rather than properties, this antinomy is completely analogous to the one just described. By definition, a predicate is "heterological" if the property designated by the predicate does not belong to the predicate itself. (For example, the word 'monosyllabic' is heterological, for the word itself is not monosyllabic.) Obviously both the assumption that the word 'heterological' is itself heterological as well as the opposite assumption lead to a contradiction. Russell and other logicians have constructed numerous antinomies of this kind.

Ramsey has shown that there are two completely different kinds of antinomies. Those belonging to the first kind can be expressed in logical symbols and are called "logical antinomies" (in the narrower sense). The "impredicable" antinomy is of this kind. Ramsey has shown that this kind of antinomy is eliminated by the simple theory of types. The concept "impredicable," for example, cannot even be defined if the simple theory of types is presupposed, for an expression of the form, a property does not belong to itself ($\sim f(f)$), is not well-formed, and meaningless according to that theory.

Antinomies of the second kind are known as "semantical" or "epistemological" antinomies. They include our previous example, "heterological," as well as the antinomy, well-known to mathematicians, of the smallest natural number which cannot be defined in German with fewer than 100 letters. Ramsey has shown that antinomies of this second kind cannot be constructed in the symbolic language of logic and therefore need not be taken into account in the construction of mathematics from logic. The fact that they appear in word languages led Russell to impose certain restrictions on logic in order to eliminate them, viz., the ramified theory of types. But perhaps their appearance is due to some defect of our ordinary word language.

Since antinomies of the first kind are already eliminated by the simple theory of types and those of the second kind do not appear in logic, Ramsey declared that the ramified theory of types and hence also the axiom of reducibility were superfluous.

Now what about Russell's second reason for ramifying the theory of types, viz., the vicious circle principle? This principle, that "no whole may contain parts which are definable only in terms of that whole," may also be called an "injunction against impredicative definition." A definition is said to be "impredicative" if it defines a concept in terms of a totality to which the concept belongs. (The concept "impredicative" has nothing to do with the aforementioned pseudo concept "impredicable.") Russell's main reason for laying down this injunction was his belief that antinomies arise when it is violated. From a somewhat different standpoint Poincaré before, and Weyl after, Russell also rejected impredicative definition. They pointed out that an impredicatively defined concept was meaningless because of the circularity in its definition. An example will perhaps make the matter clearer:

We can define the concept "inductive number" (which corresponds to the concept of natural number including zero) as follows: A number is said to be "inductive" if it possesses all the hereditary properties of zero. A property is said to be "hereditary" if it always belongs to the number $n + 1$ whenever it belongs to the number n. In symbols,

$$\text{Ind}(x) =_{\text{Df}}(f) [(\text{Her}(f) \cdot f(\text{o})) \supset f(x)]$$

To show that this definition is circular and useless, one usually argues as follows: In the *definiens* the expression '(f)' occurs, i.e., "for all properties (of numbers)". But since the property "inductive" belongs to the class of all properties, the very property to be defined already occurs in a hidden way in the *definiens* and thus is to be defined in terms of itself, an obviously inadmissible procedure. It is sometimes claimed that the meaninglessness of an impredicatively defined concept is seen most clearly if one tries to establish whether the concept holds in an individual case. For example, to ascertain whether the number three is inductive, we must, according to the definition, investigate whether every property which is hereditary and belongs to zero also belongs to three. But if we must do this for every property, we must also do it for the property "inductive" which is also a property of numbers. Therefore, in order to determine whether the number three is inductive, we must determine among other things whether the property "inductive" is hereditary, whether it belongs to zero, and finally—this is the crucial point—whether it belongs to three. But this means that it would be impossible to determine whether three is an inductive number.

Before we consider how Ramsey tried to refute this line of thought, we must get clear about how these considerations led Russell to the ramified theory of types. Russell reasoned in this way: Since it is inadmissible to define a property in terms of an expression which refers to "all properties," we must subdivide the properties (of type 1): To the "first order" belong those properties in whose definition the expression 'all properties' does not occur; to the "second order" those in whose definition the expression 'all properties of the first order' occurs; to the "third order" those in whose definition the expression 'all properties of the second order' occurs, and so on. Since the expression 'all properties' without reference to a determinate order is held to be inadmissible, there never occurs in the definition of a property a totality to which it itself belongs. The property "inductive," for example, is defined in this no longer impredicative way: A number is said to be "inductive" if it possesses all the hereditary properties of the first order which belong to zero.

But the ramified theory of types gives rise to formidable difficulties in the treatment of the real numbers. As we have already seen, a real number is defined as a class, or what comes to the same thing, as a property of fractions. For example, we saw that $\sqrt{2}$ is defined as the class or property of those fractions whose square is less than two. But since the expression 'for all properties' without reference to a determinate order is inadmissible under the ramified theory of types, the expression 'for all real numbers' cannot refer to all real numbers without qualification but only to the real numbers of a determinate order. To the first order belong those real numbers in whose definition an expression of the form 'for all real numbers' does not occur; to the second order belong those in whose definition such an expression occurs, but this expression must be restricted to "all real numbers of the first order," and so on. Thus there can be neither an admissible definition nor an admissible sentence which refers to all real numbers without qualification.

But as a consequence of this ramification, many of the most important definitions and theorems of real number theory are lost. Once Russell had recognized that his earlier attempt to overcome it, viz., the introduction of the axiom of reducibility, was itself inadmissible, he saw no way out of this difficulty. The *most difficult problem* confronting contemporary studies in the foundations of mathematics is this: How can we develop logic if, on the one hand, we are to avoid the danger of the meaninglessness of impredicative definitions and, on the other hand, are to reconstruct satisfactorily the theory of real numbers?

IV. Attempt at a Solution

Ramsey (1926) outlined a construction of mathematics in which he courageously tried to resolve this difficulty by declaring the forbidden impredicative definitions to be perfectly admissible. They contain, he contended, a circle but the circle is harmless, not vicious. Consider, he said, the description 'the tallest man in this room'. Here we describe something in terms of a totality to which it itself belongs. Still no one thinks this description inadmissible since the person described already exists and is only singled out, not created, by the description. Ramsey believed that the same considerations applied to properties. The totality of properties already exists in itself. That we men are finite beings who cannot name individually each of infinitely many properties but can describe some of them only with reference to the totality of all properties is an empirical fact that has nothing to do with logic. For these reasons Ramsey allows impredicative definition. Consequently, he can both get along with the simple theory of types and still retain all the requisite mathematical definitions, particularly those needed for the theory of the real numbers.

Although this happy result is certainly tempting, I think we should not let ourselves be seduced by it into accepting Ramsey's basic premise; viz., that the totality of properties already exists before their characterization by definition. Such a conception, I believe, is not far removed from a belief in a platonic realm of ideas which exist in themselves, independently of *if* and *how* finite human beings are able to think them. I think we ought to hold fast to Frege's dictum that, in mathematics, only that may be taken to exist whose existence has been proved (and he meant proved in finitely many steps). I agree with the intuitionists that the finiteness of every logical-mathematical operation, proof, and definition is not required because of some accidental empirical fact about man but is required by the very nature of the subject. Because of this attitude, intuitionist mathematics has been called "anthropological mathematics." It seems to me that, by analogy, we should call Ramsey's mathematics "theological mathematics," for when he speaks of the totality of properties he elevates himself above the actually knowable and definable and in certain respects reasons from the standpoint of an infinite mind which is not bound by the wretched necessity of building every structure step by step.

We may now rephrase our crucial question thus: Can we have

Ramsey's result without retaining absolutist conceptions? His result was this: Limitation to the simple theory of types and retention of the possibility of definitions for mathematical concepts, particularly in real number theory. We can reach this result if, like Ramsey, we allow impredicative definition, but can we do this without falling into his conceptual absolutism? I will try to give an affirmative answer to this question.

Let us go back to the example of the property "inductive" for which we gave an impredicative definition:

$$\mathrm{Ind}(x) =_{\mathrm{Df}} (f)\,[\,(\mathrm{Her}(f)\cdot f(\mathrm{o}))\supset f(x)\,]$$

Let us examine once again whether the use of this definition, i.e., establishing whether the concept holds in an individual case or not, really leads to circularity and is therefore impossible. According to this definition, that the number two is inductive means:

$$(f)\,[\,(\mathrm{Her}(f)\cdot f(\mathrm{o}))\supset f(2)\,]$$

in words: Every property f which is hereditary and belongs to zero belongs also to two. How can we verify a universal statement of this kind? If we had to examine every single property, an unbreakable circle would indeed result, for then we would run headlong against the property "inductive." Establishing whether something had it would then be impossible in principle, and the concept would therefore be meaningless. But the verification of a universal logical or mathematical sentence does not consist in running through a series of individual cases, for impredicative definitions usually refer to infinite totalities. The belief that we must run through all the individual cases rests on a confusion of "numerical" generality, which refers to objects already given, with "specific" generality.[1] We do not establish specific generality by running through individual cases but by logically deriving certain properties from certain others. In our example, that the number two is inductive means that the property "belonging to two" follows logically from the property "being hereditary and belonging to zero." In symbols, '$f(2)$' can be derived for an arbitrary f from '$\mathrm{Her}(f)\cdot f(\mathrm{o})$' by logical operations. This is indeed the case. First, the derivation of '$f(\mathrm{o})$' from '$\mathrm{Her}\,(f)\cdot f(\mathrm{o})$' is trivial and proves the in-

---

[1] Cf. F. Kaufmann, *Das Unendliche in der Mathematik und seine Ausschaltung* (Vienna, 1930).

ductiveness of the number zero. The remaining steps are based on the definition of the concept "hereditary":

$$\mathrm{Her}(f) =_{\mathrm{Df}} (n)\, [f(n) \supset f(n+1)]$$

Using this definition, we can easily show that '$f(0 + 1)$' and hence '$f(1)$' are derivable from 'Her$(f) \cdot f(0)$' and thereby prove that the number one is inductive. Using this result and our definition, we can derive '$f(1 + 1)$' and hence '$f(2)$' from 'Her$(f) \cdot f(0)$', thereby showing that the number two is inductive. We see then that the definition of inductiveness, although impredicative, does not hinder its utility. That proofs that the defined property obtains (or does not obtain) in individual cases can be given shows that the definition is meaningful. If we reject the belief that it is necessary to run through individual cases and rather make it clear to ourselves that the complete verification of a statement about an arbitrary property means nothing more than its logical (more exactly, tautological) validity for an arbitrary property, we will come to the conclusion that impredicative definitions are logistically admissible. If a property is defined impredicatively, then establishing whether or not it obtains in an individual case may, under certain circumstances, be difficult, or it may even be impossible if there is no solution to the decision problem for that logical system. But in no way does impredicativeness make such decisions impossible in principle for all cases. If the theory just sketched proves feasible, logicism will have been helped over its greatest difficulty, which consists in steering a safe course between the Scylla of the axiom of reducibility and the Charybdis of the allocation of the real numbers to different orders.

Logicism as here described has several features in common both with intuitionism and with formalism. It shares with intuitionism a constructivistic tendency with respect to definition, a tendency which Frege also emphatically endorsed. A concept may not be introduced axiomatically but must be constructed from undefined, primitive concepts step by step through explicit definitions. The admission of impredicative definitions seems at first glance to run counter to this tendency, but this is only true for constructions of the form proposed by Ramsey. Like the intuitionists, we recognize as properties only those expressions (more precisely, expressions of the form of a sentence containing one free variable) which are constructed in finitely many steps from undefined primitive properties of the appropriate domain according to determinate rules of construction. The difference between us lies in the fact that we recognize as valid not only the rules of construction which the intuitionists use (the rules of the so-called "strict functional calculus"), but in addition, permit the use of the expression 'for all properties' (the operations of the so-called "extended functional calculus").

Further, logicism has a methodological affinity with formalism. Logicism proposes to construct the logical-mathematical system in such a way that, although the axioms and rules of inference are chosen with an interpretation of the primitive symbols in mind, nevertheless, *inside the system* the chains of deductions and of definitions are carried through formally as in a pure calculus, i.e., without reference to the meaning of the primitive symbols.

2 1

Predicative Functions and the Axiom of Reducibility

F. P. Ramsey

IN this chapter we shall consider the second of the three objections which we made in the last chapter to the theory of the foundations of mathematics given in *Principia Mathematica*. This objection, which is perhaps the most serious of the three, was directed against the Theory of Types, which seemed to involve either the acceptance of the illegitimate Axiom of Reducibility or the rejection of such a fundamental type of mathematical argument as Dedekind section. We saw that this difficulty came from the second of the two parts into which the theory was divided, namely, that part which concerned the different ranges of functions of given arguments, e.g. individuals; and we have to consider whether this part of the Theory of Types cannot be amended so as to get out of the difficulty. We shall see that this can be done in a simple and straightforward way, which is a natural consequence of the logical theories of Mr. Wittgenstein.

We shall start afresh from part of his theory of propositions, of which something was said in the first chapter. We saw there that he explains propositions in general by reference to atomic propositions, every proposition expressing agreement and disagreement with truth-

Reprinted with the kind permission of the publishers from F. P. Ramsey, *The Foundations of Mathematics* (New York: Humanities Press and London: Routledge & Kegan Paul, 1931, 1954), Chapter 1, pp. 32–49.

possibilities of atomic propositions. We saw also that we could construct many different symbols all expressing agreement and disagreement with the same sets of possibilities. For instance,

$$`p \supset q`, `{\sim}p . \vee . q`, `{\sim} : p . {\sim}q`, `{\sim}q . \supset . {\sim}p`$$

are such a set, all agreeing with the three possibilities

$$`p . q`, `{\sim}p . q`, `{\sim}p . {\sim}q`,$$

but disagreeing with '$p . {\sim}q$'. Two symbols of this kind, which express agreement and disagreement with the same sets of possibilities, are said to be instances of the same proposition. They are instances of it just as all the 'the's on a page are instances of the word 'the'. But whereas the 'the's are instances of the same word on account of their physical similarity, different symbols are instances of the same proposition because they have the same sense, that is, express agreement with the same sets of possibilities. When we speak of propositions we shall generally mean the types of which the individual symbols are instances, and we shall include types of which there may be no instances. This is inevitable, since it cannot be any concern of ours whether anyone has actually symbolized or asserted a proposition, and we have to consider all propositions in the sense of all possible assertions whether or not they have been asserted.

Any proposition expresses agreement and disagreement with complementary sets of truth-possibilities of atomic propositions; conversely, given any set of these truth-possibilities, it would be logically possible to assert agreement with them and disagreement with all others, and the set of truth-possibilities therefore determines a proposition. This proposition may in practice be extremely difficult to express through the poverty of our language, for we lack both names for many objects and methods of making assertions involving an infinite number of atomic propositions, except in relatively simple cases, such as '$(x) . \phi x$', which involves the (probably) infinite set of (in certain cases) atomic propositions, 'ϕa', 'ϕb', etc. Nevertheless, we have to consider propositions which our language is inadequate to express. In '$(x) . \phi x$' we assert the truth of all possible propositions which would be of the form 'ϕx' whether or not we have names for all the values of x. General propositions must obviously be understood as applying to everything, not merely to everything for which we have a name.

We come now to a most important point in connection with the Theory of Types. We explained in the last chapter what was meant by an elementary proposition, namely, one constructed explicitly as a truth-function of atomic propositions. We have now to see that, on the theory of Wittgenstein, elementary is not an adjective of the proposition-type at all, but only of its instances. For an elementary and a non-elementary propositional symbol could be instances of the same proposition. Thus suppose a list was made of all individuals as 'a', 'b', . . . , 'z'. Then, if $\phi\hat{x}$ were an elementary function, '$\phi a . \phi b$ . . . ϕz' would be an elementary proposition, but '$(x) . \phi x$' non-elementary; but these would express agreement and disagreement with the same possibilities and therefore be the same proposition. Or to take an example which could really occur, 'ϕa' and '$\phi a : (\exists x) . \phi x$', which are the same proposition, since $(\exists x) . \phi x$ adds nothing to ϕa. But the first is elementary, the second non-elementary.

Hence some instances of a proposition can be elementary, and others non-elementary; so that elementary is not really a characteristic of the proposition, but of its mode of expression. 'Elementary proposition' is like 'spoken word'; just as the same word can be both spoken and written, so the same proposition can be both elementarily and non-elementarily expressed.

After these preliminary explanations we proceed to a theory of propositional functions. By a propositional function of individuals we mean a symbol of the form '$f(\hat{x}, \hat{y}, \hat{z}, \ldots)$' which is such that, were the names of any individuals substituted for '$\hat{x}$', '$\hat{y}$', '$\hat{z}$', . . . in it, the result would always be a proposition. This definition needs to be completed by the explanation that two such symbols are regarded as the same function when the substitution of the same set of names in the one and in the other always gives the same proposition. Thus if '$f(a, b, c)$', '$g(a, b, c)$' are the same proposition for any set of a, b, c, '$f(\hat{x}, \hat{y}, \hat{z})$' and '$g(\hat{x}, \hat{y}, \hat{z})$' are the same function, even if they are quite different to look at.

A function[1] '$\phi\hat{x}$' gives us for each individual a proposition in the sense of a proposition-type (which may not have any instances, for we may not have given the individual a name). So the function collects together a set of propositions, whose logical sum and product we assert by writing respectively '$(\exists x) . \phi x$', '$(x) . \phi x$'. This procedure can be extended to the case of several variables. Consider '$\phi(\hat{x}, \hat{y})$'; give y any constant value η, and '$\phi(\hat{x}, \eta)$' gives a proposition when any

---

[1] By 'function' we shall in future always mean propositional function unless the contrary is stated.

individual name is substituted for $\hat{x}$, and is therefore a function of one variable, from which we can form the propositions

$$`(\exists x) . \phi(x, \eta)', `(x) . \phi(x, \eta)'.$$

Consider next '$(\exists x) . \phi(x, \hat{y})$'; this, as we have seen, gives a proposition when any name (e.g. 'η') is substituted for 'y', and is therefore a function of one variable from which we can form the propositions

$$(\exists y) : (\exists x) . \phi(x, y) \text{ and } (y) : (\exists x) . \phi(x, y).$$

As so far there has been no difficulty, we shall attempt to treat functions of functions in exactly the same way as we have treated functions of individuals. Let us take, for simplicity, a function of one variable which is a function of individuals. This would be a symbol of the form '$f(\phi\hat{x})$', which becomes a proposition on the substitution for '$\phi\hat{x}$' of any function of an individual. '$f(\phi\hat{x})$' then collects together a set of propositions, one for each function of an individual, of which we assert the logical sum and product by writing respectively '$(\exists \phi) . f(\phi\hat{x})$', '$(\phi) . f(\phi\hat{x})$'.

But this account suffers from an unfortunate vagueness as to the range of functions $\phi\hat{x}$ giving the values of $f(\phi\hat{x})$ of which we assert the logical sum or product. In this respect there is an important difference between functions of functions and functions of individuals which is worth examining closely. It appears clearly in the fact that the expressions 'function of functions' and 'function of individuals' are not strictly analogous; for, whereas functions are symbols, individuals are objects, so that to get an expression analogous to 'function of functions' we should have to say 'function of names of individuals'. On the other hand, there does not seem any simple way of altering 'function of functions' so as to make it analogous to 'function of individuals', and it is just this which causes the trouble. For the range of values of a function of individuals is definitely fixed by the range of individuals, an objective totality which there is no getting away from. But the range of arguments to a function of functions is a range of symbols, all symbols which become propositions by inserting in them the name of an individual. And this range of symbols, actual or possible, is not objectively fixed, but depends on our methods of constructing them and requires more precise definition.

This definition can be given in two ways, which may be distinguished as the subjective and the objective method. The subjective[2]

[2] I do not wish to press this term; I merely use it because I can find no better.

method is that adopted in *Principia Mathematica*; it consists in defining the range of functions as all those which could be constructed in a certain way, in the first instance by sole use of the '/' sign. We have seen how it leads to the impasse of the Axiom of Reducibility. I, on the other hand, shall adopt the entirely original objective method which will lead us to a satisfactory theory in which no such axiom is required. This method is to treat functions of functions as far as possible in the same way as functions of individuals. The signs which can be substituted as arguments in '$\phi\hat{x}$', a function of individuals, are determined by their meanings; they must be names of individuals. I propose similarly to determine the symbols which can be substituted as arguments in '$f(\phi\hat{x})$' not by the manner of their construction, but by their meanings. This is more difficult, because functions do not mean single objects as names do, but have meaning in a more complicated way derived from the meanings of the propositions which are their values. The problem is ultimately to fix as values of $f(\phi\hat{x})$ some definite set of propositions so that we can assert their logical product and sum. In *Principia Mathematica* they are determined as all propositions which can be constructed in a certain way. My method, on the other hand, is to disregard how we could construct them, and to determine them by a description of their senses or imports; and in so doing we may be able to include in the set propositions which we have no way of constructing, just as we include in the range of values of ϕx propositions which we cannot express from lack of names for the individuals concerned.

We must begin the description of the new method with the definition of an atomic function of individuals, as the result of replacing by variables any of the names of individuals in an atomic proposition expressed by using names alone; where if a name occurs more than once in the proposition it may be replaced by the same or different variables, or left alone in its different occurrences. The values of an atomic function of individuals are thus atomic propositions.

We next extend to propositional functions the idea of a truth-function of propositions. (At first, of course, the functions to which we extend it are only atomic, but the extension works also in general, and so I shall state it in general.) Suppose we have functions $\phi_1(\hat{x}, \hat{y})$, $\phi_2(\hat{x}, \hat{y})$; etc., then by saying that a function $\psi(\hat{x}, \hat{y})$ is a certain truth-function (e.g. the logical sum) of the functions $\phi_1(\hat{x}, \hat{y})$, $\phi_2(\hat{x}, \hat{y})$, etc., and the propositions p, q, etc., we mean that any value of $\psi(x, y)$, say $\psi(a, b)$, is that truth-function of the corresponding values of $\phi_1(x, y)$,

$\phi_2(x, y)$, etc., i.e. $\phi_1(a, b)$, $\phi_2(a, b)$, etc., and propositions p, q, etc. This definition enables us to include functions among the arguments of any truth-function, for it always gives us a unique function which is that truth-function of those arguments; e.g. the logical sum of $\phi_1(\hat{x})$, $\phi_2(\hat{x})$, ... is determined as $\psi(x)$, where $\psi(a)$ is the logical sum of $\phi_1 a$, $\phi_2 a$, ... , a definite proposition for each a, so that $\psi(x)$ is a definite function. It is unique because, if there were two, namely $\psi_1(x)$ and $\psi_2(x)$, $\psi_1(a)$ and $\psi_2(a)$ would for each a be the same proposition, and hence the two functions would be identical.

We can now give the most important definition in this theory, that of a predicative function. I do not use this term in the sense of *Principia Mathematica*, 1st ed., for which I follow Mr. Russell's later work in using 'elementary'. The notion of a predicative function, in my sense, is one which does not occur in *Principia*, and marks the essential divergence of the two methods of procedure. A *predicative function* of individuals is one which is any truth-function of arguments, which, whether finite or infinite in number, are all either atomic functions of individuals or propositions.[3] This defines a definite range of functions of individuals which is wider than any range occurring in *Principia*. It is essentially dependent on the notion of a truth-function of an infinite number of arguments; if there could only be a finite number of arguments our predicative functions would be simply the elementary functions of *Principia*. Admitting an infinite number involves that we do not define the range of functions as those which could be constructed in a certain way, but determine them by a description of their meanings. They are to be truth-functions—not explicitly in their appearance, but in their significance—of atomic functions and propositions. In this way we shall include many functions which we have no way of constructing, and many which we construct in quite different ways. Thus, supposing $\phi(\hat{x}, \hat{y})$ is an atomic function, p a proposition,

$$\phi(\hat{x}, \hat{y}), \quad \phi(\hat{x}, \hat{y}) \cdot \vee \cdot p, \quad (y) \cdot \phi(\hat{x}, y)$$

are all predicative functions. [The last is predicative because it is the logical product of the atomic functions $\phi(\hat{x}, y)$ for different values of y.]

For functions of functions there are more or less analogous defini-

---

[3] Before 'propositions' we could insert 'atomic' without narrowing the sense of the definition. For any proposition is a truth-function of atomic propositions, and a truth-function of a truth-function is again a truth-function.

tions. First, an atomic function of (predicative[4]) functions of individuals and of individuals can only have one functional argument, say ϕ, but may have many individual arguments, x, y, etc., and must be of the form $\phi(x, y, \ldots, a, b, \ldots)$ where 'a', 'b', ... are names of individuals. In particular, an atomic function $f(\phi\hat{z})$ is the form ϕa. A predicative function of (predicative) functions of individuals and of individuals is one which is a truth-function whose arguments are all either propositions or atomic functions of functions of individuals and of individuals,

e.g. $\phi a . \supset . \psi b : \vee : p$ (a function of ϕ, ψ),

$(x) . \phi x$, the logical product of the atomic functions ϕa, ϕb, etc.

It is clear that a function only occurs in a predicative function through its values. In this way we can proceed to define predicative functions of functions of functions and so on to any order.

Now consider such a proposition as $(\phi) . f(\phi\hat{x})$ where $f(\phi\hat{x})$ is a predicative function of functions. We understand the range of values of ϕ to be all predicative functions; i.e. $(\phi) . f(\phi\hat{x})$ is the logical product of the propositions $f(\phi\hat{x})$ for each predicative function, and as this is a definite set of propositions, we have attached to $(\phi) . f(\phi\hat{x})$ a definite significance.

Now consider the function of x, $(\phi) . f(\phi\hat{z}, x)$. Is this a predicative function? It is the logical product of the propositional functions of x, $f(\phi\hat{z}, x)$ for the different ϕ's which, since f is predicative, are truth-functions of ϕx and propositions possibly variable in ϕ but constant in x (e.g. ϕa). The ϕx's, since the ϕ's are predicative, are truth-functions of atomic functions of x. Hence the propositional functions of x, $f(\phi\hat{z}, x)$ are truth-functions of atomic functions of x and propositions. Hence they are predicative functions, and therefore their logical product $(\phi) . f(\phi\hat{z}, x)$ is predicative. More generally it is clear that by generalization, whatever the type of the apparent variable, we can never create non-predicative functions; for the generalization is a truth-function of its instances, and, if these are predicative, so is it.

Thus all the functions of individuals which occur in *Principia* are in our sense predicative and included in our variable ϕ, so that all need for an Axiom of Reducibility disappears.

But, it will be objected, surely in this there is a vicious circle; you cannot include $F\hat{x} = (\phi) . f(\phi\hat{z}, \hat{x})$ among the ϕ's, for it presupposes

---

[4] I put 'predicative' in parentheses because the definitions apply equally to the non-predicative functions dealt with in the next chapter.

the totality of the ϕ's. This is not, however, really a vicious circle. The proposition Fa is certainly the logical product of the propositions $f(\phi\hat{z}, a)$, but to express it like this (which is the only way we can) is merely to describe it in a certain way, by reference to a totality of which it may be itself a member, just as we may refer to a man as the tallest in a group, thus identifying him by means of a totality of which he is himself a member without there being any vicious circle. The proposition Fa in its significance, that is, the fact it asserts to be the case, does not involve the totality of functions; it is merely our symbol which involves it. To take a particularly simple case, $(\phi) \cdot \phi a$ is the logical product of the propositions ϕa, of which it is itself one; but this is no more remarkable and no more vicious than is the fact that $p \cdot q$ is the logical product of the set p, q, $p \cdot q$, of which it is itself a member. The only difference is that, owing to our inability to write propositions of infinite length, which is logically a mere accident, $(\phi) \cdot \phi a$ cannot, like $p \cdot q$, be elementarily expressed, but must be expressed as the logical product of a set of which it is also a member. If we had infinite resources and could express all atomic functions as $\psi_1 x$, $\psi_2 x$, then we could form all the propositions ϕa, that is, all the truth-functions of $\psi_1 a$, $\psi_2 a$, etc., and among them would be one which was the logical product of them all, including itself, just as $p \cdot q$ is the product of p, q, $p \vee q$, $p \cdot q$. This proposition, which we cannot express directly, that is elementarily, we express indirectly as the logical product of them all by writing '$(\phi) \cdot \phi a$'. This is certainly a circuitous process, but there is clearly nothing vicious about it.

In this lies the great advantage of my method over that of *Principia Mathematica*. In *Principia* the range of ϕ is that of functions which can be elementarily expressed, and since $(\phi) \cdot f(\phi!\hat{z}, x)$ cannot be so expressed it cannot be a value of $\phi!$; but I define the values of ϕ not by how they can be expressed, but by what sort of senses their values have, or rather, by how the facts their values assert are related to their arguments. I thus include functions which could not even be expressed by us at all, let alone elementarily, but only by a being with an infinite symbolic system. And any function formed by generalization being actually predicative, there is no longer any need for an Axiom of Reducibility.

It remains to show that my notion of predicative functions does not involve us in any contradictions. The relevant contradictions, as I have remarked before, all contain some word like 'means', and I shall show that they are due to an essential ambiguity of such words and not to any weakness in the notion of a predicative function.

Let us take first Weyl's contradiction about 'heterological' which we discussed in the last chapter. It is clear that the solution given there is no longer available to us. For, as before, if R is the relation of meaning between 'ϕ' and $\phi\hat{x}$, 'x is heterological' is equivalent to '$(\exists\phi)$: $xR(\phi\hat{z})$. $\sim\phi x$', the range of ϕ being here understood to be that of predicative functions. Then

$$(\exists\phi):xR(\phi\hat{z}) . \sim\phi x,$$

which I will call Fx, is itself a predicative function.

So $\qquad\qquad$ 'F'$R(F\hat{x})$
and $\qquad\qquad (\exists\phi):$'$F$'$R(\phi\hat{x})$,
and therefore $\qquad F($'F'$) . \equiv . \sim F($'F'$)$,
which is a contradiction.

It will be seen that the contradiction essentially depends on deducing $(\exists\phi):$'F'$R(\phi\hat{x})$ from 'F'$R(F\hat{x})$. According to *Principia Mathematica* this deduction is illegitimate because $F\hat{x}$ is not a possible value of $\phi\hat{x}$. But if the range of $\phi\hat{x}$ is that of predicative functions, this solution fails, since $F\hat{x}$ is certainly a predicative function. But there is obviously another possible solution—to deny 'F'$R(F\hat{x})$ the premise of the deduction. 'F'$R(F\hat{x})$ says that 'F' means $F\hat{x}$. Now this is certainly true for some meaning of 'means', so to uphold our denial of it we must show some ambiguity in the meaning of meaning, and say that the sense in which 'F' means $F\hat{x}$, i.e. in which 'heterological' means heterological, is not the sense denoted by 'R', i.e., the sense which occurs in the definition of heterological. We can easily show that this is really the case, so that the contradiction is simply due to an ambiguity in the word 'meaning' and has no relevance to mathematics whatever.

First of all, to speak of 'F' as meaning $F\hat{x}$ at all must appear very odd in view of our definition of a propositional function as itself a symbol. But the expression is merely elliptical. The fact which we try to describe in these terms is that we have arbitrarily chosen the letter 'F' for a certain purpose, so that 'Fx' shall have a certain meaning (depending on x). As a result of this choice 'F', previously non-significant, becomes significant; it has meaning. But it is clearly an impossible simplification to suppose that there is a single object F, which it means.

Its meaning is more complicated than that, and must be further investigated.

Let us take the simplest case, an atomic proposition fully written out, 'aSb', where 'a', 'b' are names of individuals and 'S' the name of a relation. Then 'a', 'b', 'S' mean in the simplest way the separate objects a, b, and S. Now suppose we define

$$\phi x \, . = . \, aSx \quad \text{Df.}$$

Then 'ϕ' is substituted for 'aS' and does not mean a single object, but has meaning in a more complicated way in virtue of a three-termed relation to both a and S. Then we can say 'ϕ' means $aS\hat{x}$, meaning by this that 'ϕ' has this relation to a and S. We can extend this account to deal with any elementary function, that is, to say that '$\phi!$' means $\phi!\hat{x}$ means that '$\phi!$' is related in a certain way to the objects a, b, etc., involved in $\phi!\hat{x}$.

But suppose now we take a non-elementary functional symbol, for example,

$$\phi_1 x \colon = \colon (y) \, . \, yRx \quad \text{Df.}$$

Here the objects involved in $\phi_1\hat{x}$ include all individuals as values of y. And it is clear that 'ϕ_1' is not related to them in at all the same way as '$\phi!$' is to the objects in its meaning. For '$\phi!$' is related to a, b, etc. by being short for an expression containing names of a, b, etc. But 'ϕ_1' is short for an expression not containing 'a', 'b', . . . , but containing only an apparent variable, of which these can be values. Clearly 'ϕ_1' means what it means in quite a different and more complicated way from that in which '$\phi!$' means. Of course, just as elementary is not really a characteristic of the proposition, it is not really a characteristic of the function; that is to say, $\phi_1\hat{x}$ and $\phi!\hat{x}$ may be the same function, because $\phi_1 x$ is always the same proposition as $\phi!x$. Then 'ϕ_1', '$\phi!$' will have the same meaning, but will mean it, as we saw above, in quite different senses of meaning. Similarly 'ϕ_2' which involves a functional apparent variable will mean in a different and more complicated way still.[5]

Hence in the contradiction which we were discussing, if 'R', the symbol of the relation of meaning between 'ϕ' and $\phi\hat{x}$, is to have any definite meaning, 'ϕ' can only be a symbol of a certain type meaning in a certain way; suppose we limit 'ϕ' to be an elementary function by taking R to be the relation between '$\phi!$' and $\phi!\hat{x}$.

[5] Here the range of the apparent variable in 'ϕ_2' is the set of predicative functions, not as in *Principia Mathematica* the set of elementary functions.

Then 'Fx' or '$(\exists\phi) : xR(\phi\hat{z}) . \sim\phi x$' is not elementary, but is a 'ϕ_2'.

Hence 'F' means not in the sense of meaning denoted by 'R' appropriate to 'ϕ!'s, but in that appropriate to a 'ϕ_2', so that we have $\sim : 'F'R(F\hat{x})$, which, as we explained above, solves the contradiction for this case.

The essential point to understand is that the reason why

$$(\exists\phi) : 'F'R(\phi\hat{x})$$

can only be true if 'F' is an elementary function, is not that the range of ϕ is that of elementary functions, but that a symbol cannot have R to a function unless it (the symbol) is elementary. The limitation comes not from '$\exists\phi$', but from 'R'. The distinctions of 'ϕ!'s, 'ϕ_1's, and 'ϕ_2's apply to the symbols and to how they mean but not to what they mean. Therefore I always (in this section) enclosed 'ϕ!', 'ϕ_1' and 'ϕ_2' in inverted commas.

But it may be objected that this is an incomplete solution; for suppose we take for R the sum of the relations appropriate to 'ϕ!'s, 'ϕ_1's, and 'ϕ_2's. Then 'F', since it still only contains $\exists\phi$,[6] is still a 'ϕ_2', and we must have in this case 'F'$R(F\hat{x})$; which destroys our solution.

But this is not so because the extra complexity involved in the new R makes 'F' not a 'ϕ_2', but a more complicated symbol still. For with this new R, for which 'ϕ_2' $R(\phi_2\hat{x})$, since '$\phi_2 x$' is of some such form as $(\exists\phi) . f(\phi\hat{z}, x)$, in $(\exists\phi) . 'F'R(\phi\hat{x})$ is involved at least a variable function $f(\phi\hat{z}, x)$ of functions of individuals, for this is involved in the notion of a variable 'ϕ_2', which is involved in the variable ϕ taken in conjunction with R. For if anything has R to the predicative function $\phi\hat{x}$, $\phi\hat{x}$ must be expressible by either a 'ϕ!' or a 'ϕ_1' or a 'ϕ_2'.

Hence $(\exists\phi) . 'F'R(\phi\hat{x})$ involves not merely the variable ϕ (predicative function of an individual) but also a hidden variable f (function of a function of an individual and of an individual). Hence 'Fx' or '$(\exists\phi) : xR(\phi\hat{x}) . \sim\phi x$' is not a '$\phi_2$', but what we may call a 'ϕ_3', i.e., a function of individuals involving a variable function of functions of individuals. (This is, of course, not the same thing as a 'ϕ_3' in the sense of *Principia Mathematica*, 2nd ed. Hence 'F' means in a more complicated way still not included in R; and we do not have 'F'$R(F\hat{x})$, so that the contradiction again disappears.

What appears clearly from the contradictions is that we cannot

---

[6] The range of ϕ in $\exists\phi$ is that of predicative functions, including all 'ϕ_1's 'ϕ_2's, etc., so it is not altered by changing R.

obtain an all-inclusive relation of meaning for propositional functions. Whatever one we take there is still a way of constructing a symbol to mean in a way not included in our relation. The meanings of meaning form an illegitimate totality.

By the process begun above we obtain a hierarchy of propositions and a hierarchy of functions of individuals. Both are based on the fundamental hierarchy of individuals, functions of individuals, functions of functions of individuals, etc. A function of individuals we will call a function of type 1; a function of functions of individuals, a function of type 2; and so on.

We now construct the hierarchy of propositions as follows:

Propositions of order 0 (elementary), containing no apparent variable.

     ,,   ,,   1, containing an individual apparent variable.

     ,,   ,,   2, containing an apparent variable whose values are functions of type 1.

     ,,   ,, n, containing an apparent variable whose values are functions of type $n-1$.

From this hierarchy we deduce another hierarchy of functions, irrespective of their types, according to the order of their values.

Thus functions of order 0 (matrices) contain no apparent variable;

     ,,   ,,   1 contain an individual apparent variable;

and so on; i.e. the values of a function of order n are propositions of order n. For this classification the types of the functions are immaterial.

We must emphasize the essential distinction between order and type. The type of a function is a real characteristic of it depending on the arguments it can take; but the order of a proposition or function is not a real characteristic, but what Peano called a pseudo-function. The order of a proposition is like the numerator of a fraction. Just as from '$x = y$' we cannot deduce that the numerator of x is equal to the numerator of y, from the fact that 'p' and 'q' are instances of the same proposition we cannot deduce that the order of 'p' is equal to that of 'q'. This was shown above for the particular case of elementary and non-elementary propositions (orders 0 and > 0), and obviously holds in general. Order is only a characteristic of a particular symbol which is an instance of the proposition or function.

We shall now show briefly how this theory solves the remaining contradictions of group B.[7]

(*a*) 'I am lying'.

This we should analyse as '$(\exists\,"p",p)$: I am saying "p" . "p" means p. $\sim p$. Here to get a definite meaning for *means*[8] it is necessary to limit in some way the order of 'p'. Suppose 'p' is to be of the nth or lesser order. Then, symbolizing by ϕ_n a function of *type n*, 'p' may be $(\exists\,\phi_n)\cdot\phi_{n+1}(\phi_n)$.

Hence $\exists$ 'p' involves $\exists\,\phi_{n+1}$, and 'I am lying' in the sense of 'I am asserting a false proposition of order n' is at least of order $n+1$ and does not contradict itself.

(*b*) (1) The least integer not nameable in fewer than nineteen syllables.

(2) The least indefinable ordinal.

(3) Richard's Paradox.

All these result from the obvious ambiguity of 'naming' and defining'. The name or definition is in each case a functional symbol which is only a name or definition by meaning something. The sense in which it means must be made precise by fixing its order; the name or definition involving all such names or definitions will be of a higher order, and this removes the contradiction. My solutions of these contradictions are obviously very similar to those of Whitehead and Russell, the difference between them lying merely in our different conceptions of the order of propositions and functions. For me propositions in themselves have no orders; they are just different truth-functions of atomic propositions—a definite totality, depending only on what atomic propositions there are. Orders and illegitimate totalities only come in with the symbols we use to symbolize the facts in variously complicated ways.

[7] It may be as well to repeat that for the contradictions of group A my theory preserves the solutions given in *Principia Mathematica*.

[8] When I say " 'p' means p", I do not suppose there to be a single object p meant by 'p'. The meaning of 'p' is that one of a certain set of possibilities is realized, and this meaning results from the meaning-relations of the separate signs in 'p' to the real objects which it is about. It is these meaning-relations which vary with the order of 'p'. And the order of 'p' is limited not because p in $(\exists p)$ is limited, but by 'means' which varies in meaning with the order of 'p'.

To sum up: in this chapter I have defined a range of predicative functions which escapes contradiction and enables us to dispense with the Axiom of Reducibility. And I have given a solution of the contradictions of group B which rests on and explains the fact that they all contain some epistemic element.

22

Peano, Russell, and Logicism

Herbert Hochberg

THE title is admittedly pretentious for a brief and perhaps unexciting point. Both are prompted by the fact that many philosophers and mathematicians are still concerned to argue about the achievement, or lack of such, of the Russellian programme for the "reduction" of mathematics to logic. Most such arguments, I believe, are based on a misconception about what Russell, and even Peano, accomplished. Cryptically put, the confusion begins with the statement that Russell and Whitehead, after suitable definitions of Peano's primitive terms, deduced the Peano axioms.

Let 'P' represent the Peano system (with five axioms and three undefined terms, 'zero', 'number', and 'successor'); '*PM*' stand for *Principia*; 'C' refer to a set of theorems of *PM*. Russell, after introducing three defined terms, deduced C in *PM*. But, though C may well be a particular interpretation of P, it cannot be identified with P. Russell's defined terms ('Zero', 'Successor', and 'Number') are specific interpretations of the Peano primitives; they do not supply definitions for Peano's primitive terms. In short, Russell did not deduce the Peano axioms in *PM*. Hence, one should not expect that since C can be obtained in *PM* all other interpretations of P can be obtained in *PM*. This point can be missed due to Russell's use of the same signs for both

Reprinted with the kind permission of the author, the editor, and the publisher from *Analysis*, 16 (1956): 118–120.

his defined terms and Peano's primitive terms.[1] But they are radically different, just as 'point' taken as a primitive in an axiomatic system differs from its possible interpretations in terms of 'person' or 'physical point'—to recall some elementary examples. The overlooking of this simple consideration can lead to controversy over the extent of Russell's success, with particular reference to the various domains of modern algebra, *e.g.*, it is argued that one cannot "get" groups, vector spaces, etc., Russellwise.

Upon suitable interpretations (in terms of the integers, zero, and plus, for example) of the elements and operations, specific interpretations of the group axioms can be derived in *PM*. Or, to put it another way, there are arithmetical images (or models) of the group axioms. This does not mean, nor should it, that all such interpretations can be so derived nor does it mean that the group axioms can be so derived. But this is true, as we saw, for the Peano axioms as well as for the group axioms. Further, this is no "*limitation*" of *PM* in any reasonable sense of that term. It reflects a generality for all such types of "reduction." Given two axiomatic systems, I and II, where II contains primitives not in I, upon the introduction of certain (defined) terms into I it may appear that the axioms of II can be deduced as theorems of I. Actually the propositions deduced in I constitute an interpretation of II and not the system itself. The same point may be made about the achievement of Peano in the construction of the systems of integers, rationals, real numbers, etc. If we consider all such systems as separate axiomatic systems—N_1, N_2, N_3, etc.—then from P one deduces not N_1 but an interpretation of N_1, and so on "up." Again, one should not be surprised if one does not get all such interpretations.

Consequently, to say that one cannot get the axioms for groups or vector spaces from *PM* is, at best, to say something true and trivial. For, to put the logistic thesis in the light of these remarks, one should never expect to get such axiomatic systems Russellwise. To put it even stronger—it makes no sense to say that we can so get them.

The situation may be clarified by a comparison. Consider a Euclidean plane geometry (E) as an axiomatic system and the system (E') that results from an interpretation of E in terms of the real number system. The axioms and theorems of E' (with a Russellian treatment of the interpreting terms) are logical truths. But we would not want to say that the axioms of E are tautologies; consequently, we would not

[1] B. Russell, *Introduction to Mathematical Philosophy* (New York: Humanities, 1919), pp. 9-28.

say that E has been "reduced" either to logic or the real number system. The critical question is whether or not this latter situation is like the one between P and PM. In the respects relevant to this discussion I think it is. The similarity is bypassed by identifying the undefined terms 'zero', etc., of P with the defined terms 'Zero', etc., of PM. But, as stated above, there is no such identity; one set of terms simply provides an interpretation of the other set just as in the case of E and E'. The fact that on a particular interpretation we get propositions that are logical truths in no way implies that the original propositions are logical truths. The point may be reinforced by considering that just as we can have the interpretations of E that do not turn the axioms into tautologies, we can have, without too much stretch of the imagination, similar interpretations of P. Just as we have many instances of arithmetical interpretations of axiomatic systems which would never tempt us to state that such axiomatic systems have been reduced to arithmetic, we should not be tempted to state, in view of interpretations of some axiomatic systems in terms of logistic systems, that such axiomatic systems have been *reduced* to logic. The Russell-Whitehead accomplishment provides a specific interpretation of an axiomatic system in which the interpreted propositions are tautologies.

By itself this achievement does not provide an explication of the idea that arithmetical truths are tautologies. Consequently, one may ask whether or not this particular interpretation can serve as the basis for an adequate explication of arithmetical notions. That is, can a formally constructed logistic system be employed as a tool for the analysis of our ordinary arithmetical concepts? The question thus boils down to the attempt to explicate terms of our ordinary language via constructions in certain types of formal languages. Hence, however, we answer the question of the adequacy of Russell's achievement, the attempt to do so must consist of an analysis, in our ordinary language, of certain terms in formal languages and their supposed counterparts in ordinary language. The critical problems about the logistic thesis are thus neither mathematical nor formal.

23

Russell's Theory
of Types

W. V. Quine

34. The Constructive Part

We have encompassed a substantial bit of set theory, in the foregoing chapters, without settling on any considerable existence assumptions. There were 7.10 and 13.1, which gave us finite classes. Beyond
these, we have made do with *ad hoc* existence premises expressed within the theorems that used them.

In the remaining chapters I shall describe and constrast various of
the substantial systems of existence assumptions that have figured
prominently in the literature of set theory. I shall temper the historical
approach with the logical, stressing the connections of structure between the systems, and the efficacy of departures.

The divergences among the systems are profound. Some of the
systems to be studied will be incompatible even with our 7.10 and 13.1,
despite the fact that these leave the whole ontology of infinite classes
unprejudiced. In the end I shall argue for modifying such systems so
as to reconcile them with 7.10 and 13.1 while preserving their good
points.

Reprinted with the kind permission of the publishers from Willard Van
Orman Quine, *Set Theory and Its Logic* (Cambridge: The Belnap Press
of Harvard University Press), pp. 241–258. Copyright 1963, 1969 by the
President and Fellows of Harvard College.

In this chapter I shall describe one pioneer system, Russell's *theory of types* of 1908. It is a system that evolved from Russell's tentative suggestions of 1903 with the help of an idea of Poincaré's.[1]

Poincaré tried to account for Russell's paradox as the effect rather of a subtle fallacy than of a collapse of irreducible principles. He attributed it to what he called a vicious circle. The defining characteristic of the paradoxical class y is '$(x)(x \epsilon y . \equiv . x \notin x)$', and the paradox comes, as we know, of letting the quantified variable 'x' here take y itself as a value. It is, he suggested, illegitimate to include a class y, or any classes whose specification might presuppose y, in the range of a quantification that is used in specifying y itself. He called the suspect procedure *impredicative*.[2] We must not presuppose y in defining y.

Definition, in the clearest sense, is what occurs when a new notation is introduced as short for an old one. No question of legitimacy can arise in connection with definition, so long as a mechanical procedure is provided for expanding the new notation in all cases uniquely into old notation. Now what Poincaré criticized is not the definition of some special symbol as short for '$\{x : x \notin x\}$', but rather the very assumption of the existence of such a class; the assumption of the existence of a class y fulfilling '$(x)(x \epsilon y . \equiv . x \notin x)$'. We shall do better to speak not of impredicative definition but of impredicative specification of classes, and, what is the crux of the matter, impredicative assumptions of class existence.

And what now of the vicious circle? A circular argument seduces its victim into granting a thesis, unawares, as a premise to its own demonstration. A circular definition smuggles the definiendum into the definiens, in such wise as to prevent expansion into primitive notation. But impredicative specification of classes is neither of these things. It is hardly a procedure to look askance at, except as one is pressed by the paradoxes to look askance at something or other.

---

[1] Russell, 1903, Appendix B; Poincaré, 1906, p. 307. There was a suggestion of Poincaré's idea already in Richard, 1905, as Poincaré points out.

[2] The word fared oddly. In 1906 Russell spoke of a membership condition as predicative, for one or another set theory, simply to mean that for that set theory there was a class corresponding to that membership condition. Poincaré followed this use of Russell's; it just happened that the membership conditions that he wanted to declare predicative in this sense were the ones not involving the quasi-circularity that he objected to. Straightway the term acquired the latter sense, and became independent of the former. Next Russell gave the term a more technical but kindred sense, as we shall see midway in this section. In all these senses the term must be firmly dissociated from 'predicate', which I continue to use in the sense explained early in §1.

For we are not to view classes literally as created through being specified—hence as dated one by one, and as increasing in number with the passage of time. Poincaré proposed no temporal implementation of class theory. The doctrine of classes is rather that they are there from the start. This being so, there is no evident fallacy in impredicative specification. It is reasonable to single out a desired class by citing any trait of it, even though we chance thereby to quantify over it along with everything else in the universe. Impredicative specification is not visibly more vicious than singling out an individual as the most typical Yale man on the basis of averages of Yale scores including his own.

So the ban urged by Russell and by Poincaré is not to be hailed as the exposure of some hidden but (once exposed) palpable fallacy that underlay the paradoxes. Rather it is one of various proposals for so restricting the law of comprehension:

$$(\exists y)(x)(x \,\epsilon\, y \,.\, \equiv Fx)$$

as to thin the universe of classes down to the point of consistency.

Still the proposal is less arbitrary than some alternatives, in that it realizes a constructional metaphor: it limits classes to what *could* be generated over an infinite period from unspecified beginnings by using, for each class, a membership condition mentioning only preexistent classes. Metaphor aside, the distinctive feature of such a set theory is that its universe admits of a (transfinite) ordering such that every class that is specified by a membership condition at all is specified by one in which the values of all variables are limited to things earlier in the ordering.

Moving now to the details of Russell's 1908 system,[3] we put the very notion of class aside for a while; for Russell's theory starts out in other terms.

For Russell the universe consisted of individuals in some sense, and attributes and relations of them, and attributes and relations of such attributes and relations, and so on up. His own term for the attributes and relations was '*propositional functions*'. He used 'ϕ', 'ψ', ... as variables for them. To say that x has the attribute ϕ, that x bears the relation ψ to y, and so on, he used the notation 'ϕx', '$\psi(x, y)$', etc. For *abstraction* of propositional functions from sentences he simply put

---

[3] I mention the 1908 paper for its priority. But the more usual and convenient place to look for the material is in the early portions of *Principia Mathematica*.

circumflexed variables in the argument positions. Thus the attribute of loving y and that of being loved by x would be rendered respectively by '$\hat{x}$ loves y' and 'x loves $\hat{y}$', the analogues of the class abstracts '$\{x : x$ loves $y\}$' and '$\{y : x$ loves $y\}$'. The relations of loving and its converse, corresponding to $\{\langle x, y \rangle : x$ loves $y\}$ and $\{\langle y, x \rangle : x$ loves $y\}$, come out as '$\hat{x}$ loves $\hat{y}$' and '$\hat{y}$ loves $\hat{x}$', direction being determined thus by alphabetical order.[4]

When such abstracts occur in broader contexts, there is sometimes no telling whether to construe a circumflexed variable as making its abstraction from a short clause or from a longer containing clause, especially when several abstracts occur in the passage. Russell was spared this difficulty in practice, mainly because of a modified and superior notation for classes and relations—similar in essential respects to what we have been using in earlier chapters—which he introduced by contextual definition and adhered to in all elaborate work. But in expounding his basic theory let me try to make do with his basic notation, skirting its pitfalls.

He classified his individuals and propositional functions into so-called *orders* in the following way. Individuals were of order o. Certain unspecified propositional functions of individuals were of order 1; not all. For the rest, the order of a propositional function was determined by considering the abstractive expression that names it. That order was taken as the least integer exceeding the order of all bound variables therein—all circumflexed variables, that is, and all quantified ones as well. By the order of a variable was meant the order of the values it takes; and it was essential to Russell's plan that each variable be restricted, implicitly if not by a visible index, to values of a single order. Thus it was that Russell kept the propositional function from figuring as a value of the bound variables used in specifying it; the propositional function was always of too high an order to be a value of such variables.

In the above account there is a characteristic give and take between sign and object: the propositional function gets its order from the abstractive expression, and the order of a variable is the order of the values. Exposition is eased by allowing the word 'order' a double sense, attributing orders at once to the notations and, in parallel, to their objects. Ideally the order of each variable may, to begin with, be thought of as shown by a numerical superscript; the order of each abstractive expression is then computed as above; and it carries over to the propositional function thereby named. Russell's own exposition simply blurred the distinction between the abstractive expression (or even the open sentence) and the propositional function (or attribute or relation); but that is a feature which I shall not copy, and shall have occasion to deplore.

Extensionality being what separates classes from attributes, Russell's business here is clearly with attributes rather than classes. For two attributes can be of different orders and hence surely distinct, and yet the things that have them can be the same. For example, the attribute $(\phi)(\phi\hat{x} \equiv \phi y)$, with '$\phi$' of order 1, is an attribute of y and y only, and again the attribute $(\chi)(\chi\hat{x} \equiv \chi y)$, with '$\chi$' of order 2, is an attribute of y and y only; yet their orders are respectively 2 and 3.

Relations, in the sense in which Russell's propositional functions may be spoken of as attributes and relations, are so-called *relations-in-intension*; that is, they are like attributes, and unlike mere classes of ordered pairs, ordered triples, etc., in being capable of distinctness from one another even though relating exclusively the same things. They can be pictured as attributes of ordered pairs, triples, etc. (But Russell did not give them this further analysis.)

Besides propositional functions of one variable, or attributes, and propositional functions of many variables, or relations, Russell recognized also propositional functions of no variables, or propositions; his theory of orders applied to propositions as well as to propositional functions of one or more variables. But I see no value in tracing this strand of the history.

Many attributes were, for Russell, of higher order by two or more than the things having the attributes. An example was seen in $(\phi)(\phi\hat{x} \equiv \phi y)$. Another example is $(\exists \phi)(\psi\phi \cdot \phi\hat{x})$, the attribute of having an attribute that has the attribute ψ. Some attributes, on the other hand, were of just next higher order than the things having them. An example could be $(x)(\hat{\phi}x \equiv \psi x)$, the attribute of coextensiveness with ψ. Such attributes Russell called *predicative*. The connection envisaged between this technical use of the word and the use lately attributed to Poincaré is that a class abstract ('$\{x : Fx\}$') specifies its class predicatively rather than impredicatively, in Poincaré's sense, when and only when the corresponding attribute abstract ('$F\hat{x}$') names a predicative attribute. Thus Russell, in admitting attributes that are not predicative in his sense, was not yet evidently flouting

Poincaré's precept so long as none but the predicative ones were made to determine classes.

Russell of course extended the term 'predicative' to propositional functions other than attributes. He called a dyadic relation predicative if its order was just next higher than that of the things bearing the relation, or than that of the things to which the relation was borne— whichever was the higher. Correspondingly for triadic relations and beyond.

Russell's criterion of the order of a propositional function obviously presupposes that each variable be recognizably restricted to a single order. Actually he went further: each variable for attributes was meant to range only over attributes that are themselves of some one fixed order and whose *arguments*—the things having the attributes— are of some one fixed order too. Similarly each variable for relations was meant to range only over relations that are of a single order, and that admit arguments of only some one fixed order in first argument place, and arguments of just some one fixed order in second argument place, and so on. A full formal presentation of the theory would call perhaps for numerical superscripts on the propositional-function variables to indicate the order of the propositional functions concerned, and numerical subscripts to indicate the order of admissible arguments to those propositional functions; and in the case of relations the subscripts would have to be compound, to indicate the respective orders of admissible first arguments, second arguments, and so on to the appropriate number.

Russell required that the order of a propositional function exceed that of each of its arguments. When a propositional function is given outright by the abstraction notation, this restriction is already present in what was said before, viz., that the order is to exceed that of the circumflexed variables. But it is needed still as an added restriction when the propositional function merely figures as value of a variable. In such cases the restriction amounts, in terms of indices (superscripts and subscripts), to requiring that a variable's superscript exceed its subscripts. Not that Russell was so explicit.

The forms of notation 'ϕx', '$\phi(x, y)$', etc., expressing attribution were to be accepted as meaningful only if the order or orders of the argument or arguments were those appropriate to the propositional function attributed. In terms of indices this means that the superscript of the argument, or the superscripts of the several arguments, must match the subscript of the propositional function, or the respective subscripts thereof.

But in practice Russell suppressed the indices altogether by a convention of so-called *systematic ambiguity*. The convention was, in effect, that indices are to be imagined supplied in any way conformable to the foregoing grammatical restriction.

Occasions arose when Russell did want to include in his formula some information about the orders of variables, beyond the minimal requirement of grammatical conformity. Though not caring about absolute order, he wanted sometimes to indicate that the order of one or another propositional function was to be just next above that of its arguments. Rather than restore full indices for this purpose, he introduced an exclamation point after some of the occurrences of the propositional-function variable concerned, to indicate that the variable was to range over predicative propositional functions of some order or other. The notation is illustrated early in the next section.

In general it is convenient in presenting formal systems of set theory to be able to assume the standard logic of truth functions and quantifiers as a fixed substructure requiring only the addition of axioms appropriate to the special set theory in question. We cannot adhere quite fully to this line in the present instance, because of an implicit multiplicity of sorts of variables. The implicit distinctive indices are already a departure from the standard logic of quantification with its single sort of variables. However, this departure can mainly be localized in laws like '$(x)Fx \supset Fy$' and '$Fy \supset (\exists x)Fx$' which provide for change of variables. These we have to restrict to the extent of requiring that the variable in the role of 'y' be of the same sort as that in the role of 'x'; that is, that it bear the same indices.[5]

Indices, when supplied, fix the orders of such propositional functions as are referred to by the variables themselves. Indirectly they fix also the orders of propositional functions named by expressions of abstraction; for we have said that the order is next higher than that of the highest bound variable. But this account covers only the abstractive expressions in which all variables are bound, by quantifiers or circumflex accents. To be able to say in general what expressions can

---

[5] Many-sorted logic is examined further in §37, below. —Under the head of deviations from standard logic, mention might be made also of *9 of *Principia* for its general oddity of approach to quantification theory. But *9 figures only as an option to the more classical treatment in *10; moreover it hinges on orders of propositions, which I said I would not pursue.

legitimately be substituted under the law '$(x)Fx \supset Fy$' for variables bearing given indices, we have to assign an order also to abstractive expressions with free variables. It is easily seen that the further stipulation needed in this case is that the order of the abstractive expression must be reckoned as not less than that of the free variables (while still exceeding that of the bound ones); this suffices to prevent us from defeating the other restrictions by subsequent substitutions on the free variables in question. Russell was silent on this detail, but his usage conformed.

Over and above the variables (with their indices or exclamation points) and the logical notations of quantification and truth functions, the special notations of Russell's theory are the notations of attribution ('ϕx', '$\phi(x, y)$', etc.) and the use of circumflex accents for the abstraction of propositional functions. Over and above the general logical laws of truth functions and quantifiers (restricted as above), the special principle of Russell's theory is just that of *concretion* (cf. 2.1):

(i) $$(F\hat{x})y \equiv Fy, \ (F\hat{x}\hat{y})(z,w) \equiv Fzw, \text{ etc.}$$

Again it must in justice to Russell be said that he was incommunicative over these matters.

Let us see how Russell's paradox is avoided in his theory. Where ψ is the propositional function $\sim\hat{\phi}\phi$ (the attribute of not being an attribute of self) we have, by concretion, that $(\chi)(\psi\chi \equiv \sim\chi\chi)$ and hence in particular that $\psi\psi \equiv \sim\psi\psi$. But Russell's restrictions obstruct this reasoning twice over. The combination '$\phi\phi$' is ruled out as ungrammatical to begin with, since the order of a propositional function is required to exceed that of its argument. And even if it were not thus ruled out, definition of ψ as $\sim\hat{\phi}\phi$ would give ψ a higher order than its bound variable 'ϕ' and hence disallow our taking χ as ψ in the step that led to '$\psi\psi \equiv \sim\psi\psi$'.

35. Classes and the Axiom of Reducibility

We are glad to have found the theory too weak for the paradoxes. However, it proves too weak also for some reasoning in classical mathematics that we are scarcely prepared to relinquish. An example is the proof that every bounded class of real numbers has a least bound.

Let us suppose the real numbers developed in Russell's theory in a fashion parallel to the development in Chapter VI, but with attributes in place of classes, and the attribution of attributes in place of class membership. According to §18 and §19 the least bound of a bounded class z of real numbers was the class $\cup z$, or $\{x : (\exists y)(x \, \epsilon \, y \, \epsilon \, z)\}$. So, in parallel, we may expect the least bound of a bounded attribute ϕ of real numbers in Russell's system to be the attribute $(\exists \psi)(\phi \psi \cdot \psi \hat{x})$. Now the difficulty is that under Russell's doctrine of orders the least bound $(\exists \psi)(\phi \psi \cdot \psi \hat{x})$ is of higher order than the real numbers ψ falling under the attribute ϕ whose least bound is sought.

Least bounds are needed for all the classical techniques of mathematical analysis that continuity underlies. But least bounds are no good for these ends unless they are accessible as further values of the same variables that have already been ranging over the numbers whose limits are sought. A least bound of higher order does not qualify as value of such variables, and so fails of its purpose.

Russell dealt with this difficulty by propounding his *axiom of reducibility: Every propositional function ϕ is coextensive with a predicative one.* That is,

$$(\exists \psi)(x)(\psi! \, x \equiv \phi x), \quad (\exists \psi)(x)(y)(\psi! \, (x, y) \equiv \phi(x, y)),$$

and so on. It may or may not happen, given a propositional function, that there is an abstractive expression designating a co-extensive propositional function (one true of the same things) and meeting the demands of predicativity—viz., exhibiting no bound variables of higher order than all circumflexed ones. But even failing any such actual expression, there still exists, all unexpressed, such a predicative propositional function; that is the import of the axiom of reducibility.

Applied to $(\exists \psi)(\phi \psi \cdot \psi \hat{x})$, the axiom assures us that we may without loss construe 'ϕ' and 'ψ' here as ranging over predicative attributes. In other words, we may construe 'ϕ' and 'ψ' as ranging over attributes respectively of order $n+2$ and $n+1$, where n is the order represented by the 'x'. For each bounded attribute ϕ of order $n+2$, of real numbers ψ of order $n+1$, we are thus assured a least bound $(\exists \psi)(\phi! \, \psi \cdot \psi! \, \hat{x})$. Moreover, by the axiom of reducibility again, there is a predicative χ coextensive with this $(\exists \psi)(\phi! \, \psi \cdot \psi! \, \hat{x})$. Being predicative, χ will be of order just higher than that represented by its circumflexed argument place—hence $n+1$ again. So we now have the required law: any bounded attribute of real numbers of given order $n+1$ has a least bound which is of that same order $n+1$.

But the price is paid of abandoning the constructional metaphor noted early in §34, and acquiescing rather in the paradigm of the most typical Yale man. For the axiom of reducibility regales us after all with attributes unspecifiable except by quantifying over attributes whose order is as high as their own. Whatever sense of security from paradox we may have drawn from the constructional metaphor is now, therefore, forfeited. Still the old proofs of paradox continue, it seems, to be effectively obstructed. In particular the obstruction to Russell's paradox remains just as it was.

The foundational portion of Whitehead and Russell's *Principia Mathematica*, taking up barely the first two hundred pages, contrasts markedly with the main body of that work. Propositional functions are in evidence only in the foundational part; thereafter the work proceeds in terms rather of classes and relations-in-extension. Talk of classes and relations-in-extension is founded on talk of propositional functions, by means of contextual definitions, somewhat as follows. As a preliminary step, the notation of membership is explained as merely an alternative notation for the attribution of a predicative attribute:

(i)   '$x \epsilon \phi$' for '$\phi!x$'.

Thus far, no classes. But then class abstraction is defined in context thus:[6]

(ii)   '$G\{x{:}Fx\}$' for '$(\exists \phi)((x)(\phi!x \equiv Fx) . G\phi)$'

and quantification over classes is defined thus:[7]

(iii) '$(a)Ga$' for '$(\phi)G\{x{:}\phi!x\}$',   '$(\exists a)Ga$' for '$(\exists \phi)G\{x{:}\phi!x\}$'.

The effect is this: classes are the same as predicative attributes except that when we talk of them as classes we waive distinctions between coextensive ones. The waiving of such distinctions is accomplished in (ii). For to say that anything ('G') is true of a class $\{x{:}Fx\}$ is, according to (ii), to say that it is true of *some* predicative attribute ϕ—no matter which—such that $(x)(\phi!x \equiv Fx)$. In this way Russell provides for proof of the law of existensionality:

(iv) $(x)(x \epsilon a . \equiv . x \epsilon \beta) . a \epsilon \kappa . \supset . \beta \epsilon \kappa$

[6] A construction having substantially the effect of (i) and (ii) is to be found already in Frege, 1893, pp. 52 ff.

[7] This 'a' of Russell's is a quantifiable class variable, and so not to be confused with the schematic use of 'a' to which we have become accustomed in Chapters I–X. Readers of my *Mathematical Logic* have been used to yet a third use of 'a': as a syntactic variable for variables. Russell's use will be limited to the present paragraph.

for classes without having had to assume the corresponding law for
attributes, or even for predicative attributes. As remarked, it is only
on the score of this law that there is point in distinguishing classes
from attributes.

Talk of dyadic relations-in-extension is provided for by definitions
parallel to (i)–(iii). The special variables for such relations are 'Q', 'R',
etc., and the notation for saying that x bears R to y is 'xRy'. So the
definitions are these:

(v)   '$x\phi y$' for '$\phi!(x, y)$',

(vi) '$G\{xy : Fxy\}$' for '$(\exists\phi)((x)(y)(\phi!(x, y) \equiv Fxy) . G\phi)$',

(vii) '$(R)GR$' for '$(\phi)G\{xy : \phi!(x, y)\}$',
                '$(\exists R)GR$' for '$(\exists\phi)G\{xy : \phi!(x, y)\}$'.

As they stand, (ii) and (vi) are unsatisfactorily ambiguous on the
score of how much text to reckon to 'G' in any particular application
of these definitions. Russell added a convention covering this point.

The doctrine of orders becomes much simplified insofar as we confine our attention to individuals, predicative attributes of individuals,
predicative attributes of such attributes, and so on; for the orders of
these things are respectively 0, 1, 2, ... The corresponding thing happens for classes, since classes are just predicative attributes minus the
distinctions between coextensive ones. In this connection Russell favors the word 'type' instead of 'order'; thus individuals are of *type* 0,
and classes whose members are of type n are classes of type $n + 1$.

Dyadic relations-in-extension come through with two-dimensional
types: the type of a relation is fixed only when we specify the type
of the things bearing the relation and the type of the things to which
the relation is borne. The bidimensionality of these types gives rise to
a staggering proliferation. The type of a relation of things of type m
to things of type n may be called (m, n); the type of a class of such
relations may be called $((m, n))$; and the type of a relation of such
classes to such classes is then $(((m, n)), ((m, n)))$.[8] Orders, of course,
were far worse. Russell spared himself such indices by his device
of systematic ambiguity, or, as he comes to call it, *typical* ambiguity;
but it is a device that we must view as roughly expository only, while
thinking of the real system as relating the full luxuriance of complex
indices. For when the indices are complex, as required for relations, the
plan of leaving them tacit proves too flexible. Whitehead and Russell

8 So Carnap, *Logical Syntax*, p. 85.

found that to avoid Burali-Forti's paradox they had to restore type indices at points in the argument.[9]

We saw that Russell's constructivistic approach foundered in the real numbers, and that by then resorting to his axiom of reducibility he gave up constructivism. Now we must note further, while not questioning the wisdom of giving up the constructivism, that this was a perverse way of giving it up. For the axiom of reducibility implies the superfluousness of the very distinctions that give it substance. The argument is as follows.

If Russell's system with its axiom of reducibility is free of contradiction, then we may be sure that no contradiction would ensue if we were simply to repudiate all but predicative orders. We can declare the order of every attribute to be the next above that of the things having the attribute; and correspondingly for relations-in-intension. Given any reference to an attribute of order $n + k$ that is an attribute of objects of order n, we have merely to take that notation as referring rather to a coextensive attribute of order $n + 1$ by a systematic reinterpretation of Russell's notation; and correspondingly for relations-in-intension. For Russell's axiom of reducibility tells us that a coextensive attribute or relation-in-intension of the desired order, a predicative one, exists every time. If the axiom is foreseen, the better course is to obviate all need of it by talking of simple *types* of attributes and relations-in-intension from the start rather than of orders in any distinctive sense; there is an excuse for orders only if a weak constructive theory is to be adhered to and the axiom of reducibility withheld.[10]

One senses from a reading of Russell how he was able to overlook this point: the trouble was his failure to focus upon the distinction between "propositional functions" as attributes, or relations-in-intension, and "proposition functions" as expressions, viz., predicates or open sentences. As expressions they differed visibly in order, if order is to be judged by indices on bound variables within the expression. Failing to distinguish sharply between formula and object, he did not think of the maneuver of letting a higher-order expression refer outright to a lower-order attribute or relation-in-intension.

Russell had also an independent motive for retaining the extra orders. He thought these distinctions were helpful against a class of para-

[9] *PM*, vol. 3, p. 75.

[10] This argument was advanced at greater length in pp. 5–8 of my dissertation (Harvard, 1932) and in "On the Axiom of Reducibility." And there is something of it in Hilbert and Ackermann, 1928 edition, pp. 114 ff.

doxes not considered in foregoing pages: the paradoxes known nowadays as *semantic*. One of these, due to Grelling,[11] arises from the reflection that a predicate may be true of itself (like 'short', which is a short word, or 'English', which is English, or 'word', or 'predicate', or 'pentasyllabic'), or it may not (like 'long', 'German', 'verb', 'monosyllabic', and indeed most predicates). We get the paradox by asking whether 'not true of self' is true of itself. Another such paradox has come down from antiquity as the Epimenides paradox or the paradox of the liar. Its traditional forms can be variously quibbled over; the essential logic of it can perhaps be put most forcefully thus:

'yields a falsehood when appended to its own quotation'
yields a falsehood when appended to its own quotation.

This tells us how to form a certain sentence, and tells us further that it is false; but the sentence which it tells us how to form is itself; so it is true if and only if false. A third semantical paradox, attributed to G. G. Berry, turns on the reflection that there are only finitely many English syllables; hence only finitely many natural numbers each of which is specifiable in fewer than 24 syllables; and hence a least natural number not specifiable in fewer than 24 syllables. But I have just specified it in 23 syllables. The literature also contains further semantic paradoxes.[12]

The notion that Russell's orders were relevant to such paradoxes is not one that I know how to make plausible while maintaining a distinction between attributes and open sentences, which he confused under the head of propositional functions. It seems clear in any event that by rights the semantic paradoxes should be blamed on special concepts foreign to the theory of classes or propositional functions: on denotation (or "truth of") in the case of Grelling's paradox, on falsehood (and hence truth) in the case of the Epimenides, and on specifiability in the case of Berry's. These three culpable notions are important ones, and the semantic paradoxes create a crisis with respect to them analogous to the crisis that Russell's paradox creates with respect to the notion of class membership. The notions of denotation, truth, and specifiability must be subjected to some sort of intuitively unanticipated restriction, in the light of these paradoxes, just as class existence must in the light of Russell's paradox and others. But the semantic paradoxes are of no concern to the theory of classes. This

---

11 In Grelling and Nelson. The paradox has been wrongly attributed to Weyl.
12 See Whitehead and Russell, vol. 1, pp. 60–65.

point was made in a way by Peano even before Russell's theory appeared, and it was urged by Ramsey in his critique of Russell's theory.[13]

Russell's theory, with its discrimination of orders for propositional functions whose arguments are of a single order, came to be known as the "ramified theory of types"; and Ramsey's position was that it should be reduced to the so-called "simple" (or, in Sheffer's quip, "ramsified") theory of types. He did not, indeed, make his case as strong as he might. Sharing Russell's failure to distinguish clearly between attribute and expression, he in turn evidently missed the really decisive point: that the axiom of reducibility guarantees outright the dispensability of the ramified theory.

It must be remembered moreover that the simple theory of types, whether urged on this latter ground or in Ramsey's less decisive way, had already been the explicit working theory of Whitehead and Russell's *Principia Mathematica* anyway. Once Russell's contextual definitions of classes and relations-in-extension were at hand, the ramified substructure dropped from sight; all thought thenceforward was of types, in the simple sense, of classes and relations-in-extension.[14] Thus what Ramsey was urging, and I a few pages back, was in effect just the disavowal of an ill-conceived foundation.

One may as well dispense not merely with the initial ramification of orders of attributes and relations-in-intension, but with the attributes and relations-in-intension themselves. One may as well simply take Russell's classes and relations-in-extension as starting point, subject to the so-called simple theory of types to which they are already subject in *Principia*. As long as the ramification of orders is retained, so that two coextensive attributes may differ in order, there is evident need to distinguish coextensive attributes and hence to call them attributes instead of classes; but this reason for starting with attributes instead of classes lapses when we drop the ramification.

Russell had also a philosophical preference for attributes, and felt that in contextually defining classes on the basis of a theory of attributes he was explaining the obscurer in terms of the clearer. But this feeling was due to his failure to distinguish between propositional functions as predicates, or expressions, and propositional functions as attributes. Failing this, he could easily think that the notion of an at-

---

[13] Peano, 1906, p. 157; Ramsey, pp. 20–29. Ramsey cites the Peano passage.

[14] "If we assume the existence of classes, the axiom of reducibility becomes unnecessary" (Whitehead and Russell, vol. 1, p. 58).

tribute is clearer than that of a class; for that of a predicate is. But that of an attribute is less clear.[15]

In Hilbert and Ackermann (1938, 1949) and elsewhere we find a notation reminiscent still of Russell's old theory of propositional functions. For classes and relations we find '*F*', '*G*', etc., with suppressible indices, and then instead of '*x* ε *a*' and '*xRy*' we find '*F*(*x*)' and '*G*(*x, y*)', reminiscent of Russell's '*φx*' and '*ψ*(*x, y*)'. But the reminiscence is misleading. The values of '*F*', '*G*', etc. are no longer propositional functions but rather classes and relations-in-extension, by the only criterion: coextensive ones are identified.

This notation has the fault also of diverting attention from major cleavages between logic and set theory. It encourages us to see the general theory of classes and relations as a mere prolongation of quantification theory in which the hitherto schematic predicate letters are newly admitted into quantifiers and into other positions that were hitherto reserved to '*x*', '*y*', etc. (thus '(*F*)', '(∃*G*)', '*H*(*F, G*)'). The existence assumptions, vast though they are, can become strangely inconspicuous; they come to be implicit simply in the ordinary old rule of substitution for predicate letters in quantification theory, once we have promoted those letters to the status of genuine quantifiable variables. Any comprehension statement, say of the form:

$$(\exists F)(x)(Fx \equiv \ldots x \ldots),$$

simply follows by such substitution from:

$$(G)(\exists F)(x)(Fx \equiv Gx),$$

which in turn follows from '(*x*)(*Gx* ≡ *Gx*)'.[16]

Such assimilation of set theory to logic is seen also in the terminology used by Hilbert and Ackermann and their followers for the fragmentary theories in which the types leave off after finitely many. Such a theory came to be called the predicate calculus (Church: functional calculus) of *n*th order (not to be confused with order in Russell's

15 See above, Introduction. I have treated themes of this section more fully in "Whitehead and the Rise of Modern Logic"; also in *Word and Object*, pp. 118–123, 209 ff. See also Church, *Introduction to Mathematical Logic*, pp. 346–356.

16 This point, which I raised in "On Universals," p. 78, had escaped Hilbert and Ackermann; they adopted comprehension axioms too (1938, p. 125). They mentioned that they could instead have resorted to a primitive notation of abstraction (which was Russell's way), but not that they could have dispensed with both. In 1949 (pp. 133 ff.) the surviving author adopted rather a rule of so-called definition, tantamount still to a primitive notation of abstraction.

sense), where n is how high the types go. Thus the theory of individuals and classes of individuals and relations of individuals was called the second-order predicate calculus, and seen simply as quantification theory with predicate letters admitted to quantifiers. Quantification theory proper came to be called the first-order predicate calculus.

It was a regrettable trend. Along with obscuring the important cleavage between logic and "the theory of types" (meaning set theory with types), it fostered an exaggerated if foggy notion of the difference between the theory of types and "set theory" (meaning set theory without types)—as if the one did not involve outright assumption of sets the way the other does. And along with somewhat muffling the existence assumptions of the theory of types, it fostered a notion that quantification theory itself, in its 'F' and 'G', was already a theory about classes or attributes and relations. It slighted the vital contrast between schematic letters and quantifiable variables.

The notational style that I am deploring was in essential respects Russell's, of course, before it was Hilbert and Ackermann's. It was associated with failures to discriminate propositional functions as open sentences from propositional functions as attributes. Of those failures various ill consequences were noted in recent pages; and the notions last deplored are just an attenuated continuation of the series.

Speaking of slighting the contrast between schematic letters and quantifiable variables recalls the virtual theory, where I let schematic letters 'a' and 'R' simulate class and relation variables. That mimicry, however, was the contrary of a muffling of existence assumptions. It was a simulation of existence assumptions, and it was overt.

24

On Logicism

John L. Pollock

BERTRAND Russell expended a great deal of effort trying to establish the truth of logicism—the thesis that mathematics can be reduced to logic. The crowning achievement of this work was *Principia Mathematica*, co-authored by Whitehead.[1] At least as late as 1938, when Russell wrote the introduction to the second edition of *Principles of Mathematics*[2], he still believed in logicism. In that introduction, Russell wrote: "The fundamental thesis of the following pages, that mathematics and logic are identical, is one which I have never . . . seen any reason to modify." On the basis of Russell's work, together with more recent work that has built upon Russell's work, many people have been completely convinced of the correctness of logicism. The point of this paper is to show that, great though Russell's work in logic was, neither it nor the work that followed it has established that logicism is correct, because in fact logicism is incorrect.

Logicism, formulated precisely, consists of two principles:

(1) All concepts of mathematics can be defined in terms of the

I would like to express my indebtedness to Ian Mueller for his very helpful comments on an earlier version of this paper which was read at the meeting of the Western Division of the APA in Cleveland, May, 1969.

[1] A. N. Whitehead and Bertrand Russell, *Principia Mathematica* (Cambridge, 1910–1913).

[2] Russell, *Principles of Mathematics*, 2nd ed. (Cambridge, 1938).

concepts of logic, and accordingly all statements of mathematics can be translated into statements of logic;

(2) Under this translation, all truths of mathematics become truths of logic.

At one time logicism was an extremely popular theory and was regarded as being very profound, thanks largely to the efforts of Russell. Logicism seems to explain mathematical knowledge by saying that it has the same source and justification as logic. This seemed to considerably simplify the epistemological problem of explaining mathematical knowledge, for the following reasons. Prior to 1931, it was simply assumed by most people that logic was axiomatizable. In fact, it was generally supposed that logic had been axiomatized by Russell himself in *Principia Mathematica*. Consequently, logicism was interpreted as lending considerable support to the conventionalist theory of mathematical truth. However, this turned on a mistaken conception of logic. In 1931, Gödel published his famous incompleteness theorem,[3] which says in essence that neither mathematics nor logic (insofar as logic includes higher-order logic and set theory) can be completely axiomatized. The result is that logicism, even if correct, can no longer be regarded as an explanation of mathematical knowledge, because Gödel's result shows in effect that we don't understand our knowledge of principles of logic any better than we do our knowledge of mathematics. Since Gödel, the appearance of any connection between logicism and conventionalism has largely dissolved.[4] Consequently, many (perhaps most) people are now inclined to regard logicism as true, and as of some interest in itself, but as not having any interesting implications about anything else and as not helping at all to explain our a priori knowledge of mathematics.

Although it may not be as interesting as it once seemed, the question whether logicism is true remains to be answered. In this paper it will be demonstrated that logicism is false. Most attempts to refute logicism have concentrated on principle (2). I shall concentrate instead on principle (1).

If by "logic" we merely mean "first-order logic," then logicism

[3] Kurt Gödel, "Über formal unentscheidbare Sätze der Principia Mathematica und verwandter Systeme I", *Monatshefte für Mathematik und Physik*, 38 (1931).

[4] For a more complete discussion of conventionalism, and the extent to which Gödel's theorem shows it to be false, see my "Mathematical Proof," *American Philosophical Quarterly* (July, 1967).

is clearly false. This is because first-order logic is axiomatizable, and hence any mathematical theory that can be reduced to it will be axiomatizable. But by Gödel's theorem, not all mathematical theories can be axiomatized, so not all mathematical theories are reducible to first-order logic. (In point of fact, it is questionable whether any interesting ones are.) Logicism is only plausible if we include either set theory or higher-order logic as logic. Logical validity for higher-order logic is definable in set theory, so insofar as mathematics is reducible to higher-order logic, it is also reducible to set theory. Consequently, the truth of logicism reduces to the question whether mathematics is reducible to set theory.

Considerable evidence to the effect that mathematics can be reduced to set theory comes from the fact that all of the concepts of *classical* mathematics *have* been reconstructed in set theory and the proofs of the major theorems do indeed go through in set theory. This is essentially what the bulk of Russell's work goes to show. However, this does not yet establish the truth of logicism. Two points must be made here. First, to say that the classical theorems become theorems of set theory is merely to say that those truths of classical mathematics that *have been proven* can also be proven in set theory. This does not imply that *all* truths of classical mathematics are truths of set theory. The attitude one takes in connection with this further question depends in part on one's attitude towards set theory. Some mathematicians and philosophers are inclined to believe that no sense can be made of "true" in set theory unless this just means "derivable from the axioms". For these people set theory is just axiomatic set theory. This position would entail the rejection of logicism, because it is demonstrably false that all truths of classical mathematics are theorems of axiomatic set theory. This results from Gödel's incompleteness theorem; axiomatic set theory, being an axiomatic theory, cannot contain all of classical mathematics. However, the position that "true" in set theory just means "derivable" seems untenable, for the following reason. The analysis of arithmetical statements in set theory is intuitively correct. For example, "$2 + 3 = 5$" can be correctly analysed as meaning that given any two disjoint sets X and Y, if X has two elements (i.e., X can be put into a one-one correspondence with the set $\{\emptyset, \{\emptyset\}\}$) and Y has three elements, then the union of X and Y has five elements. Thus given any true arithmetical statement there is a true statement of set theory having the same meaning. But by Gödel's theorem, no axiomatic set theory can contain all of those latter set-theoretic truths as theorems. Consequently, the concept of truth for set theory must be broader than that of what is derivable from the axioms.

Nevertheless, there does seem to be something peculiar about the concept of truth for set theory. Although there are a number of set-theoretic principles that we want quite definitely to call true, there are some, like the axiom of choice, the continuum hypothesis, and the axiom of inaccessible ordinals, whose truth values we don't even know how to go about determining. Furthermore, there are different, incompatible, axiomatizations of set theory, but it is hard to see what could possibly count as showing that one of these axiomatizations is correct and all the others incorrect. The choice between these competing axiomatizations seems to be at least partly a matter of convention. But this implies that there is no objective standard of truth and falsity that can be applied to sentences of set theory to decide between different axiomatizations.

However, even if there really is no objective standard for deciding whether to accept certain principles of set theory (and I am not altogether convinced of this), this does not mean that truth does not make sense for set theory. On the contrary, many sentences of set theory are quite definitely true or false. The situation is just that there are *some* that may be neither true nor false. If this is correct, it must mean simply that we do not have a completely sharp concept of a set—that our concept of a set is open-textured in certain respects. The result is that our incomplete concept of a set suffices to determine the truth values of a great many principles of set theory, but it leaves some principles undecided. To decide these latter principles we must sharpen our concept of a set, and how we do this is largely a matter of convention. Different equally acceptable axiomatizations of set theory will agree on those matters that are objectively true or false, but will decide some of these previously undetermined matters in different ways.

The result of all this will be that it does make sense to talk about truth in set theory, and this concept of truth will be broader than the concept of derivability from any set of axioms, but it may not be the case that every sentence of set theory has a determinate truth value. Some sentences will be objectively true and others objectively false, but some may be neither. These latter sentences can only be given a truth value by further explicating our concept of a set. On this picture, the language of set theory is not bivalent—not every sentence is either true or false.

The failure of bivalence for set theory (if it really does fail) does not have any clearly detrimental effect on logicism. Although some sentences of set theory may not have a truth value, those that express truths of mathematics should still be objectively true. In fact, seeing that a sentence of set theory expresses a truth of mathematics is one way of seeing that it is true. Accordingly, it is not implausible to suppose that all truths of classical mathematics can be translated into truths of set theory. And on the ground that the translations that have been given seem intuitively correct, I would be strongly inclined to affirm this. Thus I have no argument with those people who assert that all of classical mathematics can be reduced to set theory.

If logicism makes no stronger claim than that *classical* mathematics can be reduced to set theory, then it is true. But this weak form of logicism, while mathematically interesting, is not philosophically interesting. Logicism, as a philosophical theory, is a thesis about Mathematical Truth, not about some restricted subclass of mathematical truths. The only philosophically interesting version of logicism is the strong form which refers not just to the concepts of classical mathematics, but to *all* mathematical concepts, and asserts that they are all definable in set theory. This strong form of logicism is false.

Consider a formal language for set theory. This can be taken to be an applied predicate calculus with identity in which the only non-logical symbol is "ϵ", standing for the relation of class membership. The thesis of logicism asserts that all mathematical concepts can be defined in this language. Unless this is to be trivially false, we must make a distinction between a mathematical object (e.g., a particular number, or function), and a concept of that mathematical object. To say that a mathematical object can be defined in the language of set theory means that there is some uniquely referring expression of this language (a *term* of this language) which denotes that object. Clearly not all mathematical objects can be defined in this language. This results from the simple fact that there are only denumerably many expressions in the language of set theory (i.e., as many expressions as there are natural numbers) but there are nondenumerably many mathematical objects. Thus if logicism is to be interesting it cannot be taken as asserting that all mathematical objects are definable in the language of set theory.

A much more interesting formulation of logicism is obtained as follows. There is, or at least there appears to be, an absolute concept of definability, which is to be contrasted with definability within any particular formal language. The absolute concept is just the concept of something being definable somehow, by some legitimate means, within mathematics. It is not at all clear that all mathematical objects are definable in this sense (i.e., that it is possible to have concepts for all mathematical objects). In fact, it is a rather natural conjecture that the set of definable mathematical objects is denumerable, in which case it follows immediately that not all mathematical objects are definable. Although this concept of absolute definability is distinct from the concept of definability within any particular formal language, there remains the possibility that it can be *analysed* in terms of definability within some particular formal language. This is just what logicism proposes—absolute definability can be analysed as definability within the language of set theory.[5] It will now be demonstrated that this is false.

Consider a Gödel numbering of the expressions of the language of set theory (that is, an assignment of non-negative integers to the expressions in such a way that each expression is assigned a different integer). If ϕ is an expression of the language, let $\#_\phi$ be the Gödel number of ϕ. An *open formula* is a formula of this language containing at least one occurrence of a variable not bound by a quantifier. If an open formula contains n such variables, the formula is called an *n-formula*, and can be thought of as symbolizing a complex relation (or if $n = 1$, a complex predicate). Now consider 1-formulas. An object is said to *satisfy* a 1-formula if, and only if, the predicate symbolized by the 1-formula can be truly predicated of that object. Let us define a function F which, to the Gödel number of each 1-formula, assigns the smallest ordinal number not satisfying that 1-formula if there are any that do not satisfy it, or assigns 0 if all ordinal numbers satisfy the 1-formula.[6] That is, if θ is a 1-formula, then

$$F(\#_\theta) = \begin{cases} \text{the smallest ordinal number not satisfying } \theta \text{ if there is} \\ \text{an ordinal number not satisfying } \theta; \\ \text{0 otherwise.} \end{cases}$$

Clearly the function F is a perfectly well-defined mathematical concept. In particular, its extension is not one of the "overly large" sets that lead to the set-theoretic antinomies (the domain of F is a subset of

---

[5] Analogously, prior to Gödel many people felt that absolute provability could be analysed as provability within some particular axiomatic theory, such as that of *Principia Mathematica*.

[6] By "ordinal number" I mean both the finite ordinals and the transfinite ordinals.

the set of non-negative integers, and the range of F is a bounded set of ordinals). Thus there is no temptation to say that no such function as F exists, and there seems to be no other ground upon which one might object that F is not really definable. But it will now be shown that F cannot be defined within the language of set theory.

Not all ordinal numbers are denoted by terms of our set-theoretic language, for the simple reason that there are only denumerably many terms but nondenumerably many ordinals. In general, if a is an ordinal that is denoted by some term, let a be a term denoting a. Every natural number can be defined in set theory, so given a natural number n (which is a finite ordinal) there will always exist a term n denoting it.

Given these definitions, to say that F can be defined within set theory is to say that there is a 2-formula ϕ of our set-theoretic language such that, for each 1-formula θ, if $n = \#_\theta$ and a is an ordinal number to which we can refer in our set-theoretic language, then $F(n) = a$ iff $\phi(n, a)$ is true. Let us suppose that, contrary to what is to be proven, F can be defined within set theory, using some 2-formula ϕ. It will be shown that this supposition leads to a contradiction. Following Gödel, it is a simple matter to construct within the language of set theory a 1-formula ψ such that $\psi(n)$ is true iff n is the Gödel number of some 1-formula. Now consider the 1-formula $(\exists n)(\psi(n)$ & $\phi(n, x))$. Let us abbreviate this as "Σ". An ordinal number a satisfies Σ iff there is a 1-formula θ such that a is the smallest ordinal number not satisfying θ. There are only denumerably many 1-formulas in the language of set theory, so there are only denumerably many ordinal numbers satisfying Σ. It is a theorem of set theory that there are non-denumerably many ordinal numbers. Consequently, there is an ordinal number β which is the first ordinal number not satisfying Σ. That is, $\beta = F(\#_\Sigma)$. Furthermore, β is denoted by a term β of the language. Such a term is

$$\cup \{x; \text{Ord}(x) \ \& \sim\!\Sigma(x) \ \& \ (\forall y)[(\text{Ord}(y) \ \& \ y < x) \supset \Sigma(y)]\}.^7$$

Let $k = \#_\Sigma$. Then $\phi(k, \beta)$ is true. But then, $(\exists n)(\psi(n)$ & $\phi(n, \beta))$ is true, i.e., $\Sigma(\beta)$ is true. But β is defined to be the first ordinal number not satisfying Σ, so by definition, $\Sigma(\beta)$ is false. Thus we are led to a contradiction. Therefore, the function F cannot be defined within set theory. The definition of F makes essential use of concepts

---

7 This is because this term denotes $\cup \{\beta\}$, which is β.

that cannot be defined within the relatively impoverished language of set theory—namely, the concept of an object satisfying a formula of the language of set theory.

The heuristic idea behind the above argument is based on a logical paradox originally mentioned by Russell.[8] Consider the smallest undefinable ordinal. That ordinal is defined as "the smallest undefinable ordinal." Hence the smallest undefinable ordinal is definable, which is a contradiction. Analogously, it is easily verified that the ordinals definable in the language of set theory are just those satisfying Σ. If a satisfies Σ, then it is the smallest ordinal not satisfying some formula θ, and hence a is definable in that way. Conversely, if a is definable then it is denoted by some term g. Then a is the smallest (in fact, the only) ordinal not satisfying the formula "$x \neq g$", and hence a satisfies Σ. Consequently, β defined as above is the smallest ordinal not definable in the language of set theory.

It should be pointed out that this argument, unlike Russell's, is not a paradox. There is no contradiction at all in supposing that such a function as F exists—in fact, it seems clear that it does. The contradiction turns on the assumption that F is definable in set theory, and hence merely shows that F is not so definable.

It might well be objected that the above argument employs mathematical concepts that Russell was not thinking about when he defended logicism. In attempting to establish the truth of logicism, Russell only considered classical mathematics. But this misses the point that logicism is a theory about the general concept of mathematical truth, not just about some restricted subclass of mathematical truths. To be philosophically interesting, logicism must talk about *all* truths of mathematics, and so interpreted, logicism is false. Not all mathematical concepts can be defined within set theory. Set theory must be regarded as just one more mathematical (or logical) theory alongside all the others. Set theory is not the queen of mathematical theories to which all the others can be reduced. Like any mathematical theory, it may bear important relations to other mathematical theories. In particular, it bears important relations to the classical theories of the natural and real numbers. But it cannot be regarded as containing all of mathematics.

[8] "Mathematical Logic as Based on the Theory of Types," *American Journal of Mathematics*, 30 (1908): 222–262.

25

Russell's Reduction of Arithmetic to Logic

Herbert Hochberg

SEVERAL problems are connected with Russell's "reduction" of elementary arithmetic to logic. In this paper I am concerned with only one of them, which, while not technical like those surrounding the theory of types and the axiom of infinity, is a fundamental one. The problem may be put simply. Aside from any technical issues relating to the logicists' reconstruction of the Peano postulates and concepts, why has Russell "reduced" elementary arithmetic to logic and not merely mapped the Peano system onto *Principia Mathematica* or, at best, constructed an interpretation of the Peano system? The question is particularly pointed if one does not feel that, via the bridge afforded by analytical geometry, one may also reduce, for example, Euclidean plane geometry to logic. To justify this feeling one must point out distinguishing features which make one mapping a reduction and the other merely a mapping. Here I shall attempt to defend the Russell reduction in the case of elementary arithmetic and argue that there are distinguishing features which, first, substantiate his claims about arithmetic and, second, need not force the logicist to claim that the same type of analysis applies in the case of a geometry.

Russell's program must be understood as embodying a philosophical thesis in response to distinct philosophical or metaphysical questions. In the case of arithmetic there are two questions. First, what entities, if any, are the arithmetical propositions about? Or, to put it differently, what constitutes the ontological ground for the truths of arithmetic? Second, what kinds of truths are the true propositions of arithmetic?

To get at these questions we must first note that three distinct sets of propositions and signs are involved. First, there is the set of propositions and signs that constitute *ordinary* arithmetic. Among them are signs like '7', '5', '+', etc. and truths like '7 + 5 = 12'. These signs and statements are, in one definite sense, unproblematic with respect to their meaning. Questions about their meaning can be answered in terms of their ordinary use and context. Part of this context consists of their role in mathematics proper and part in the applications of mathematics—from the esoteric uses in science to the most mundane actuarial functions. One crucial feature stands out—as Russell noted—namely, in applying numbers to things, we attribute them to groups or collections of things. Thus, we may be said to ordinarily treat numbers as attributes of collections. We will return to this later; for the moment we need only note that it is a feature of our ordinary use of numerical concepts.

A second system of signs and sign sequences involved is the Peano system of postulates and theorems. This system can be considered in two ways. To get at what is essential it will be harmless if we take liberties with both the Peano system and history. Assume that, at the time of Euclid, a number of geometrical truths about triangles, circles, etc., were known but not organized into an axiomatic system. Assume next that Euclid supplied such an axiomatics for such propositions, and, in so doing, added some new ones and selected some as axioms or basic propositions so that a number of the known truths turned out to be theorems. In one sense one may say that the propositions, known prior to Euclid's work, are exactly *the same* as those incorporated into his system. The same terms are used, the applications are the same, etc. However, in another sense, one may say that Euclid, in changing the contextual setting for such terms and sentences involving them, changed the significance and hence the meaning of the signs and propositions. In Euclid's axiomatic system, the *same signs* and sentences may occur but with a different meaning. So long as we are clear how we use 'meaning' and 'same' here, there is no problem and nothing to argue about. Similarly, in one sense, we may say that Peano supplied an organized axiomatics for our ordinary arithmetical propositions. So taken, he enriched the context for arithmetical concepts and propositions. But there is a second way of looking at the Peano system. We may take it as an abstract axiomatic system of which ordinary arithmetic, organized in a certain way, is an interpretation. We then have an abstract axiomatic system, whose primitive signs are uninterpreted marks, *and* a system of ordinary arithmetic, whose signs need no interpretation due to the meaning supplied by the rich context of the ordinary use and application of such signs.[1] Noting the two ways in which the Peano system may be taken is important for the issues at hand, but, once noted, we may forget, for our discussion, its role as an organized version of ordinary arithmetic and consider it to be an abstract axiomatic system.

The third relevant system of signs is that portion of Russell and Whitehead's *Principia Mathematica* which is involved in the interpretation of the Peano system that they proposed. Just as the signs in the Peano system differ from those of ordinary arithmetic, the "number signs" of *PM* differ from both of these. The "meanings" of the number signs of *PM*, in a clear sense of 'meaning', are precisely specified in terms of their definitions by means of the logical primitives of *PM*. Such signs are thus neither abstract marks nor those of ordinary arithmetic.

Let us call the three systems '*OA*', '*PA*', and '*RA*', respectively, and use a lower case '*p*' and '*r*' as subscripts for the respective arithmetical signs of the Peano and Russellian systems, that is of *PA* and *RA*. Thus, '7', '7_p', and '7_r', are three signs and not one. Consequently, to say either that Peano defined '7' or that Russell defined '7' or '7_p' is at best false. What one should say, if he seeks to defend Russell's philosophy of arithmetic, is that by means of *RA* Russell solved the philosophical problems raised about arithmetic that we mentioned above. In terms of our example, Russell used '7_r' and *RA* to interpret '7_p' and *PA* and answer metaphysical questions raised in connection with '7' and *OA*. Just what this means and involves must be spelled out and defended. Since the key to Russell's solution is his handling of the ontological questions, we will get into them by taking up some points about ontological issues in general.

Consider an object, *o*, that has the property *white* and a philosopher who, in providing an ontological analysis of the object and specifying

[1] For a detailed discussion of abstract axiomatic systems and interpretations of them see my "Axiomatic Systems, Formalization, and Scientific Theories," in *Symposium on Sociological Theory*, ed. L. Gross (New York: Harper & Row, 1959), pp. 407–436.

the ground or basis for the truth of the sentence '*o* is *white*', recognizes in his ontology, first, a universal referred to by the term '*W*', a particular or substratum referred to by 'o_1', a nexus of exemplification which connects universals to particulars and which is reflected in a clarified language by juxtaposition of subject and predicate terms, and a fact, which is indicated by the sentence 'Wo_1' and which contains W, o_1, and the nexus. The ordinary claim that it is the case *that o is white* is thus reflected in such an ontological position by adhering to several different ontological kinds. (One could say "kinds of entity," but some philosophers distinguish universals and particulars as entities from the nexus which, while not an entity, has some sort of ontological status.) A different philosopher will contend that the ordinary fact can be reflected and the ordinary object analyzed without recourse to such an extensive ontology. We thus arrive at a metaphysical conflict between alternative ontologies. How such a conflict may be resolved, or if it is resolvable at all, are not questions we need take up here in any detail. We need only note, first, that Occam's razor functions as a basic principle in constructing an ontology, and, second, that an adequate ontology must *fit* the ordinary facts and objects. A mapping or coordination helps explain what is meant by "fitting" ontological analyses to ordinary facts. A philosopher, advocating the ontological analysis we just considered, coordinates to the notion of the ordinary object *o* that of a complex entity of which o_1 and W are constituents. Likewise, he coordinates the universal W to the property *white* and the fact that o_1 exemplifies W to the ordinary fact, or, if you will, truth that *o* is *white*.[2] Thus, an ontological position consists of a set of interrelated concepts and statements together with a coordination procedure which maps these onto ordinary notions and statements. What is required, of course, is that the philosophical statements mapped onto the ordinary ones be both equivalent in truth value and relevant to the philosophical issues raised in connection with

---

[2] To speak of coordinating the universal white to the property white may well be misleading here. One may hold that the property is a universal. Thus, one coordinates the *metaphysical concept* of a universal to the *ordinary concept* of a property. He does not correlate one *thing* with another. That is, one coordinates different concepts (notions, meaningful expressions) which are embedded in different contexts, just as in the case of the object *o* and its analysis. However, some philosophical gambits involve the coordination of different things, a bare substratum, o_1, to an object, *o*, for example. Such positions literally *introduce special things* in order to analyze *ordinary* things. There is much to be clarified here, but that would involve an essay in itself.

the ordinary statements. Truth functional equivalence does not pose a problem; the relevance of proposed analyses does. But this latter question is not fruitfully discussed in general. Hence, we shall return to it later in a specific context for the issues at hand.

By offering an ontological analysis of the object *o* and the specifying of a ground of truth for the sentence '*o* is *white*', one does not hold that the object is not *real*, since only its constituents are real. Nor, does one hold that the object really is composed of universals and substrata *instead* of chalk, wood, atoms, or what have you. The sort of constituents of the object that we have been talking about are mentioned in connection with a specific set of questions, which are not requests for a compositional analysis in any ordinary sense. Similarly, if one was concerned with other philosophical problems, one might talk about a chair as a pattern of sensa or a history of momentary physical time slices, about a self as a set of experiences related in certain ways, and so on. Again, if one is careful, he does not thereby deny that, in one sense, there are chairs, selves, continuants, and so forth, since, in another context, they are construed or analyzed according to a philosophical position. In short, one must not confuse the two distinct contexts, one philosophical, the other ordinary, since one speaks of chairs, selves, numbers, etc. in both and uses the one to answer questions and problems raised about the other. Keeping the two contexts distinct should also prevent one from making the misleading claim that the one context, the philosophical one, provides the *real meaning* for the concepts of the other, the ordinary one. This question of "meaning" is central and we shall return to it later. For the moment an analogy may be helpful.

A common use of the term 'reduction' occurs when one speaks of macro-theories being reduced to micro-theories. One example would be in the case of a macro-behavioral theory being reduced to a physiological one; another classical example is the reduction of a macro-theory of gases to a particle theory. One also speaks of states of the respective systems being reduced to corresponding micro-states. Thus, the fact that a gas has a certain temperature is reduced to the fact that the particles which *constitute* the gas are in a certain state. In a straightforward sense of 'formal', such reductions are formally the same as the philosophical or ontological analyses we considered. Two sets of statements and terms are coordinated in such a way that the one set is mapped onto the other. In the case of the scientific theories there are several relevant features that lead one to speak of "reduction." For example, the particles are taken to be literally physical parts of the macro-objects. Further, the coordinating statements are either discovered or hypothetical physical laws, and the basic laws of one theory become deductive consequences of those of the other, taken together with the coordinating statements. But even in such cases, it is misleading to hold that the gas does not have a temperature, *really*, since there is *ultimately* only the particle state or that for a gas to have a certain temperature *really means* that it is in a certain particle state. Of course one can so legislate his use of such terms that the claims are stipulated to be true. But such legislation provides no resolution for the philosophical puzzles generated by our use of such terms. A first step at a solution involves noting, and not confusing, the various senses of terms like 'real' and 'mean' that are germane to the issues.[3]

The statements that there is one and only one even natural number between 7 and 9 and that 7 plus 5 equals 12 are truths that belong to the ordinary arithmetical context. Thus, we ordinarily claim that *there are numbers* with certain characteristics. If one then raises the questions, "What do we mean when we say a number exists?" and "Why is '7 + 5 = 12' true?", an appropriate response might be along the lines Wittgenstein goes through in *Remarks on the Foundations of Mathematics* and earlier in the *Tractatus*. One sort of answer to these questions lies in understanding the context of ordinary mathematical usage; learning the language game of arithmetic and its applications to physical objects and situations. Similarly, if one asks what an object is or what a property is and how objects and properties are connected, one could explain the ordinary context for the use of such concepts. But none of these explanations constitute an ontological or philosophical analysis.[4] To provide such an analysis one must take

[3] For a further discussion of these issues see my "Intervening Variables, Hypothetical Constructs, and Metaphysics," in *Current Issues in the Philosophy of Science* (New York: Holt, Rinehart & Winston, 1961), pp. 448–460; "Physicalism, Behaviorism, and Phenomena," *Philosophy of Science*, 26 (1959): 93–103; and G. Bergmann, *Philosophy of Science* (Madison: University of Wisconsin Press, 1957).

[4] This is not to say that such explanations and explorations of the ordinary context are not relevant to proposed ontological analyses. For surely a presupposition of an adequate analysis of the ordinary context is an understanding of its subtleties. Moreover, some philosophical disputes are certainly about what belongs to the ordinary context. For example, see the dispute between D. A. T. Gasking, "Mathematics and the World," and H. N. Castañeda, "Arithmetic and

such questions in another way. Taken in this other way, to ask what is a number or what number signs indicate or why "$7 + 5 = 12$" is true is to ask for the location, in one's ontology, of the things and relations which ground the truths of arithmetic. Russell located such a ground in terms of classes and logical truths about classes. What ontological status classes and logical truths have and what philosophical problems may be raised about such notions is not relevant here, though it is, of course, a basic part of the whole story. The point that is relevant here is that the way one deals with such questions about classes and logic provides, on the Russellian approach, a solution to the ontological problems about arithmetic. But proposing the Russellian solution invites the raising of our original question in another form: 'Are numbers *really* classes?'

Consider the problem of universals. A philosopher argues that there are universals on the basis of holding that no nominalistic account can adequately ground the true ascription of one and the same predicate to two objects or the fact that two objects have the *same* property. If this line is cogent, one seems forced to accept universals, just as one seems forced to accept a special tie or nexus of exemplification, or something similar, in order to avoid Bradley's regress. By contrast, one seems to argue for the construing of the ground of arithmetical truths in terms of relations among classes on the basis of parsimony. One does not seem forced to accept Russell's thesis as one does seem forced to accept universals and the nexus of exemplification. Yet, the appearance is deceptive. For, given the adherence to principles like Occam's razor, in the absence of any equally cogent and parsimonious alternative, one is forced to Russell's solution. Hence, if we ask "Why is Russell's achievement more than a mere mapping?" a reply is forthcoming, in part, in that the logistic thesis provides the most parsimonious ontological grounding for the truths of arithmetic. But this needs to be spelled out. To do so I shall consider some objections and alternatives to the logistic program, which return us to the question 'Are numbers really classes?'

Suppose one objects to the Russell program on the basis of the old adage that a thing is what it is and not another thing. In short, numbers are numbers, not classes. Russell is claiming that one sort of thing, a

---

Reality," as to whether or not there are alternative arithmetics as there are alternative geometries. Both papers are reproduced in *Philosophy of Mathematics*, ed. P. Benacerraf and H. Putnam (Englewood Cliffs, N.J.: Prentice-Hall, 1964), pp. 390–417.

number, is another sort of thing, a class. This may result in a more parsimonious ontology, but it involves a grotesque procedure of "reducing" something to something else. Just as a phenomenalist is involved in the absurd claim that a physical object, such as a train, is a collection of sense data or a physicalist makes the ridiculous assertion that awarenesses, experiences, and all mental states are really bodily states, the logicist claims that numbers are classes and arithmetical truths really logical truths. To avoid such illicit reduction one must recognize numbers as a category of entity and ground the truths of arithmetic in terms of relations holding among such entities. One thus recognizes arithmetical entities and, as it were, arithmetical facts.

Such a line assumes that we start from the implicit or explicit acceptance of the fact that there are numbers. But, in the sense in which this is true, it is irrelevant. We all admit that there is an even natural number between 7 and 9. This does not mean that we hold, either implicitly or explicitly, to a philosophical position recognizing an entity which stands in a three-term relation to two other entities denoted by the signs '7' and '9'. Nor does it mean that we are forced to adopt such a position on *that basis alone*. This would be like holding that, since one can buy two shirts of the same color, some form of Platonism must be adopted and all forms of nominalism rejected, on the basis of that fact alone. Here we should not be misled by its being the case that we might be led to an ontology recognizing numbers as basic entities or some form of Platonism on the grounds that such views alone serve to adequately analyze and ground the ordinary truths like '7 + 5 = 12' and 'Those shirts have the same color'. Clearly what is involved here is a very complicated procedure of *fitting* one alternative to the ordinary facts and successfully refuting the competing views. But this is not done in the simpleminded way of either pointing out that we say there are numbers and that objects have the same color in our ordinary use of number signs and color words or that we accept such claims as obvious truths. To think otherwise is, in effect, to fuse ordinary language analysis with ontological analysis and, in so doing, trivialize both. Whether numbers are entities and if so what kind, are precisely the philosophical questions which we answer by fitting a metaphysical position to the ordinary facts. But this involves much more than reciting commonplace truths. The truths of arithmetic, which we start from, do not, by themselves, imply that numbers are entities, or that they are classes, or that they are not classes. To reject the Russellian thesis on the ground that arithmetic is about numbers, not classes, is to be overly simplistic about philosophical questions in general and not merely about those relevant to arithmetic.

The objection we have just considered may be raised in an apparently more cogent form. Instead of merely asserting that numbers are numbers and being indignant about Russell's presuming to reduce one thing to another, one might hold that no statements about classes may be taken as "reconstructions" of arithmetical statements, since the two kinds of statements do not "mean" the same thing. To dissolve this form of the objection we must separate three aspects of it or, perhaps better, three different senses of 'meaning' that are involved in it.

First, there is the simple point that the intentions and mental states relevant to the one set of statements differ from those relevant to the other. Thus, what we *have in mind* on occasions when we ordinarily use arithmetical notions and assert arithmetical truths will not, generally, be what one has in mind when he uses the correlates of such notions and statements, which are offered by a particular philosophical position, in the context of a philosophical analysis. While this is unquestionably true, it is also, I submit, irrelevant. Consistently pursued, such an approach will merely lead one to a version of the so-called paradox of analysis and to the self-defeating rejection of every philosophical and ontological analysis. If the fact that such an approach is self-defeating and paradoxical is not taken as sufficient grounds for rejecting it, we may part company from its advocates on the basis that such a requirement (intentional equivalence, if I may so put it) for a philosophical analysis being sufficient for or fitting the ordinary facts is overly puritanical and stringent. Being so, it does not provide a reasonable ground for the rejection of Russell's reconstruction of arithmetic or of any other proposed philosophical analysis.[5]

A second strand of the objection is closely related to the first. One may reject a thesis like Russell's by holding that the proper answers to the philosophical questions surrounding arithmetic are to be arrived at by exploring the subtleties of the ordinary conceptual context of arithmetical propositions and notions. To understand what numbers are it suffices to understand how to use arithmetical concepts as they relate to each other, as well as in measuring, counting, etc. *The meaning* of arithmetical concepts is given by such a context, rather

[5] For some related comments on the paradox of analysis see G. Bergmann and H. Hochberg, "Concepts," *Philosophical Studies*, 8 (1957): 19–27.

than by definitions or reconstructions in Russellian fashion within the system of *PM*. Statements belonging to the one context cannot, therefore, be construed in terms of statements belonging to the other.

On the basis of such an argument, one not only recognizes that '7' and '7_r' are different terms belonging to different contextual settings but also claims that in no sense is '7_r' *relevant* to the "meaning" of '7'. One does more than insist on the distinction between the ordinary and the philosophical contexts and claims more than that the two give distinct meanings to their respective concepts. For, in effect, such a line of argument claims that philosophical puzzles are answered or dissolved by merely exploring the details and subtleties of the ordinary contextual setting. What one does is hold that only the ordinary context is significant or, to put it another way, that there are no ontological problems to be answered by specifying a ground for the arithmetical truths. One thus refuses to raise certain questions or, putting the same thing still differently, one takes ordinary arithmetic to constitute its own ontological ground. The same approach is naturally applied to other philosophical problems. Using it, one does not solve the problems of universals and predication by recognizing entities of a certain kind but dissolves them by exploring the ways in which we use predicates and verbs.

It is, perhaps, ironic that the first way of rejecting the Russellian analysis, on the basis that arithmetical statements do not mean the same thing as statements about classes, leads to an abundant ontology with the recognition of special arithmetical entities; while the second objection, on the ground that arithmetical concepts are unique and to be understood only in their own context, leads to the rejection of any ontological questions about arithmetic. The first has affinities to an extreme form of Platonism and is reminiscent of Meinong; the second has similarities to the formalistic standpoint that Russell attacked and is generally the approach implicit in Wittgenstein's comments about arithmetic. Both share certain features with the so-called intuitionist philosophy of mathematics. But, historical connections aside, both gambits may be rejected as critiques of Russell's approach. The first may be rejected in that it relies on a requirement that is too stringent and, in effect, rejects any analysis; the second in that it refuses to consider the questions Russell sought to answer. This brings us to the third aspect or sense of 'meaning' that is relevant to these objections and to the question of whether or not Russell showed that numbers are really classes.

Recall two statements that we discussed earlier:

(1) *o* is *white*.
(2) *o* contains a particular o_1 which exemplifies the universal *W*.

It is clear that (1) and (2) will differ in intentional contexts. It is also clear that (2) does not belong to any ordinary, nonphilosophical context, and that if we restrict ourselves to such contexts we shall never utter a sentence like (2), let alone raise a question as to whether it provides an analysis for, or meaning to, (1). In these senses (1) and (2) *mean quite different things*. But, if we do raise problems about universals, particulars, and predication, then a further sense of 'meaning' becomes relevant. The *analysis* a philosopher gives of (1), which is schematically expressed by (2), may be taken to provide such a further sense of 'meaning'. In this sense one may hold that (1) and (2) mean the same thing, according to one specific metaphysical position. Hence, it should also be clear that the difference in meaning between (1) and (2) and the fact that (1), but not (2), has an ordinary nonphilosophical use are irrelevant to the adequacy of (2) as a proposed analysis of (1). What goes for the problem of universals goes for Russell's analysis of arithmetic. Certain statements about classes in the system of *PM* can be taken to mean the same thing as the arithmetical statements of *OA* with which they are correlated, in the sense that they are offered as purported ontological analyses in response to ontological questions about *OA*. This is why the two objections we considered above are not relevant to the question of the success, or lack of it, of Russell's analysis.

What is relevant is, first, whether the mapping is technically adequate, and, second, whether it can be used to cogently answer the philosophical questions. The question of the technical adequacy is not our concern here. Defending the philosophical cogency of the Russell analysis amounts to pointing out how it jibes with or fits the ordinary context of arithmetic, arguing that it is the ontologically most parsimonious alternative, refuting *philosophical* objections to it, and establishing the inadequacies of proffered alternatives. The technical adequacy and ontological parsimony I have taken for granted here. I have tried, however, to rebut some objections, and, in so doing, argue against some alternatives. We shall return to those alternatives and to another as well, shortly. Now, I should like to point to those features of the ordinary context that show Russell's analysis to both jibe with it and be relevant to it.

One outstanding fit with the ordinary context is that feature we noted earlier and which Russell stressed. We ordinarily apply numbers to groups or classes of objects. Construing numbers as classes of classes accurately reflects such usage. A second fit is with our pre-analytic notion that arithmetical truths are somehow necessary or conceptual truths rather than empirical ones, for, on Russell's analysis, they are correlated to logical truths. If one recalls that phrases like "necessary truth" and "conceptual truth" are themselves analyzable, along lines quite compatible with Russell's approach, in terms of the notion of *logical truth*, the point becomes even more forceful.

Russell's analysis also preserves, as he noted, the ordinary notion that arithmetical signs are not mere abstract marks or symbols but meaningful signs associated with definite concepts. Russell, however, seems to have thought that he was supplying *the* meaning to our ordinary arithmetical signs by a set of definitions in *RA* just as, in another context, he thought he was supplying *the meaning* to signs like 'Pegasus' and 'the present king of France'. In both cases he puts matters in a misleading way and invites the Wittgensteinian response about arithmetic and Strawson's criticism of the Theory of Descriptions. But, in both cases Russell is essentially correct in that the philosophical analyses he gives of the respective problems can be cogently put.[6] Here, the point is not that he supplies *the meaning* to ordinary arithmetical expressions and statements, but that *according to his analysis*, as well as *according to our ordinary usage*, arithmetical expressions are not mere abstract sign designs. No attempt to solve the philosophical problems surrounding arithmetic which takes arithmetical expressions to be uninterpreted, abstract sign designs can jibe with this obvious feature of the ordinary context. This disparity goes along with another. Taking arithmetical statements as uninterpreted formal patterns precludes taking them as true statements.

Russell also made this point. But, thinking that he was supplying *the meaning* to the ordinary arithmetical terms, he put both claims a bit differently:

> ... it fails to give an adequate basis for arithmetic. In the first place, it does not enable us to know whether there are any sets of terms verifying Peano's axioms; it does not even give the faintest suggestion of any way of discovering whether there are such sets. In the second place, as

---

[6] I have attempted to do so for the theory of descriptions in "Strawson, Russell, and the King of France," in this volume.

already observed, we want our numbers to be such as can be used for counting common objects, and this requires that our numbers should have a *definite* meaning, not merely that they should have certain formal properties. This definite meaning is defined by the logical theory of arithmetic.[7]

By contrast, the Russellian analysis not only jibes with the more specific ordinary notion that arithmetic truths are a special kind of truth, but with the more obvious idea that some arithmetical statements, such as '7 + 5 = 12', are true, while others, such as '7 + 5 = 13', are false.

There is another, and decisive, respect in which the Russell reconstruction fits the ordinary context. Perhaps it is no more than an elaboration of the last mentioned point. Measuring and counting are the two basic applications of arithmetic to empirical situations. Our ordinary use of arithmetical concepts in measuring and counting take for granted that such concepts have a *definite* meaning and that certain arithmetical statements are true. Counting is a rather obvious case. What we do is establish a 1 — 1 correlation between a set of numbers and, say, a set of people. It is understood that the numbers are *arranged* in the standard way; that is, that certain arithmetical truths hold. *We do not treat the arithmetical terms and statements as uninterpreted sign designs which we interpret* in terms of signs referring to people and relations among them. When we count a group of people consisting of Jones, Smith, and Brown, we do not interpret the sign '1' in terms of the sign 'Jones' or hold that '1' refers to Jones or "means" Jones (or 'Jones' for that matter). The same is true in cases of measurement. Consider a simple case of measuring, where we merely establish a rank ordering among minerals, in terms of the relations *harder than* and *equally hard*, and where these relations are specified in terms of a scratch test. What we do is discover that a set of numbers and the relations > and =, taken in the standard arithmetical way, share certain logical properties with the minerals and the relations *harder than* and *equally hard*.[8] This enables us to coordinate to each statement about a mineral, or kind of mineral, being harder than another (or equally

7 B. Russell, *Introduction to Mathematical Philosophy* (London: Allen & Unwin, 1953), p. 10.

8 See G. Bergmann and K. W. Spence, "The Logic of Psychophysical Measurement," in H. Feigl and M. Brodbeck, *Readings in the Philosophy of Science* (New York: Appleton-Century-Crofts, 1953), and C. G. Hempel, *Fundamentals of Concept Formation in Empirical Science, International Encyclopedia of Unified Science* (Chicago: University of Chicago Press, 1952), 2:7.

as hard as another) a statement about a number being greater than another (or a statement of numerical equality). We do not treat the arithmetical statements as abstract, uninterpreted sign sequences and the empirical statements about the minerals as interpretations of them. If we speak of interpretations at all in such a context, we might think of the arithmetical statements and the empirical ones about the minerals as both being interpretations of an abstract set of sentences. Thus, we discover that the two systems of statements share "certain formal properties." Such a set of abstract sentences, taken in a certain context, would specify what it is to be a rank ordering, just as a set of formalized or abstract axioms can be taken to specify what it is for an interpreting system to be a group in mathematics.

The use of arithmetic in both counting and measuring dramatically contrasts with the application of a geometry in empirical matters. *In applying a geometry, we interpret it.* In other words, the ordinary context for geometrical statements reveals that we take them to be either empirical statements or sentential forms belonging to abstract axiomatic systems, which have certain logical and mathematical features. Thus, to apply a geometry is to give an interpretation to an abstract axiomatic system, which is quite unlike what we do in counting and measuring. This shows that the ordinary context for geometrical statements would be ignored or distorted if we took a mapping of, say, Euclidean plane geometry onto *PM* to be an analysis on a par with Russell's logistic *reduction* of arithmetic.[9]

The philosophical problems that arise in connection with geometry —'What are geometrical statements about? What kinds of truths are the axioms and theorems of a geometry? *How do we reconcile alternative geometries?*'—can be answered, and must be answered, in terms of the distinction between a geometry as an abstract axiomatic system and a geometry as a set of physically interpreted laws or hypotheses.[10] Taken in the one sense, no ground of truth is required for the statements of a geometry, since one deals with uninterpreted sign sequences

[9] Unfortunately, some logicists of a formalistic bent have thought that just because Russell constructed a mapping he solved the philosophical problems of arithmetic. The embarrassing gap is sometimes covered by saying that Russell reconstructed *the meaning* of the arithmetical terms and statements in "the logical, not the psychological sense of the term 'meaning'." C. G. Hempel, "On the Nature of Mathematical Truth," in Benacerraf and Putnam, *Philosophy of Mathematics*, p. 375.

[10] This is spelled out in Hochberg, "Axiomatic Systems, Formalization, and Scientific Theories," in *Symposium on Sociological Theory*.

and not statements that are true or false; taken in the other sense, we deal with *merely* another set of empirical laws or purported laws. Such a resolution of the philosophical problems raised by geometries fits with the ordinary context for geometrical propositions. We can even put it more emphatically. The fact that there are alternative geometries in the ordinary mathematical context requires a solution along the lines we just considered. There is no other way of resolving the apparent conflict between Euclidean and non-Euclidean geometries (as well as the same type of conflict among the various non-Euclidean geometries). To suggest that each geometry is about a special type of idealized set of entities (Euclidean triangles, Riemannian triangles, etc.) as arithmetic is about a unique sort of entity—numbers—transforms an extreme form of Platonism into a kind of philosophical lotus-eating. This gambit, I suspect, we may reject without further discussion. It does, however, reflect detrimentally on the view we considered earlier which rejected the Russellian reduction of arithmetic to logic on the ground that "numbers are numbers and not anything else." Moreover, note, again, the similarity between such an extreme form of Platonism and the Wittgensteinian advocacy of the logical independence of different language games (and the implicit holistic theory of meaning he advocates). Is there "really" a difference between inventing special entities for every language game to be about and insisting on the unanalyzability of any system in terms of any other? More on this point shortly.

In the ordinary context there are alternative geometries. There are not, in any similar or reasonable sense, alternative arithmetics.[11] Thus, to treat arithmetic along the lines that one may use to resolve the philosophical problems raised by geometries would be mistaken. This fact not only strongly supports the Russellian "reduction" of arithmetic to logic, but it provides the careful logicist with a satisfactory basis for rejecting any similar reduction of a geometry to logic.[12]

[11] Gasking has attempted to argue that there are alternative arithmetics and Castañeda has neatly pointed out how silly some of his arguments are. Gasking and Castañeda, in *Philosophy of Mathematics*.

[12] Some logicists, like Quine, are so entranced with the formal possibilities of a mapping that they put arithmetic and geometry in the same category and "reduce" both to logic. W. V. Quine, "Truth by Convention," in Benacerraf and Putnam, *Philosophy of Mathematics*, p. 339. If one becomes truly intoxicated by such mappings, he may conclude that all statements are reducible to logic and hence that there is no real difference between logical truths and empirical truths. This is probably one underlying cause of Quine's celebrated attack on the synthetic-analytic distinction, proxy functions notwithstanding.

We have considered some ways in which the Russellian analysis is supported by features of the ordinary context of arithmetic. There is yet another point in favor of Russell's analysis, but it is, perhaps, more problematic. Recall our earlier discussion of the reduction of some scientific theories to others. In some cases, of such reduction the axioms of the theory which is reduced will be correlated to theorems of the reducing theory. This, of course, strengthens the sense of the term 'reduction', since there is an obvious sense in which theorems are *derived* from axioms. On Russell's program, the axioms of Peano's system, whether taken as an abstract axiomatics of which ordinary arithmetic is an interpretation or as an organized version of ordinary arithmetic, correspond to theorems of *PM*. This means that his reduction is one in the stronger sense that I just mentioned. This can be taken to answer yet another way of taking the question about grounding the truths of ordinary arithmetic. For, one sense of grounding a set of truths is to specify other truths from which they logically follow. With all the qualifications implied by our discussion so far, Russell may be said to have grounded arithmetic in this sense as well. That is, he grounded the truths of arithmetic in a sense in which some of the truths of logic have no ground. Alternatively, logical truths and concepts might have an ontological ground in a sense in which those of arithmetic do not, if the former, not being "reducible" in turn, are taken to be ontologically grounded by basic entities and relations among them. Here we make use of the idea that the primitive concepts of a metaphysical position reveal its ontology.

Some further comments may be made about the alternatives to Russell's analysis. Concerning the gambit that seeks to establish a unique ontological status for numbers, we might note that the style of argument employed against Russell's analysis of the ontological problems of arithmetic would also lead one, if he were consistent, to reject the "construction" of other numbers on the basis of the natural numbers as well as Russell's avoidance of possible or fictional entities, like Pegasus and the king of France in 1969, by means of the theory of descriptions. Thus, just as one can seemingly reject '$7_r + {_r} 5_r = 12_r$' as an analysis of '$7 + 5 = 12$' on the ground that they do not mean the same thing, one can reject '$(\exists x)[\phi x \,\&\, (y)(\phi y \supset y = x) \,\&\, \psi x]$' as an analysis of 'the ϕ is ψ' on the same ground. One might then take expressions like 'Pegasus' and 'the present king of France' as primitive or incapable of definition or analysis, just as one may take some arithmetical expressions to be primitive. If one philosophizes within the restrictions

Russell imposes on himself, one can be led to recognize, in the fashion of Meinong, entities corresponding to such primitive notions, assuming one treats sentences involving them as meaningful assertions, which are true or false on the basis of certain facts.[13] If one does not so philosophize, he, in effect, gives up his gambit and transforms it into the Wittgensteinian alternative we also considered. This comment requires some unpacking.

The key to dealing with ontological or metaphysical issues is to be concerned with language in its referential use. Hence, we are concerned with how language is connected to the world so that statements are descriptive or true of it. One obvious, simple, and cogent way of establishing the link between language and the world is to have the primitive terms and categories of a language refer to objects in and indicate features of the world. Here, one may fruitfully think in terms of a schematic or idealized language constructed solely for the purpose of reproducing or reconstructing or, if you will, containing correlates of the ordinary truths of fact, logic, and mathematics. An ontology or metaphysical position is specified by the things one takes one's terms to be linked to and the ways in which one connects the terms. This is one crucial point that is behind the so-called reference theory of meaning. To accept primitive terms but refuse to recognize a corresponding entity or feature of reality is to refuse to play the philosophical game.[14] One way of attempting to make such a refusal intellectually respectable is to attack the reference theory of meaning and advocate a holistic or contextualist theory of meaning as an alternative. This is the sum and substance of the Wittgensteinian gambit. But it is one thing, and a legitimate one, to hold that the ordinary context and use of terms provide their "meaning." It is another thing, and an illegitimate one, to confuse this sense of 'meaning' with

[13] This is a long story in itself, and hence what I have said is cryptically, rather than accurately, put. For the details of the story see my "Strawson, Russell, and the King of France," in this volume; "On Referring and Asserting," *Philosophical Studies*, 20 (1969), 81–88; "Professor Quine, Pegasus, and Dr. Cartwright," *Philosophy of Science*, 24 (1957): 191–203; and "On Pegasizing," *Philosophy and Phenomenological Research*, 17 (1957): 551–554.

[14] Just as Quine refuses to play when he holds that a nominalist may admit primitive predicates so long as he does not take them as substitutable for variables or at the level of language where one has quantifiers. Thus, his celebrated ontological criterion "to be is to be the value of a variable" is merely a way of verbally, as opposed to "really," avoiding a commitment to universals.

the advocacy of a holistic *theory of meaning* as a solution to the ontological problems. Actually, this latter move has different variants. One can take it, as we noted earlier, to be an explicit refusal to consider philosophical problems. Or, a philosopher can, in the style of something like Bradley's absolute idealism, *consciously* accept the metaphysical pattern of holism and introduce some sort of Absolute as the ontological ground of "everything." Alternatively, one can speak, like Quine, of tying language as a whole to "experiences." Here, it is characteristic to speak of meaning only in terms of the whole system, but, nevertheless, Quine also speaks of anchoring parts of the language to experience. If we probe into this notion of *tying* or *anchoring*, it becomes apparent that the holistic talk about meaning merely avoids the issues, since we return to the question of the *reference* of language. Whether we talk about reference as meaning or not is really beside the point and not worth arguing about. Thus, the Quinean gambit can be taken to *implicitly* refuse to take up the issues, even though Quine seems concerned with "ontological commitments." The point is really elementary: to raise ontological issues in connection with "the meaning" of language is to ask about the connection of language to what it is about. One who insists on speaking of 'meaning' in such a way as to explicitly or implicitly avoid such questions about the referential use of language avoids, not dissolves, the issues. These comments should help to explain why the advocate of "numbers are numbers" should be led either to accept *possible* entities like Pegasus or reject ontology altogether, via the Wittgensteinian route; they also further explain what is meant by saying that the Wittgensteinian critique of Russell is irrelevant.

There is yet another feature worth noting about what I have characterized as the Wittgensteinian critique. In structure and style of argument it is basically the same as the extreme Platonistic critique. Yet, an advocate of it rejects ontological issues and positions. In spite of this, if we project an ontology onto it, by considering its primitive concepts and features to be ontologically significant, it will not only share a style of argument but an ontology with the extreme form of Platonism. Need one bother to paraphrase the comment to the effect that he who ignores history is forced to relive it, or, in this case, reproduce it?

We may also note here that what I have called an extreme form of Platonism need not preclude taking terms for some natural numbers as construed or defined in terms of others. Thus, '2' might be held to be definable in terms of '1', 'successor', and the notion of natural number. In other words, a modification of the view might involve taking, in effect, only Peano's primitives (or an alternative set of primitive concepts) as ontologically significant. Along this line, one might hold that '2' can be taken to mean 'the successor of 1', even though '1' cannot be taken to mean 'the class of all first level unit classes' and '+2' cannot be taken as indicating a class of pairs of natural numbers.

Another alternative to Russell may be briefly dismissed. Ayer,[15] following a line elegantly stated by Hahn,[16] has argued that arithmetical truths are true by definition. While attractive, the line is incoherent. Either all arithmetical terms will be defined or not. *If they are*, then the thesis *reduces* to Russell's or something like what Russell did. For, every arithmetical truth will then be stateable without using any arithmetical terms. It is then completely misleading to speak of definitions alone as the ground of truth for arithmetical statements. *If they are not*, then one is left with some statements employing arithmetical terms as primitives. He must then take such statements to "define" such terms. But this is clearly "definition" in the sense of "implicit definition," and is, in effect, no different from the advocacy of the Peano postulates, taken as an abstract axiomatic system, as a "philosophy of arithmetic." This, as Russell showed, is unsatisfactory.

One may be dissatisfied with my purported defense of Russell, since he may feel that all that I have done is stipulate that the sort of mapping Russell constructed provides a sense of meaning for arithmetical statements and, since it does, he has "reduced" arithmetic to logic. Thus, one may feel that I have done no more than repeat, in a roundabout fashion, the claim of Hempel's which I criticized above.[17] I do not think that such a criticism is justified.[18] Nevertheless, I understand the sense of dissatisfaction. For, taking the Russell "reduction" to be a mapping that is cogent, on the grounds I appealed to, is not nearly as

15 A. J. Ayer, *Language, Truth, and Logic* (New York: Dover, 1952), p. 82.

16 H. Hahn, "Logic, Mathematics and Knowledge of Nature," in *20th-Century Philosophy: The Analytic Tradition*, ed. M. Weitz (New York: The Free Press, 1966), pp. 222–235. Perhaps, however, Hahn only means to advocate the Russellian analysis and is not stating a view similar to Ayer's.

17 See fn. 9 above.

18 If nothing more, being clear about just what Russell has done and why it is philosophically relevant is one thing; to cover up a philosophical problem, or pass it by, with the use of a phrase like "the logical meaning" or "a logical reconstruction" is another.

strong a claim as Russell appeared to make. But we must note that what goes for Russell's reconstruction of arithmetic goes for all ontological analyses. It is then in a very limited sense that a metaphysical position purports to tell us what is "really" what. Unfortunately, perhaps, that is the way it is.

26

Logic and Ontology in Russell's Philosophy

E. D. Klemke

As I conceive it, the main question in the philosophy of logic is: What is the relationship between logic and ontology? That is, does logic have ontological status, or at least, ontological implications; and if so, what are they? I shall here examine the various views held by Bertrand Russell in answer to this question.

The question as stated above is fairly broad and general. It breaks down into several more specific questions:

(1) What is the nature of logical truth?
Or what is the nature of the truths (or laws) of logic?
Are they truths at all?
And if so are they analytic or synthetic? A priori or a posteriori?

(2) What are logical truths about?
What entities, if any, are referred to by the laws of logic?

(3) What is the nature of logical form?
Which terms, if any, of language express or indicate logical form?
Can such terms be distinguished from nonlogical terms?
What elements, if any, of logical syntax indicate logical form?

(4) What is the ontological status of logical form?
What entities, if any, are referred to by logical terms?

What features of the world, if any, are indicated by logical syntax?

That there may be other issues which rightfully belong in a consideration of logic and ontology, I shall not deny. But these are the only ones with which I shall be concerned in this study. I shall begin with an examination of Russell's answers to (3) and (4). Later I shall turn to (1) and (2).

I

In the Preface to *The Principles of Mathematics*, Russell states that this work has two main objects. One is to give proof of the logistic thesis "that all pure mathematics deals exclusively with concepts definable in terms of a very small number of fundamental logical concepts, and that all its propositions are deducible from a very small number of fundamental logical principles."[1] The other main object is to present a "discussion" or "explanation" of these fundamental *logical* concepts "which mathematics accepts as indefinable."[2] The first task is one in the philosophy of mathematics. The second is one that falls within the range of our subject matter. Part One of Russell's book is devoted to this endeavor. Before going into his discussion in detail, we may note that already in the preface, Russell indicates an answer to some of the questions contained in the clusters of questions I have designated (3) and (4). First, according to Russell, there are certain "concepts" which are fundamental logical concepts. Strictly speaking, these are indefinables, although it is possible to give some elucidation or explanation of them. But, second, all of these indefinables have ontological status. Hence the inquiry into the nature and number of the logical concepts is not merely a linguistic one. Russell is very explicit on this matter. He writes: "The discussion of indefinables . . . is the endeavour to see clearly, and to make others see clearly, the *entities* concerned, in order that the mind may have that kind of acquaintance with them which it has with redness or the taste of pine-

---

[1] Bertrand Russell, *The Principles of Mathematics*, 2nd ed. (New York: W. W. Norton, 1964), p. xv.
[2] *Ibid.*, p. xv.

apple."[3] Thus in our inquiry we are concerned with what entities are involved with regard to the fundamental logical concepts. Furthermore, since these are indefinables, we shall be seeking the ultimate and irreducible entities which constitute the subject matter of the philosophy of logic.

In the opening sentence of Chapter I, Russell writes: "Pure mathematics is the class of all propositions of the form '*p* implies *q*', where *p* and *q* are propositions containing one or more variables, the same in the two propositions, and neither *p* nor *q* contains any constants except logical constants."[4] We are not now concerned with the adequacy of this definition. (Russell later recognized that it is too narrow and revised it in the Introduction to the second edition.) Our question has to do with the logical constants: What are they? Russell goes on to say that "logical constants are all notions definable in terms of the following: implication, the relation of a term to the class of which it is a member, the notion of *such that*, the notion of relation, and such further notions as may be involved in the general notion of propositions of the above form."[5] Russell is not always careful in distinguishing symbols from their references. But in view of the passage I quoted above (referring to entities) we may assume that, by 'logical constants', Russell is referring, not to the *signs* for implication, class-membership, etc., but to whatever entities are referred to by such signs. Immediately following the passage I quoted above, Russell acknowledges the difficulty in getting ourselves or others to "see clearly" the entities concerned, and says that it is "easier to know that there must be such entities than actually to perceive them."[6] These frequent references to entities or to concepts—which, as we shall see, are also entities—make it clear that, for Russell, logical constants are not mere words but the ontological simples indicated by logical terms.

In a later passage, Russell enlarges the class of logical constants (or indefinables) to include: formal implication, material implication, the relation of a term to a class of which it is a member, the notion of such that, the notion of relation, and truth.[7] Russell also later adds proposi-

---

[3] *Ibid.*, my italics.
[4] *Ibid.*, p. 3.
[5] *Ibid.*
[6] *Ibid.*, p. xv.
[7] *Ibid.*, p. 11.

tional functions and classes to this list.[8] And still later he speaks of denoting and all the ways of denoting as primitives.[9]

Now since all of these are primitive logical constants, strictly speaking, they cannot be defined. Or, as Russell says, "the logical constants themselves are to be defined only by enumeration, for they are so fundamental that all the properties by which the class of them might be defined presuppose some terms of the class."[10] But why can we not define, say, implication? (or better, 'implies'?) One can put forth what appears to be a definition: 'If p implies q, then if p is true then q is true'—that is, the truth of p implies the truth of q. Similarly, 'If p implies q, then if q is false then p is false'—that is, the falsity of q implies the falsity of p. But these are merely "new implications" and not a definition of implication.[11] But why can we not define implication (or 'implies') as follows: ' 'p implies q' = df. 'either p is false or q is true' '? Russell replies: It is true that 'p is false or q is true' is equivalent to 'p implies q'. But equivalence means mutual *implication*. Hence, "this still leaves implication fundamental, and not definable in terms of disjunction."[12] On the other hand, Russell holds that disjunction is definable in terms of implication.[13] He holds the same for negation.[14] Apart from the difficulties in Russell's "definitions," there are many problems connected with the widely accepted view that certain logical terms are definable via others.[15] One might also argue that Russell's view suffers from the failure to provide any criterion for distinguishing logical from nonlogical terms.

To sum up the discussion thus far: According to Russell, logical terms do have ontological status. They refer to logical constants which are entities capable of being grasped by our minds. Those logical terms which represent indefinables cannot be defined except in the sense of what is (misleadingly) called definition by enumeration (e.g., implication, class-membership, etc.). Other logical terms can be defined via the primitives (e.g., 'or' via 'implies'). The subject matter of logic,

[8] *Ibid.*, pp. 13, 18.
[9] *Ibid.*, p. 27.
[10] *Ibid.*, pp. 8–9.
[11] *Ibid.*, p. 14.
[12] *Ibid.*, p. 15.
[13] *Ibid.*, p. 17.
[14] *Ibid.*, p. 18.
[15] For an account of some of these difficulties, see Gustav Bergmann, *Logic and Reality* (Madison: University of Wisconsin Press, 1964), Chapters 2–4.

then, consists not of mere words, but of those notions or entities which such words refer to.

II

Thus far, in my consideration of (3) and (4) I have been concerned only with questions pertaining to *logical terms*. Before taking up Russell's later views on this issue, let us examine Russell's early views on those other questions in (3) and (4) which pertain to logical *syntax*. Russell devotes some very difficult and confusing chapters to this topic in *The Principles of Mathematics*. He says that he will take up some problems of "philosophical grammar."[16] Perhaps some of what follows will be more evident if we bear in mind a principle upon which Russell explicitly relies in this work, namely: "Every word occurring in a sentence must have *some* meaning."[17] The reason given for this is that "a meaningless sound could not be employed in the more or less fixed way in which language employs words."[18]

After discussing the difference between grammatical distinctions on the one hand and logical or philosophical distinctions on the other, Russell introduces his puzzling notion of a term. We are told that a term is "whatever may be an object of thought, or may occur in any true or false proposition, or can be counted as *one*."[19] He says that 'term' is synonymous with the words 'unit', 'individual', and 'entity'. Thus "every term has being, i.e., *is* in some sense."[20] From this it follows that "a man, a moment, a number, a class, a relation, a chimaera, or anything else that can be mentioned, is sure to be a term."[21] Russell then says that a term has all the properties commonly assigned to substances or substantives. Thus, every term is a "logical subject." Furthermore "every term is immutable and indestructible."[22] Each term is numerically identical with itself and numerically diverse from every other term. Russell then distinguishes between two kinds of terms: *things* and *concepts*. Things are indicated by proper names, whereas concepts are designated by all other words. Furthermore, among con-

16 *Ibid.*, p. 42.
17 *Ibid.*
18 *Ibid.*
19 *Ibid.*, p. 43.
20 *Ibid.*
21 *Ibid.*
22 *Ibid.*, p. 44.

cepts, Russell distinguishes those which are indicated by adjectives from those which are indicated by verbs. The former he refers to as *predicates* or *class-concepts;* the latter are almost always *relations.*

Russell then introduces a discussion of propositions and maintains that, for many propositions, it is possible to distinguish the subject of the proposition and an assertion about that subject. Russell then at first proposes to use the expression 'term' in 'term of a proposition' to designate those terms which can only be subjects of a proposition. Thus take the proposition that Socrates is human. It has one term; the other two terms are a verb and a predicate. But Russell is not consistent on this point. Later he insists that concepts are terms and that they are no less substantial than substantives are.

Russell's usage here is confusing. One might be inclined to think that he is distinguishing between terms as terms of a proposition or sentence and terms as referents. Thus we might say (if this were so) that the subject term of a proposition indicates a thing, and the predicate term of a proposition indicates a concept—either a class-concept or a relation. But this cannot be what Russell intends. For he says that "predicates . . . *are* concepts"[23] not 'predicates indicate concepts'. Furthermore he says "Socrates *is* a thing"[24] not ' 'Socrates' indicates a thing'. Further, we are told that the reason why Socrates is a thing is that "Socrates can never occur otherwise than as a term in a proposition."[25] Note that it is Socrates and not his name which occurs in a proposition. Hence we cannot defend any view by which (according to Russell) terms and propositions are linguistic whereas things and concepts are their referents. Terms are things or concepts. And propositions include things and concepts as their parts. Propositions do not contain words. They contain "the entities indicated by words."[26] But if propositions include things and concepts, then does Russell equate propositions with actual states of affairs or facts? No. For one thing, terms can occur in false propositions. Presumably there are no false facts.[27] Second, terms are immutable and indestructible. Hence actual states of affairs which are not eternal, etc., cannot consist of terms.

To summarize: According to Russell, every word of a sentence

[23] *Ibid.*, p. 45, my italics.
[24] *Ibid.*, my italics.
[25] *Ibid.*
[26] *Ibid.*, p. 47.
[27] *Ibid.*, p. 46.

must have a meaning.[28] Its meaning is the *referent* of the word. These referents are called *terms*. Every term has being. Anything that can be mentioned is a term—whether a man or a chimaera. Each term is immutable and indestructible. There are two kinds of terms—things and concepts. Terms are terms of propositions; they occur in propositions. Terms which are concepts are just as substantial and real as those which are things. Propositions do not contain words, but contain those entities represented by words. That is, a proposition combines eternal and immutable entities.

But all this seems very odd and leads to a genuine difficulty. Take a singular proposition. Upon Russell's analysis, it is not a series of words (a sentence) but consists in an eternal and immutable thing related to an eternal and immutable concept. But suppose I utter the sentence 'Socrates is mortal'. Apart from the problem as to how the sentence is related to the proposition, presumably what I intend to assert by it is the claim that a noneternal thing has a certain property! How can I do this if all terms are immutable and indestructible entities? Russell indicates part of the answer in his discussion of 'I met a man in the street'. If I assert this, I am referring to an actual creature of flesh and blood, not some eternal, indestructible entity. How do I do this? According to Russell, the proposition contains the concept man, but it is not *about* that concept. This *concept denotes* a particular being, the existent man, and by so denoting, the proposition is about that existent man.[29] Apparently, then, words do not denote, only concepts do. Thus we may say that the sentence 'I met a man in the street' indicates a proposition, i.e., a relation of eternal entities. One of these entities is the concept man. Yet the proposition is not about the concept, but about the particular man I met. And the proposition is about that man by virtue of the fact that the *concept, a man*, denotes that particular man.

Once again, Russell's view is: All words must have meanings by virtue of standing for something other than themselves. These referents are terms. Propositions contain, not words, but the entities, i.e., terms, indicated by words. On the other hand certain concepts such as *a man* may have meaning in another sense in that they may denote noneternal things, such as actual bipeds.

28 *Ibid.*, p. 42.
29 *Ibid.*, p. 47.

III

I shall turn now to a somewhat later work of Russell's, one which is of great importance for the philosophy of logic, his "The Philosophy of Logical Atomism."[30] Russell claims that he is going to put forth a certain logical doctrine and on the basis of this a metaphysics, namely, logical atomism. According to Russell, logical atomism is "the view that you can get down in theory, if not in practice, to ultimate simples out of which the world is built, and that those simples have a kind of reality not belonging to anything else."[31] Russell states that this view is called *logical* atomism because the atoms and their components which are arrived at as a result of analysis are logical atoms and not physical atoms.[32] This ontology is then linked with a certain method, that of analysis. According to Russell, we start with data which are undeniable but which are vague and ambiguous. "The process of sound philosophizing . . . consists mainly in passing from those obvious, vague, ambiguous things . . . to something precise, clear, definite, which by reflection and analysis we find is involved in the vague thing we start from, and is . . . the real truth of which that vague thing is a shadow."[33]

What are these atoms which we "get down" to, and what are their components? The atoms are of two main kinds: *facts* and *beliefs*. Or, since beliefs are a type of fact, we might call them nonintentional and intentional facts. Facts are not particular things, but what whole sentences refer to. They are objective and part of the real world. In addition to the major division already referred to, Russell has many ways of classifying and subdividing facts. (a) There are singular facts (e.g., the fact referred to by 'this is white') and general facts (those referred to by universal propositions). (b) There are also positive and negative facts. (c) There are logical (completely general) and nonlogical facts. All of the facts thus far mentioned fall under nonlogical facts. A completely general fact of logic would be, for example, the fact

---

[30] Russell, "The Philosophy of Logical Atomism," in *Logic and Knowledge*, ed. R. C. Marsh (New York: Macmillan, 1956), pp. 177–281. This work consists of eight lectures given in 1918.

[31] *Ibid.*, p. 270.

[32] *Ibid.*, p. 179.

[33] *Ibid.*, pp. 179–180.

referred to by 'For every x, if x is a member of A and A is included in B, then x is a member of B'.[34]

Now it may seem that the end result of analysis consists in arriving at these various kinds of facts. But this is not so. Facts are not the *ultimate* ontological simples, for they are complex entities, of the form ϕx, xRy, etc. The ultimate simples are those which make up facts, namely, particulars on the one hand and qualities and relations on the other. But if the latter are the ontological simples, why bring in facts at all? The answer which Russell gives is that facts are essential in ontology. To do ontology is to give an account of the world. In order to give that account, one cannot simply enumerate the various kinds of things—particulars, qualities, and relations. Particulars have qualities and stand in relations. That they have qualities and relations are facts. Hence facts must be brought in if we wish to give a complete account of the world.[35] Another reason is merely suggested for holding that facts as well as components are needed in ontology. It is this: strictly speaking, the distinction beween simples and complexes holds only for singular facts. General facts cannot be analyzed into their constituents in the way in which the fact that this is white can be analyzed as containing an individual named by 'this' and a quality or universal named by 'white'.

Thus far we have dealt only with atomic facts—using the term in a broad sense.[36] Or if we limit atomic facts to singular facts, then thus far we have spoken only of atomic and general facts. But the use of 'atomic' suggests that there might also be *molecular* facts. Are there such compound facts? Russell's answer is not entirely clear. At first he claims that there are no molecular facts in the sense of disjunctive facts, etc., but there are *negative* facts. There are, of course, molecular propositions[37] of the form 'p or q', 'if p, then q', 'p and q', etc., but no molecular facts. About the only argument which Russell gives for this claim is this: "I do not suppose there is in the world a single disjunctive fact corresponding to 'p or q'. It does not look plausible that in the actual objective world there are facts going about which you could describe as 'p or q'." But he adds: "But I would not lay too much stress on what strikes one as plausible: it is not a thing you can

34 *Ibid.*, pp. 182–184.
35 *Ibid.*, p. 183.
36 *Ibid.*, p. 199.
37 In this work, by 'proposition' Russell means sentence.

rely on altogether."[38] Russell opts for the view that the truth or falsity of a proposition of the form of '*p* or *q*' depends on *two* facts and not a single disjunctive fact. I shall shortly bring up an objection to Russell's view—one which arises (as he saw) from within his own position.

We have seen that, although Russell denies that there are molecular facts, nevertheless he insists that there are negative facts. Russell's main argument has to do with the case of false positive propositions. For example, take the false and positive proposition 'Socrates is alive'. What makes it false? According to Russell, "it is false because of a fact in the real world,"[39] the fact of Socrates' *not* being alive. An alternative view, that what makes a false positive proposition false is there being *no fact at all* (rather than a negative fact), apparently never occurred to Russell.

Let us turn now to a consideration of general facts. If Russell was prepared to throw out molecular facts, why does he insist on there being general facts? First, if there were no general facts, then (*A*) 'Everything is mortal' would be equivalent to (*B*) '*a* is mortal and *b* is mortal . . . and *n* is mortal'. But you cannot arrive at (*A*) unless you have the proposition: '*All* men are among those I enumerated'. Hence, "You can never arrive at a general proposition by inference from particular propositions alone. You will always need at least one general proposition in your premises."[40] But one might object: "This only shows that there must be general *propositions*. Why must there also be general *facts*?" Russell answers: "When you have enumerated all the atomic facts in the world, it is a further fact about the world that those are all the atomic facts there are about the world, and that is just as much an objective fact *about* the world as any of them are."[41]

I now turn to the difficulty which I mentioned above. The acceptance of general (universal) facts seems to imply the necessity for molecular facts as well. For example, take the proposition (*A*) 'All humans are mortal'. This has the form (*A'*) '(*x*) (if *x* is human, then *x* is mortal)'. By universal instantiation we get the proposition (*B*) 'If Socrates is human, then Socrates is mortal'. If (*A*) or (*A'*) refers to a general fact, then the question arises: Why doesn't (*B*) refer to a

[38] *Ibid.*, p. 209.
[39] *Ibid.*, p. 214.
[40] *Ibid.*, p. 235.
[41] *Ibid.*, p. 236.

molecular fact? Russell answers: "I do not feel sure that you could not get round that difficulty. . . . If it cannot be got round, we shall have to admit molecular facts."[42]

I mentioned above that, for Russell, there are also completely general facts of logic which are referred to by logical propositions. Since this topic more properly comes under the heading of those questions which I have designated as (1) and (2), I shall defer consideration of it until later.

IV

I have thus far examined the structure of Russell's ontology as presented in the logical atomism lectures. Let us now specifically take up Russell's views regarding our main questions (3) and (4). First, what is Russell's view regarding the ontological status of logical terms? I shall separate the question into two parts, the first part dealing with 'not' and the second dealing with the other logical terms.

At first glance it might appear that Russell holds that 'not' has ontological status because of his espousal of negative facts. But that would be an erroneous inference. For Russell introduces negative facts to account for the falsity of false, positive propositions, not to account for negative propositions. As we saw above, he holds that the only thing that can account for the falsity of 'Socrates is alive' (a false positive proposition) is the negative fact of Socrates' not being alive. In Russell's view, a negative proposition, whether true or false, does not require a negative fact in order to account for its truth or falsity. It merely requires the same fact as the unnegated proposition. How can this be? The answer Russell gives is: "There are *two* propositions corresponding to each fact."[43] Let us take it as a fact that Socrates is dead. Then we have two different propositions which could be uttered: 'Socrates is dead' and 'Socrates is not dead'. According to Russell, there is *one* fact in the world which makes the one true and the other false. But although there is in each case only one fact, and for each fact two propositions, one true and the other false, there are (according to Russell) two different *relations* that a proposition may have to a fact: "the one the relation that you may call being true to

42 *Ibid.*, p. 237.
43 *Ibid.*, p. 187.

the fact, and the other its being false to the fact. Both are essentially logical relations which may subsist between the two."[44] Again, there are many problems here. Precisely what are these two relations? Why not hold that in the case of a negative false proposition, there is no relation to a fact at all? Etc. I shall not stop to consider all these difficulties but merely point out that, in Russell's view, he sees no need to hold that negation has ontological status. But of course the relation, being false to a fact, must have such status. One might wonder whether the latter is any more plausible than the former.

Let us turn now to the remaining logical constants—'and', 'or', etc. There are two passages in which Russell explicitly denies that such terms have ontological status. In the first, while speaking about the features of a logically perfect language (a topic which I shall treat at length later) he says that, in such a language, each word will name one and only one simple object—except for words such as 'or', 'not', etc., "which have a different function."[45] In the second, after introducing the customary truth-table for inclusive disjunction, Russell says: "You must not look about the real world for an object which you can call 'or' and say, 'Now, look at this. This is "or".' There is no such thing."[46] Unlike descriptive terms, which get their meaning by referring to objects, the meaning of disjunction, etc., is explained by the truth-tables for such terms. To be sure, the truth-tables may (as Russell says) explain the meaning of 'or', etc., but this is not incompatible with the thesis that logical terms may have ontological status, even if their "mode of being" is not that of objects, the referents of descriptive terms.

V

Let us now turn to another question which occurs in (3)–(4). What, if anything, about the world is indicated by logical syntax? Russell's answer is: a great deal. However, for Russell, this is not true for any natural languages, all of which contain logical imperfections. But it does hold with regard to a logically perfect language. What are the features of such a language? First, there is an isomorphism or identity of structure between any proposition and the fact it repre-

[44] *Ibid.*
[45] *Ibid.*, p. 197; cf. p. 196.
[46] *Ibid.*, p. 210.

sents. "The objective complexity in the world . . . is mirrored by the complexity of propositions." Second, the words of a logically perfect language "correspond one by one with the components of the corresponding fact"—except for logical words. There is exactly "one word and no more for every simple object." Third, anything that is not simple can be expressed by a combination of simple terms. Fourth, the logical structure of facts which are asserted or denied may be seen "at a glance." Fifth, the vocabulary of any such language will be "very largely private to one speaker."[47] As an example of such a language, Russell refers to the syntax of *Principia Mathematica* supplemented by a "vocabulary," that is, a set of descriptive terms all of which refer to sense-data and their properties.[48]

It is evident that Russell relies on two principles, both of which are made explicit in the lectures. The first is the reference theory of meaning, according to which the meaning of a term is the object to which it refers.[49] The second is the principle of acquaintance, according to which a simple term is meaningful if and only if it refers to an object of direct acquaintance; and a complex term is meaningful if and only if it is analyzable into meaningful simple terms.[50]

What features of the world, then, are expressed by the syntactical features of a logically perfect language? First, as we have seen, the syntactical structure of any sentence mirrors the objective structure of the fact it represents. A proposition of the form 'Fx', for example, 'This is white', represents the fact of an individual having a quality. A proposition of the form 'xRy', for example 'a is to the left of b', represents that an individual stands in a relation to another individual.[51] Second, the geometrical shapes and/or syntactical features are representative of the two main ontological kinds, individuals, and characters (including relational ones). If we call qualities monadic relations, then a character is always indicated by a relational sign, whereas an individual is indicated by a proper name, the sign(s) for the term(s) of a relation.[52] Third, certain expressions do not, in isolation, stand for any referents. Upon a proper analysis of propositions in which they occur, they are not in fact actual constituents of such

47 *Ibid.*, pp. 197–198.
48 *Ibid.*, p. 198.
49 *Ibid.*, p. 186.
50 *Ibid.*, pp. 196, 194–195.
51 *Ibid.*, p. 198.
52 *Ibid.*, pp. 198–200.

propositions. These expressions are known as "incomplete symbols." Definite descriptions and class-signs are among the most important examples of such symbols.[53]

Since Russell's theory of descriptions is a familiar one, I shall be brief regarding it. One of the reasons for formulating the theory is to account for the problem of what I shall call apparent names. Consider the significant and true proposition 'Romulus did not exist'. Russell says: "If Romulus himself entered into our statement . . . [it] would be nonsense, because you cannot have a constituent of a proposition which is nothing at all. Every constituent has got to be there as one of the things in the world, and therefore if Romulus himself entered into the propositions that he existed or that he did not exist, both these propositions could not only not be true, but could not be even significant, unless he existed. That is obviously not the case." Hence, "although it *looks* as if Romulus were a constituent of that proposition, that is really a mistake."[54] Russell's account is thoroughly confusing. Since propositions are merely symbols for him in this work, what he intends to say is that the term 'Romulus' does not actually function as a proper name of an individual in 'Romulus does not exist'. Instead of being a name, 'Romulus' is a "truncated description" standing for "the person who did such and such things," or "the person who was called 'Romulus'."[55] This is not a matter of replacing one type of name with another type of name. Russell argues that a definite description (a phrase of the form 'the so-and-so') cannot be a name. There are three main arguments presented by Russell for this claim.

(1) Take Russell's example, 'the author of *Waverley*'. One can understand the meaning of this complex symbol even if one had never heard it before, as long as one had known the meaning of 'the', 'author', 'of', and '*Waverley*'. But one could not understand the meaning of a proper name (e.g., 'Scott') if one had not heard it before, because "to know the meaning of a name is to know who it is applied to."[56] (2) If 'the author of *Waverley*' were a name, then the proposition 'Scott is the author of *Waverley*' would be like the proposition 'Scott is Sir Walter'. That is, its truth would not depend on any other fact except the fact that a certain person was *called* 'the author of *Waverley*'. A name is merely what a man is called. But Scott was the

[53] *Ibid.*, pp. 241–254.
[54] *Ibid.*, p. 242.
[55] *Ibid.*, p. 243.
[56] *Ibid.*, p. 244.

author of *Waverley* even when no one called him thus. And further-more he was the author only by virtue of having written *Waverley* and not because someone may have called him the author. (3) If 'the author of *Waverley*' were a name, then 'Scott is the author of *Waverley*' would have to be either false or tautologous upon substituting a proper name for the definite description. If we substitute either 'Scott' or 'Sir Walter', we get a tautology, either 'Scott is Scott' or 'Scott is Sir Walter'. Whereas if we substitute a name for anyone who is not Scott we get a falsehood. Hence 'Scott is the author of *Waverley*' cannot be a tautologous identity statement.[57]

From this it follows that when a definite description occurs in a proposition, "there is no constituent of that proposition correspond-ing to that description as a whole. In the true analysis of the proposi-tion, the description is broken up and disappears."[58] Upon the correct analysis, the proposition 'The author of *Waverley* exists' says two things: 'There is at least one thing which is author of *Waverley* and there is at most one'. 'The author of *Waverley* is human' adds to the preceding 'and that thing is human'. The logical translation is familiar, hence I omit all the details.[59]

Definite descriptions constitute one class of "incomplete symbols," that is, symbols which have no meaning in isolation but acquire mean-ing only in a context, the context of a proposition, but which do not refer to any constituents corresponding to them.[60] Other incomplete symbols are symbols for classes and for relations taken in extension. All have a meaning in use and do not have any meaning in isolation. That is, they do not stand for any entities in the world. Class symbols are introduced as *defined* signs—definable via propositional functions. By this means, a statement which appears to be about a class is actually a statement about a propositional function being satisfied. "In that way you find that all the formal properties that you desire of classes, all their formal uses in mathematics, can be obtained without supposing . . . that there are such things as classes, without supposing, that is . . . that a proposition in which symbolically a class occurs, does in fact contain a constituent corresponding to that symbol."[61]

57 *Ibid.*, pp. 244–247.
58 *Ibid.*, p. 248.
59 *Ibid.*, pp. 249–252. See also the Introduction to Russell and A. N. Whitehead, *Principia Mathematica* (Cambridge: The University Press, 1910).
60 *Ibid.*, p. 253.
61 *Ibid.*, p. 266.

Russell's treatment of these issues in *Introduction to Mathematical Philosophy*[62] is very similar to that in "The Philosophy of Logical Atomism." Hence I shall not repeat the points which I have made above.[63]

VI

Thus far, still limiting the discussion to questions (3) and (4), I have examined Russell's views in *The Principles of Mathematics* (1903) and "The Philosophy of Logical Atomism" (1918). Let us now turn to some later works of Russell's and consider his position with regard to these same questions.

I shall begin with the Introduction to the second edition of *The Principles of Mathematics* (1938). First, let us again start with Russell's views about the logical constants. Russell states that there are three main questions to ask with regard to the logical constants. "First, are there such things? Second, how are they defined? Third, do they occur in the propositions of logic?"[64]

One. Are there logical constants? Russell says that in one sense of this question, the answer is clearly yes. He makes but does not explain a distinction between a logical proposition and its symbolic expression. In the latter, there clearly are certain words or signs which "play a constant part, i.e., make the same contribution to the significance of propositions wherever they occur."[65] Examples are words such as 'or', 'and', 'not', 'if-then', etc. He goes on to say: "In some cases, this is fairly obvious: not even the most ardent Platonist would suppose that the perfect 'or' is laid up in heaven, and that the 'or's' here on earth are imperfect copies of the celestial archetype."[66] Russell then criticizes his earlier interpretation of the thesis that 'every word occurring in a sentence must have some meaning', whereby this was construed to mean that every word must name some term or entity. He says: "That a word 'must have *some* meaning'—the word, of course, being not gibberish, but one which has an intelligible use—is not always true

[62] Russell, *Introduction to Mathematical Philosophy* (London: Allen & Unwin, 1919), Chapters 13–18.
[63] See also Russell, *Our Knowledge of the External World* (New York: W. W. Norton, 1929, New American Library, 1960), Chapter 2.
[64] Russell, *The Principles of Mathematics*, p. ix.
[65] *Ibid.*
[66] *Ibid.*

if taken as applying to the word in isolation. What is true is that the word contributes to the meaning of the sentence in which it occurs: but that is a very different matter."[67] Russell then suggests that logical terms are to be treated like descriptions and class-symbols, that is, as incomplete symbols: "their *uses* are defined, but they themselves are not assumed to mean anything at all."[68]

Two. If we now consider logical constants to be linguistic terms and moreover terms which do not refer to objects, how are they to be defined? Russell briefly draws a parallel to his way of dealing with such things as points of space, instants of time, and particles of mater by "substituting for them logical constructions composed of events." "I do not mean that statements apparently about points or instants . . . are false, but only that they need interpretation which shows that their linguistic form is misleading, and that when they are rightly analyzed, the pseudo-entities in question are found to be not mentioned in them."[69] For example, 'Time consists of instants' does not, according to Russell, mention time or instants. Rather it must be "interpreted." If we first define as the "contemporaries" of an event *x* those events which end after it begins and begin before it ends, and as the "initial contemporaries" of *x* those events which are not wholly later than any other contemporaries of *x*, then we may interpret 'Time consists of instants' as 'Given any event *x*, every event which is wholly later than some contemporary of *x* is wholly later than some initial contemporary of *x*'. Russell then merely adds: "A similar process of interpretation is necessary in regard to most if not all, purely logical constants."[70] But he does not explain how this is to be done or why it is true for some and not all logical constants.

Three. Do logical constants occur in propositions? Russell says that this question is more difficult than it seemed at first sight. But it is no longer clear what the question even means, since Russell has apparently abandoned the view of propositions as relations among eternal terms. He says that after we try to reduce the number of undefined logical constants, we find that at least two are needed as primitives—incompatibility ('not-both') and generality ('all'). He maintains that what was said earlier about 'or' applies to incompatibility as well, and

---

[67] *Ibid.*, p. x.
[68] *Ibid.*
[69] *Ibid.*, p. xi.
[70] *Ibid.*

adds that "it would seem absurd to say that generality is a constituent of a general proposition."[71]

Upon the basis of this discussion it seems clear that Russell now (1938) holds that logical constants are merely linguistic. Indeed, he says: "Logical constants, therefore, if we are to say anything definite about them, must be treated as part of the language, not as part of what the language speaks about. . . . It will still be true that no constants except logical constants occur in the verbal or symbolic expression of logical propositions, but it will not be true that these logical constants are names of objects, as 'Socrates' is intended to be."[72]

VII

Let us now turn to a somewhat later work of Russell's, *An Inquiry Into Meaning and Truth*.[73] Of the various issues which fall under our questions (3) and (4), I shall focus on the issue of logical terms and their meaning. Russell refers to terms such as 'not', 'or', 'but', etc., as conjunctions and maintains that conjunctions have no meaning "in isolation," but "presuppose the existence of language."[74] That is, they are attached to propositions ('not-p') or used to connect propositions ('p or q'). Russell holds that the same is true for 'all', 'some', and 'the', except that these three presuppose propositional functions rather than propositions.[75] All such logical terms are contrasted with object-words which are words the meaning of which "we learn by directly acquiring an association between the word and the thing."[76] Logical terms do not refer to objects presented to us in our experience. Nevertheless Russell holds that they may yet have a relation to experience. Consider 'or'. You cannot show anyone examples of 'or's in the world. If you ask a child 'Will you have pudding or pie?' and the child replies 'Yes', you cannot produce an entity which is pudding-or-pie. Yet 'or'

[71] *Ibid.*

[72] *Ibid.*, pp. xi–xii.

[73] Russell, *An Inquiry Into Meaning and Truth* (London: Allen & Unwin, 1940. Reprinted, Harmondsworth, England: Pelican, 1962). All references are to the latter edition.

[74] *Ibid.*, p. 61.

[75] *Ibid.*

[76] *Ibid.*, p. 66.

has a relation to experience, namely, the experience of choice.[77] Thus, *psychologically*, 'or' "corresponds to a state of hesitation."[78] "When we use the word 'or', we do so, as a rule, because we are in doubt and wish to decide on alternative."[79] But "nothing in the non-linguistic or non-psychological world is 'indicated' by a disjunction."[80] The same holds for other logical words such as 'not', 'some' or 'all'. They cannot be interpreted except to make reference to a state of mind.[81]

VIII

Thus far in my treatment of Russell's philosophy I have been concerned solely with questions (3) and (4). I now turn at last to questions (1) and (2). What is the nature of logical truth, and what entities if any are referred to by the truth of logic?

Surprisingly, little is said on these topics in *The Principles of Mathematics*. Of course, a good deal is said about *mathematical* propositions, namely that they are all deducible from a small number of fundamental logical principles.[82] But our question has to do with these fundamental (and indeed all) *logical* propositions. If we were given an adequate characterization of mathematical truths, then we could assume that the laws of logic have the same characteristics. Now Russell frequently says that the propositions of mathematics are of the form 'p implies q', that p and q contain variables, and that p and q contain no constants besides logical constants.[83] And at one point he says that the truths of mathematics are a priori. "The fact that all mathematical constants are logical constants, and that all the premises of mathematics are concerned with these, gives, I believe, the precise statement of what philosophers have meant in asserting that mathematics is *a priori*."[84] Since the propositions of mathematics are deducible from the logical "premises" (axioms?), presumably the latter must also be a priori, if the former are. But are the laws of logic analytic a priori or synthetic a priori, according to Russell? I think that the

[77] *Ibid.*, p. 69.
[78] *Ibid.*, p. 79.
[79] *Ibid.*, p. 81.
[80] *Ibid.*, p. 79.
[81] *Ibid.*, pp. 86, 88. Cf. pp. 200–202, 227.
[82] Russell, *The Principles of Mathematics*, pp. xv, 5.
[83] *Ibid.*, pp. 3, 8.
[84] *Ibid.*, p. 8.

customary answer is: analytic a priori, of course. But this is not as obvious as it may seem. Indeed, in a passage near the end of the book, Russell says that Kant rightly perceived that the propositions of mathematics are synthetic, even though he held that the propositions of logic are analytic. Russell comments: "It has since appeared that logic is just as synthetic as all other kinds of truth."[85] He does not however elaborate on this, and in a footnote he refers us to his *Philosophy of Leibniz*, Section 11.

Turning to that passage, we find a discussion of Leibniz's view that all the propositions of logic, arithmetic, and geometry are analytic.[86] Russell cites some examples of propositions which were held to be thus by Leibniz and says: "These instances suffer from one or other of two defects. Either the instances can be easily seen to be not truly analytic—this is the case, for example, in Arithmetic and Geometry —or they are tautologous, and so not properly propositions at all."[87] Examples are '*A* is *A*', 'The equilateral rectangle is a rectangle', etc. Russell then says: "Most of these instances assert nothing; the remainder can hardly be considered the foundations of any important truth. Moreover, those which are true presuppose . . . more fundamental propositions which are synthetic.[88] Russell then claims to show this by the following. Except for "pure tautologies" such as '*A* is *A*', the subject of analytic propositions must always be complex, a collection of attributes, and the predicate must be some part of this collection. But "this collection . . . must not be any haphazard collection, but a collection of compatible or jointly predicable predicates. . . . Now this compatibility, since it is presupposed by the analytic judgment, cannot itself be analytic."[89] Thus, according to Russell, propositions such as 'The equilateral rectangle is a rectangle' cannot possibly be "wholly analytic," for "they are logically subsequent to synthetic propositions asserting that the constituents of the subject are compatible."[90]

But this passage is confusing. Because the discussion is limited to Leibniz, the only examples considered are subject-predicate proposi-

[85] *Ibid.*, p. 457.

[86] Russell, *A Critical Exposition of the Philosophy of Leibniz* (London: Allen & Unwin, 1900, 1937), pp. 16–22. Russell acknowledges that Leibniz did not actually use the term 'analytic'.

[87] *Ibid.*, pp. 16–17.

[88] *Ibid.*, p. 17.

[89] *Ibid.*, p. 18.

[90] *Ibid.*, p. 22.

tions. Now even if we can accept Russell's argument that *these* are "logically subsequent" to synthetic propositions, this would not be a proof that *logic* is just as synthetic as all other kinds of truth, i.e., that all the laws of logic are synthetic. There may be good reasons for accepting such a thesis, but it does not seem to me that Russell has provided any.

IX

A very interesting discussion of questions (1) and (2) occurs in *The Problems of Philosophy* (1912).[91] In a chapter devoted to "Our Knowledge of General Principles," Russell maintains that there are a number of such principles which cannot be proved or disproved by experience, even though they are accepted and used in arguments which begin from what is experienced. Among such principles are the principle of induction, the truths of mathematics, and a number of "self-evident logical principles," such as *modus ponens*, the law of identity, etc.[92] Russell maintains that our knowledge of any such logical principle is a priori, i.e., "*logically* independent of experience (in the sense that experience cannot prove it)."[93] Russell then concludes that it is evident that "there are propositions known *a priori*, and that among them are the propositions of logic and pure mathematics."[94]

He then turns to the question 'How is such a priori knowledge possible?' He discusses and rejects the Kantian view that "anything we shall ever experience must show the characteristics affirmed of it in our *a priori* knowledge, because these characteristics are due to our own nature."[95] He then considers and also rejects the widely held view (from Kant on) that a priori knowledge is in some sense mental. More specifically, he examines the claim that the laws of logic (or certain ones among them) are laws of *thought*, "concerned rather with the way we must think than with any fact of the outer world."[96] He takes as an illustration the law of non-contradiction, 'Nothing can both be

---

[91] Russell, *The Problems of Philosophy* (Oxford: The University Press, 1959).
[92] *Ibid.,* pp. 71–72.
[93] *Ibid.,* p. 74.
[94] *Ibid.,* pp. 80–81.
[95] *Ibid.,* p. 86.
[96] *Ibid.,* p. 88.

and not be'. This is commonly intended to say that nothing can at the same time both have and not have a certain quality. For example, a tree cannot both be a beech and also not be a beech. In Russell's view, what makes it at first sight feasible to call this logical principle a law of thought is the fact that it is by thought rather than by any "outward observation" that we are convinced of its necessary truth. "When we have seen that a tree is a beech, we do not have to look again in order to ascertain whether it is also not a beech; thought alone makes us know that this is impossible."[97] Nevertheless, Russell maintains that this view that the principle is a law of thought is erroneous.

> What we believe when we believe the law of contradiction [*sic*], is not that the mind is so made that it must believe the law . . . . *This* belief is a subsequent result of psychological reflection, which presupposes the belief in the law of contradiction. The belief in the law . . . is a belief about things, not only about thoughts. It is not, e.g., the belief that if we *think* a certain tree is a beech, we cannot at the same time *think* that it is not a beech; it is the belief if the tree *is* a beech, it cannot at the same time *be* not a beech. Thus the law of contradiction is about things, and not merely about thoughts; . . . the law of contradiction itself is not a thought but a fact concerning things in the world.[98]

But why *must* this be so? "If this, which we believe when we believe the law of contradiction, were not true of the things in the world, the fact that we were compelled to *think* it true would not save the law . . . from being false; and this shows that the law is not a law of thought."[99]

Russell goes on to maintain that the same thing holds for all other a priori judgments; for example, 'two and two are four'. This is not a statement that our minds are so constituted as to believe that two and two are four. No fact regarding the constitution of our minds could make it *true* that two and two are four. "Thus our *a priori* knowledge . . . is not merely about the constitution of our minds, but is applicable to whatever the world may contain."[100]

But from Russell's discussion thus far, it would seem that the laws of logic and all other truths which are known a priori are about such things as ordinary objects in the world, beech trees, tables, etc. But

[97] *Ibid.*
[98] *Ibid.*, pp. 88–89.
[99] *Ibid.*, p. 89.
[100] *Ibid.*

Russell immediately denies this and says: "The fact seems to be that all our *a priori* knowledge is concerned with entities which do not, properly speaking, *exist*, either in the mental or in the physical world."[101] And what are these entities? Universals, things which do not exist in space or time, but which nevertheless *subsist* or have being.[102] Russell claims to have proved both that there are such entities as universals and that their reality is not merely mental. And he further claims that our knowledge of universals solves the problem of a priori knowledge, the problem as to how knowledge which is necessary and independent of experience yet also significant and about the real is possible. Such knowledge is possible because *"All a priori knowledge deals exclusively with the relations of universals."*[103] Since the laws of logic are known a priori, it follows that they are about universals, those timeless and unchanging entities in the realm of subsistence.

In answer to our questions (1) and (2) we may then summarize: According to Russell, the laws of logic are a priori and they are about real entities, universals. Are they analytic a priori or synthetic a priori? The answer clearly is: they are synthetic. Since they are about actual entities they are significant and not merely analytic. They do not merely concern the relations of ideas (in Hume's sense), nor are they merely verbal. They deal with objective relations among objectively real entities. But precisely how are the laws of logic about universals? What universals are related, for example, in the law of non-contradiction? We are given no answer to these questions. Most of Russell's illustrations concern mathematical truths such as 'two plus two equals four.' We are told that this deals exclusively with the universals, *two*, *four*, etc. Presumably in some analogous sense the laws of logic relate the universals *not*, *and*, *or*, etc.

X

Questions (1) and (2) are treated briefly in "On Scientific Method in Philosophy."[104] Russell maintains that philosophical propositions

101 *Ibid.*, pp. 88–90.
102 *Ibid.*, p. 100.
103 *Ibid.*, p. 103.
104 Russell, *Mysticism and Logic* (Garden City, N.Y.: Doubleday, 1957), pp. 93–119.

are propositions of logic and that the latter are general and "may be asserted of each individual thing." But "not only must they be concerned with all things, but they must be concerned with such properties of all things as do not depend upon the actual nature of the things that there happen to be, but are true of any possible world, independently of such facts as can only be discovered by our senses."[105] This means that logical propositions must be a priori, that is propositions which "can be neither proved nor disproved by empirical evidence," which "would be equally true however the actual world were constituted."[106] In being concerned with everything there is, such propositions must not mention any particular thing or predicate or relation. An example of such a proposition is: "If x is a member of the class a and every member of a is a member of β, then x is a member of the class β whatever x, a, and β may be."[107] A similar view is given in *Our Knowledge of the External World*.[108] However, in this work Russell holds that all such propositions of pure logic are self-evident as well as general.[109]

XI

Let us turn once again to the 1918 lectures, "The Philosophy of Logical Atomism," focusing now on (1) and (2). As we saw earlier, Russell makes a distinction between particular (or better: singular) facts and general facts, and also maintains that there are "the completely general facts of the sort that you have in logic, where there is no mention of any constituent whatever of the actual world, no mention of any particular thing or particular quality or particular relation, indeed . . . no mention of anything."[110] One of the chief characteristics of logical propositions, then, is that "they mention nothing." As an example of such a proposition, Russell cites: 'If one class is part of another, a term which is a member of the one is also a member of the other'. Russell says that all the words of any such statement of a logical proposition "really belong to syntax." That is, "they are words

[105] *Ibid.*, p. 106.
[106] *Ibid.*
[107] *Ibid.*, p. 107.
[108] Russell, *Our Knowledge of the External World*, pp. 50–53.
[109] *Ibid.*, p. 51.
[110] Russell, "The Philosophy of Logical Atomism," in *Logic and Knowledge*, p. 184.

merely expressing form or connexion, not mentioning any particular constituent of the proposition in which they occur."[111] This is a very puzzling passage. First, Russell seems here to *distinguish* words from propositions, whereas on the very next page he says that a proposition is merely a symbol and consists in words. Second, strictly speaking, Russell cannot maintain that there is no mention of anything in a logical proposition. If there are completely general facts of logic, and if logical propositions express such facts, then obviously logical propositions must mention general facts. It may be true that they do not refer to particular things, but it cannot be true that they refer to nothing. Hence we must search for some other characteristic by which to distinguish logical (or completely general) propositions from non-logical propositions.

Later, Russell offers another characteristic: Logical propositions (and propositional functions) "contain only variables and nothing else at all."[112] "Every logical proposition consists wholly and solely of variables, though it is not true that every proposition consisting wholly and solely of variables is logical."[113] But this won't do. First, as Russell realizes, by the second part of this statement, even if the first part were true, this would only mean that consisting wholly of variables is a necessary and not a sufficient condition for being a logical proposition. But second, is it true that logical propositions contain only variables and nothing else? Russell asks us to consider the stages of generalization in the following sequence:

$$\text{Socrates loves Plato}$$
$$x \text{ loves Plato}$$
$$x \text{ loves } y$$
$$x \, R \, y$$

He says: "When you have got to $x \, R \, y$, you have got a schema consisting only of variables, containing no constants at all."[114] But surely such schemata as '$x \, R \, y$' are not logical propositions, in the sense of being *truths* of logic. No, Russell says that "When you have got down to those formulas that contain only variables, like $x \, R \, y$, you are on the way to the sort of thing that you can assert in logic."[115]

111 *Ibid.*
112 *Ibid.*, p. 237.
113 *Ibid.*
114 *Ibid.*, p. 238.
115 *Ibid.*

He then gives as an example of a proposition of logic the following: (A) '$x\,R\,y$ implies that x belongs to the domain of R'. But does this contain only variables? Does it not contain 'belongs' and 'domain', etc.? Russell says no: "It is only the habit of using ordinary language that makes those words appear. They are not really there. That is a proposition of pure logic. It does not mention any particular thing at all. This is to be understood as being asserted whatever x and R and y may be. All the statements of logic are of that sort."[116] But this is thoroughly confusing. First, surely the occurrence of 'belongs' etc. in (A) is not just a matter of English or ordinary language. A symbolic translation of (A) would have to have some counterpart for 'belongs', 'implies', etc. and in order to even interpret (A), such terms would have to be constants and not variables. Suppose we transcribe (A) as

$$(A')\quad x\,R\,y \supset x\,\epsilon\,D\,{}^{\backprime}R.$$

Unless some terms were constants, how would we know that (A') is to be interpreted as (A) rather than as: '$x\,R\,y$ and x is identical with the so and so'? Hence, second, it is not obvious that the propositions of logic do not mention anything, even if they do not refer to particular things. Third, even if we clear up these difficulties and accept (A) as an example of a law of logic, surely not all laws of logic are of this sort. Assertions such as (A) seem to be laws only in the sense that they present logical forms, that is, syntactical principles. But they do not appear to be propositions in the sense in which we speak of the *laws* or *truths* of logic. Hence we must search for some other characteristic which holds of logical propositions which are laws of logic and not mere assertions of syntactical forms.

After several pages of wrestling with the issue, Russell comes up with such a characteristic. He says: "Everything that is a proposition of logic has got to be in some sense or other like a tautology."[117] But what does this mean? "It has got to be something that has some peculiar quality, which I do not know how to define, that belongs to logical propositions and not to others." He gives the following as examples of logical truths:

> If p implies q and q implies r, then p implies r.
> If all as are bs and all bs are cs, then all as are cs.
> If all as are bs, and x is an a, then x is a b.

[116] *Ibid.*, p. 239.
[117] *Ibid.*, p. 240.

And he says: "These are propositions of logic. They have a certain peculiar quality which marks them out from other propositions and enables us to know them *a priori*. But what exactly that characteristic is, I am not able to tell you."[118]

XII

In his *Introduction to Mathematical Philosophy* (1919),[119] Russell again takes up the question of the nature of logical truths. We are told that in logic we do not deal with any particular things or properties; rather "we deal formally with what can be said about *any* thing or *any* property."[120] He then asks the question, 'What are the constituents of a logical proposition?' He again considers propositions whose general form may be represented by '*x R y*' and says that "as a first approximation" we may accept the view that "*forms* are what enter logical propositions as their constituents."[121] He then states that one of the marks of a logical proposition is that it is concerned only with such forms. But this time he is more explicit in noting that logical propositions also contain symbols which "express" logical constants but then, oddly, claims that logical constants are "in essence the same thing" as forms.[122] He then puts forth as a necessary but not sufficient condition that all logical propositions "can be expressed wholly in terms of logical constants together with variables."[123] He then seeks for some further condition whereby we can have a criterion (both a necessary and a sufficient condition) for logical propositions. He first says that all logical propositions have a characteristic "which used to be expressed by saying that they were analytic, or that their contradictories were self-contradictory."[124] But this is not an adequate "mode of statement," for the law of contradiction is merely one among other laws of logic; and furthermore the proof that the denial of some proposition is self-contradictory requires other logical principles besides the law of contradiction. Russell nevertheless believes that the essential

---

118 *Ibid.*
119 Russell, *Introduction to Mathematical Philosophy* (London: Allen & Unwin, 1919).
120 *Ibid.*, p. 196; cf. p. 198.
121 *Ibid.*, p. 199.
122 *Ibid.*, p. 201.
123 *Ibid.*, p. 202.
124 *Ibid.*, p. 203.

characteristic of logical propositions that we are seeking "is the one which was felt, and intended to be defined, by those who said that it consisted in deducibility from the law of contradiction."[125] And he again refers to this characteristic as that of being a tautology.

Finally Russell puts forth a criterion for logical propositions. In addition to their being known a priori, they can be expressed wholly in terms of variables and logical constants, and they are all tautologous. But again he claims that he does not know how to define 'tautology', and he mentions in a footnote that his former pupil, Wittgenstein, was "working on the problem" but that he does not know whether Wittgenstein solved it.

XIII

I shall now briefly turn once again to the Introduction to the second edition of *The Principles of Mathematics*, this time stressing Russell's answers to questions (1) and (2). Russell again notes that all logical propositions are tautological and that their verbal expressions can contain no constants except logical constants.[126] Furthermore, he states that all logical propositions must be completely general, in the sense that they do not mention particular things or qualities, and that they must be true "in virtue of" their form. He now states that the latter characteristic is "the fundamental characteristic" of logical propositions but he concludes his discussion by saying: "I confess, however, that I am unable to give any clear account of what is meant by saying that a proposition is 'true in virtue of its form'."[127]

It seems clear from the context of this discussion, as well as that in the *Introduction to Mathematical Philosophy*, that Russell was groping for a criterion which was formulated later by W. V. Quine and which has been commonly accepted. According to this criterion, all logically true propositions are those in which only logical constants occur essentially and all other terms occur vacuously. (A term occurs essentially in a proposition if replacing it by another could turn the statement into a falsehood; otherwise it occurs vacuously.)[128] The

[125] *Ibid.*
[126] Russell, *The Principles of Mathematics*, pp. ix, xi.
[127] *Ibid.*, p. xii.
[128] W. V. Quine, *Mathematical Logic*, rev. ed. (New York: Harper & Row, 1951), p. 2

difficulty with this criterion is that it rests upon the notion of logical constant. But what is the criterion by which we may distinguish logical terms from nonlogical terms? Some (for example, Carnap) identify nonlogical terms with descriptive terms and then maintain that a term is a logical term if it is not a descriptive term. It is not clear that this criterion will serve to distinguish all logical from nonlogical terms. But if it does, then Quine's criterion for logical truths serves as the criterion which Russell was trying to formulate.

Epilogue

LOVE, KNOWLEDGE, AND PITY

by Bertrand Russell

THREE passions, simple but over-whelmingly strong, have governed my life: the longing for love, the search for knowledge, and unbearable pity for the suffering of mankind. These passions, like great winds, have blown me hither and thither, in a wayward course, over a deep ocean of anguish, reaching to the very verge of despair.

I have sought love, first, because it brings ecstasy—ecstasy so great that I would often have sacrificed all the rest of life for a few hours of this joy. I have sought it, next, because it relieves loneliness—that terrible loneliness in which one shivering consciousness looks over the rim of the world into the cold unfathomable lifeless abyss. I have sought it, finally, because in the union of love I have seen, in a mystic miniature, the prefiguring vision of the heaven that saints and poets have imagined. This is what I sought, and though it might seem too good for human life, this is what—at last—I have found.

With equal passion I have sought knowledge. I have wished to understand the hearts of men. I have wished to know why the stars shine. And I have tried to apprehend the Pythagorean power by which number holds sway above the flux. A little of this, but not much, I have achieved.

Love and knowledge, so far as they were possible, led upward

Reprinted with the kind permission of Little, Brown & Co., Atlantic Monthly Press, from Bertrand Russell, *The Autobiography of Bertrand Russell*, 1967.

toward the heavens. But always pity brought me back to earth. Echoes of cries of pain reverberate in my heart. Children in famine, victims tortured by oppressors, helpless old people a hated burden to their sons, and the whole world of loneliness, poverty, and pain make a mockery of what human life should be. I long to alleviate the evil, but I cannot, and I too suffer.

This has been my life. I have found it worth living, and would gladly live it again if the chance were offered me.

—From *The Autobiography of Bertrand Russell*

Selected Bibliography
WORKS ON BERTRAND RUSSELL

Compiled with the assistance of
G. Moor, R. Reed, and R. Birnbaum

Aiken, H. D. "Mr. Demos and the Dogmatism of Mr. Russell." *The Journal of Philosophy* 43 (1946): 214–217.

Aiken, L. W. *Bertrand Russell's Philosophy of Morals*. New York: Humanities Press, 1963.

Aldrich, V. C. Review of P. A. Schilpp, ed., *The Philosophy of Bertrand Russell*. *The Journal of Philosophy* 42 (1945): 594–607.

Ayer, A. J. Review of *My Philosophical Development*. *Spectator* 202 (1959): 703.

Benjamin, A. C. "Is Empiricism Self-Refuting?" *The Journal of Philosophy* 38 (1941): 568–573.

Bentley, A. F. "Logicians' Underlying Postulations; Russell's Approach." *Philosophy of Science* 13 (1946): 3–19.

Bergmann, Gustav. "Russell on Particulars." *The Philosophical Review* 56 (1947): 59–72. Reprinted in *The Metaphysics of Logical Positivism*, pp. 197–209. Madison: University of Wisconsin Press, 1954.

———. "Russell's Examination of Leibniz Examined." *Philosophy of Science* 49 (1956): 145–159. Reprinted in *Meaning and Existence*, pp. 155–188. Madison: University of Wisconsin Press, 1960.

———. "The Revolt Against Logical Atomism." *The Philosophical Quarterly* 7 (1957): 323–339, and 8 (1958): 1–13. Reprinted in *Meaning and Existence*, pp. 39–72. Madison: University of Wisconsin Press, 1960.

Berlin, I. Review of *History of Western Philosophy*. *Mind* 56 (1947): 151–166.

Black, Max. "Russell's Philosophy of Language." In Schilpp, ed., *The Philosophy of Bertrand Russell*, pp. 227–256.

Black, V. "Good Reasons and Reasonable Acts." *The Journal of Philosophy* 52 (1955): 181–189.

Boas, G. Review of *History of Western Philosophy. The Journal of Historical Ideas* 8 (1947): 117–123.

Bode, Boyd H. "Russell's Educational Philosophy." In Schilpp, ed., *The Philosophy of Bertrand Russell*, pp. 619–642.

Boodin, John Elaf. "Russell's Metaphysics." In Schilpp, ed., *The Philosophy of Bertrand Russell*, pp. 475–510.

Borkowski, Ludwik. "Reduction of Arithmetic to Logic Based on the Theory of Types." *Studia Logica* 8 (1958): 283–295.

Bouwsma, O. K. "Russell's Argument on Universals." *The Philosophical Review* 52 (1943): 193–199.

Brightman, E. S. "Russell's Philosophy of Religion." In Schilpp, ed., *The Philosophy of Bertrand Russell*, pp. 537–556.

Broad, C. D. "Is There Knowledge by Acquaintance?" *Proceedings of the Aristotelian Society*, Supplement 2 (1919): 206–220.

———. Review of *The Philosophy of Bertrand Russell. Mind* 16 (1947): 355–364.

Brown, H. C. "A Logician in the Field of Psychology." In Schilpp, ed., *The Philosophy of Bertrand Russell*, pp. 445–474.

Buchler, Justus. "Russell and the Principles of Ethics." In Schilpp, ed., *The Philosophy of Bertrand Russell*, pp. 511–536.

Butler, R. J. "The Scaffolding of Russell's Theory of Descriptions." *The Philosophical Review* 63 (1954): 350–364.

Caton, C. E. "Strawson on Referring." *Mind* 68 (1959): 539–544.

Chisholm, R. M. "Russell on the Foundations of Empirical Knowledge." In Schilpp, ed., *The Philosophy of Bertrand Russell*, pp. 419–444.

Church, Alonzo. "A Formulation of the Simple Theory of Types." *Journal of Symbolic Logic* 5 (1940): 56–68.

Cory, D. "Are Sense-Data in the Brain?" *The Journal of Philosophy* 45 (1948): 533–548.

Cross, R. N. Review of *History of Western Philosophy. Hibbert Journal* 45 (1947): 193–201.

Demos, R. "Mr. Russell and Dogmatism." *The Journal of Philosophy* 42 (1945): 589–594.

Dewey, John. "Propositions, Warranted Assertibility, and Truth." *The Journal of Philosophy* 38 (1941): 169–186.

Donagan, A. "Recent Criticisms of Russell's Analysis of Existence." *Analysis* 12 (1951–52): 132–137.

Edwards, Paul. "Bertrand Russell's Doubts about Induction." *Mind* 58 (1949): 141–163. Reprinted in A. Flew, ed., *Logic and Language*, pp. 59–84. Garden City, New York: Doubleday & Co., 1965.

Edwards, Paul; Alston, William P.; and Prior, A. N. "Russell, Bertrand Arthur William." In Paul Edwards, ed., *The Encyclopedia of Philosophy*, vol. 7 (New York: Macmillan, 1967), pp. 235–258.

Eisler, R. "Scientific Inference According to Bertrand Russell, K. R. Popper and Feliz Hausdorff." *Hibbert Journal* 47 (1949): 375–381.

Evans, M. "Naturally Immaterial"; reply to article in *Kenyon Review* by Bertrand Russell. *Sewanee Review* 51 (1943): 131–147.

Feibleman, James. "A Reply to Bertrand Russell's Introduction to the Second Edition of *The Principles of Mathematics*." In Schilpp, ed., *The Philosophy of Bertrand Russell*, pp. 155–174.

———. *Inside the Great Mirror; A Critical Examination of the Philosophy of Russell, Wittgenstein and Their Followers*. The Hague: M. Nijhoff, 1958.

Findlay, J. N. "Is There Knowledge by Acquaintance?" *Proceedings of the Aristotelian Society*, Supplement 23 (1949): 111–128.

Fritz, C. A. *Bertrand Russell's Construction of the External World*. London: Routledge & Kegan Paul, 1952.

Gale, R. M. "Russell's Drill Sergeant and Bricklayer and Dewey's Logic." *The Journal of Philosophy* 56 (1959): 401–406.

Geach, P. T. "Russell's Theory of Descriptions." *Analysis* 10 (1950): 84–88. Reprinted in M. Macdonald, ed., *Philosophy and Analysis*. New York: Barnes & Noble, 1954.

———. "Russell on Meaning and Denoting." *Analysis* 19 (1958–59): 69–72.

Gödel, Kurt. "Russell's Mathematical Logic." In Schilpp, ed., *The Philosophy of Bertrand Russell*, pp. 123–154.

Gotlind, E. *Bertrand Russell's Theories of Causation*. Upsala: 1952.

Ghyka, M. "Bertrand Russell and Scientific Philosophy." *Personalist* 28 (1947): 129–139.

Hallden, Sören. "Certain Problems Connected with the Definition of Identity and of Definite Descriptions Given in *Principia Mathematica*." *Analysis* 9 (1948–49): 29–33.

Hamilton, R. Review of *Philosophy and Politics*. *Hibbert Journal* 46 (1947):81–84.

Harre, R. "Dissolving the 'Problem' of Induction." *Philosophy* 32 (1957): 58–64.

Hart, H. L. A. "Is There Knowledge by Acquaintance?" *Proceedings of the Aristotelian Society*, Supplement 25 (1949).

Hartshorne, C. Review of Schilpp, ed., *The Philosophy of Bertrand Russell*. *Journal of Religion* 25 (1945): 280–284.

Hay, W. H. "Bertrand Russell on the Justification of Induction." *Philosophy of Science* 17 (1950): 266–267.

Hempel, Carl G. "On Russell's Phenomenological Constructionism." *The Journal of Philosophy* 58 (1966): 668–670.

Hochberg, Herbert. "Peano, Russell, and Logicism." *Analysis* 16 (1956): 118–120.

———. "Descriptions, Scope, and Identity." *Analysis* 18 (1957–58): 20–22.

———. "St. Anselm's Ontological Argument and Russell's Theory of Descriptions." *The New Scholasticism* 33 (1959): 319–330.

———. "Things and Descriptions." *American Philosophical Quarterly* 3 (1966): 1–9.

Hoensbroech, F. "On Russell's Paradox." *Mind* 48 (1939): 365–368.

Hook, Sidney. "Bertrand Russell's Philosophy of History." In Schilpp, ed., *The Philosophy of Bertrand Russell*, 643–678.

Hughes, G. E. "Is There Knowledge by Acquaintance?" *Proceedings of the Aristotelian Society*, Supplement 23 (1949): 91–110.

Jager, R. "Russell's Denoting Complex." *Analysis* 20 (1959–60): 53–62.

Jeffreys, H. "Bertrand Russell on Probability." *Mind* 59 (1950): 313–319.

Johnson, W. E. *Logic*, Pt. II. Cambridge: University Press, 1922. Chapters III and VI.

Kneale, W. C. "The Objects of Acquaintance." *Proceedings of the Aristotelian Society* 34 (1933–34): 187–210.

———. Review of *Human Knowledge*. *Mind* 58 (1949): 369–378.

Laird, John. "On Certain of Russell's Views Concerning the Human Mind." In Schilpp, ed., *The Philosophy of Bertrand Russell*, pp. 293–316.

Lejewsky, Czeslaw. "A Re-examination of Russell's Theory of Descriptions." *Philosophy* 35 (1960): 14–29.

Lewy, C. "On the 'Justification' of Induction." *Analysis* 6 (1938–39): 87–90.

Lindeman, E. D. "Russell's Concise Social Philosophy." In Schilpp, ed., *The Philosophy of Bertrand Russell*, pp. 557–578.

Linsky, Leonard. "Reference and Referents." In C. E. Caton, ed., *Philosophy and Ordinary Language*, pp. 74–89. Urbana: University of Illinois Press, 1962.

———. "Substitutivity and Descriptions." *The Journal of Philosophy* 58 (1966): 673–684.

———. *Referring*. London: Routledge & Kegan Paul, 1967. Chapter IV.

Lovejoy, A. O. *The Revolt Against Dualism*. Chicago: Open Court, 1930. Chapters VI and VII.

Malcolm, N. Review of *Human Knowledge: Its Scope and Limits*. *The Philosophical Journal* 59 (1950): 94–106.

Martin, R. M. "On the Berkeley-Russell Theory of Proper Names." *Philosophy and Phenomenological Research* 13 (1952–53): 221–231.

McGill, V. C. "Russell's Political and Economic Philosophy." In Schilpp, ed., *The Philosophy of Bertrand Russell*, pp. 21–54.

McKenney, J. L. "Concerning Russell's Analysis of Value Judgments." *The Journal of Philosophy* 55 (1958): 382–389.

McLendon, H. J. "Has Russell Answered Hume?" *The Journal of Philosophy* 49 (1952): 145–159.

———. "Has Russell Proved Naive Realism Self-Contradictory?" *The Journal of Philosophy* 53 (1956): 209–302.

Monro, D. H. "Russell's Moral Theories." *Philosophy* 35 (1960): 30–50.

Moore, G. E. "Is There Knowledge by Acquaintance?" *Proceedings of the Aristotelian Society*, Supplement 2 (1919): 179–193.

———. "Russell's 'Theory of Descriptions'." In Schilpp, ed., *The Philosophy of Bertrand Russell*, pp. 175–226.

———. *The Commonplace Book of G. E. Moore, 1919–1953*, Casimir Lewy, ed. London: Allen & Unwin, 1963. Notebook II, Item 4, and Notebook V, Item 13.

Nagel, Ernest. "Mr. Russell on Meaning and Truth." *The Journal of Philosophy* 38 (1941): 253–270.

———. "Russell's Philosophy of Science." In Schilpp, ed., *The Philosophy of Bertrand Russell*, pp. 317–350.

Pap, Arthur. "Logic, Existence and the Theory of Descriptions." *Analysis* 13 (1952–53): 97–111.

Parker, D. H. "Knowledge by Acquaintance." *The Philosophical Review* 54 (1945): 1–18.

Pears, D. *Bertrand Russell and the British Tradition in Philosophy*. New York: Random House, 1968.

———. "Logical Atomism: Russell and Wittgenstein." In A. J. Ayer, et al., *The Revolution in Philosophy*, pp. 41–55. London: Macmillan, 1956.

Popper, Karl R. and Hansdorff, F. "Scientific Inference According to Bertrand Russell." *Hibbert Journal* 47 (1949): 375–381.

Quine, W. V. "On the Axiom of Reducibility." *Mind* 45 (1936): 498–500.

———. "On the Theory of Types." *Journal of Symbolic Logic* 3 (1938): 125–139.

———. *From a Logical Point of View*. Cambridge, Mass.: Harvard University Press, 1953. Chapters I, V, and VI.

———. "Russell's Ontological Development." *The Journal of Philosophy* 63 (1966): 657–667.

———. *Set Theory and Its Logic*. Cambridge, Mass.: Harvard University Press, 1963, 241–265.

Quinton, A. "Russell's Philosophical Development." *Philosophy* 35 (1960): 1–13.

Ramsey, F. P. *The Foundations of Mathematics*. New York: Harcourt, 1931. Chapters I and II.

Reeves, J. W. "The Origin and Consequences of the Theory of Descriptions." *Proceedings of the Aristotelian Society* 34 (1933–34): 211–230.

Reichenbach, H. "Conversation between Bertrand Russell and David Hume." *The Journal of Philosophy* 46 (1949): 545–549.

———. "Bertrand Russell's Logic." In Schilpp, ed., *The Philosophy of Bertrand Russell*, pp. 21–54.

Ritchie, A. D. Review of *History of Western Philosophy*. *Mind* 55 (1946): 256–262.

———. Review of *Human Knowledge: Its Scope and Limits*. *Nature* 163 (1949): 267–268.

Russell, L. J. Review of *An Inquiry into Meaning and Truth*. *Mind* 53 (1944): 332–340.

Schilpp, P. A., ed. *The Philosophy of Bertrand Russell*. Evanston: Northwestern University Press; 3rd ed., New York: Harper & Row, 1963.

Schoenman, Ralph. *Bertrand Russell, The Philosopher of the Century*. Boston: Little, Brown, 1967.

Searle, J. R. "Russell's Objections to Frege's Theory of Sense and Reference." *Analysis* 18 (1957–58): 137–142.

Sellars, Wilfrid F. "Presupposing." *The Philosophical Review* 63 (1954): 197–215.

Shearn, Martin. "Whitehead and Russell's Theory of Types—A Reply." *Analysis* 11 (1950–51): 45–48.

———. "Russell's Analysis of Existence." *Analysis* 11 (1950–51): 124–131.

Sommers, Fred. "Types and Ontology." In P. F. Strawson, ed., *Philosophical Logic*, pp. 138–169. Oxford: Oxford University Press, 1967.

Smart, H. R. "Cassirer versus Russell." *Philosophy of Science* 10 (1943): 167–175.

Smart, J. J. C. "Whitehead and Russell's Theory of Types." *Analysis* 10 (1949–50): 93–96.

———. "The Theory of Types Again." *Analysis* 11 (1950–51): 131–133.

Smullyan, A. F. "Modality and Description." *Journal of Symbolic Logic* 13 (1948): 31–37.

———. Review of *Logic and Knowledge*. *The Philosophical Review* 67 (1958): 237–242.

Stace, W. T. "Russell's Neutral Monism." In Schilpp, ed., *The Philosophy of Bertrand Russell*, pp. 351–384.

Strawson, P. F. "On Referring." *Mind* 59 (1950): 320–344. Reprinted in Flew, ed., *Essays in Conceptual Analysis*, pp. 21–52. London: Macmillan, 1956.

———. "A Reply to Mr. Sellars." *The Philosophical Review* 63 (1954): 216–231.

———. "Identifying Reference and Truth-Values." *Theoria* 30 (1964): 96–118.

Thayer, H. S. "Two Theories of Truth: The Relation between the Theories of John Dewey and Bertrand Russell." *The Journal of Philosophy* 44 (1947): 516–527.

Ushenko, A. P. "Russell's Critique of Empiricism." In Schilpp, ed., *The Philosophy of Bertrand Russell*, pp. 385–417.

———. "Reply." *The Journal of Philosophy* 52 (1956): 819–820.

Wang, Hao. "Russell and Philosophy." *The Journal of Philosophy* 58 (1966): 670–673.

Warnock, G. J. *English Philosophy Since 1900*. London: Oxford, 1958. Chapter III.

Watson, G. "Bertrand Russell and Basic Propositions." *Personalist* 28 (1946): 140–146.

Whittaker, E. T. Review of *Philosophy of Bertrand Russell*. *Nature* 155 (1945): 128–131.

Wiener, Phillip R. "Method in Russell's Work on Leibniz." In Schilpp, ed., *The Philosophy of Bertrand Russell*, pp. 277–292.

Weitz, Morris. "Analysis and the Unity of Russell's Philosophy." In Schilpp, ed., *The Philosophy of Bertrand Russell*, pp. 55–122.

Wilson, N. L. "Description and Designation." *The Journal of Philosophy* 50 (1953): 369–383.

———. "In Defense of Proper Names against Descriptions." *Philosophical Studies* 4 (1953): 72–78.

Wisdom, John. "Bertrand Russell and Modern Philosophy." In *Philosophy and Psychoanalysis*, pp. 195–209. Oxford: Blackwell, 1953.

Wood, A. *Bertrand Russell, The Passionate Sceptic*. London: Allen & Unwin, 1957.

Index*

Analysis:
   primitives of, 35
   reconstruction and, 41, 51–57,
      141
   reduction and, 29, 400–406
Aristotle, 106

Bentham, J., 51
Bradley, F., 89–90
Bundling:
   problem of, 21
   theory of, 99–100

Carnap, R., 13
Cavell, S., 104–105
Church, A., 262
Classes:
   and concepts, 6
   as incomplete symbols, 6
   nature of, 374

Descriptions, 9–10, 320–322
   and individuals, 78–80
   and meaning, 245–248
   and ontology, 119, 429–430
   and particulars, 113

Descriptions (*continued*)
   elimination of, 227–229
   Frege on, 211–212, 258–261
   Meinong on, 120–127
   primary occurrence of, 226–
      229
   Russell on, 127–135, 257–258
   Strawson on, 223–225

Existentialism, 111–112
Extensionality, 376

Facts, 9, 11–12, 38
   and meaning, 211
   and reference, 232–235, 258–
      261
   atomic, 44–45
   relational, 93–94
   Russell on, 98–99, 210, 263–
      266
Functions, 7, 374–375
   and descriptions, 130–132
   and types, 376–377

Geach, P. T., 206
Gödel, K., 389–393

* Compiled by G. Moor

DATE DUE